DATE DUE

NOV 2 8 1996	

BRODART, INC.   Cat. No. 23-221

Urbanization and
Urban Systems in India

Urbanization and
Urban Systems in India

R. RAMACHANDRAN

DELHI
OXFORD UNIVERSITY PRESS
BOMBAY CALCUTTA MADRAS
1989

Oxford University Press, Walton Street, Oxford OX2 6DP

New York Toronto
Delhi Bombay Calcutta Madras Karachi
Petaling Jaya Singapore Hong Kong Tokyo
Nairobi Dar es Salaam
Melbourne Auckland
and associates in
Berlin Ibadan

SBN 0 19 562140 9

Phototypeset by Indraprastha Press (CBT),
4 Bahadur Shah Zafar Marg, New Delhi 110002.
Printed by Crescent Printing Works Pvt. Ltd., New Delhi 110001
and published by S. K. Mookerjee, Oxford University Press
YMCA Library Building, Jai Singh Road, New Delhi 110001

Dedicated to my father
V. S. Ranganatha Iyer,
scholar, teacher and critic

Contents

Tables

Figures

Preface

This book is an attempt to present the salient aspects of urbanization in India from a geographical point of view. It is written essentially for the benefit of Indian students of urban geography, particularly at the post-graduate level. At the present time, Indian students are compelled by circumstances to read a rapidly proliferating volume of American and British textbooks, wherein the western city and western perceptions of non-western cities dominate. By and large, the vast majority of Indian students have no comprehension of the American or European cultural environment. The result is that the western textbooks on urban geography only tend to confuse the understanding of both the Indian and western urban scenes. It is hoped that this book will provide guidance to the average student of urban geography in India and help to put the problems of urbanization in India in a perspective that will perhaps instil greater insight and appreciation. The book should also prove useful to students in sister social science disciplines, particularly sociology, political science and town planning. Western scholars and students of the Indian urban scene may perhaps discover new facets that have escaped their notice.

Although geographical studies on Indian towns and cities are not inconsiderable, the author has depended heavily on the works of historians, sociologists, demographers and political scientists to provide a holistic view of urbanization and the problems it has generated in the past few decades in India. The author firmly believes that no social scientist today can afford to work in isolation and ignore the contributions of sister disciplines. In particular, it has become increasingly clear that a geographer ought to study the literature in the entire range of social science disciplines on urban affairs before undertaking serious research in his own field. While each discipline has a unique contribution of its own, it nevertheless benefits from the aspects highlighted by the other disciplines. This book owes much to the scholarly labours of a large number of Indian social scientists on urban problems in the country.

This book has a deliberate bias both in its conceptualization and its execution. There is a strong bias in favour of an Indian point of view on all aspects of urbanization in India. The study deliberately ignores western contributions to the study of urbanization, unless they are directly meaningful from the Indian point of view. It must, however, be made clear at the outset that what is presented here is really the author's perception and understanding of urban problems. There are obviously several Indian perspectives on urbanization. Further, a book written in the English language cannot but acknowledge the profound western intellectual heritage, a heritage to which the author is deeply indebted. Nevertheless, the language and the spirit of the book have only a transient relationship, of the same nature as the relationship between 'body' and 'soul' in the Indian tradition. The author attaches no particular significance to the language in which the book is written; what is important is the spirit in which it is written.

An important motive for this work has been enjoyment. It is the product of over a decade of teaching a course on urban geography to post-graduate students at the University of Delhi. It has grown spontaneously out of this enjoyable experience with very keen young students. My debt of gratitude to them would be amply re-paid if students in coming years find this book enlightening and useful.

The preparation of a book for publication entails much labour, time and skill. The staff of the Oxford University Press, Delhi, have given all of these in generous measure to make this book a reality. The final typing of the manuscript was done efficiently by Mr G. D. Khandpal, and Mr Bachi Ram Arya has skilfully prepared the figures, often working against the clock. To all these people I feel a deep sense of gratitude. Finally, my family (which consists of my wife and two daughters) has shown fortitude in the face of my undue affection for 'the book' and the long hours I have bestowed on it. I would like to reassure them that I do care for them no less than for my work.

16 February 1989
New Delhi

R. RAMACHANDRAN
Professor of Geography
Delhi School of Economics
Delhi University

CHAPTER 1

The Study of Urbanization

Towns and cities have acted as focal points in the cultural landscape of India for nearly five millennia, though with some significant breaks in between. They continue to play a major role in India's emergence as a premier industrial and political power in the world. India is often portrayed as a land of villages and hamlets; nevertheless, in reality, it is equally a land of towns and cities. With over 12,000 settlements with populations of 5,000 persons or more, India has an urban infrastructure of gigantic magnitude. In 1981, India's urban population surpassed that of the United States. In terms of the absolute number of urban settlements and size of the urban population, India is possibly the largest urbanized nation in the world today. India's urban population in 1981 was slightly more than 159 million, which is greater than the total population of all but three other countries in the world. Even if numbers do not tell the entire story, they have a significance of their own. India's recognized urban settlements, numbering 3,245 in 1981, are at various stages of technological and cultural modernization, with a remarkable unevenness of development in the different states and regions of the country. The landscape of urban settlements in India provides a veritable laboratory for the study of the complex inter-relationships among the people and between the people and the physical and cultural environments in which they live.

The study of urbanization in India by its very nature involves several dimensions of analysis. Fundamentally, these include a time dimension covering a period of nearly 5,000 years; a spatial dimension that spans 2,800 kilometres east to west and 3,300 kilometres north to south, and a socio-cultural dimension that covers a wide spectrum of people of diverse ethnic origins, speaking a variety of languages and having an abiding faith in some of the world's oldest religious traditions. A fourth dimension relevant to the study of Indian urbanization has to do with the economic and political processes that have shaped and are continuing to shape the basic character of urban life in India. In particular, we cannot fail to recognize the fact that India is emerging into a strong and viable nation-state based on the principles of socialism, secularism and democracy and is building up a strong scientific and technological framework.

Given this broad analytical framework, the task of the student of urbanization in India is not an easy one, nor could one individual undertake to reveal all the insights into India's past, present and future patterns of urbanization. This book has, therefore, a much more limited objective: it attempts to make an appraisal of urbanization in India from a geographer's point of view. It should, however, be emphasized that geographers share the domain of urban studies with other social sciences.

GEOGRAPHICAL APPROACHES
TO THE STUDY OF URBANIZATION

A geographer's primary interest is in the study of the inter-relationships between people and their habitats. In an urban setting, the habitat comprises not merely the territory of the city and its hinterland but also the spatial linkages between a large number of urban and rural settlements within the region. Apart from distance relationships, geographers also focus on the environment of the habitat which includes the climate, landform features, surface and groundwater sources, drainage, soils and vegetation. The environmental setting plays a key role in the desirability of an urban place as a residential area and to a large extent conditions its future growth. Cities are products of man and environment interacting in a heuristic process of adaptation and response. The net result is a highly variable and complex matrix of human and environmental attributes which are in a constant process of change. This aspect of change links geography with history in exploring the past and the present aspects of the city. Fundamentally, however, geographers have approached the study of urbanization from three viewpoints: (a) locational, (b) regional, and (c) spatio-structural. The significance of these three basic approaches is explored in greater depth in the following paragraphs.

Locational Approach

At a synoptic level, urban places are just points on a map of the natural and cultural landscape. Geographers have in the past devoted much attention to the question as to why a place is located where it is. They have attempted to study the interplay of physical characteristics of the landscape such as rivers, mountain gaps, the juxtaposition of differing landscapes such as a piedmont and a plain, or the presence of lakes or the sea. Simultaneously, the cultural setting is not altogether ignored. The role of a place in the evolution of the culture of the people of the region, the inter-connections between places on the economic and social plane, and the productive activities in the peripheral region of the city are all taken into account in explaining the location of a place. Whether it is Nasik on the banks of the Godavari, Varanasi on the Ganga, or Simla or Shillong in a picturesque mountain setting, the location of a city is a significant aspect in itself and cannot be ignored in any study of urbanization.

Interest in site characteristics and situational aspects later gave rise to the study of the role of cities in the cultural landscape. A city is a capital of a kingdom or an empire, a centre of pilgrimage, a port city, a fishing town or an industrial centre; all these attributes of cities are related intrinsically to their location. This has led to an emphasis on the classification of towns based on functional and locational attributes as a necessary but preliminary stage in the detailed study of the processes of urbanization.

It is only in recent times, however, that geographers have become aware of the empirical regularities in the size and spacing of towns and cities. The aggregate patterns of towns in a larger landscape is not haphazard but follows a rather neat spatial and statistical pattern. Smaller towns are spaced close together while larger cities are far apart, and every region has a few large cities and a number of smaller towns. Enquiry into this aspect has led to the emergence of both behavioural and normative theories of city location, which have given us a greater insight into the urbanization process itself.

The locational approach, in short, is not a static but a dynamic method of enquiry and, as yet, it cannot be fully asserted that we have exhausted the full potential of this approach. In particular, the locational approach offers a useful framework for generating normative theory which in turn has significant implications for the spatial planning of emerging urban landscapes.

Regional Approach

A city is the focal point of a wider region and every town and city
has its concomitant tributary area. Town and city exist not only
on their individual productive base but also on the basis of mutual
exchange of goods and services between the city on the one hand
and the rural villages on the other. The study of the relationship
between the city and its region from ancient times to the recent
historical past, highlighted the contribution of the city as the cultural
and economic focus of the region and at the same time underlined
the dependence of the city on the country for the surplus production of food and raw materials. The city flourished on the wealth of
surplus production in the surrounding region, we were told.
However, this notion no longer holds good and the city today is as
much a producer and supplier of goods and services as the villages
are producers and suppliers of goods. The relationship is one of
mutual dependence—a symbiotic relationship in which the city
and the country are partners at large.

Geographers, fascinated as they were with the study of the
relationship between the city and its region, initially focused attention on the problem of delimiting the boundaries of the city region,
an exercise which is far more difficult and complicated than it
appeared to be at first sight. The city region is essentially a functional region, where the functional relationships between city and
region are manifold and where each specific function of the city
has an associated regional dimension. Together, all the functions
that link the city to the country produce a mass of boundaries,
some at shorter and others at longer distances from the city. A
coherent explanation of this rather confusing array of city regions
was not possible until a normative theory of the functional inter-
relationships between city and region was evolved, which, by
introducing the notion of hierarchy, isolated the clusters of functions and corresponding regions in a regional setting. Furthermore,
in India, where over 70 per cent of the population lives in rural
areas, the relationship between the villages and the small and
medium towns, and in a more indirect way the larger cities, underlies a very important process of communication and diffusion of
socio-economic development. Rural-urban linkages, as yet faintly
understood in India, provide the grass-root network for bringing
about the much needed technological transformation of the rural
hinterlands.

The regional approach to the study of urbanization has at least two other facets. The first has to do with the immediate rural-urban fringe of the larger cities. Here the city inexorably dominates the countryside which is eventually brought into its fold. The rural way of life gives way to the urban life-style, as the urban population spills over into the fringe villages. The fringe of the city offers avenues of investigation of the concomitant effects of urbanization as it occurs at the very doorstep of the city. The second facet has to do with the analysis of the levels of urbanization and aspects of the processes of urbanization in the different regions in the country. The inter-regional and intra-regional variations in urban patterns and processes are studied in relation to the contextual aspects of environvent, economy and society. This approach yields a number of interesting, but rather general, insights into the processes of urbanization in the country.

The regional approach is naturally a major focus of geographical research and is in many ways a very important approach to the study of urbanization. The regional approach, by linking the study of the rural with the study of the urban landscapes, provides a meaningful framework for understanding and also for planning for socio-economic development of both rural and urban areas.

Spatio-structural Approach

The city is also a physical entity occupying several square kilometres of area. In the daily lives of people, it functions as an organismic whole, although comprising of interdependent and interacting component parts. The city has several focal points within it—the main market, the railway station and bus stand, the secondary markets, and professional, educational and medical institutions; all these focal points are linked with the residential areas of rich and poor alike. Religious, linguistic and ethnic minorities have traditionally sought refuge in the city. The city is heterogenous in terms of its population composition and has a variegated and complex land-use structure. It is unified by its network of planned or unplanned roads and the various modes of transportation and communication. The city comes to life with the spatial mobility of its people engaged in their day-to-day activities to satisfy their economic, social and cultural needs. Land, roads, buildings and people, all form part of the city structure. Each component unit performs a significant role, so that the city may function harmoniously and perform its wider role as a focal centre of the region and the nation. The study of the internal characteristics of cities covers a wide spectrum of attributes ranging from the movement of pedestrians to the emergence of large industrial complexes within the urban periphery. If there is one thing that interests the geographer most, it is that every phenomenon in the city is related to all other phenomena in both the spatial and temporal dimensions. Geographers study the variations in the flow of vehicles and people between various locations within the city. They may focus on the intricate patterns of land-uses in commercial, industrial and residential areas. They examine the spatial segregation of the city's population into zones, localities and *mohallas*. They study the distribution of population density within the city or the decline of land values from the city centre to the periphery.

Every facet of the city's internal structure is worthy of detailed study. Yet, the wider perspective of how everything fits into a coherent pattern fascinates the student who is concerned with the underlying structural patterns within the city, which is not readily apparent from the visible city landscape. Such enquiries have led to descriptive theories and analytical frameworks which offer a rather oversimplified explanation for the underlying city structure. Not more than the deceptive tip of the iceberg has been uncovered in this search for theory and a lot more lies ahead for the inquisitive and imaginative student of urban geography.

Every discipline approaches its problems of research and enquiry within a broad framework or paradigm. We have outlined the geographical paradigm within which students have, by and large, pursued their enquiry into problems of urbanization in India. Nevertheless, paradigms change with time in every discipline, and geography is no exception. In a minor way this has already been alluded to in the discussion of the various geographical approaches to the study of urbanization.

THE RISE OF URBAN STUDIES
IN INDIA

Urban studies in India, within the framework of social science disciplines, is just over six decades old. Interest in towns and cities was initially stimulated among Indian social scientists by Patrick Geddes in the University of Bombay in 1915, and the study of urban problems was taken up by geographers and sociologists to some extent in the 1920s. However, substantive research on urban problems in India belongs to the post-Independence period in all the social science disciplines. A review of research on urban problems in the areas of geography, sociology, economics and public administration has been prepared in a series of volumes sponsored by the Indian Council of Social Science Research. In addition to this we have significant contributions made by town planners since the early 1960s. What follows is a very brief overview of the contributions of the various social science disciplines in the area of urban studies in India. Geographers should examine in great detail the literature in the sister social science disciplines when they initiate independent research.

Geographical Studies

In the late 1920s and the early 1930s a dozen or so articles on urban geography were published in the Journal of the Madras Geographical Association. These articles dealt with the distribution of urban settlements within administrative areas as well as a descriptive analysis of the location and growth of individual towns and cities in South India. The major spurt in urban studies took place in the early 1950s when the centre of gravity of urban geographical studies shifted from Madras to Calcutta and later to Varanasi. The growth of urban geography in India is well reflected in the number of articles on urban geography appearing in leading professional journals in geography published from Madras, Calcutta and Varanasi. (Since the 1950s, Varanasi has emerged as the primary centre of urban studies in India.) In all the leading professional journals in India, the proportion of articles on urban geography began to increase. The spatial diffusion of urban studies is further reflected in the emergence of new journals in centres such as Bombay, Hyderabad and a larger number of centres in the Ganga plain area. By the late 1960s, urban studies had become very popular with geographers in the country. Urban studies were reported in journal articles of towns and cities from Assam to Gujarat and from Kashmir to Tamil Nadu, covering the entire length and breadth of the country. The first full-length book on urban geography in India appeared in the middle of the 1950s, in the 1960s as many as six new books were published, and the number increased to nearly 40 in the 1970s. Considering the size of the country and the number of urban places in it, the volume of literature on urban affairs is indeed meagre. There is certainly a lot more work to be done. Nevertheless, the pace of geographical studies on the Indian urban scene has increased significantly in the past decade and all indications are that it will continue to do so.

The earliest urban geographical studies in India were essentially descriptive in nature and focused on the origins and characteristics of individual towns and cities. The stress on the historical roots of urban centres is natural in a country where urbanization is deeply rooted in history and even pre-history. The geographical component in the early studies emphasized the role of towns as ports, pilgrimage centres, and as administrative and cultural foci. Attempts were made to explain the loss and gain in the status of towns, both within the historical and the environmental framework. Site characteristics received considerable attention, and locations with respect to natural and physical landscape features received special mention. On the structural side, the lay-out of the streets and the role of the commercial hub of the city were described in some depth. However, the majority of the studies were exploratory in nature and lacked an analytical framework. By and large, research was confined to archival sources of information and there was little or no evidence of field observation or survey.

The 1950s saw the emergence of urban geography as a full-fledged area of specialization in Indian geography. The focus shifted from a descriptive to an analytical frame, although studies of individual cities still dominated the thinking of geographers. A major point of departure from the past was the emphasis on primary sources of information collected through actual field-work in the towns and cities. Conceptually, two sets of problems were investigated: the relation of the city to its hinterland and the internal structure of cities in terms of generalized functional zones. This approach to urban studies was well grounded in the Varanasi school of geography which provided the venue for a luxuriant growth of urban studies. Looking back, however, one discerns a disconcerting lack of initiative in the studies of this genre in exploring new themes and methods for urban research.

By the early 1960s, Indian urban geography had grown out of its colonial linkage with British geography, and the peer group from whom Indian geographers sought guidance shifted from Europe to America. In line with American urban studies, the focus of urban research in India moved away from the study of individual cities to the problems of classification of urban centres in a regional and national perspective. Before the enthusiasm for town classification could subside, a new and massive wave of ideas based on a normative theory of central places overwhelmed the thinking of Indian urban geographers, who began to look for central place systems in every region, without quite understanding the implications of this approach. As a result, much of this research is essentially imitative and lacking in relevant and innovative applications of the original theory. Given the Indian urban system, which is far from an ideal normative system of cities, the search for systems by and large became a futile exercise in the mechanical application of quantitative and statistical methods to prove what was already well known.

The normative central place concepts, however, found a more fertile area for research in planning for rural area development. The relationship between urban centres and rural development began to have a significant impact on the planner's thinking in the late 1960s. This led to the study of growth centres and growth points in the early 1970s. Aspects of the nature of linkages between villages and towns were studied in a more meaningful fashion. This was made possible by the generous research grants from the University Grants Commission and the Indian Council of Social Science Research, particularly for conducting field-work. Simultaneously, detailed sample surveys of households were carried out for a few cities, notably Vijayawada and Bangalore. The conducting of systematic, rather than unstructured and observational, field surveys received strong encouragement during this period. More and more studies by individual researchers began to demonstrate the value of primary data collection through interview procedures. These studies generated valuable data on the movement of people within a city, the characteristics of dwellings, and information on people's perception of the city's landscape. Other studies focused on the rural-urban fringe and identified the inter-village and intra-village differences in the impact of metropolitan expansion and its consequences. The importance of urban surveys in the preparation of long-term plans for metropolitan areas was demonstrated in a number of studies relating to the metropolitan cities of Hyderabad, Calcutta and Delhi. By the late 1970s, urban geography had emerged as a strong subdiscipline within geography, being no longer dominated by the thinking of British and American geographers. The 1980s have witnessed the blossoming of an independent outlook and innovative enquiry on the part of Indian students of urban geography.

Non-geographical Studies

Urban studies in the other social science disciplines in India show parallel development starting primarily from the 1950s. Indian sociologists of the Bombay school had made pioneering studies in the western region of India as early as the 1920s, but, as in geography, substantive studies were mainly a product of the late fifties. The earlier studies followed a pattern already well established by social anthropologists in the study of Indian village communities. Caste, kinship, religion and social institutions formed the main aspects of enquiry. An attempt was made to evaluate the similarities and differences between rural and urban society in India. Comparison of social institutions and customs among rural and urban communities showed remarkable parallel development of social hierarchy in both areas. The joint family and the institutions associated with *jati* and *varna* were present in the city as much as the villages; but occupations changed with the identifiable levels of administrative, commercial and industrial activity in the city. Traditional occupational bonds such as the *jajmani* system, appropriate to an agricultural society, were irrelevant in the urban context. Nevertheless, those at the bottom of the social order in the village remained virtually in the same position in the city, thereby indicating the irrelevance of the western concept of social mobility. In the 1960s the primary interests of the urban sociologists changed somewhat. Social change became the main focus of study. The stresses and strains that the various segments of urban society faced were lucidly portrayed and the increasing impact of westernization, particularly on metropolitan society, was brought out in unmistakable terms. A tendency for imitative research along lines set by American sociologists was, however, evident, both in the choice of new problems for investigation and the use of quantitative and statistical methods. There was considerable stress on studies on aspects of the sociology of education, medical sociology and industrial sociology. Popular movements in urban areas and urban unrest were also investigated.

Urban economics is as yet a comparatively unexplored field in India. Despite the fact that the country has a large number of professional economists (in fact several times larger than the number of geographers or sociologists), there are fewer studies on urban economics. In the 1920s, the growth of towns was studied as part of economic history, the account being largely demographic and historical rather than economic in nature. In the mid-1950s, however, noted economists conducted urban economic surveys of individual cities focusing on aspects such as household income and expenditure, employment and unemployment and related factors. These studies were sponsored by the National Planning Commission. In addition to this, the National Sample Surveys provided a mass of data at the national level for rural and urban areas for several points in time. Analyses of these data by economists have indicated the widening gap between rural and urban populations in terms of income levels. At the same time they also indicate the increase in income disparities within urban areas. However, the macro-level analysis has not been adequately supported by micro-level studies of individual cities. The study of the economic base of cities has largely been ignored, although there are studies on sectors such as large-scale, small-scale and cottage industries. Further studies on the economics of urbanization and urban management are very few in number and the contribution of economists to city planning is immeasurably poor in relation to their contributions to national and state-level planning.

With the vast wealth of Census data there is no dearth of demographic studies on Indian cities which cover considerable common ground among the disciplines of economics, sociology and geography. These studies have provided a well articulated demographic profile of Indian cities at the national, regional and local levels. Aspects such as population growth, density distribution, age and sex composition, literacy and occupations and to some extent rural-urban migrations have been studied. Inter-regional and intra-regional variations in demographic characteristics have been explored more often in a lengthy descriptive style with scant interest in developing an analytical framework. Data appear to dominate the perception of the researchers on urban demographic problems. However, data seem to fail wherever crucial issues are involved. There are hardly any data on social stratification in terms of *jati, varna* and religious groups, and similarly data are lacking in relation to rural-urban migration and the factors relating to the migrational process. Furthermore, those interested in demographic studies rarely get out into the field to check the accuracy of the data or to collect more meaningful information on aspects that a national census cannot cope with. A study imprisoned within the four walls of the Indian Censuses, cannot achieve anything other than a few mundane and stale generalizations about the status of urban demographic problems in India.

Political scientists, particularly those interested in public administration, have during the past decade or so endeavoured to examine in some depth the urban polity and its colonial and post-Independence ramifications on city developement and in particular city planning. The failure of the experiment in local self-government both under British rule and in the post-Independence period, for entirely different reasons, has been adequately highlighted. Urban management under a multiplicity of agencies has generated unresolvable conflicts of interests and responsibility, leading to an inefficient and incompetent municipal administration. The way out of this mess is not a clear one, for the choice lies inevitably between grass-root democracy and an administration dominated by bureaucrats.

Historians, and in fact more specifically archaeologists, have evidenced a keen interest in the Harappan urban civilization and the diffusion of chalcolithic cultures and the later iron age cultures in India. These studies, conducted mostly in the 1960s and 1970s, provide an ever-expanding body of information on the possible origins and diffusion of settlements in general and urban settlements in particular in the Indus and Ganga plains, in the Deccan and in the extreme south of India. Apart from the scattered but unfortunate attempts to mix up mythology with pre-history, the archaeological studies in themselves demonstrate meticulous care in the methods and in the interpretation of facts. More recently, historians have taken over from the archaeologists, the study of the Aryan and Dravidian phases of urbanization from about the sixth century BC. There is a vast wealth of historical material on ancient and medieval India still awaiting analysis and interpretation, and the number of historical studies of urbanization are few in number. Apart from the Mughal phase of urbanization in northern India, on which a number of studies exist, studies on urbanization in the medieval period are few, an unfortunate gap indeed in our knowledge of medieval urban India for which there are adequate sources of information. Further, there is a lack of interest among historians in a systematic analysis of urbanization in various historical periods both in northern and southern India and more so in the South. Unfortunately, Indian historians tend to focus exclusively either on the north or the south of India, thus demonstrating a lack of national perspective or even expertise—a failing which is of critical importance in the understanding of urbanization processes in both the ancient and medieval periods.

Town planners were a rarity in India before Independence, but after 1947 their number and their contribution to the study of urban development problems has been phenomenal, particularly since the 1960s. However, studies by town planners in India have two major failings. Firstly, town planners rarely step out of the metropolitan fringe of the million cities into the arena of the small cities and towns; secondly, they are too deeply rooted in western town planning notions to begin to understand the Indian reality. Too much emphasis on the western art of town planning, focusing on law, regulation, land zoning, beautification and landscaping have left the Indian city folk bewildered at what is being done for them. Standards and norms, imported wholesale from the West, have no relevance in a country with an entirely different cultural and economic setting. In recent times, there has been discussion on the need to change the norms and standards to suit Indian conditions. However, what is actually needed is a break from the western approach to town planning and a fresh look at city planning in India starting with the smaller cities and towns. Such a development is perhaps in the offing, if the experience of hundreds of town planners who have been seasoned under Indian reality in the various state town planning departments is reflected in the thinking of the articulate town planners.

To sum up, we may assert with some confidence that the literature on Indian urbanization acquired variety, range and maturity by the early 1980s. We have reached the take-off stage in the intellectual pursuit of the meaning and significance of urbanization in India.

SOURCE MATERIALS AND METHODOLOGY

Urban studies are very much circumscribed by the nature and availability of the source materials and the methodology of analysis. In this section, we attempt a rather brief overview of source materials and methodology used by geographers in urban studies. The source materials and methodology vary according to the issues being investigated and more detailed references to these are made in the substantive chapters of this book. The following paragraphs emphasize merely the general sources of information and the major methodological issues in urban geography.

Secondary Sources

India has very rich sources of information for urban studies. The

Census volumes, both at the national level and the state and district levels, despite the limitations of a large data collecting organization, provide a mine of information on rural and urban places for a period of just over one hundred years. This wealth of information has been and will continue to be used by geographers and other social scientists. The Census is in most cases the only source of information that can be used in a macro- and even meso-level spatial analysis of urban patterns. It is also the main source of information for temporal studies focusing on the recent past. The Census also provides data on intra-city spatial units; however, in this case, it is often difficult to find maps showing the exact boundaries of the wards, localities or Census enumeration blocks for which data are given. Another major problem with the Census is the rather limited range of information provided by it. At the lowest spatial level, the Census provides information on the following: (a) population totals along with sex-wise distribution, (b) number of houses and households, (c) number of workers, male and female, for each of nine categories recognized by it, (d) the number of scheduled caste and scheduled tribe persons, and (e) the number of literate persons, male and female. Data on language and religion are available for some cities, particularly the largest cities, while information on age structure and migration status is not available for individual cities. There is no point in dwelling upon areas on which the Census does not throw any light, for these are inevitably very large; on the other hand, one could and should ask if all the available information has been properly and adequately analysed. Apparently, there is considerable scope for improvement in this aspect. For urban geographers in particular, and for others as well, changes in the Census definition of urban areas and in actual boundaries of the urban areas pose serious problems for those interested in temporal analysis.

Apart from the Census volumes, there is a large body of archival material on Indian cities, in the British and medieval periods in particular. This source has been rather sparingly used by geographers in the past. Unlike the situation for European cities, detailed land-use maps, or for that matter, even good base maps for individual cities are not always available (in recent times, the town planning departments have prepared base maps for a number of Indian cities and towns, and in some cases detailed maps are also available for localities within cities). Areal photographs of Indian cities are all but unavailable, even if such photographs exist for specific points in time with some government departments. This does very much inhibit the zeal of the student of urban geography, for he cannot even get started with his research, for want of the basic minimum infrastructure for carrying out his studies. However, in a number of cases students have through their own efforts succeeded in obtaining access to rare maps and other source materials which are generally inaccessible to the public.

Primary Sources

The strength of geographical urban studies in India has, in the ultimate analysis, to depend heavily on primary data collection and analysis. In this area, geographers have two alternative methods before them. The first is the method of field observation which involves walking through the city streets and preparing notional maps and notes on city land-uses, flow of people and vehicles, and the morphological characteristics of residential and non-residential structures. This approach somewhat parallels the participant observer technique used by social anthropologists. The merit of this method lies in objectivity of measurement through observation, where the object being observed does not interact with the observer. Physical objects in the city's landscape would not tell lies but city people could. The techniques of field observation and recording have been well discussed in geographical literature and there is no need to recapitulate them here. A second approach, which has increasingly been employed by geographers during the past decade or so, is rigorous random sample surveys of dwellings, households, commercial or industrial establishments or their customers. Such surveys involve interviews using structured or unstructured schedules. This method, with its limited accuracy and reliability, still has a number of advantages in the Indian context and will probably become increasingly indispensable to the student of urban studies. Geographers are, however, rather poorly trained in conducting interviews, unlike the students of some of other disciplines such as sociology and social work. On the other hand, there is the advantage of a strong field-work tradition in geography through observation and unstructured personal enquiry. There is, nevertheless, a very urgent need for geographers to improve their field techniques with the use of appropriate statistical methods of spatial sampling, estimation and testing hypotheses.

Statistical Methods

In the 1960s statistical and mathematical techniques gained popularity among geographers in western countries as well as in India. Much of the quantitative thrust in urban geography, which formed the pioneer fringe for introduction of these techniques, has been highly productive in terms of new insights into problems hitherto only vaguely understood or not investigated. The application of statistical methods has resulted in a more rigorous analysis of secondary and primary data often through the use of electronic calculators or even computers. While calculators are becoming fairly common in geographical laboratories, access to computers is available only in a handful of metropolitan university departments. Few geographers in India can write programmes for data analysis or mapping, although Indian scientists in general have a high international reputation for computer software development. It is the lack of facilities and the high cost of computer use that inhibits the geographer's involvement in the use of this sophisticated tool of data analysis.

Having said this, there is an equal need to point out the pitfalls of a statistical and quantative approach to the study of urban problems. Quantitative methods are essentially tools of analysis and are not by themselves capable of generating a theory or even offering meaningful explanations for urban problems. Going by past experience, there is a strong tendency among geographers to become slaves rather than masters of quantitative techniques. This has resulted in a futile exhibition of statistical jargon without commensurate compensation in terms of new insights into the study of urban problems. Such a situation can be seen in the study of the factorial ecology of cities, where sophisticated statistical methods are used to produce facile generalizations. What makes the fundamental difference in the application of advanced statistical methods is a thorough grasp of these techniques; otherwise, instead of the researcher occupying the driver's seat, the techniques may take over. The results can be catastrophic for both the researcher and the discipline.

THE NEED FOR REORIENTATION
OF URBAN RESEARCH IN INDIA

The study of urban problems by geographers has followed a rather stereotyped pattern in India in the past few decades. Studies of individual cities have generally followed a set pattern from which only a few have deviated in any significant way. Similarly, the techniques of urban analysis developed in the West have led to a proliferation of mechanical applications devoid of originality and stifling in the repetitiveness of their oversimplified generalizations about the patterns of urbanization in India. There is a strong need to break from the path followed in the past and to look for new avenues of fruitful research. Urban geographers will have to put more and more emphasis on the study of the current urban problems of the country which differ in fundamental terms from urban problems elsewhere in the world, in view of the distinctive features of our social, economic and political systems. In the light of this, we suggest three useful avenues for further research by Indian geographers: (a) problem oriented studies, (b) policy oriented studies, and (c) evaluation studies. It should be understood that it is not the intention, nor is it possible, to identify all the potential avenues of research in urban geography.

Problem Oriented Studies

Urbanization has in the past three decades exposed the weaknesses of infrastructure and urban spatial characteristics of towns and cities. The recent perceptions of the role of the city as an industrial centre providing employment to the unemployed, as a growth point stimulating development in its hinterland and as a Utopia for the rural poor and those afflicted by natural or man-made calamities, have brought in their wake myriads of problems which the cities are unable to cope with. The proliferation of slums, the inadequacies of city transport, the rising land and property values, the legendary insufficiency of water and electricity, are all manifestations of changing circumstances in urban areas. The spatial allocation of amenities and infrastructure is uneven within our cities, with appalling conditions of living in some areas, contrasted with luxury and high living in others. The misery of the slums does not however deter the rural poor from coming into the city; the perceptions of the poor and also the rich are often widely off the mark. The paradox is that to the rich the city's landscape is filthy and ugly, needing urgent urban surgery, while to the poor the city is still full of vitality and variety, and is highly liveable (compared to the dull and static atmosphere of the village). There is a need to adopt a behavioural approach to the study of urban problems. It is not merely the physical reality *as it exists* that needs to be studied, but also the reality and the need for change *as perceived* by various sections of urban society. This implies a shift from the observational approach to field survey to the interview method. People are the main sources of information in the city; after all, cities exist for the people. In order to study the problems meaningfully, there is a need to give up preconceived and prejudiced notions of the city's landscape and society. Western, including Marxian, views have little relevance to the Indian situation. For the uncommitted and free researcher, innovation and ingenuity will find ample scope in a nation of massive and complex urban problems.

Policy Oriented Studies

It is not enough to understand urban problems as they occur; we also ought to be able to visualize an urban future for the country, consistent with the reality of the Indian situation and within the framework of the political, social and economic constraints under which we operate. We need to develop norms for various urban amenities, land-use, street layouts and the like, which are not mere imitative translations of prescriptions for the other countries of the world, but are generated from within our own experience. In other words, we need a normative approach, in addition to, and in fact consistent with, a behavioural approach to urban problems.

A variety of problems confront the city and city region planner. There has to be a policy regarding the hierarchical and functional specializations of towns and cities consistent with India's development goals. The question of what is appropriate in the Indian context needs careful examination in the light of the real world urban experience. Again, the problems of the rural-urban fringe and of the haphazard industrial and residential growth in urban areas call for policies which ought to take into account the political, administrative and economic constraints imposed by the rapid physical expansion of larger cities. Towns with a population of less than 100,000 have, until recently, been largely ignored by planners and policy makers. The role of these towns must be studied in the context of socio-economic development to generate an appropriate policy framework. Urban housing, particularly for the poor and the less privileged sections of society, needs careful study to generate policy measures in an area that has significant political overtones. At the other end of the spectrum are policies relating to the urban super-rich class whose growing mountain of black money has pushed land prices to the skies in metropolitan centres. On the credit side, black money has contributed to the much needed growth in city infrastructure. It is an important source of finance for the increase in the stock of housing in our cities, and its role in the development of industry and commerce, where it also originates, cannot be underestimated. It is not often realized that the housing and employment conditions in Indian cities would be a lot worse but for the operation of the parallel economy. An urban policy must be courageous enough to recognize the forces at work in Indian cities, whether these are due to poverty or super-affluence. Indian cities demonstrate the coexistence of extremes of every kind. Imaginative research on policy should highlight the inherent contradictions of our urban society and strive to work out the path of least resistance to a better future.

Evaluation Studies

Investment in urban infrastructure over the post-Independence period runs into several thousand crores of rupees. There are a large number of central government schemes, some which come under the national five year plans as well as state supported schemes for the improvement of urban areas. These range from housing schemes for refugees, industrial workers and the poorer sections of society to schemes for slum clearance, development and relocation, and also schemes for the provision or improvement of electricity supply, transportation, water supply and sewerage facilities in urban areas. Yet, hardly any attention has been paid by geographers to the study of these programmes of urban improvement. The success or failure of policies and plans depends on their implementation. Evaluation of development schemes would generate the feedback for framing policy and for planning new programmes. Geographers have the capability and the responsibility to undertake evaluation studies on urban development schemes.

It is quite amazing that although over 400 city master plans have been prepared in various parts of the country, not a single one has been evaluated by geographers in terms of the objectives it has set before itself and in terms of the actual content of the plan. Geographers' traditional interest in city land-uses ought to stimulate their concern about the master plans, which are essentially physical plans of a city for a period of 20 to 25 years. Every master plan contains a proposed land-use map showing the areas identified for various categories of land-use along with the zoning regulations for each category of land-use. Such a land-use map of the planning area is in effect a blueprint for the future development of land-use in the city. Copies of city master plans, it is true, are not readily available, but there is still a lack of will to undertake the evaluation of plan documents which have been prepared with considerable skill, but are nevertheless vulnerable to failure at the implementation level.

A PREVIEW

The temporal and spatial aspects of urbanization at the national and inter-city levels form the main focus of this book. It does not deal with aspects of the internal structure of Indian cities, which in view of its vastness of scope would need the space of another book. In particular, the book emphasizes the processes of urbanization and the nature of interdependence among urban centres and between urban centres and their hinterlands—in other words, on the characteristics of urban systems in India. The history of urbanization in India from prehistoric times to the present is explored in chapter 2 and this is followed by a discussion on the processes of urbanization in chapter 3. The locational aspects of urbanization form the main thrust of the five succeeding chapters. Starting with the fundamental problems of city definition, several issues are explored successively, such as the spatial patterns of urbanization in the country, the classification of cities, the normative theories of settlement location, and issues and methodologies in the empirical analysis of settlement systems in India. The approach is essentially at the macro level covering the entire country. The next two chapters are devoted to a study of the city and its relations with its surrounding region. This is done at two levels—the area of dominance of the city and the peripheral area around the city where the direct impact of the city is felt in day-to-day life. The final chapter examines the fundamental issues involved in framing a national urbanization policy.

SELECTED READING

Bose, Ashish: 'Administration of Urban Areas', in ICSSR: *A Survey of Research in Public Administration*, Vol. I, Allied Publishers, Bombay, 1973, pp. 193–248.

Bose, A. N.: 'Urban Economics: A Trend Report', in ICSSR: *A Survey of Research in Economics*, Vol. VI, Allied Publishers, Bombay, 1980, pp. 1–37.

D'Souza, Victor S.: 'Urban Studies: A Trend Report', in ICSSR: *Survey of Research in Sociology and Social Anthropology,* Vol. I, Popular Prakashan, Bombay, 1974, pp. 115–57.

Gosal, G. S.: 'Urban Geography: A Trend Report', in ICSSR: *Survey of Research in Geography,* Popular Prakashan, Bombay, 1972, pp. 203–13.

Hoselitz, B. F.: 'Survey of the Literature on Urbanisation in India', in Turner, Roy, ed.: *India's Urban Future,* Oxford University Press, Bombay, 1962, pp. 425–43.

Raju, S.: 'Parochialism in Urban Geography', *Annals, National Association of Geographers of India,* Vol. 5, No. 1, 1985, pp. 51–6.

Rao, M. S. A., ed.: *Urban Sociology in India,* Orient Longman, New Delhi, 1974, pp. 1–13.

CHAPTER 2

The History of Urbanization

The Indian subcontinent shares, with Mesopotamia and the Nile valley, a long history of urbanization. The first phase of urbanization in the Indus valley is associated with the Harappan civilization dating back to 2350 BC. The cities of this civilization flourished over a period of more than 600 years up to about 1700 BC and this was followed by a prolonged period of over a thousand years in which we have no evidence of urban development. From around 600 BC, we again come across towns and cities associated with the two major, but closely related, cultural streams of India, namely the Aryan civilization of the North and the Dravidian civilization of the South. From this period onwards, for about 2500 years, India has had a more or less continuous history of urbanization. However, we know from historical evidence that there were both periods of urban growth and periods of urban decline. Thus cities grew in number and in size during the Mauryan and post-Mauryan periods (from 300 BC to AD 600), both in northern India as well as in the extreme South. Cities declined and were largely neglected during the post-Gupta period, that is from AD 600 to about AD 1000 in northern India. In southern India, on the other hand, urbanization attained a zenith during the period from AD 800 to 1200. Urbanization on a subdued scale flourished in northern India under the influence of Muslim rulers, who came to India from Afghanistan and beyond from around AD 1200, and attained a second climax during the Mughal period, when many of India's cities were established. The British came to India at a time when India was perhaps the most urbanized nation in the world, and the early part of British rule saw a decline in the level of Indian urbanization. During the latter half of British rule, Indian cities regained some of their lost importance; further, the

British added several new towns and cities, in addition to generating newer urban forms in the existing cities. The post-Independence period has witnessed urbanization in India on a scale never before achieved.

The story of urbanization in India in historical times is a story of spatial and temporal discontinuities. The earliest urban developments were confined to the Indus valley and the adjoining parts of Rajasthan, Punjab and to some extent western Uttar Pradesh. Other parts of the country remained outside the pale of urbanization. In the early historical period, urbanization took place in the middle Ganga plains and in the southern part of the Indian peninsula, while the areas in between had no known cities. During much of the historical period, vast parts of the country were untouched or only partly affected by urbanization. Spatial discontinuities in urbanization continue to be an important aspect even in modern India.

The causative factors behind urbanization varied from time to time, leading to not one but several urbanization processes at different points in time. In the prehistoric period, urbanization was synonymous with the origin and rise of civilization itself, thus manifesting itself essentially as a cultural process. In the historical periods, from ancient times to the British period, urbanization was inextricably related to the rise and fall of kingdoms, dynasties and empires, and thus in effect urbanization during this period was essentially a political process. In recent times, urbanization has been associated with industrialization and economic development. In this sense, urbanization is essentially an economic process.

Many well known cities of prehistoric and historic times exist today in the form of small mounds or ruins. This is true of such great cities as Mohenjodaro, Harappa, Nalanda, Taxashila and Vijayanagar. Other ancient and historical cities survive to this day—among them are Pataliputra, Madurai, Kancheepuram, Varanasi and Delhi, to name only a few. In most of these historical cities, the past has been partly or totally obliterated; in some cases the old structures and street layouts are still in evidence. The beautiful temples of southern cities belong to the 12th or 13th centuries, while the monuments of the Mughal period belong to the 16th and 17th centuries. In Varanasi, which is perhaps India's oldest existing city, there is no trace of structures dating back more than 300 years. The present urban landscape of India is replete with cities having their origins at various points in the historical past; Nasik, Jaipur, Moradabad, Kanpur and Simla, for example, testify to their widely different socio-cultural origins. The emergence of industrial cities such as Bokaro, Bhilai and Rourkela, has added another dimension to the already variagated nature of Indian urbanization.

It is difficult, if not impossible, to describe the history of Indian urbanization in any meaningful fashion, without a simplification of the time periods of analysis. On the basis of the temporal discontinuities in Indian urbanization we have, for the sake of convenience, divided the urban history of India into five time periods as follows:

(1) the prehistoric period—2350 to 1800 BC,
(2) the early historical period—600 BC to AD 500,
(3) the medieval period—AD 600 to 1800
   (including the Mughal period—AD 1526 to 1800),
(4) the British period—AD 1800 to 1947, and
(5) the post-Independence period.

Students of history may not agree with the terminology used for these time periods or with the limits prescribed for them. There are, in effect, several difficulties in defining time periods for detailed study. For one thing, there are spatial discontinuities in the history of urbanization. For example, the medieval period was a period of anticlimax as far as urbanization in the Ganga plains is concerned; on the other hand, this period witnessed a very high level of urbanization in the South. The three major port cities of India, namely, Bombay, Madras and Calcutta, which we have inherited from British colonial rule, were established long before AD 1800. Nevertheless, periodization is a necessary first step in any historical analysis. What follows is a more detailed description and analysis of urbanization in the five given time periods in which the spatial variations in urbanization in different parts of the country are also taken into account.

THE PREHISTORIC PERIOD
(2300 BC TO 1800 BC)

The beginnings of urbanization in the Indian subcontinent go back to 2350 BC (about 4500 years ago) to the Indus valley region. Even prior to this, there is ample archaeological evidence of palaeolithic and neolithic settlements in northern, central and southern India and in the border regions of Afghanistan and Baluchistan. In all these areas, the practice of agriculture and the domestication of animals were clearly in evidence. Together with these developments we also have evidence of wheel-thrown pottery and painted ware of great artistic beauty. The variety and range of tools used by these village people show progressive improvement, particularly in terms of the materials out of which they were made. Thus, stone implements gave way to copper and later to bronze implements. It is at this stage of cultural and technological development that the larger village settlements showed distinct urban attributes; thus ushering in an era of urbanization.

Nature of the Evidence

Our understanding of the origins of the earliest cities is based entirely on archaeological evidence obtained from excavation of the ruins of the early settlements. We have, from this evidence, a fairly thorough understanding of the physical aspects of city development, such as the spatial extent of the cities, the layout of their streets, the types of structures and dwellings, and the materials of which they were made. We have concrete evidence of pottery showing variations in the technique of its production and the artistry of its appearance, of tools made of stone and metals, and of articles such as clothing, food grains, and the various types of domesticated animals. Writing in baked tabloids provides additional information about the social and cultural life of the people, although the writing as such has not so far been deciphered. We have a few skeletal remains of humans from which inferences regarding their racial origins can be drawn. There is, however, no literary evidence. Though the archaeological evidence, unlike literary evidence, uncovers the truth as it was, and cannot lie, the lack of literary evidence is a serious handicap in our understanding of the prehistoric societies in their totality. An important aspect of the evidence has to do with the problem of dating the ruins. This is normally done by either of two methods—the stratigraphic method or the radio-carbon dating method. Each has its pitfalls and the actual dating by all reckoning can only be approximate. However, vertical digging in the same area provides a chronological sequence of evidence on human habitations.

Diffusion versus Independent Origin

Opinions differ as to the manner in which the earliest cities in the

Indus valley region originated. Earlier archaeological studies, mainly by western scholars, were emphatically of the view that the central idea of the urban way of life came to the Indus valley from Mesopotamia, possibly by chance migration of people. Evidence in support of this includes the rather abrupt beginnings of city life in Mohenjodaro and Harappa, where vertical digging of the sites has revealed no transitional phase of cultural development. The salient features of the civilization in Mesopotamia and in the Harappan cities are the same—these include wheel-turned pottery, the art of writing, the location of the urban settlements on the banks of rivers, the practice of agriculture and so on. Besides, the Indus valley is not far from Mesopotamia, where cities existed nearly a thousand years before the Harappan cities, thus allowing sufficient time for the diffusion of the idea from Mesopotamia to the Indus valley. Interaction between the two areas, at least in the later stages of the Harappan civilization, is indicated by the presence of Harappan coins in Sumerian cities and Sumerian coins in the port city of Lothal, a Harappan city.

However, except for contemporary trade, the evidence of diffusion of the city way of life becomes unsustainable on closer examination. Harappan agriculture was purely rain-fed and dependent in part on the natural flooding of the plains. No elaborate irrigation works existed. The motifs, shapes, and artistic expressions on pottery and other objects in the Harappan civilization are distinctly of indigenous origin. The system of writing, as yet undeciphered, is obviously different from its Mesopotamian counterpart. Harappan cities are bereft of defensive walls and other aspects of city structure differ markedly from the Mesopotamian cities. Coins and weights are entirely new and are of a different design. There is thus no doubt that the city way of life was not transplanted in toto by people migrating from Mesopotamia to the Indus valley. However, certain specific ideas, such as the techniques of making copper from its ore and of wheel-turned pottery could have been borrowed from West Asia. The growing evidence appears to favour the indigenous origin of the Harappan cities, with some diffusion of ideas from West Asia.

The People of the Harappan Civilization

Any civilization is a product of its people. Who were the Harappans? A rather unnecessary but persistent question is whether the

Harappans were Aryans or Dravidians,[1] the two major ethno-
cultural groups in India. This question needs to be answered at
two levels. Firstly, at the social and cultural level, the main point
to be emphasized is that of discontinuity. The Harappan culture
pre-dates the early Aryan culture of northern India and the
Dravidian culture of the South by nearly a thousand years. The
high level of meticulously planned urban spatial organization
revealed in the Harappan culture is nowhere in evidence, either in
the South or in the North, even after a thousand years. There is no
continuity in writing, the art of pottery, or in the detailed technology of agriculture. However, aspects of Harappan culture could
have filtered through other transitional cultures into both the
Aryan and Dravidian realms. Neither the Aryans nor the Dravidians can claim, on the basis of the present evidence, any direct
inheritance to the Harappan cultural traditions. At the second
level, there is concrete evidence from human skeletal remains in
the ruins of Harappan cities. From this a number of racial types
have been identified—proto-Australoid, Mediterranean, Mon-
goloid and Alpine, of which the Mediterranean is predominant.
The presence of different racial elements points towards a composite culture, with influences coming from far and wide. But as both
the Aryans and the Dravidians belong to the the Mediterranean
group, no meaningful conclusions can be derived from this evidence. The origins and later dispersal and absorption of the
Harappan people are likely to remain shrouded in mystery.
Nevertheless, experts are hardly in a position to contradict the
layman's view that the Harappan culture and people were products of the Indian subcontinent who in course of time fused into
the slowly evolving composite Indian culture.

The Harappan Culture

The Harappans were primarily an agricultural people. Like the
Mesopotamians, the Harappan people settled on fertile plains
where flood waters provided a means of natural irrigation.
However, unlike the Mesopotamians, the Harappans did not
develop an elaborate system of irrigation, involving weirs and
channels. The plough was not known to the Harappans; instead

[1] The terms 'Aryan' and 'Dravidian' today connote linguistic families rather than
ethnic groups. However, in early times, the 'Aryans' were a distinct ethnic group. The
term 'Dravidian' originates from the word 'Tamizhar', which denotes Tamil speaking
people.

they used the harrow for tilling the soil. Barley, wheat, peas and sesamum were the chief crops. In addition, cotton and rice, unknown in other parts of the world then, were also grown. Domesticated animals were sheep, cattle, buffaloes, pigs, dogs and camels. Among the metals, copper and bronze were used for tool making, while iron was absent. Wheel-turned pottery is a distinctive feature of this culture. Further, gold and silver were used for making items of jewellery and vessels. Stone and bronze sculptures and terracotta animals, birds, snakes, fish, spindles and toys, testify to a high degree of artistic development. Cotton textiles were a very important industry. The art of writing was known and a script using about 250 characters or signs was in use. A system of weights and measures based on binary and decimal modes was current. The figures on seals reveal the worship of deities of both sexes— male forms such as the linga and the bull representing perhaps Shiva, and nude female figurines representing the mother goddess.

The Harappan culture has all the attributes of a fully developed urban society supported by rural villages around the larger urban centres. The city proper supported a class of non-farmers. At the head of this society was a high priest or king supported by a coterie of nobles. The uniformity of culture throughout the length and breadth of the Indus valley region, reveals the role of a central political influence, or in other words the existence of an empire, ruled possibly from the twin capitals of Mohenjodaro and Harappa. Such a political organization calls for a high degree of social stratification and hierarchy. However, evidence in this regard is indirect and circumstantial, as will be seen in the following sections.

City Structure and Planning

The two cities of Mohenjodaro and Harappa represent the climax of urban development attained in the Harappan culture. Both these cities are now in Pakistan. There were, however, other cities in the region, some in India, which do not show the same degree of development. These towns were smaller and perhaps functioned, not as capital cities, but as regional centres. Lothal, the third major city of this period was a major port on the Gulf of Cambay. The other cities and towns were located at Kalibangan and Banwali in Rajasthan and Haryana respectively, Surkotada in Kachchh and Rangpur and Rojdi in the Kathiawar peninsula. All these towns are located in India. In addition, the ruins of over a hundred

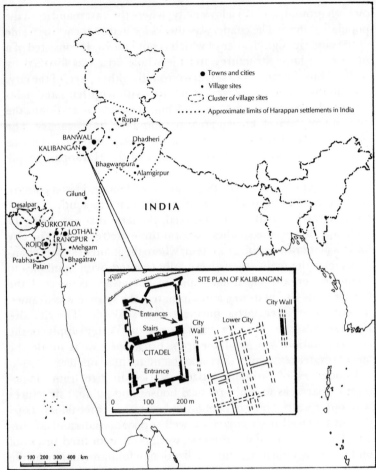

FIGURE 2.1. Harappan Towns and Cities in India 2300–1800 BC.

lesser sites of Harappan settlements probably representing larger villages have also been discovered in India (Figure 2.1).

The purpose of this section is to examine the salient urban morphological characteristics of the major cities and towns, and aspects of the settlement system as such will be explored in the following section. The two most important cities, namely, Mohenjodaro and Harappa, show remarkable similarities in their urban morphology. Each is located on the banks of a navigable river—Mohenjodaro on the Indus and Harappa on the river Ravi. The city proper consisted of two component parts: (1) a citadel, built on high ground, and (2) a lower city, where the vast majority of the population lived. The citadel was always located on the western side of the city, the significance of which is not known. It consisted of a number of large structures and the whole area was fortified by walls. Thus the citadel stood apart from the other parts of the city. Within the citadel, there were structures with large halls and palatial residences for the nobles and high priests. In addition, the citadel had the well known great bath and the state granary. The nature of the structures testifies to the fact that the citadel was indeed the real capital where the rulers of the Harappan people resided.

The lower city, or the city proper, was built on a grid iron pattern, where the streets were aligned east-west and north-south. A three-level hierarchy of streets is observed, the largest streets being 14 metres wide and the smallest around three metres wide. The city had an elaborate drainage system, where the main drainage channels along the main streets were fully covered, with manholes to facilitate periodic cleaning. Pipes of earthware connected the houses to the street drains and ultimately the sewage was drained into the river, after partial purification in soak-pits. The city also had a separate storm water drainage system. Water supply for the city population was available from brick-lined wells inside the larger residences, which were about a metre in diameter.

Residences of ordinary citizens varied in size from single-roomed barracks to multi-roomed houses and palatial structures with outer walls. Some of the houses had two or three floors. Thus the city had well-to-do citizens as well as poor artisans and labourers. All the residential structures were built with fired bricks of uniform size, indicating standardization, a fundamental principle in the mass production of bricks. Individual houses also had baths and privies, thus providing basic urban amenities.

The two cities extended over an approximate area of more than two square kilometres and had an estimated population of around 30,000 persons. Mohenjodaro is the older and larger of the two cities and it was rebuilt at least nine times in a span of six to eight hundred years. However, the rebuilding did not disturb the basic pattern of street layout, except in the later phases, when the rigid patterns were not strictly adhered to. Harappa is apparently a city built at a later point in time, as its sudden appearance on the landscape indicates, and it was perhaps built as a secondary capital to satisfy the needs of an expanding empire.

Lothal, located near a distributary of the Sabarmati river, was actually a sea port at the mouth of the Gulf of Cambay. It probably started as a fishing village and emerged as a major trading port under the influence of the Harappan empire. Through Lothal, the Harappans established trade links with the outside world, in particular with the Mesopotamian cities. Besides trade, Lothal was also a centre of industry, as indicated by the presence of a variety of items like ivory objects, cotton goods, objects used in warfare such as daggers, spearheads and so on. The city was partly destroyed by floods in 2000 BC after which it lost its importance. A major flood around 1900 BC resulted in its final destruction.

Unlike the other two Harappan cities, Lothal was surrounded by a mud brick wall, which probably was a protective device against floods. On the other hand, Lothal had a structure similar to the other two cities. It consisted of two parts—the raised city in the west containing the major palatial buildings housing the ruling class, and the lower town with a market centre in the north, an industrial sector in the west and a residential area in the northwestern part. There was a large dockyard in the eastern part, connected by an artificial channel to the river. In addition to Lothal, the Harappan people had several other port towns at Suktagendor, Sotka-koh, Bhagatrav, Tuda and Somnath.

Among the smaller towns, Kalibangan in Rajasthan has a typical Harappan city structure with lower and upper city areas, a grid pattern of streets without drains and buildings of inferior quality, indicating both a lower status of the town, as well as a declining phase of urbanization. Another sea port, on a smaller scale than Lothal, was located on the Makran coast in Baluchistan, having a dockyard in addition to the citadel and lower town. The other smaller towns did not have citadels, indicating their lower status in the urban hierarchy. Thus, the Harappan towns and cities revealed variations in form, structure and functions.

The total picture and scale of urbanization in the Harappan civilization is yet to emerge as newer sites are discovered and investigations made. Nevertheless, considering the spatial extent of the Harappan culture, which extended from Baluchistan to western Uttar Pradesh, towns and cities were indeed few in number and probably accounted for less than five per cent of the total Harappan population.

City and Country Relations

The Harappan empire encompassed a few large cities, a number of smaller towns, and a very large number of rural villages. The relations between the urban centres and the villages may be inferred from the mass of archaeological evidence. It would appear from the evidence, that the rural villages were mainly concerned with agriculture, although a few industries such as pottery making and textiles for ordinary wear were also present. The city produced a greater variety of goods, both luxury items such as jewellery, expensive clothing, and artistic ware, and articles of everyday use, including metalware and tools. Thus the cities were as much centres of production of goods as the villages. Agriculture was unimportant in the city; but, on the other hand, the city had a class of people who enjoyed leisure and power and were responsible for the welfare and security of the entire society. The villages and the cities shared a common culture in terms of language, religion, customs and beliefs. The city provided the leadership at the cultural, political and economic levels. There was no conflict of interests between the city and the country and the relationship was one of mutual co-operation and harmony.

The emergence of the earliest cities generated a 'little tradition' based on common beliefs and mythology, which unified rural and urban society. This society was literate, in the sense that the art of writing was known and records of various transactions between the country and the city were maintained. The ruler of the empire acted also as the chief priest and was responsible not only for the maintenance of law and order, but also for dispensing justice to the entire population. Thus, the relationship between the city and country encompassed all aspects of life—cultural, political and economic.

The Decline of Harappan Cities

The Harappan cities flourished during the period 2400 BC to about 1900 BC. From then on, till about 1700 BC, the urban settlements became smaller and their general condition deteriorated. The physical extension of the houses into the well planned streets, the partitioning of houses and courtyards, the mixing up of residential and non-residential uses, and the deterioration in quality of the drainage systems, all point towards slow urban decline. This decline may partly be explained by the growth of population and the increasing pressure on the city's available land area. The progressive decline occurred over a period of two centuries, until ultimately the cities were abandoned for some reason still unknown to us.

The decline and eventual disappearance of the Harappan civilization is often put down to either natural disaster or deliberate destruction by an invading army. The probable natural causes for the disappearance of this culture are floods, droughts and pestilence. Most Harappan cities were located on the banks of major rivers and were highly vulnerable to devastation by floods; however, floods could not have destroyed all the cities at one time. Harappan agricultural technology even at its zenith was weak—the plough was not known and metals such as copper and bronze were sparingly used for tool making. It is quite possible that a general decline in the fertility of the land aggravated by frequent droughts destroyed the very base of the urban superstructure which was dependent on agricultural surpluses. The increasing pressure of population in cities, with concomitant overcrowding and poor sanitary conditions at the later stages, could have produced devastating pestilence, thus reducing the population and sapping its vitality.

An alternative view holds that the Harappan culture was destroyed by invasion by an outside people, believed to be the early Aryans. In the *Rig Veda*, there is an account of the destruction of many walled settlements, which the Aryans called 'purs'. There is also archaeological evidence from Baluchisthan of the sudden destruction of villages by invaders coming from southern Russia and Turkistan. The Harappan cities lacked defensive structures and easily fell to the invaders. These invasions probably began by 1800 BC. The early Aryans, being essentially a rural folk, made no efforts to revive the cities.

Whether the Harappan culture was ultimately destroyed by nature or by man, it undoubtedly came to an end by about 1800 BC. Harappan town planning, so highly developed as to be the envy of even modern-day town planners, never again reappeared in the Indian subcontinent. It is indeed unfortunate that the successors to the Harappan culture did not make any attempts to carry forward the levels of perfection in town planning attained by the Harappans.

THE EARLY HISTORICAL PERIOD
(600 BC TO AD 500)

The second phase of urbanization in India began around 600 BC. The architects of this phase were the Aryans in the North and the Dravidians in the South. These parallel and independent urban developments are later culturally interlinked by large-scale migration of Aryan people to southern India, particularly the brahmanas and Jain and Buddhist monks, starting from around 300 BC. These migrations initiated a process of Sanskritization of the Dravidian South, resulting in the emergence of a composite culture. Thus, during the later historical periods, the cities of the North and the South were intimately tied to each other through cultural and economic interaction.

The second phase of urbanization is in many ways more important to us, because from this time onwards, urbanization became a permanent feature of the Indian landscape. The oldest existing cities in India—Varanasi and Patna (Pataliputra) in the North and Madurai and Kancheepuram in the South, originated around 500 BC and are symbolic of India's long urban heritage.

The early historical period covers nearly a thousand years of urban history. This period may be divided into three parts in northern India, consisting of the post-Vedic period, the Mauryan period and the post-Mauryan period. These periods indicate the early origins of urbanization, its climax in the Mauryan period, and later its decline. In southern India, urbanization originated in the pre-Sangam period and rose to great heights during the Sangam period, which saw the emergence of literary classics in Tamil.

The Nature of Evidence

Unlike the first phase of prehistoric urbanization, the second phase of Aryan and Dravidian urbanization is substantiated by the great literary texts of this period. The *Rig Veda* is the oldest of our great religious texts and it belongs to the pre-urban phase of Aryan culture. The *Rig Veda* is followed by a number of Vedic texts such as the *Dharmashastras* and *Dharmasutras* belonging to the period 600 to 300 BC, wherein references are made to the presence of urban places. Panini's great grammatical work also belongs to this period and so do the various Jain and Buddhist religious texts written in the Pali language, using the Brahmi script or its variants. The *Arthasastra* of Kautilya provides a wealth of information on the urban centres of the Mauryan period. The great epics, the *Ramayana* of Valmiki and *Mahabharata* of Vyasa muni were written in the post-Mauryan period, although the actual events may have belonged to much earlier times. The *Kamasutra* of Vatsayana, *Mahabhashya* of Patanjali, *Manusmriti* and the *Puranas* provide a mine of information on urbanization during the post-Mauryan phase. The literary evidence during the later time periods tends to exaggerate and glorify cities and much of the description is fictional rather than factual. Archaeological evidence in support of the existence of early Aryan cities is not altogether lacking; nevertheless, there are no spectacular remains of ancient cities comparable to the Harappan phase. This is mainly because the Aryans used wood and other perishable materials for building their cities, thus leaving behind very little archaeological evidence.

For southern India, literary evidence exists in the Tamil language. The earliest phase of Tamil literature is known as the Sangam period, dating back from 500 BC to AD 200. This phase of Tamil literature includes the *Tolkappiam*, a grammatical work, the epics of *Silappadikaram* and *Manimekhalai*, the philosophical work of *Tirukkural* and a number of other works. All these texts together provide a picture of the emergence of early Tamil kingdoms and of urban centres, besides information on Tamil society and culture. The literature during this period also shows indirect and direct influences of Jainism and Buddhism, and of the brahmanical religion of northern India.

Urban Origins in the Post-Vedic Period

The *Rig Veda* describes the Aryans as a pastoral and agricultural people of rural origin and the proud destroyers of an alien culture. The pro-rural bias of the *Rig Veda* finds sympathetic echo in the later brahmanical texts such as the *Dharmasastras* and *Dharmasutras*. The Aryans came to India in several migrational waves and over a period of several centuries between 2000 BC and 1500 BC. They first settled in the valley of the Indus and its tributaries and later, in the post-*Rig Vedic* period, their domain was extended to the upper Yamuna and Ganga plains. The pre-urban phase of Aryan occupation of northern India is well documented in the so-called painted grey ware culture described by archaeologists. This wheel-turned pottery is distinct from the ochre coloured and red ware pottery of the later phases of Harappan culture. The Vedic pre-urban Aryans were also familiar with the use of the plough and of metals such as copper, bronze and iron.

For nearly a thousand years from 1500 to 600 BC, the pre-urban Aryans lived in enclosed rectangular villages, divided into four segments by two main streets which crossed each other in the centre. Four gates located in each of the four cardinal directions provided entry into the village. The lands around the village were communally owned and used for cultivation and grazing. Their society was essentially egalitarian with no marked distinctions between the various sections of the population.

By the post-Vedic period, 800 to 600 BC, the centre of the Aryan homeland had shifted to the upper Yamuna and Ganga basins, which were inhabited by the two principal Aryan tribes, the Kurus in the area around Delhi and the Panchalas in the upper Ganga-Ghaghara doab near Bareilly. There were many other Aryan tribes, who fought incessant wars among themselves and with the non-Aryan groups. The territorial feuds led to the emergence of small kingdoms, which necessitated the building of capital cities and palaces, and the rise of elitist classes of nobles, militia and priests. The earliest cities of this period were Hastinapura, Sravasthi, Kapilavastu, Ujjain, Mahishamati, Champa, Rajgir, Ayodhya, Varanasi and Kausambi. The location of most of these cities is supported by archaeological evidence in addition to the literary evidence (see figure 2.2 later).

According to the *Aitareya* and *Taitareya Upanishads*, the Aryan country or Arya Varta was divided into eight *janapadas* or tribal territories. Later, through territorial conquest and expansion, the *janapadas* increased in number and size and in time 16 *mahajanapadas* came to be recognized. This process of expansion and consolidation of Arya Varta continued into the later periods. Territorial expansion increased the power of the kings, who could now make land grants and impose taxes, while the role of the popular assemblies, a characteristic feature of the early Vedic period, vanished. The king was assisted by the brahmanas; the art of writing was still unknown and there is no direct evidence of it as yet. The Ashokan edicts are the earliest written records of India which have been deciphered. These were written either in the Brahmi or Kharosthi script in the Prakrit language. Panini's *Astadhyayi*, however, belongs to an earlier period (*c.* 500 BC) and this work must have required the use of a written script. It is possible, therefore, that the art of writing existed earlier than 500 BC.

The cities of the post-Vedic period were few and far between.

Mention has been made of about a dozen cities of this period, which is a comparatively small number for the large area in which Aryans had already settled. However, it is important to note that cities emerged and began to play a key role in Aryan society which changed from an egalitarian society to one with marked differences within the various sections of people. In particular, the kings and the kshatriyas wielded greater power and influence than before. This produced a tussle for supremacy between the kshatriyas and the brahmanas. In early Vedic times, the brahmanas, with their mystico-religious source of power, enjoyed enormous influence among the masses. The emergence of the cities resulted in the rise of secular power of the kshatriyas. This struggle resulted in the emergence of kshatriya religious movements as exemplified by the rise of Jainism and Buddhism. The new religious movements were essentially urban oriented. They not only held city life as legitimate, but in fact went so far as to praise it. This is very evident from the Buddhist and Jain texts. As opposed to this, the later Vedic literature is totally contemptuous of urban places and urban people. It assigned a lower status to the vaishyas, who played a key role in urban commerce. Thus the emergence of cities juxtaposed the brahmanical spiritual power against the secular forces represented by the kshatriyas and the economic power of the vaishyas. In this struggle, the secular forces emerged triumphant and the brahmanical religion was driven almost into oblivion. It was saved partly by historical circumstances and partly by the acceptance by the brahmanas of the superiority of the kshatriyas in all secular matters. This acceptance is evident in the epics where kshatriyas are portayed as incarnations of god.

The emergence of cities in the post-Vedic period is to be attributed, in the final analysis, to economic forces. The Aryans were essentially an iron-age people, while the Harappans were unaware of iron. Iron tools are an important component of the Aryan period. Iron was used for making axes, saws and agricultural implements. The use of iron was important in many ways for setting the stage for urbanization. First, it made it possible to clear the thick forests of the Ganga plains for cultivation. The early Aryan settlements were located close to the foothills of the Himalayas as far east as southern Nepal and from this region they expanded southwards along the river valleys. The use of iron was of vital importance in widening the area of settlement. Secondly, the use of iron ploughs and draught animals, mainly oxen, helped to generate a large surplus of food which contributed to the emergence of cities. Thirdly, iron was important in the manufacture of horse-driven chariots for warfare and ox-driven carts for transportation. These also contributed to the increased mobility of the population and helped trade and commerce, a basic economic factor leading to urbanization.

A further point to be remembered here is that the Aryans had spent over a thousand years in India before city life emerged. Naturally, there was considerable contact between the Aryan and non-Aryan people inhabiting the same area. The Vedic literature refers to the non-Aryans as *panis, dasas* or *dasyus*. Grudging credit is given to these ethnic groups for their skills in trade and warfare. The fact was that, in many areas such as trade, crafts, industries and architecture, the local population had superior skills. Even in agriculture the pre-Aryans were the first to introduce the transplantation method in rice cultivation, thereby increasing productivity. Thus, the contribution of the pre-Aryan population to the emergence of cities cannot be denied. Moreover, even at this time, the pre-Aryan component of the population was probably larger than the Aryan component. However, through the process of Sanskritization, the Aryan and pre-Aryan cultures fused to form a richer and more varied Indian culture.

The houses of this period, both in the villages and in the cities, were made of mud walls, timber and thatch. Baked bricks were also in use, but rather sparingly, as is evident from the poverty of archaeological finds of buildings in the early cities of this period in Kurukshetra and Hastinapura. The paucity of archaeological evidence is also due to the small number of field investigations that have been carried out so far.

The Mauryan Period

This period is extremely rich in terms of literary sources of information, the most important being Kautilya's *Arthasastra,* the Buddhist texts and the travel accounts of Fa-Hsien and Megasthenes. We have, as a result, a voluminous account of urbanization and city life during this period. Some, at least, of the literary accounts are gross exaggerations, as many a city is described as having insurmountable walls, deep moats, wide streets, large gates, sky-rocketing mansions, busy markets, parks and lakes. Furthermore, all cities are described in a similar literary style with little variation in content. The archaeological excavations provide far more convincing evidence of urbanization during the period. This period also witnessed the introduction of aspects of Greek architecture and scientific knowledge in India's urban landscape, brought about by Alexander's invasion in 326 BC.

The Growth of Cities. From the post-Vedic period to the Mauryan period, there is once again a major eastward shift in the position of the Indian cultural heartland. By this time, the lower Ganga plains had been fully inhabited and the centre of gravity had shifted from the Kuru and Panchala country around Delhi to the Magadh region in Bihar. The smaller *janapadas* gave way to the *mahajanapadas* around 600 BC, which gave rise to the Magadhan empire around 300 BC. However, the concept of *janapadas* as politico-administrative units continued to be accepted and their number increased from eight in the post-Vedic period to over 230 by about AD 500. All the *janapadas* continued to be administered or sometimes ruled by local kings from a capital city located in the centre of each *janapada*. The growth of *janapadas* and empires encouraged urbanization. The cities increased in number, size, and the complexity of their internal structure and functions. The relations between the city and countryside also underwent important changes.

Types of Towns. The complexity of urbanization during the Mauryan period is indicated by the presence of different types of towns in addition to the capital or administrative city. The Buddhist texts give a typology of cities of this period. The more important categories of towns were: *Rajadhaniya nagara, Sthaniya nagara, Kharvata, Kheta, Putabhedana, Nigama, Pattana* and *Dronamukha*. The first four are administrative towns at four hierarchical levels, the *Rajadhaniya* being the capital city and the largest of all cities. The *Sthaniya nagara,* according to Kautilya, was the capital of a *janapada*, which at this time had the status of a province within an empire. The *Kharvata nagara* was the focal point of about 200 villages—smaller than a *Sthaniya nagara* which covered 800 villages. The *Kheta* was a small town comparable to the *Kharvata* but it was located in a hostile territory within the empire and therfore treated with disdain by the rulers.

The last four types refer to commercial cities. Of these, the *Putabhedana* was a large commercial centre specializing in wholesale trade. The *Nigama* was an ordinary market centre (the term itself refers to an organization of merchants). The *Pattana* was a coastal trading town, while the *Dronamukha* was located at the mouth of a river and served as a port city.

Other types of towns mentioned are *Khadavara,* a military camp and *Nivesa,* an encampment. Both these were of a temporary nature. In addition, there were cities of a permanent character, specialized centres of learning and religion, arts and crafts, and medicine. The well known educational cities of Taxashila and Nalanda, however, belong to the post-Mauryan period.

The Internal Structure of Cities. The cities of this period resembled the early Aryan villages. They were all walled cities, rectangular or square, with four gates, one in the centre of each side. The city was surrounded by moats and walls, in some cases in a successive concentric manner. In the city were the king's palace, the council hall, the royal store house, buildings used for dramatic arts and sports, business quarters, and residences of ordinary people. Larger cities had market places and rest-houses for travellers.

Kautilya in his *Arthasastra* describes in some detail the internal structure of capital cities. These descriptions are normative rather than actual. Nevertheless, they do provide an insight into the thinking on city planning during this time. According to Kautilya, a capital city should have three royal highways in the east-west direction and three in the north-south direction, dividing the city into 16 sectors, each sector having a specific type of land-use. These specific land-uses included the following: the palaces of the king, the ministers and the priests; the houses of dealers in flowers and perfumes; residences of warriors; warehouses and workshops; stables for elephants, camels and horses; records and audit offices; the labour colony; the royal armoury; residences of merchants; living quarters of courtesans and dancers; residences of craftsmen in wool, leather, etc.; the royal treasury and mint; the residences of brahmanas and temples; houses of metal workers and workers in jewellery; and so on. The city's internal structure had acquired great variety and complexity. The city showed distinct levels of segregation in terms of occupations. Brahmanas, kshatriyas, and vaishyas lived in separate sectors of the city. The kshatriyas and brahmanas lived in the better areas of the city which were located in the north and north-east. The vaishyas lived in the southern parts of the city, while the sudras, who comprised the bulk of the artisan class, lived in the western part of the city. This section was also the industrial area of the city.

The streets had a standard width of about eight metres and formed a grid. The residents had to make their own arrangements for the disposal of rubbish. The larger houses had courtyards, pounding sheds, and latrines for the common use of the tenants. Security was a major obsession with the city fathers and, consequently, a complete record of the city population was maintained and the activities of strangers monitored.

City Administration. Kautilya's *Arthasastra* gives details of Mauryan urban administration. The city was under the charge of a *nagaraka* or mayor, just as the village was under the charge of the village headman or *mukhya*. However, the mayor was subordinate to the *samaharta* or the minister in charge of municipal affairs. The duties of the *nagaraka* included the inspection of the city's water supply and the maintenance of the roads, public grounds, subterranean passages and the city's defences such as the wall, tower and moat. The town was divided into four wards, each in the charge of a *sthanika*, and each ward was divided into *gopas* which consisted of between 10 and 40 households. The arrival and departure of visitors to the city—guests of city residents, travellers, sadhus, merchants— were kept track of by the city's espionage network. The citizens were forbidden to move about the city in the night. The city also had a police force. According to Megasthenes, the city was ruled by a committee of 30 members, subdivided into six committees of five members each. These committees were in charge of: (1) factories, (2) foreigners, (3) births and deaths, (4) markets, weights and measures, (5) inspection of manufactured goods, and (6) sales tax. According to Kautilya, however, these functions were performed not by committees but by *adhyakshas* or superintendents appointed by the ruler. The city legal system consisted of courts at three levels: the locality, the caste and the clan level. In addition to these courts, the various occupational guilds also settled disputes among their members.

City Industry. The Mauryan city was also a centre of the manufacturing industry. Each specific industry was allotted a certain area within the city. In addition, the city was often surrounded by craft villages. These villages were more or less homogeneous in terms of occupation and specialization in some activity. Thus, there were villages of reed makers, salt makers, potters and so on. Within the city itself, there was a great variety of crafts and industries. The sixty-odd industries mentioned may be grouped into 11 categories as follows: (1) textiles, (2) carpentry and woodwork, (3) metal work including smiths and jewellers, (4) stone work, (5) glass industry, (6) bone and ivory work, (7) perfumery, (8) liquor and oil manufacture, (9) leather industry, (10) clay works including pottery, terracotta figure making, modelling and brick making, and (11) other miscellaneous industries such as making garlands, combs, baskets and musical instruments, and painting. An advanced system of guilds or *shrenis* of industrial labour regulated the manufacture of goods. The guilds of merchants dealing in various goods were called *nigamas*.

Urban Society. The urban society of this period was stratified more or less along the lines of the rural society. Caste and occupation were the primary indicators of status, and individuals spent their life within this framework. Mobility to a higher status in society was possible, but rare. The major segments of the urban society were: (1) the king and his higher administrative and military officials, (2) priests, (3) lower administrative and military officials, (4) independent professionals such as physicians, scribes, accountants and teachers, (5) the mercantile community, (6) artisans and craftsmen, (7) public entertainers such as musicians, dancers, actors and prostitutes, and (8) persons performing a variety of services, such as *dhobis*, barbers and domestic servants.

The Post-Mauryan Period

Cities, and along with them the urban way of life, began to decline from around the 5th century AD. This is lucidly described by Fa Hsien and Hiuen Tsang who visited India during the periods AD 405–11 and AD 630–44, respectively. The accounts of these foreign travellers about the state of urban centres are further supported by Indian writers, notably Vatsayana, and the overwhelming archaeological evidence available to us today. The literary accounts describe the utter ruin and abandonment of a number of well-known cities of the earlier period. The list of cities that were in a state of decline includes: Taxashila, Mathura, Sravasthi, Kausambi and Pataliputra. In spite of the adverse conditions for urban growth during this period, a few cities still managed to maintain their former splendour, for example, the cities of Kanauj and Nalanda.

The reasons often attributed for the decline of urban centres in the post-Mauryan period are many and varied: (1) The frequent recurrence of natural calamities such as famines, pestilence, fire, floods and earthquakes, took a heavy toll of urban population. (2) The political factor was no less important. The decline of well-administered empires and their replacement by the rule of feudal chiefs resulted in the exploitation of peasants and artisans alike. Capital cities, particularly the larger ones, were abandoned, as they no longer served as seats of government. (3) Foreign invasions, particularly those of the Hunas who entertained anti-Buddhist sentiments, resulted in the deliberate destruction of many Buddhist centres in north-western India and also in the Ganga plains, though to a lesser extent. (4) In addition to the foreign invaders, the internecine wars between feudal chiefs also contributed to the destruction of urban places. (5) Many cities in the Mauryan period had emerged directly as a consequence of the rise of Buddhism, and with its decline in the post-Mauryan period, many urban centres also lost their former importance. (6) The prosperity of earlier times was essentially due to a very productive agricultural base and the growth of crafts and industries. These had been protected and encouraged by kings. With the decline of the empires and kingdoms and the rise of petty feudal chiefs, agriculture and industry became less productive, and concomitantly urban centres began to decline.

Urbanization in South India

The story of the second phase of Indian urbanization, up to this point, has largely been confined to the North. However, the extreme southern part of India, which comprises the two states of Tamil Nadu and Kerala, witnessed an independent process of urbanization resulting in the emergence of a distinctly Dravidian[2] (as different from Aryan) culture.

The first phase of urbanization in India, namely the Harappan phase, had resulted in the establishment of urban centres as far south as the mouths of the rivers Narmada and Tapti and in the Malwa plateau. There is distinct archaeological evidence of the spread of Harappan culture deep into the Deccan plateau. However, as in northern India, there is no continuity between the Harappan phase of urbanization and the Dravidian phase of urban development. The origins of the Dravidian phase of urbanization may be traced to around the 5th century BC. Unlike the Aryan phase of urbanization, the origins of the Dravidian phase are not fully

[2] The word *dravida* was first used in Sanskrit around the 8th century AD. In this context it referred to a region rather than a people or a language. In early Tamil literature the world *dravida* was not used at all. However, in recent times, it has found acceptance in Tamil literature.

understood and there is a need for further archaeological and historical enquiry in this direction. Nevertheless, the rough contours of the Dravidian phase of urbanization may be delineated from the available archaeological and literary evidences.

The Pre-urban Phase. The earliest human settlements in South India, from archaeological evidence, date back to 2300–1800 BC. These settlements were located on the tops of granitic hills, on hill slopes and on plateau surfaces. Evidence of the domestication of cattle, sheep and goats and the cultivation of grain crops is found on these settlement sites. Handmade pottery and stone axes are also found, but the use of metals was not known. Terracotta objects and rock paintings are also traced to this period. In summary, one could characterize this period as the neolithic phase of rural settlements.

Between 1800 and 1500 BC, the rural settlements show further advancement with the use of metals and wheel-turned pottery. There are distinct signs of Harappan influence during this phase, although no urban settlements have so far been discovered. A characteristic of this period is the occurrence of circular hutments made of wattle and daub on wooden frames with mud floors. Objects made of copper and bronze made their first appearance during this period. This chalcolithic culture developed further during the succeeding period (1400 to 1050 BC), as evidenced by the increasing use of metals and wheel-turned pottery. Horses appear on the scene for the first time, indicating greater mobility of the people. A large number of sites belonging to this period have been excavated in the states of Tamil Nadu and Karnataka. At that point in time, the stage was set for the emergence of urban centres.

The Urban Phase. From the early chalcolithic settlements, there arose a distinct Dravidian culture with Tamil as the spoken language. The other Dravidian languages of today, such as Kannada, Telugu and Malayalam, originated at later points in time (roughly the 10th century AD onwards) as a result of Aryan influences in the South. The fact that the Dravidian culture attained a very high level, with urbanization as a concomitant process, is attested by the vast body of classical works in the Tamil language in what is known as the 'Sangam' literature. The position of Tamil in the South corresponds to that of Sanskrit in the North. However, while Sanskrit ceased to be a spoken language long ago, Tamil continues to be a spoken language to the present day.

The early Tamil literature of the Sangam period consists of

works on grammar, collections of early poetry, epics and discussions on philosophy and culture. The earliest works, such as the *Tolkappiam* and its predecessors could have been written only in an urban context. The two major Tamil epics, namely, *Silappadikaram* and *Manimekhalai* deal with urban societies in the Pandya and Chera kingdoms. Thus, the classical Tamil literature provides ample evidence of an independent urban civilization in the South. The major Tamil cities were Madurai, Vanji, Urayur, Puhar and Korkai, which served as the capital cities of the early Tamil kingdoms of the Pandyas, Cholas and Cheras. Megasthenes, the Greek ambassador at the court of the Mauryan king, mentions the southern cities of Madurai and Kancheepuram and the Pandyan kingdom in the 4th century BC. Kautilya in his *Arthasastra* refers to the trade between the Mauryan empire and the cities of Madurai and Kancheepuram in the 3rd century BC. Pearls, metals (particularly gold) and fine textile products were imported from the South into the Mauryan empire. The literary evidence indicates the existence of cities in South India as far back as the 4th and 3rd century BC. Naturally, then, Dravidian cities did not come about all of a sudden, nor did the Tamil culture and its literature emerge out of a vacuum. There are indications that city life perhaps emerged in the South even before the 3rd century BC. However, the evidence available to us is not conclusive.

Salient Features of Urbanization. From early times, the Tamil country, which included the two southern states of India, was divided into four *mandalams*—equivalent to the *mahajanapadas* of the North, though differing from the *janapadas* in terms of their non-tribal origins. The *mandalams* were further subdivided into smaller territorial units called *nadus* and *kottams*. A king ruled over the *mandalams*, while chieftains ruled over the smaller territorial units and paid tribute to the king. Accordingly, a system of cities emerged with capital cities at their apex and smaller towns forming the focal points of the lower territorial orders. In addition, there were a number of port cities, specializing in international trade.

In the early Tamil cities the king's palace and the temples were enclosed within four walls, but the cities as a whole did not have walls. In the main city, the buildings were made of bricks and tiles, cemented by mortar. The poor, however, lived in huts made of thatch with mud floors. Different communities lived in segregated streets. The major components of Tamil society in the Sangam period were the Parpanars (brahmanas), Arasars (nobles), Vellalars (peasants) and the Vaniyars (traders). Tamil society was not divided into four *varnas* as in the North, but the idea of the *varnas* spread into the South at a later stage. Even today the majority of the people in the South practise burial, which is a Dravidian tradition; while cremation is practised by the migrants from North India. The social customs, particularly in relation to marriage, are distinctly different from the Aryan, and these practices, as they existed in the Sangam period, are lucidly described in the early Tamil literature.

The major cities of the period were Puhar, the Chola port and coastal capital, Uraiyur, the Chola inland capital, Korkai, the Pandya coastal capital, Madurai, the Pandya inland capital, Musiri, the Chera port, and Vanji or Karur, the Chera inland capital. Thus a distinctive feature of the southern kingdoms was the existence of two capital cities for each kingdom. Kanchi (Kancheepuram of today) was the inland capital of the Tondai-mandalam, the fourth territorial unit of the Tamil country (figure 2.2).

The southern cities carried on a flourishing trade with the Arabs, and later the Greeks and the Romans. Early contact with the Hebrew kingdoms of Sumeria (in Mesopotamia) around 1000 BC is indicated by the use of Tamil words in Hebrew for peacocks and monkeys. The Pandya kings sent emmissaries to the Roman court in the second century AD, and the presence of numerous kinds of Roman coins in South India testifies to the volume of trade between the South Indian ports and Europe.

Distinctive Aspects of Dravidian Urbanization. In general South India, and particularly the Tamil country, shows remarkable continuity in urban traditions from the 5th century BC to the present. While some of the earlier urban centres such as Uraiyur, Puhar and Korkai exist only as ruins today, others, particularly Madurai and Kancheepuram, have withstood the vagaries of Indian history remarkably well. One major factor contributing to this continuity is the near absence of foreign invasions which characterize the history of North India. The South was protected from the Muslim invasions of the medieval period, and although Aryan influences penetrated into the region from as early as the 5th century BC, the South always maintained a cultural identity of its own. Aryan influences, starting with the Buddhist and Jain monks who were based primarily at Kancheepuram in Tamil Nadu and Nagarjuna-konda in Andhra Pradesh, were eventually absorbed within the

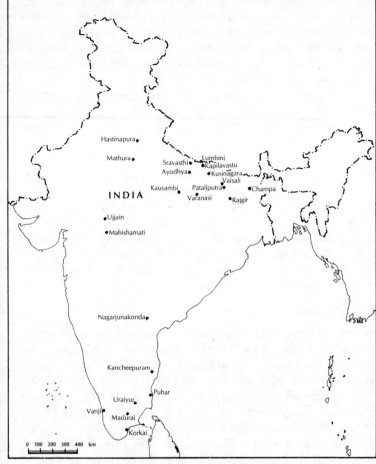

FIGURE 2.2. Ancient Aryan and Tamil Cities 600–300 BC.

local traditions. The process of fusion of the Aryan and Dravidian traditions did not generate a cultural hiatus, while in the North such a hiatus emerged inevitably as a result of the conflict between Islamic and Aryan traditions and cultures.

URBANIZATION IN THE MEDIEVAL PERIOD
(AD 600–1800)

The decline of urban centres that began in the Gupta period (5th century AD) continued during the succeeding centuries in northern

India, which witnessed during this period the political disintegration of the larger empires and the emergence of unstable dynastic regimes. The decline of Buddhism gave rise to the revival of Hinduism. The concept of Bharatavarsha now included the entire South as well as the North. Sankaracharya of Kaladi in the 8th century AD, who contributed in large measure to the revival of Vedic religion, travelled widely over the country and established four *maths* in the four corners of Bharatavarsha—Joshimath in the Himalayan region, Puri in Orissa, Dwarka in Gujarat and Sringeri in Karnataka. These centres have emerged as urban places of great religious importance wielding enormous influence all over India. The most significant aspect of these places is their continuity through history to present times. During the period under discussion, the decline of urban centres in the North was paralleled by the emergence of powerful Hindu kingdoms and urban centres in South India. Urbanization in North India, on the other hand, further suffered from Muslim invasions from the North-west. The story of urbanization during this period is a story of turmoil in the North and rapid growth in the South.

Sources of Information

The literary sources of information on urbanization for this period for northern India are rather scant. The twenty-odd books of Al-beruni, an Uzbek traveller who studied the Hindu way of life in India between AD 1017 and 1030, and the memoirs of Ibn Batuta, a diplomat traveller who visited India during 1333–42, constitute the primary sources of information. The travel accounts of Marco Polo who visited some of the cities of the South in 1288 are another useful but limited source of information. The literary evidence is further supported by archaeological evidence as in the case of Delhi, Agra and other urban centres in the North. For South India, there is, however, a vast body of literature in Tamil. Much of this literature is of a religious nature. A major work of this period is the *Ramayanam* written by the poet Kamban in the 9th century AD. By this time, South India had been substantially Sanskritized by the Aryan brahmanas who migrated there to seek favours, and in particular generous land grants, from the Hindu kings.

The Rise of Urbanization in the South (AD 600–1300)

In the late Vedic period (800 to 400 BC), two major centres of urbanization were prominent—the northern centre located in the middle

Ganga basin and the southern one in the Tamil country. During the Mauryan period, urbanization spread to the lower Ganga valley, Orissa, Gujarat and Maharashtra, and much of the extensive territory lying between the two original centres of urbanization was dotted with cities. Cities such as Nasik, Puri, Cuttack, Broach (Bharuch), Ujjain and Machilipatnam, served as a link between the northern and southern urban foci. During the medieval period (AD 800–1300) urbanization in the entire South—the region south of the Vindhya mountains—received a strong stimulus and numerous cities came into existence. Urbanization during this period is closely identified with the rise and decline of kingdoms and dynasties. A major feature of the history of South India during this period was the remarkable influence of brahmanical religious customs and rituals and the role of the Sanskrit language. Beginning with the Satvahanas, the Chalukyas, the Rashtrakutas and even the Pallavas, the South saw the emergence of kingdoms whose ruling dynasties were brahmanas. This largely explains the Aryan influence on the South and the dominance of the temple and the religio-political elite in southern cities.

The major kingdoms in the South during this period were the Chalukyas in Karnataka who ruled this territory between AD 600 and 800. Their capital at Vatapi (present-day Badami) was a major city of this time. The Ishvakus established their rule in the Krishna-Godavari region and built many cities, including Nagarjunakonda and Dharanikota, which are in ruins today, as well as the cities of Vijayawada, Rajahmundry and Nellore which stand to the present day. About the same time, the Pallavas of Kancheepuram rose to power (AD 500–800). They were followed by the Cholas, who ruled òver the Tamil country for over 400 years from AD 900 to 1300. The cities in the South grew in number and included a large number of cities which are still well known today including Tanjore, Kumbakonam, Tiruchirappalli, Cuddalore, Nagapattinam and Tiruchendur, to name but a few. A major feature of all these cities is the presence of one or more temples which dominate the urban landscape. Indeed, the size of an urban place could be estimated by the size of its dominant temple. Even today the approach of major cities in the South is indicated by the appearance of the temple *gopuram*.

The Chalukyas and the Pallavas were replaced by the Rashtrakutas in the Deccan. They ruled from Malkhed (near Sholapur) in Maharashtra for about 200 years (AD 750–972). The famous Ellora caves belong to this period. Other dynasties that ruled over this region were the later Chalukyas with their capital at Kalyani, the Hoysalas of Belur, the Kakatiyas of Warangal and so on. Each kingdom was remarkable not only for the emergence of its capital city, but also for its numerous administrative and commercial centres. A large number of cities that originated during this period continue to exist today.

The medieval South Indian city had a distinct urban morphology which still holds for southern cities. The major feature of the city was the temple, which served as the focal centre. Around the temple there were one or more concentric squares of streets. The inner squares were occupied by the upper castes, particularly the brahmanas. The lower castes lived in the periphery of the city and often the lowest castes were not allowed to come near the temple. Streets leading outwards from the four gates (*gopurams*) of the temple were mostly devoted to commercial activity and served as arterial roads of the city, linking the inner city with the periphery and the rural region beyond.

Muslim Rulers and Urbanization in the North (AD 1000 to 1526)

Between AD 600 and 1000 urbanization in North India continued to make slow progress under the patronage of petty Hindu kingdoms. The Hunas, who destroyed many cities in the early historical period had by this time merged with the locally powerful Rajput clans. The Rajput kings established numerous towns in Marwad, Mewad and Malwa. The Palas of Bengal contributed to the urbanization of the Ganga delta. The old and established urban centres in the Ganga plains saw ups and downs with the rise and fall of countless dynasties.

The slow political disintegration in North India set the stage for Muslim invasions from Afghanistan. The initial forays were most disastrous for Indian cities. Thus, the seventeen invasions of Mahmud of Ghazni ravaged the cities of north-west and western India including the cities of Gujarat. However, the new Muslim rulers of India soon established themselves with their capital at Delhi. The earliest dynasty was the so-called Slave dynasty of Qutb-ud-din Aibak. They were followed by the Khiljis, Tughluqs and later the Lodis. These successive dynasties built new cities within the present site of Delhi. Thus, within a span of a few hundred years, the city of Delhi built by Ananga Pala Tomara was replaced by that of Qutb-ud-din; later a new city was built nearby at Siri (now in ruins) by the Khiljis. The Tughluqs built an entirely enclosed township at Tugluqabad and still later Jahanpanah and Ferozabad came into existence to the north of the site of ancient Indraprastha. The Lodis shifted the capital from Delhi to Agra in 1506.

Al-beruni and Ibn Batuta mention nearly fifty cities of importance during this period. Their lists show hardly any new city, most of the cities having existed long before this period. Urbanization by this time had reached every corner of northern India from Chittagong in the far east to Baroda (Vadodara) in the west and from Srinagar in the north to Dhar in the Malwa Plateau. However, there were many areas in between, where cities were non-existent. In relation to the previous time period, urbanization in the medieval period was rather subdued. The few capital cities established by the Muslim rulers, however, showed distinct signs of prosperity as reported by Ibn Batuta. The two leading urban centres of northern India from this time onwards were Delhi and Agra; and while Agra has lost much of its former glory as capital of an empire, Delhi continues to enjoy a premier position even today. Other major cities in the North during this period were Mathura, Thaneshwar, Allahabad, Varanasi, Pataliputra, Gwalior, Ujjain, Dhar, Somnath, Meerut, Panipat, Broach, Baroda and Srinagar.

Cultural Hiatus in Indian Urbanization. This period marks a major cultural shift in the Indian urban scene. For the first time, the Islamic influence made its distinct impact on the urban landscape. Mosques, forts, palaces, reflect Islamic art and values and the traditions of Central Asia, the Arabs, and more specifically the Persians. As early as the Mauryan period, Indian cities saw the impact of foreign influences, primarily Iranian and Greek, in the arts and sciences, but these were absorbed into the indigenous culture. While the foreigners (*yavanas*) for a time were disliked, nevertheless, they were ultimately absorbed within the *varna* system of Indian society. Such a fusion of cultures unfortunately did not occur following the Muslim invasions of India. The cultural thrust during this period was altogether of a different kind. It divided the people and the society into two camps for all time—the Muslims and the non-Muslims. Thus a cultural hiatus came into existence in India's urban landscape. At least in the initial stages, the Muslims were confined to the cities, while the villages followed the ancient religious traditions. A new Muslim urban culture arose, with the king, nobles and the military at its apex. Persian was invariably the court language and fashions were determined by Persian customs and manners. The ruling classes were mainly from Afghanistan, with smaller numbers of Turks and Mongols. Eventually, all these ethnic subgroups were absorbed into an Indian Muslim society that consisted predominantly of converts. Thus, while the ethnic gap was narrowed, the cultural gap remained as wide as ever as between the Muslims and the Hindus. This cultural hiatus was conspicuous within all the cities as well as between the cities and their hinterlands. The city, by this time, had become the focal point of an alien culture. While the city had a large or even dominant Muslim population, the villages were by and large predominantly Hindu. The anti-urban bias of the Vedic tradition received renewed support, and Hinduism began to shift to its original rural traditions. The *bhakti* movements of the 12th and 13th centuries in South India, which later spread to North India as well, tended to highlight the rural brahmanical tradition and provided a shield against alien urban influences. City and country were largely alienated from each other during this period, a phenomenon that was further strengthened under the British.

Urbanization in the Mughal Period (AD 1526–1800)

The Mughal period stands out as a second high watermark of urbanization in India, the first occurring during the Mauryan period. The country (essentially northern India including Pakistan and Bangladesh) attained a high level of political stability and economic prosperity under the Mughals over a period of about 300 years—a period long enough to establish cities on a sound footing. The Mughal period saw the revival of older established cities, the addition of a few new cities and the building of an impressive array of monumental structures in almost every major city of northern India, whose urban landscape today bears unmistakable testimony to the grandeur of Mughal architecture.

   Sources of Information. The literary sources of information for this period are interestingly all in foreign languages including Persian (which was the official language of the Mughal administration), English and other European languages. Abu-l Fazl, a courtier of Akbar (1556–1605) wrote two books—*Ain-i-Akbari* and *Akbarnama*. These form the major source of information, apart from numerous Mughal administrative records available to us. In addition to this, we have the accounts of foreign travellers and emissaries, such as Ferishta (1599), Pelsaert (1620–7), Bernier (1658–67), Tavernier (1641–65), Manucci (1656) and Thevenot (1666). The written documents are further supported by the rich archaeological remains of Mughal cities.

The Extent and Level of Urbanization. The Mughal empire covered the whole of northern India from Assam to Gujarat, including present-day Pakistan and Bangladesh. The empire was divided into 15 *subas* (provinces), which were further subdivided into 105 *sarkars* or districts. According to Abu-l Fazl, there were 2,837 towns in 1594; only the larger cities numbering around 180 are, however, actually mentioned in his works. All the provinces, whether Bengal in the East, Berar, Khandesh or Malwa to the South, Gujarat in the West, or Lahore, Multan or Kashmir in the North, contained many cities of importance, besides numerous small towns and large villages of some consequence.

The overall urban system of this time was dominated by 16 large cities: Agra, Sikri, Delhi, Ahmedabad, Cambay, Ellichpur, Burhanpur, Ajmer, Ujjain, Mandu, Awadh, Lucknow, Varanasi, Jaunpur, Bihar and Cuttack. Of these, four have survived as large cities of today: Delhi, Ahmedabad, Lucknow and Varanasi; Jaunpur, Ujjain and Burhanpur are still one-lakh cities. Some of the cities mentioned above, for example, Sikri, have all but vanished, and all except Sikri had existed long before the Mughals came to India. The contribution of the Mughals to urbanization in India cannot be measured in terms of the number of new cities that they established—there were few of these, such as Moradabad. But, on the other hand, the Mughals contributed in a large measure to the revival of existing urban centres.

At the southern fringe of the Mughal empire, the rise of the Marathas, the Bahmani kingdoms and Vijayanagar empire, and finally the Nizam of Hyderabad, stimulated urban growth. Golconda, Hyderabad, Bijapur and Aurangabad are outstanding examples of urban development during this period. In addition, Pune became the centre of Maratha power and the city developed into a metropolis of great cultural and political importance.

Apart from the capital and administrative towns, the smaller towns received support from a class of feudal chiefs to whom the Mughal emperors gave large land grants. It does appear that, at least to some extent, the Mughal emperors were aware of the yawning cultural gap between the rural masses and the city rulers. In order to bring about closer contact, the intermediate functionaries were dispersed into different parts of the empire. These petty feudal lords helped in the process of land resettlement and the building of small towns. From the literary evidence, it becomes clear that the smaller urban places, noted for their crafts-men, and for the large houses of the nobles and their henchmen, prospered considerably. All this led to an ever-expanding urban system, with a hierarchy of settlements, each performing a number of economic, administrative and military functions.

The Development of Capital Cities. An integral and major aspect of urbanization, at every point of time in history and pre-history, is the scale and character of the capital cities. It is here that the maximum ·attention is paid and vast sums of money and labour invested. The capital city is invariably the largest and the most impressive city of the time, and the three Mughal capital cities were no exception. The capital originally established in Delhi in 1526, shifted to Agra, and then, during Akbar's time, an entirely new city was built at Fatehpur Sikri, which lasted for barely 15 years. Later, under Shahjahan, the capital returned to Delhi with the building of Shahjahanabad—a planned city of great beauty and charm.

These three capitals differ from each other in many ways. Fatehpur Sikri is unique among capital cities of the world in that its location was based on irrational considerations; the result was its abandonment within a period of 15 years mainly on account of inadequate water supply. Agra, however, was a large city even before Sikander Lodi made it his capital. When the Mughals took over, they altered the appearance of Agra by building an impressive fort city. (The Taj lies outside the city proper.) A major charac-teristic of Mughal cities was the building of forts in which the entire royal entourage lived. The city of the ordinary people lay outside the fort, often surrounded by a wall as in the case of Shahjahanabad in Delhi. Unlike Agra, Shahjahanabad is a well planned city with a wide central avenue leading to the main gate of the Red Fort. On one side of this avenue—the Chandni Chowk—is a mosque, the Jama Masjid, a symbol of Islamic culture. The chowk constituted the main market, while on either side of the central avenue were located the residences of nobles. The city proper is divided into *mohallas* or localities, where the streets are narrow. The poorest people lived near the outer wall. Shahjahanabad may be described as the urban jewel of the Mughal empire.

The Internal Structure of Cities. Certain basic elements characterize the internal structure of cities and towns of this period. The first and the most conspicuous element was the palace of the king or the feudal lord of the area, which was located either on a river bank or on high ground towards one end of the city. The palaces were the largest structures in the city with a number of buildings enclosed within a fort. The second major element was the mosque—the Jama Masjid—which became the cultural focal point of the Muslim reisdents of the city and continues to play the same role even today. The third element, not always present, was the outer wall, defending the city from invaders. All cities had gates for regulating entry. Some cities, in particular the city of Agra, grew beyond the outer wall, indicating rapid and uncontrolled growth. The fourth aspect has to do with the lack of planning of the city's road network. Except for Shahjahanabad, none of the Mughal cities had a regular or planned network of roads and streets. In fact, the internal structure of the Mughal cities was haphazard with overlapping residential, commercial and industrial land-uses. The entire area of the city was closely built with a very high density of population; new growth was accommodated in the suburbs, which were strung along the roads leading to the main gateways of the outer wall. Every city of this period had a market centre—the main chowk or crossroads of the city. Adjoining the market centre were the homes of craftsmen and the centre of the local industry. The markets sold a variety of goods—textiles, food, metal and wooden objects, and so on, and attracted customers both from within and outside the city.

The larger residences and buildings of the Mughal cities were built of brick and mortar, while the smaller ones, which constituted the larger part of the city, were made of mud, wood and thatch. The cities by and large were poor in appearance and unclean or even filthy. This is indeed to be expected, as cities such as Delhi and Agra housed nearly 5,00,000 people. The poverty of the masses was clearly in evidence in all the cities; narrow, dusty streets and the lack of basic amenities such as drainage and water supply made living conditions intolerable. Some cities, however, were relatively better off than others. Thus, Hyderabad, Ahmedabad and Broach were described as better cities, while the cities of the Ganga plains were poor and shabby in appearance. Most towns in this period looked like overgrown villages. To most European visitors of this time, Indian cities were rather unimpressive. The contrast between the rich and the poor in the cities was extreme—a phenomenon which continues to mar our urban scene even to the present day.

Industry and Urbanization. A major factor contributing to urbanization in the Mughal period was the growth of traditional industries such as textiles (cotton, silk and woollen) and metal work, and various arts and crafts. North Indian cities hummed with industrial activity. Whether in Dacca, Varanasi or Ahmedabad, industry was a major urban activity and the markets of all the cities were full of goods of high quality. This is amply testified by European travellers in India during this period. The crafts and industry were patronized by the rich. The craftsmen, however, came from the poorer sections of urban society. In earlier time periods, the craftsmen were Hindu; but during the course of Muslim rule from AD 1000, and in particular during the Mughal period, the skilled craftsmen were converted to Islam. This occurred partly in response to the pressure from the ruling elite and partly as an escape from the low caste status assigned to craftsmen in Hindu society. However, the economic conditions of the craftsmen did not improve even after their conversion to Islam. They continued to be exploited and this state of affairs has remained unchanged to the present. Nevertheless, industrialization and urbanization proceeded simultaneously and generated a large number of small towns in addition to the many provincial and administrative capitals of the period.

External trade was another major contributing factor in urbanization during this period. Indian-made goods were much sought after in West Asian, South-east Asian and European markets. A number of trade centres emerged, particularly at the periphery of the Mughal empire. The main centres were Cambay, Surat, Burhanpur, Satgaon, Chittagong, and Hooghly. Cambay and Surat were by far the most important trade centres of this time. The traders belonged to three communities—the Bohra Muslims, the Hindu Banyas, and the Parsis. Traders had appointed agents in other parts of the world, particularly in South-west Asia and South-east Asia. Burhanpur in Malwa was a major centre of trade between the Mughal empire and the kingdoms of the Deccan. Trade and industry thus contributed immeasurably to urbanization during this period.

Urbanization in the Deccan and the South (AD 1300–1800)

In the onward march of the Muslim cultural invasion of India, the Deccan acted as a buffer zone between the extreme South and the North. The two southernmost states never formed part of the northern Muslim empires. The Muslim influence there was confined to sporadic forays, for example, the invasion of the Pandya kingdom and the destruction of Madurai city in the 13th century by Malik Kafur. On the other hand, northern parts of Karnataka, Andhra Pradesh and the whole of Maharashtra were outside the direct control of the Muslim rulers of the North, including the Mughals. This region was divided into a number of Muslim and Hindu kingdoms. The Bahmani kingdoms of Ahmadnagar, Bijapur and Golconda had to meet with the stiff opposition of the Vijayanagar kingdom with its capital at Hampi. The Marathas rose to power in the 17th century and established Pune as their capital; further, they also exercised control over parts of the extreme South as far as Madurai and Tanjore. They helped to rebuild the Hindu temples and protect the urban centres of the far South.

A number of major cities grew up in the Deccan. Of these Golconda (now in ruins near Hyderabad), Bijapur, Ahmadnagar, Gulbarga, Badami, Kolhapur, Pune, Hampi (now in ruins) and Hyderabad are notable examples. These cities were built on a grand scale, with monumental structures in the centre in the form of mosques or palaces. They often had planned street layouts, as in Hyderabad, and large market centres—the Char Minar area of Hyderabad. Some of these were walled cities, reflecting the sense of insecurity felt by the smaller kingdoms in relation to their giant northern counterparts. A number of these cities continue to occupy positions of great importance even today. Hyderabad and Pune are million cities, while Ahmadnagar, Bijapur, Gulbarga and Kolhapur are all one-lakh cities.

The urban character of the Deccani cities presents a mixed picture of Hindu and Muslim dominance. Ahmadnagar, Bijapur, Golconda and Hyderabad were the capitals of Muslim kings, while Hampi and Pune symbolized revival of Hindu political power. The rural population in the Deccan remained predominantly Hindu in its composition, and the Muslim influence on the whole was confined to the cities. Thus, the contrast between the city and the country widened and the city had only a marginal significance to the masses in the rural areas.

In the far South, the ancient kingdoms of the Cholas, Pandyas, Hoysalas, Gangas and Rastrakutas had all come to an end. This was a period of the 'Kalabras' which in Tamil is synonymous with confusion. The far South experienced a period of urban stagnation, if not decline, during this period. The Marathas, and to some extent

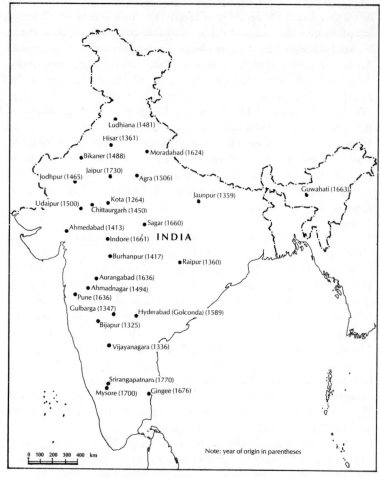

FIGURE 2.3. Selected Medieval Indian Cities.

other local kings and chieftains, helped to sustain the earlier prosperity of the temple cities of the South. While the South did not
experience the cultural trauma of the North, it nevertheless suffered
from the weakness of its political set-up.

Captive Urbanization

Despite the laudable efforts of Akbar to bring about cohesion
between the Hindu and Muslim societies of India, the intra-urban
as well as rural-urban cultural hiatus continued to persist during
the Mughal times. While the Muslim influence penetrated to the

smaller towns during the Mughal period, the conflict between the two cultures remained unabated. The cultural hiatus is highlighted by the fact that there were as many as 29 major uprisings even during Akbar's time. The village and the city were divided on the basis of religion and each group followed its own ways. In the major cities, the Hindu population was substantial; they even formed a majority in some cities. Communal tension was a common feature of this time, as it is, unfortunately, even today. In large measure, the present communal riots in urban India have their origins in the Mughal period. The important point that emerges is that the socio-cultural hiatus not only characterized rural-urban relations, but also the relations of people within the city itself. The city thus emerges as a hotbed of social heterogeneity and tension. Riots broke out periodically, disrupting the normal quiet, peace and harmony.

The people of the Hindu-Muslim city are still captives within the four walls of their experience—an experience derived from history, of doubt and distrust. At the present time, a large number of Muslims live in segregated areas within the cities, thus generating cities within cities. These islands of humanity are cut off from the rest and cannot expand to accommodate their increasing numbers. The city becomes a prison for its residents, where walls of prejudice isolate groups from the mainstream. To liberate the captive cities would require a total restructuring of their living quarters and the elimination of spatial segregation within the city.

URBANIZATION IN THE BRITISH PERIOD
(1800–1947)

The European phase of India's urban history has its beginnings, ironically, in the period during which Mughal supremacy was at its height. The Portuguese were the first to establish new port towns in India—Panaji in Goa in 1510 and Bombay in 1532. They were followed by the Dutch—Machilipatnam in 1605 and Nagapattinam in 1658; and the French—Pondicherry in 1673 and Chandranagore in 1690. The British established themselves in Madras in 1639 and Calcutta in 1690. All these European settlements, and the European presence as traders in a large number of existing Indian ports and inland cities, continued throughout the Mughal period; but without having any marked impact on the level of urbanization in India. It is only in the early 19th century that the British established a firm territorial hold in India, and India came under the British crown in 1858. From that time, until 1947, the British exercised unquestioned sway over the entire subcontinent including the 500-odd princely states. The entire country, without exception, came under one political umbrella. This was unprecedented in Indian history. The course of urbanization after 1800 in all parts of India was determined by British colonial economic policies and social attitudes.

Sources of Information

The Euroepan presence from the 16th century onwards is well documented, and the volume of literary sources since the inception of the East India Company is indeed vast. Nevertheless, our understanding of the processes of urban growth and decline during the early phase, that is, upto the year 1872, is fragmentary and in part speculative in nature. In 1872 India's first census of population was carried out, and since then censuses have been taken regularly at intervals of 10 years, providing direct information on the growth of towns and cities in India. The scope of census information on urbanization has also steadily increased since the time of the earliest censuses in the 19th century. Even today the census constitutes the basic source of information on urbanization and its various facets.

Urban Decline in the 19th Century

The consolidation of territorial power by the British in 1800 and the end of a period of political instability brought about, surprisingly, a period of stagnation and decline of urban centres in India, which lasted for well over a century. The 19th century urban scenario stands out in contrast to the Mughal period of urban growth. The main reasons for the decline of cities during this period are: (1) the lack of interest on the part of the British in the prosperity and economic development of India, and (2) the ushering in of the industrial revolution in England in the latter half of the 18th century, thus altering the very complexion of urbanization in England, and in India at a later stage.

Around 1800, India had 16 cities with a population of one lakh or more, and about 1500 towns spread over all parts of the country. Only a third of the towns and cities were located in the Ganga plains: western and southern India were comparatively more urbanized, while eastern India was the least urbanized. The overall level of urbanization in 1800 is estimated to be approximately 11 per cent. Varanasi was the largest city in India in 1800, followed by Calcutta; Surat, Patna, Madras, Bombay and Delhi had populations of only 1,50,000. Among these cities, only three (Calcutta, Madras and Bombay) were entirely new cities established by the British; the rest had their origins in Mughal or earlier times.

A major feature of the early 19th century was the decline of the pre-British cities. Prominent among the cities that lost their former importance were Agra, Delhi, Lucknow, Ahmedabad, Srinagar, Cambay, Patna, Gaya, Baroda, Indore and Tanjore. This is by no means a complete list of cities which declined during this period. By 1872, when the first Census was undertaken, the urban population of India had declined from 11 per cent in 1800 to 8.7 per cent in 1872. There were only 16 cities with a population of one lakh or more and, in all, only 43 places had a population of 50,000 or more. Calcutta had by this time become the premier city of India with a population of nearly 8 lakhs, and while the pre-British cities showed a marked decline in population, the British cities of Calcutta, Bombay and Madras showed remarkable growth.

The decline of a large number of urban places in India during the 19th century was primarily due to the negative attitude of the British towards the traditional industries of India, particularly the cotton textile industry. This attitude was largely a result of the industrial revolution in England and the growth of the textile industry in Manchester. By the end of the 19th century, England had emerged as a major industrial economy of the world and India was the main market for British goods. India's traditional urban centres, which depended on the export of its industrial products, declined rapidly as a consequence.

Another factor contributing to the decline of the urban centres of the pre-British period was the introduction of the network of railroads in India, starting from 1853. By 1900, the rail network had been fully developed and covered all parts of the country. The introduction of the railways resulted in the diversion of trade routes into different channels and every railway station became a point of export of raw materials, thus depriving some of the earlier trade centres of their monopoly in trade. Many trading points on the Ganga river, which was an important trade channel, lost their importance. A good example is that of Mirzapur.

On the positive side, the railways contributed to the growth of the metropolitan cities and even some of the major inland towns. The railways also helped in the introduction of modern industry in the metropolitan cities of Calcutta, Bombay, Madras and Kanpur. The 19th century also saw the emergence of a new class of towns in the hill areas of the Himalayas and the South.

By 1901, after a century of British occupation of India, India's level of urbanization, remained at around 11 per cent; the 19th century had witnessed a period of decline of urban centres until about 1870, and thereafter a slow upward growth in the level of urbanization. In 1901, India had 25 cities with one lakh or more persons and 69 cities with a population of 50,000 or over. In all there were 1,917 towns in India in 1901.

Facets of British Influence on Urbanization

The largely negative impact of the British on the Indian urban scene in the 19th century has to be viewed in the light of the overall impact of British rule over the entire period from 1800 to 1947. While urban stagnation or slow growth was a feature of this period until about 1931, urbanization began to show signs of rapid growth thereafter. In 1941, which marks the last Census before Independence, there were 49 one-lakh cities in India, and in all around 2,500 towns. Apart from the overall level of urbanization, the British impact was considerable in terms of the morphology of Indian cities and their functional character. During the 150 years of British rule, India's urban landscape went through a radical transformation.

The major contributions of the British to the Indian urban scene were: (1) the creation of the three metropolitan port cities, which emerged as the leading colonial cities of the world, (2) the creation of a chain of hill stations in the Himalayan foothills and in South India, and the introduction of tea and coffee plantations which produced a number of small settlements with distinct urban characteristics in Assam and elsewhere, (3) the modification of the urban landscape of the existing cities with the introduction of (a) the Civil Lines and (b) the Cantonments, (4) the introduction of the railways and modern industry which led to the creation of new industrial townships such as Jamshedpur, Asansol, Dhanbad and so on, and (5) the improvements in urban amenities and urban administration. These major facets of British influence are examined in greater depth below.

1. The Metropolitan Cities. By the start of the 20th century,

Calcutta, Bombay and Madras had become the leading cities of India; although none of these had a population of a million. The older cities of the Mughal period had all dwindled into small towns and cities. Thus, Delhi, Varanasi, Ahmedabad, Agra and Allahabad had populations of around 2,00,000 only, while Calcutta, the leading city, had a population of over 9 lakhs. Further, the landscape of the colonial cities showed distinct signs of European influence.

Calcutta, Madras and Bombay were leading administrative, commercial and industrial cities. The city's focal point was the central commercial area, with tall, European-style buildings, representing the banks and headquarters of commercial and industrial houses. Numerous streets and by-lanes specialized in various products—clothing, furniture, medical supplies, electrical and other gadgets, apart from areas devoted to entertainment. The chief commercial area was also the city's focal point of rail and road transportation. Suburban railways, tram cars and city buses gave the colonial cities a new status, unmatched by the traditional cities of the interior.

The city's administrative nerve centre was no less impressive. Dalhousie Square in Calcutta and Fort St. George in Madras were close to the central commercial area, but each was a major second focal-point in the city. Both the central market area and the administrative area had massive buildings which were British variants of Roman styles. To the native Indians, these structures provided a glimpse into European culture, while for the Europeans, they were reminders of their home. The metropolitan cities had no remarkable structures reflecting Indian traditions; the only features that were entirely Indian were the shabby and crowded residential quarters where the greater part of the Indian population of these cities lived.

In 1911, the capital of the British Indian empire was shifted to Delhi, and an entirely new city—New Delhi—was built. This new city was completed by about 1935. New Delhi had a modern commercial area, with a magnificent administrative complex not far away. It was a sprawling city of bungalows with large compounds and wide streets lined with trees, which on the whole provided a cultural landscape satisfying European taste. New Delhi stands in sharp contrast to the now overcrowded and rather dilapidated Shahjahanabad, the city of the Mughals.

2. *Hill Stations and Plantation Settlements.* The hill station is an

inheritance from the British period. It is a permanent feature today, though it has been thoroughly Indianized during the post-Independence period. The British, coming from a cool temperate climate, found the Indian summer season inhospitable and even considered it a threat to good health and longevity. They found an escape in the hills, where they spent the greater part of summer. Even the national capital was shifted from Delhi to Simla for six months of the year. The hill stations, located at elevations of 1,500 to 3,000 metres above sea level, attempted to replicate the ambience of the English countryside, for which the English in India longed, nostalgically.

The first hill stations were established as early as 1815, and by 1870 there were over 80 hill stations in four different areas in India, serving the four major metropolitan cities of Calcutta, Delhi, Bombay and Madras. These areas were: (a) Simla-Mussoorie-Nainital near Delhi, (b) Darjeeling-Shillong near Calcutta, (c) Mahabaleshwar in the Western Ghats near Bombay, and (d) the Nilgiri-Kodaikanal area in Tamil Nadu.

The hill stations originally catered to the needs of the British population in India, which consisted mainly of civilian and military personnel and their dependents. In course of time, a substantial native population migrated to these towns, seeking employment in providing the various services which the British needed. The British built schools, hospitals, hotels and clubs for the exclusive use of Europeans. Women and children of European origin outnumbered the men, who were compelled to spend longer times in the plains. In due course, the Indian princely families followed the British to the hill stations, where they established their summer palaces. The hill stations also eventually served the needs of European business executives working in private industrial and business houses, and Christian missionaries.

For the vast masses of Indians in the plains, the hills had a spiritual sanctity. They were considered as places for quiet contemplation and for withdrawal from wordly concerns. The Himalayan region, in particular, had mythological significance, apart from its being the source of the sacred river Ganga. As early as the 8th century, Adi Sankaracharya had established temples in Badrinath, Kedarnath and Amarnath. In the South as well, the hills formed appropriate locations for temples and places of worship. The British viewpoint, however, differed considerably. The hill station, for the British, was a temporary home away from home. For a people accustomed to a different climate, the hill station was also a definite need. Today hill stations exist primarily as recreational and tourist centres catering mainly to the needs of the new urban elite.

The tea and coffee plantations generated yet another type of settlement in the plains of Assam and in the hill areas of Kerala, Tamil Nadu and Karnataka. These settlements were brought about by both voluntary and forced migration of poor labourers from Bihar and Bengal in the case of the estates in Assam, and from neighbouring districts in the case of tea and coffee plantations in the hills of southern India. The plantation settlements were never very large in size, but had distinct urban characteristics in the presence of processing plants, workers' residences and associated commercial establishments.

3. Civil Lines and Cantonments. The urban landscapes of a large number of Indian towns and cities, which originated long before the arrival of the British, were, nevertheless, modified substantially during the British rule. The modifications are most noticeable at the administrative centres of the British Raj—the provincial capitals, the district headquarters, and the tehsil-level administrative centres. The 'Civil Lines' were a new addition to all but the smallest administrative centres, while cantonments were most often built near major towns for considerations of security. The civil lines and the cantonments existed as adjuncts to the 'native' city to accommodate the British civilian and military personnel. The civil lines contained the administrative offices and courts as well as residential areas for the officers. The civil line and cantonment areas invariably had large open spaces, and roads were built according to a plan, with the administrative buildings occupying a central position. The civil lines area stood apart from the native city, which was overcrowded and lacked basic amenities. The British residences, sprawling bungalows with large compounds, are a typical colonial heritage.

Unlike the civil lines, cantonments are found in fewer places. The cantonments are, however, very conspicuous around the large cities. In all 114 cantonments were built during the late 19th and early 20th century, of which about five per cent were located in hill areas and functioned, more or less, as adjuncts to the hill stations. They were concentrated in the plains of the Punjab and western Uttar Pradesh, while the four southern states together had only five cantonments. The cantonments were originally built for hous-

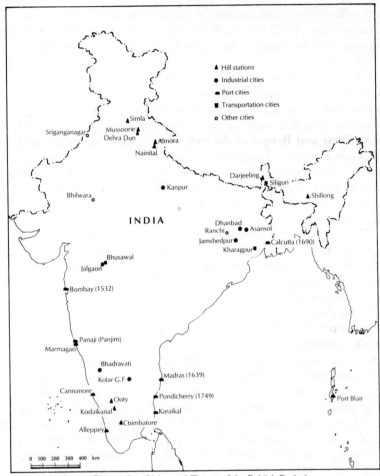

FIGURE 2.4. Cities and Towns of the British Period.

ing British officers and men of the armed forces. Indian soldiers were housed in separate areas within the cantonment. In both British and Indian barracks spatial segregation in terms of rank was strictly enforced.

The civil lines and cantonments highlight the social distance deliberately maintained by the British from the mass of Indian urban dwellers. The British, even more than the Muslim rulers, were conscious of their alien identity and hardly attempted to acquaint themselves with the people over whom they ruled. The city thus became more firmly divided within itself, and the social distance between the urban and rural areas increased.

4. Railways, Industrialization and Urbanization. The introduction of railways in India in the latter half of the 19th century contributed to the emergence of a national network of urban places, in which the metropolitan cities formed the primary foci, supported by the one-lakh cities which acted as satellite centres. The railways contributed in no small measure to the enlargement of trade and the introduction of modern industry and thus indirectly helped the process of urbanization, although the impact of the railways was not strongly in evidence until the 1930s.

The most direct contribution of the railways to the growth of the existing cities was the railway station. The railway station, soon became a focal point of the city, rivalled only by the main market centre. The cities began to grow in the direction of the railway station and even the main market began to shift towards this area. The result was haphazard urban growth from the city centre towards the railway station. The railways also introduced, in a number of larger towns, railway colonies to accommodate their administrative and engineering staff. The railway colonies have become an integral part of many Indian cities. The enlargement of the railway network also led to the establishment of railway workshops and the employment of large numbers of workers. As a result of this development, new railway towns emerged in various parts of the country, for example, Jamalpur in Bihar, Waltair in Andhra, Bareilly and Meerut in Uttar Pradesh, Nagpur in Maharashtra and so on.

The industrial revolution that originated in England in the latter half of the 18th century, took a full hundred years to reach India. The early factory industries to emerge in India were the cotton textile industry in Bombay and Ahmedabad, jute in Calcutta and coal mining in the Damodar basin. There was some scattered development of the cotton textile industry in other parts of India, as well. Kanpur and Jamshedpur were the only truly industrial cities to emerge during the British rule; Kanpur specialized in the leather and woollen textile industries, while Jamshedpur, established in 1907, was the main iron and steel centre in India until 1947. Industrial development in India before Independence was indeed very modest. Most industries were located in existing towns, principally the colonial metropolitan cities of Bombay, Calcutta and Madras. Calcutta and Bombay were the only cities in which distinct industrial areas developed.

5. *Urban Amenities and Urban Administration.* One of the major benefits of British rule was the improvement in civic amenities in some, at least, of India's major cities. Piped water supply, street lighting, domestic electricity supply, sewerage, modern shopping areas and in some cases parks and playgrounds for recreation were established in a number of cities. However, it must be admitted that at the time of Independence, the vast majority of India's towns and cities did not have electricity, leave alone piped water supply and sewerage. The conditions in many places, particularly with respect to water supply and sewerage, continue to be poor even to this day. During the British period, civic amenities were provided only in the civil lines area and the cantonment. The native city remained outside the pale of modernization. Urban administrative bodies were established to look after the civic amenities (and to introduce local or grass-root democracy) in a number of cities from 1881. These municipalities were primarily concerned with the collection of local taxes, the maintenance of roads, removal of garbage and night soil, primary education and public health. Town planning was not introduced during the British period, although legislation for the improvement of slum areas was enacted in the first two decades of the 20th century in Bombay and other provinces.

Urbanization in the Princely States

During the entire period from 1800 to 1947, a substantial part of India was outside the direct jurisdiction or rule of the British government in India. In 1947, there were as many as 548 princely states, some of which were as large as the British provinces, for example, Hyderabad and Mysore. The only direct British impact on urbanization in the princely states was seen in the institution of the Residency and cantonments in the capital cities of some of the states. In Hyderabad, Mysore and other major cities, the Residency and the adjoining areas grew more rapidly than the rest of the city, partly as a result of the comparative security and freedom from arbitrary rule that these areas offered. The smaller towns in the princely states continued to stagnate during this period. With a few exceptions, the princely states were generally backward in terms of their level of economic development. This is reflected in the lower levels of urbanization in these states.

The New Urban Ethos

In the British period, Indian cities became the focal points of westernization. Schools, colleges and universities trained men and women in western thought and languages. A new western oriented urban elite emerged. Their dress, eating habits, and social behaviour reflected western values and attitudes. The educated sought jobs under the British government and, in general, emulated the British in all walks of life. This process of westernization, firmly rooted in India during the British period, has continued to guide the destiny of the urban elite even four decades after Independence. It is indeed the central aspect of social change in modern India. With the process of westernization, there has been a concomitant alienation of the urban elite from the urban and rural masses. The gap between city and countryside has become wider and the rural-urban conflict continues to plague the Indian social and political system.

THE POST-INDEPENDENCE PERIOD

Urbanization has entered a new and more important phase in the post-Independence period. In contrast with the British period, which witnessed a period of urban stagnation, the post-Independence period is notable for rapid urbanization, particularly of the one-lakh and million cities. There has been nearly a threefold increase in India's urban population, from 62 million in 1951 to 159 million in 1981. The proportion of urban population to total population has increased at a slower pace from 17.6 per cent in 1951 to 23.7 per cent in 1981. The number of cities with a million or more persons has increased from 4 to 12 in the same period. The major changes that have occurred in India's urban scene in the post-Independence period are: (1) the influx of refugees and their settlement, primarily in urban areas in northern India, (2) the building of new administrative cities, such as Chandigarh, Bhubaneshwar and Gandhinagar, (3) the construction of new industrial cities and new industrial townships near major cities, (4) the rapid growth of one-lakh and million cities, (5) the stagnation, and in some cases decline, of small towns, (6) the massive increase in squatters and the proliferation of slums in the million cities, and the emergence of the rural-urban fringe, and (7) the introduction of city planning and the general improvement in civic amenities.

The Refugee Influx and Urbanization

In the period immediately following Independence, there was a massive influx of refugees into India, in two principal streams: (1) the refugees from West Pakistan, who found their way to Delhi, the national capital, the adjoining state of Punjab (including modern-day Haryana) and to a lesser extent western Uttar Pradesh; and (2) the refugees from East Pakistan who settled down in Calcutta and its suburbs and in Assam and Tripura. In all 14 entirely new towns were built to accommodate the refugees, of which only one was in West Bengal, five in Uttar Pradesh, four in Punjab, three in Gujarat and one in Maharashtra. In addition, refugee colonies (new townships) were established near existing cities. These new urban additions were generally designated as model towns, and 19 places in Punjab, Haryana and Delhi were selected for locating these townships. In contrast, the refugees from Bangladesh settled primarily in the rural areas of West Bengal, Assam and Tripura. Thus, the impact of the refugees on urbanization was far greater in the northern states of India than in the eastern and and southern states.

New State Capitals

The partition of India in 1947 and the states' reorganization of 1956, resulted in the creation of linguistic states, without suitable capital cities. Some of these states built, with central assistance, new capital cities, the most notable and the most lavishly built among these being Chandigarh. Chandigarh has a western look, and stands out as an anamolous marvel among Indian cities. The other new administrative capitals are Bhubaneshwar in Orissa, Gandhinagar in Gujarat, and Dispur in Assam. These towns have added a significant new dimension to Indian town planning.

Industrial Cities

India has become the world's tenth largest industrialized nation. This has come about largely in the post-Independence period, and in particular since 1956. Among the most notable outcomes of industrialization in the post-Independence period are the steel cities of Rourkela, Durgapur, Bhilai Nagar and Bokaro, each of which has a population of one lakh or more persons. Other new industrial cities are the refinery towns of Barauni, Noonmati, Haldia and Ankleshwar; the fertilizer towns at Sindri, Mittrapur,

Legend:
- ⊘ State capitals
- ● Industrial cities
- ⊙ Port cities
- ▲ Plantation towns
- ♟ Refugee towns
- ○ Other cities

INDIA

Naya Nangal
Chandigarh
Yamunanagar
Modinagar
Itanagar
Kohima
Kandla Gandhinagar Murwara
Bokaro Steel City Durgapur Aizawl
Ankleshwar Haldia
Durg-Bhilai Rourkela
Bhubaneshwar
Ulhasnagar Jagdalpur Paradeep
Ichalkaranji
Neyveli
Valparai
Karaikudi
Rajapalayam

0 100 200 300 400 km

FIGURE 2.5. Important Cities and Towns of the Post-Independence Period.

Naya Nangal and Namrup; port towns such as Kandla and
Paradeep; and aluminium towns like Korba and Ratnagiri. The
number of industrial townships or company towns located in close
proximity to existing major cities is too large to be listed here.
There are over one hundred such townships in India today. In
addition, there are over 500 industrial estates on the periphery of
one-lakh cities. Industrial growth in India during the past three
decades has indeed been impressive and so has its impact on city
development.

Metropolization

A remarkable feature of urbanization during the post-Independence period has been the rapid growth of the one-million and one-lakh cities. The number of such cities has increased from 76 in 1951 to 219 in 1981. The proportion of urban population living in the one-lakh cities has increased from 38 per cent in 1951 to 60 per cent in 1981. In absolute terms the population living in one-lakh cities has increased from 39 million in 1951 to 94 million in 1981—a phenomenal growth indeed. The unenviable result of this growth is the widening gap between the cities and the smaller towns in terms of opportunities for employment, education and medical facilities. Further, the rapid and more or less unplanned and haphazard growth of the cities has imposed severe strains on housing, water supply, sewage and sanitation in the cities—a problem that has become chronic and assumed alarming proportions.

Stagnation and Decline of Small Towns

A concomitant phenomenon of metropolization is the decline or stagnation of the smaller towns. The decline has been most conspicuous in the case of very small towns with a population of less than 20,000, and to a lesser degree in towns of 20,000 to 50,000. The total number of urban places in India has increased from 2,844 in 1951 to 3,245 in 1981, while the number of small towns with populations of less than 20,000 has declined from 2,345 in 1951 to 2,020 in 1981. The contribution of these towns to the total urban population has also declined from 32 per cent in 1951 to 19 per cent in 1981. It is important to note that small towns play a crucial role in rural development and, to a large extent, the decline of the small town is an indication of the failure of the planners to bring about any development in rural areas. The trend of declining small towns ought to be a major cause for worry for the National Planning Commission.

The Growth of Slums and the Rural-Urban Fringe

The rapid growth of the one-million cities, in particular, has brought in its wake a large set of problems. Perhaps, the most important of these is the problem of housing for the poorer sections of society. Many have flocked to cities in search of employment. The available housing accommodation in the city is far too expensive, and the poor have by and large settled down in an illegal way on vacant public or private land. Ugly thatched huts, tenements constructed with an odd mixture of assorted materials, and the use of pavements for dwelling are all characteristic features of metropolitan cities in India today. Further, the big cities have expanded physically into the peripheral villages in an unplanned and haphazard manner. Thus, a rural-urban fringe has emerged around most of the larger cities. The provision of basic amenities, such as piped water supply, sewerage, drainage and paved roads to the slum dwellers and the fringe villages, poses a major problem to the city administration. There is increasing demand for these services, while the people, particularly in the slums and fringe areas contribute nothing by way of taxes. Further, the municipality is called upon to provide services to areas that are under illegal occupation. Political exegencies have compelled the administration to legalize squatter colonies and provide them with some, at least, of the basic amenities. The inherent contradictions of this chaotic situation in our urban areas pose tremendous challenges to the urban planner and the city administrator alike.

City Planning

The post-Independence period saw the beginnings of city planning in India. The Town and Country Planning Organization, established by the central government, prepared the Master Plan for Delhi in 1957. It also prepared model legislation for town planning for state governments to enact. The 1960s saw the emergence of town planning departments in different states in the country. With the help of central grants, these departments have prepared over 500 master plans for individual cities. However, few city master plans have been implemented with vigour. The metropolitan cities such as Delhi, Bombay, Madras and Calcutta have succeeded to some extent in executing massive housing programmes, the construction of commercial complexes, the creation of new industrial areas, and the re-location and rebuilding of slum areas. All this activity has altered the urban landscape of the big cities in a significant way. The experience gained by the Metropolitan Development Authorities provides the basic infrastructure for planned urban development in the future.

SELECTED READING

Ali, S.M.: *Geography of the Puranas,* Peoples Publishing House, 1966.

Bhatia, S.S.: 'Historical Geography of Delhi', *Indian Geographer,* Vol. 1, 1956, pp. 17–43.

Bhattacharya, B.: *Urban Development in India,* Shree Publishing House, Delhi, 1979.

Davis, Kingsley: 'Urbanisation in India: Past and Future', in Turner, Roy, ed.: *India's Urban Future,* Oxford University Press, Bombay, 1962, pp. 3–26.

Gadgil, D.R.: *Industrial Evolution in India in Recent Times,* Oxford University Press, Delhi, 1974, pp. 134–47.

Habeeb, Atiya: 'Urban Growth: A Historical Perspective', *Travaux et Documents de Geographie Tropicale,* CEGET, 1981, pp. 31–57.

Habib, Irfan: *An Atlas of the Mughal Empire: Political and Economic Maps with Detailed Notes, Bibliography and Index,* Oxford University Press, New Delhi, 1982.

King, A.D.: *Colonial Urban Development,* Routledge & Kegan Paul, London, 1976.

Naqui, H.K.: *Urbanisation and Urban Centres under the Great Mughals,* Indian Institute of Advanced Study, Simla, 1972.

Neelakanta Sastri, K.A.: *A History of South India,* Oxford University Press, Bombay, 1966.

Raj Bala: 'Spatial Perspective on Urbanization in India from the Ancient to the Early Modern Period', *Transactions, Institute of Indian Geographers,* Vol. 3, 1980, pp. 21–9.

Schwartzburg, J.E.: *A Historical Atlas of South Asia,* The University of Chicago Press, Chicago, 1978.

Subramaniam, N.: *Sangam Polity,* Asia Publishing House, Bombay, 1966.

Thakur, V.K.: *Urbanisation in Ancient India,* Abhinav Publications, New Delhi, 1981.

Ved Prakash: *New Towns in India,* Monograph No. 8, The Cellar Book Shop, Wyoming, Detroit, 1969.

CHAPTER 3

Urbanization Processes

Ever since 2500 BC, urban places have played an important role in the evolution of India's cultural, political, economic and social life. Throughout this long period—4500 years—the proportion of the country's total population living in urban areas has fluctuated between five and twenty-five per cent. These statistics, however, hide the more significant events of the rise and fall of individual cities and of systems of cities which made lasting impressions on the country's cultural and social advancement. The influence of cities, past and present, on our way of life, cannot by any standards be considered as a simple, unidimensional process. On the other hand, the emergence, spatial spread, growth and decline of cities, have meant different things at different points in time and space. There are, in fact, not one but several processes of urbanization at work at any given point in time and space. These processes are interdependent and inter-related, yet varied in terms of their underlying causes and the manifestations of their impact. The history of urbanization in India reveals, broadly, four processes of urbanization at work throughout the historical period. These are: (a) the emergence of new social relationships among people in cities and between people in cities and those in villages through a process of social change; (b) the rise and fall of cities with changes in the political order; (c) the growth of cities based on new productive processes, which alter the economic base of the city; and (d) the physical spread of cities with the inflow of migrants, who come in search of a means of livelihood as well as a new way of life. All these processes have been enriched by the influences of other world cultures, in particular those from West Asia and Europe.

URBANIZATION AS A
SOCIO-CULTURAL PROCESS

Cities are social artifacts. They originated as a result of the emergence of the ruling classes—people who controlled and regulated the distribution of goods and services within the society as a whole. The rulers were supported in this task by the literati—the educated upper class of people, the militia, and a host of servants and occasionally slaves. Thus, the early tribal or folk societies were transformed into peasant or feudal societies in which the urban foci played a crucial role. Sometimes the change from a tribal society, in which no urban centres were present, to a peasant or feudal society occurred as a result of invasion by people of a different ethnic stock. In such a situation, the urban rulers were invariably outsiders, while the rural people represented the original population. In this situation, the relations between country and city were characterized by servitude of the rural people to the urban dwellers. When foreigners invaded a peasant or feudal society, the existing urban places underwent considerable social change, depending on the role played by the foreigners. The foreigners from other cultures came as merchants, mercenaries, or as rulers with their vassals. They brought with them their customs, dress, religion and social values. Out of this cross-cultural interaction a new society emerged, in which the foreigners eventually became indistinguishable from the local population. In recent times, the mobility of people between and within countries and the flow of information through the mass media, are all contributing towards change in urban as well as rural society. However, in the process, the urban places act as transmitters and interpreters of foreign influences. The city today stands apart from the countryside, in terms of the higher degree of its acceptance of foreign and cross-cultural influences. The city is a melting pot of people with diverse ethnic, linguistic and religious backgrounds. Seen in this light, urbanization is a socio-cultural process of transformation of folk, peasant or feudal village societies.

India has a continuous history of urbanization since 600 BC. Over this period the country has witnessed major cultural influences which have shaped the character of its urban societies. Although a wide range of cultural influences have made their imprint—the Greeks, the Iranians, the central Asians, Turks, Arabs and Europeans—three major socio-cultural processes have had an overwhelming significance. These are Aryanization, Persianization and Westernization.

Aryanization

It is important to emphasize, at the outset, that between the Harappan phase of urbanization (2300 to 1800 BC) and the Aryan phase of urbanization (800 to 600 BC), there was a wide gap of a thousand years. This discontinuity in urbanization is not only temporal and spatial, but even more significantly, socio-cultural. Consequently, in the following discussion on urbanization as a socio-cultural process, the Harappan phase is largely ignored. Instead, the second phase of urbanization is taken as the starting point in the evolution of Indian urban society.

For nearly a thousand years (1500 to 600 BC) the Aryan tribes lived as a rural agricultural and pastoral people in the plains of the Indus and, later, the Yamuna and the Ganga. The Aryans, who used iron tools and implements, were able to clear land for cultivation and to subjugate the non-Aryan population, who probably belonged to the chalcolithic and stone age cultures. This composite society was dominated by the Aryan tribes. The Aryans, who had still not mastered the art of writing, had, nevertheless, developed an advanced religio-mystical culture dominated by the brahmanas, whose ritualistic interpretations of life held the population together. The transformation of this rural society into an urban society took place around 600 BC, with the rise of the secular power of the kshatriyas. The incessant wars between the Aryan and non-Aryan tribes enhanced the role of the warrior class. Military organization and centralization of tribal power became more important than mystic spiritualism. This gave rise to the emergence of *janapadas*—tribal territories—with 'purs' or fortified settlements as their centralized capitals. Thus, the first Aryan cities came into being. Soon, the tribal *janapadas* expanded to include more territory by conquest and the *mahajanapadas* developed. Towns became larger and more conspicuous. The rise of secular power in urban areas was a direct threat to the brahmanas who wielded spiritual power. The brahmanas opposed urbanism in unequivocal terms. The city was portrayed as an evil influence, while the rural way of life was glorified. The kshatriyas tried to break the brahmanical influence on the rural masses and this led to the establishment of Buddhism and Jainism which repudiated the ritualistic religion of the brahmanas. Both Buddhism and Jainism looked upon urbanism with favour and soon attracted people with urban occupations, such as the crafts, trade and transport, to their fold. By this time, writing had been invented and the Brahmi script was widely used. The brahmanas were left with no choice but to compromise with the rise of urbanization and with the secular power of the kshatriyas. They did so with a flourish in the epics—in the Ramayana and Mahabharata the kshatriyas were given pride of place as incarnations of God. However, the brahmanas retained the highest ritualistic rank for themselves in the *varna* system. Out of this compromise emerged the great Aryan tradition which spread to the four corners of India and abroad in course of time. Thus, urbanization was influenced by, and at the same time shaped, the Aryan traditions.

The Aryan city was not entirely inhabited by ethnic Aryans; it had in fact a majority of non-Aryans, namely, sudras, who formed the lowest class as artisans, servants and craftsmen. In addition, the traders, who later are identified as vaishyas, formed an important class of people. The vaishyas were among the richest people in the city, to whom the brahmanas and kshatriyas looked for support. In the city, the four *varnas* became interdependent, and the acceptance of the Great Epic Tradition helped to unite urban society.

The Aryan phase of urbanization generated three types of cities: (a) the capital cities, where the secular power of the kshatriyas was dominant; (b) the commercial cities dominated by the vaishyas; and (c) the sacred cities, which, for a time, were dominated by Buddhists and Jains, who were kshatriyas, and later by brahmanas. The brahmanas, however, continued to wield great influence in the rural areas and they continued their opposition to urbanization and the urban way of life.

From about 500 BC, the Aryans, in particular the brahmanas, and Jain and Buddhist monks, migrated to different parts of the country, towards the south, east and west from the Ganga plains. Their migrations resulted in introducing an urban culture in all these areas. Aryanization thus refers not to an ethnic but to a cultural transformation of people in different parts of India. The majority of the people who were thus influenced consider themselves Aryans, although they are not Aryans in the ethnic sense.

It is, however, possible that the ethnic Dravidians, in the extreme south of India—present-day Tamil Nadu to be specific—had developed an urban way of life even before Aryan influence began to penetrate there. Nevertheless, from 500 BC onwards, urbanization in South India shows clear signs of Aryan cultural influences. Thus, the kings of the southern kingdoms patronized the northern brahmanas and obtained recognition and even legitimacy for their own dynasties in the eyes of the people. The temples and art forms of South India reflect Aryan influence in unmistakable terms. Concomitantly with Aryanization, urbanization also spread rapidly in the South and attained great heights under the numerous dynasties of Hindu rulers including the Pallavas, Cholas, Pandyas, the Chalukyas and the Rashtrakutas.

The process of Aryanization of Indian society was completed nearly two thousand years ago. With Independence, the Hindu kingdoms which highlighted the Aryan urban ideals also came to an end. But throughout the pre- and post-Independence period, the innumerable *jatis*—endogamous ethnic groups—which comprise Indian society, have tried to enhance their status in the *varna* system; in particular, they tried to emulate the brahmanas and kshatriyas, the latter more commonly; and to claim a new status in society, higher than they originally had. Thus, sudras who rose to power and became kings claimed the status of kshatriyas, and many other groups laid claim to higher status in the *varna* scale on the real and imagined achievements of their leaders. This process has been termed, for the lack of a better word, sanskritization. The process of sanskritization goes on today in our urban areas, not in terms of claims of higher status in the *varna* system, but in terms of adoption of social customs, manners and behaviour. The lower *jatis* imitate the upper ones. Thus the numerous *jatis* that inhabit the cities of today are engaged in a process of imitation and competition for enhanced status. Urbanization provides an anonymous venue for such a process of social change.

Persianization

A second major social and cultural influence on the Indian urban scene was brought about by Muslim rulers from the 10th century AD until the advent of the British in AD 1800. The urban centres in India acquired an entirely new social and cultural character with the change of rulers. The city became Islamic and its architecture and its society reflected Islamic traditions brought to India from West Asia by the Afghans, Turks and Mongols. Throughout this long period, Persian was the official language of state. Persian culture, through its rich language and literature, its art forms and social customs, dominated the behaviour of the urban elite.

Through the elite it spread to the other classes of people in the city and, to a far lesser extent, the rural areas. A new language was born out of this cross-cultural impact—Urdu. The Hindus, who often formed a majority even in the cities, were influenced by this development. Their language, culture and behaviour underwent significant changes. The kshatriyas and the vaishyas in the cities who had more intimate contacts with the Muslim rulers, became, over a period, their partners in arms and administration. Thus, urbanization developed a dual focus—Hindu and Islamic.

The influence of the brahmanas in the cities, which was never very significant, was further eroded; however, in the rural areas their influence increased. The rural population was culturally isolated from the city and the brahmanical antagonism to the urban way of life found a new acceptance among the rural folk and reinforced their faith in their ancient religion.

Persianization, as an urban cultural influence, was confined, by and large, to the Ganga plains and the Deccan. Its influence waned rapidly with distance from Delhi, the capital city of the period. There was hardly any impact of Persianization in the states of Kerala, Tamil Nadu, Assam or Manipur. On the other hand, the majority of the cities of northern India show remarkable evidence of Persianization of their culture.

Westernization

The last, but not the least important socio-cultural influence on Indian urbanization came from the British who ruled over India for nearly 150 years. Westernization is clearly visible in various aspects of city life today—in administration, in education, and in the language of social interaction of the city people and their dress and mannerisms. A person who does not share some, at least, of the outward signs of westernization is considered as a rustic. Urbanism is clearly identified with westernization. The urban personality is a curious and variable mixture of western and Indian values and modes of behaviour. The complexity and confusion of values is largely responsible for the urban chaos in India. The scale of western cultural impact was greater than that of Islamic and Persian cultural influence; the western influence was secular rather than religious. The latter aspect led to the decline of traditional values and recognition of the equality of men, irrespective of their ethnic or religious background. Westernization has also penetrated to the rural areas, although to a far lesser extent. The rural people who come to the city imbibe some of the values of the urban dwellers. A thorough understanding of the role of Indian and western value systems in our urban society is a necessary pre-condition for the study of Indian urbanization processes today.

URBANIZATION AS A
POLITICAL-ADMINISTRATIVE PROCESS

From about the 5th century BC to the 18th century AD, urban centres in India emerged, declined or even vanished with the rise and fall of kingdoms and empires. Pataliputra, Vijayanagar, Delhi, Bijapur, Golconda, Madurai and Kancheepuram are all examples of cities that flourished, decayed, and sometimes revived in response to changes in the political scene. Many historical Indian cities no longer exist today. Some of these were the leading cities of India in their time. The ruins of cities at Hampi in Karnataka, Malkhed and Kalyani in Maharashtra, and Achichatra, Sravasthi and Kausambi in Uttar Pradesh testify to the processes of urbanization of the past. Throughout the historical period, the capital cities occupied a position of primacy among all cities. The wealth and well-being of a kingdom was measured by the scale and grandeur of its capital city. At a lower level, the provincial and lower administrative capitals owed their importance to political and administrative processes within kingdoms. While commercial and port cities also flourished during the historical period, it is the capital and administrative cities that dominated the urban scene in terms of their numbers and population.

During British rule over India, the administrative factor played an important role in the process of urbanization. The provincial capitals, the district headquarters, and the tehsil towns grew in importance and overshadowed the earlier urban centres. The administrative towns began to acquire a new urban form in the presence of the civil lines and cantonments. The national capitals, and some of the provincial capitals as well, shifted to the hill stations, such as Simla, Darjeeling, Shillong and Ootakamund during the summer, thus generating a new class of transient capital cities.

After Independence, the political-administrative aspect of urbanization is seen in the emergence of new state capitals in Chandigarh, Bhubaneshwar and Gandhinagar, for example. The number of states in India has been increasing and the political pro-cesses in the country could well bring about further division of larger states on administrative and political grounds. If this happens, new state capitals, and the related urban paraphernalia, will inevitably emerge. At a lower level, there has been a constant subdivision of districts and thus the number of districts in India has almost doubled since Independence. Naturally, the new district headquarters have acquired a higher status and this is reflected in their rapid growth. The Community Development Programme, started in 1952, has generated a new class of rural service centres, catering to the developmental needs of the rural villages. There are 5,026 Community Development Blocks in India, and although the majority of the headquarters of the Blocks are not recognized as urban places as such, they do in effect perform some at least of the functions of urban places. In course of time, these centres will become full-fledged urban places.

Clearly, therefore, administrative and political developments have played an important role in urbanization in the past and they continue to be relevant today. The administrative or political factor often acts as an initial stimulus for urban growth; which is then further advanced by the growth of commercial and industrial activities.

URBANIZATION AS AN ECONOMIC PROCESS

A classical view of urbanization characterizes an urban place as an economic parasite thriving on the agricultural surplus produced in its hinterland. This view, which had, perhaps, some value when considering the emergence of ancient cities from a predominantly peasant society, is no longer tenable in the post-industrial revolution period. Today, the city is a focal point of productive activities. It exists and grows on the strength of the economic activities existing within itself. It does, in addition, provide services and goods to its hinterland; and to a large extent, it is the hinterland that is economically dependent on the city. Farmers have to go to the city to obtain new seed varieties, fertilizers, for the purchase of tractors, or repair of agricultural equipment. They also go to the city to buy a variety of consumer goods—transistor sets, bicycles, watches, clothing, footwear and electrical items. The city offers a variety of goods and services and these are sold both within and outside the city. It does not and cannot exist by itself. Its economic relations with its hinterland and other cities of the nation and the world are important to it. It is the level and nature of economic activity in the city that generates growth and, therefore, further urbanization. Looked at from this angle, urbanization in modern times is essentially an economic process.

The nature of economic activities in a town or city, in simple terms, relates to production at three levels: primary, secondary and tertiary. The character of urbanization depends very much on the type of economic production going on in the city.

Primary Production and Urbanization

Primary production has to do with agriculture, fishing, forestry and mining. It is well known that, particularly since AD 1850, a large number of mining towns have emerged in India. The entire coal region extending over Bengal, Bihar and Orissa has a number of mining towns; the chief among which are Jharia, Raniganj, Keonjhar and Asansol. The list of mining towns would run into hundreds; they include not only coal mining towns, but also towns specializing in the mining of iron ore, manganese, bauxite, copper, gold and petroleum. Thus, specialized mining towns exist all over the country from Rajasthan to Assam, and Tamil Nadu to Kashmir. Today mining employs a high level of technology and the workers in mines include not only a large number of unskilled but also a significant number of highly skilled workers. The workers often come from far off places; in the process, the mining towns stand out as cultural islands within their respective regional milieu. Further, the mining towns have their unique urban attributes and are clearly distinguishable.

Unlike mining, fishing and forestry have not generated many urban places in India. It is, however, well known that in a large number of coastal towns and cities, along both the western and eastern coasts of India, fishing is a major productive activity. In addition, there are a large number of settlements of fishermen which are generally thought of as villages; although in actual fact, they ought to be considered as urban places. These settlements attract not only traders in fish and fish products, but also other traders who cater to the needs of the fishermen; ancillary productive activities include boat building and repair and the repair of fishing equipment. With the introduction of deep sea fishing, particularly along the west coast, motorized boats and specialized equipment are now playing a more important role. With these developments, settlements of fishermen have acquired a distinct urban character.

India's forests have traditionally been sources of a variety of products—from timber and firewood to animal skins and lac. A number of towns have emerged at the edge of the forests, dealing in forest produce. As against the traditional urban centres based on forestry, there are new towns where the manufacture of plywood, paper or furniture forms the main productive base. Examples are Dandeli in Karnataka, Baypore in Kerala, Sirpur Kagaz Nagar in Andhra Pradesh and Balarshah in Maharashtra. The number of such towns is much larger than one would imagine and they have played an important role in Indian urbanization.

Agriculture, particularly of the commercial variety, has also given rise to many urban centres in India. The tea plantations of South India, Assam and West Bengal have generated nearly a thousand settlements, often relatively small, for housing the plantation workers. These settlements also have modern factories for the processing of tea. The labour force often comes from distant places—for example, the Santals in Assam and the Tamils in the Kerala highlands. The plantation settlements are in no sense rural villages. In their layout, community life, and economic activity, they are indeed true urban centres. The people here are wage earners, in much the same sense as people in other towns and cities. In fact, the urban amenities enjoyed by the plantation settlements, in terms of housing, water supply, electricity and so on, are often unavailable in many Census towns.

Finally, the small towns in India—with a population of less than 20,000—have a substantial and sometimes even a major part of their work force engaged in agriculture. In fact, out of a total of 2,122 towns in India in 1961, Asok Mitra recognizes no less than 656 towns as being agricultural towns, where the dominant economic activity is cultivation. There is in fact no inherent contradiction between agricultural activity and urban character. The modern Indian farmer may live in the city and commute to the village to work on the farm; he may use tractors and other machinery and often his level of technical knowledge and expertise is no less than that of the factory worker. A substantial number of India's innovative and prosperous farmers live in towns. Agriculture is in effect just another economic activity, requiring certain specialized skills. With increasing mechanization and decreasing labour-intensity in agriculture, the relationship between agriculture and urbanization needs a thorough review. That agriculture is a non-urban occupation is no longer tenable in India today. The

Green Revolution in Punjab has vitalized and generated a number of small towns, which provide a variety of amenities to the new rich class of farmers. A similar situation is noticeable in the Guntur-Vijayawada districts of Andhra Pradesh, in the Coimbatore-Salem districts of Tamil Nadu, as well as in the sugar belt of Maharashtra, and the Rajasthan canal area.

The key to the emergence of a class of primary activity oriented urban centres is technological change from traditional to modern methods of farming, fishing and forestry. India's small towns are likely to emerge as new foci of an urban revolution on the heels of an agricultural or primary activity oriented revolution. The provision of infrastructure for these towns can stimulate agriculture or any other primary activity and at the same time raise the level of urbanization. The process of urbanization through modernization of primary activities is an ongoing and potentially most significant urbanization process in India.

Secondary Production and Urbanization

From Kautilya's *Arthasastra* we find that industry and trade were vital components of the urbanization process as early as the 4th century BC. As many as 64 industries producing textiles, metal products, leather products, glass, woodwork and pottery are mentioned by Kautilya. The artisans engaged in these trades organized themselves into guilds to protect their economic interests. Such was the versatility and diversity of secondary productive activities in that period, that there were no parallels to Indian cities anywhere else in the world. Products made in Indian cities found markets both in India and abroad. Thus, industrial urbanization thrived in periods of political stability over a wide region, and there were at least two of these in the long span of Indian history—the Mauryan period and the Mughal period. Over both these periods, urbanization attained very high levels. During the early phase of British rule, political stability and the rule of law was established, but Indian urbanization declined; the reason undoubtedly was the erosion of the Indian industrial base by the growing commercial interests of the British. However, both indigenous and British industrial entrepreneurs contributed to the urbanization process during the later phase of British rule. There can be no doubt that secondary production has been a major factor in India's urbanization throughout our long history.

With the revival of secondary productive activities since Independence, when the legitimate interests of this sector were firmly protected by the government, urbanization has been gaining momentum along with industrialization. After more than four decades, India now possesses a diversified industrial base and is poised to emerge as an industrial nation of high rank in the world. The effects of industrialization on Indian urbanization processes will become increasingly evident in the coming decades. Industrialization has already contributed to the rapid growth of the one-lakh cities and the million cities. Calcutta, Bombay, Delhi and Madras are major industrial centres today. To this list may be added other million cities such as Ahmedabad, Kanpur, Bangalore and Hyderabad. Industrial estates and townships have proliferated at the peripheries of metropolitan cities. Around Delhi, for example, industrial belts have been established beyond the limits of the Union Territory of Delhi, taking advantage of accessibility to the metropolitan city as well as concessions offered by state governments. There is a distinct tendency for industries to grow along major arterial roads connecting big cities. This has led to urban industrial corridor development. There are distinct axes of urban industrial development along the Calcutta-Bombay and the Delhi-Madras routes. Such development will increase in the decades ahead.

The most conspicuous examples of urbanization directly as a result of secondary activity are Durgapur, Bhilai and Rourkela. Jamshedpur also had its beginnings as an industrial township in 1912. Modinagar in Uttar Pradesh, Bhadravati in Karnataka, Chittaranjan in West Bengal and Naya Nangal in Punjab are other examples of urban development directly related to industrialization. There are innumerable examples of such towns and cities in every state in India. There is no doubt that secondary urbanization has made a strong impression on the Indian landscape. However, this does not mean that all urban places in India are being industrialized and, thus, further urbanized. There are indeed a large number of Indian cities which do not have even a single factory establishment of moderate size. On the other hand, factories registered under the factories act, which includes small scale industries, are found in most towns, with few exceptions. This means that industrialization is a contributing factor, though not necessarily an important or dominant factor, in the growth of all towns and cities in India. The contribution of industry to employment—salaried jobs, in fact—is a major force attracting rural folk to the city. However, as yet the total employment in the organized sector in India is less than 10 million, as compared to 15 million persons employed by the central and state governments. The unorganized manufacturing sector employs nearly 25 million workers. The overall employment in secondary activities is not only substantial in absolute terms, but also significant in relation to India's total urban population of 159 million in 1981. Nevertheless, unemployment is a major source of violence and crime in Indian cities. This reflects, in part, the weaknesses in the development of the urban industrial sector. It is to be expected that in the initial stages of a process such as industrialization progress will be slow and almost imperceptible. India has reached a point of take-off in industry and the future decades will demonstrate more substantial growth and a significant change in the urban industrial landscape.

Indian cities are not adequately equipped to handle the problem of rapid growth in industrial land-use. As a result, industries are likely to be allocated space in an unplanned and haphazard fashion. This becomes evident from the fact that even for those towns and cities for which master plans have been prepared, it has not been possible to implement them. Industrial urbanization brings with it a host of problems for planners and administrators.

Tertiary Production and Urbanization

In villages tertiary production is relatively less important; nevertheless, the tertiary sector exists in any village and is represented by the village money lender, *purohit,* astrologer, medical man, *dhobi,* and other service classes. In urban areas, these activities become more varied and employ a larger proportion of the population. The nature and variety of tertiary services available in a town depends on the socio-economic conditions of life and the level of technology.

From ancient times, tertiary services have played a major role in the urbanization process. The earliest cities of the world came into existence essentially in order to provide tertiary services to their hinterland. It is often thought that the earliest cities developed as parasites thriving on the surplus food produced in the rural hinterland. This is not really valid, because the relationship between the city and its hinterland is a two-way relationship. The rural folk in the hinterland parted with their surplus production in return for security in times of external aggression and security from thugs and dacoits. Apart from this, the city provided other services and, in particular, leadership and guidance in several walks of life—religion, education, medicine and entertainment. Apart from the king and the nobility, the tertiary sector was represented by priests, medical men, musicians, dancers, traders, story-tellers and so on. The people of the city, among whom there were always some strangers and migrants, were also provided with basic services. The city streets were kept clean, the streets were guarded by night watchmen, the city water supply was regulated and protected, and steps were taken to prevent fire hazard. Transport of goods and people was the occupation of a class of people, who served both the traders and the public. The modern city has all these services and more. The range of tertiary services has expanded to include educational institutions, hospitals, cinema houses, law courts, banks and financial institutions, shops selling a wide variety of goods, and finally the bureaucracy to regulate the entire gamut of socio-economic relationships. It is true that in the process of development, the tertiary activities in a city assume a more dominant role than primary or secondary production. In developed countries, employment in the tertiary sector is greater than the combined employment in the primary and secondary sectors.

The growth of tertiary activities in a city contributes in a direct way to city growth. In every city, a part of the city tertiary activity is meant for its own population, but a second and perhaps more significant part, exists for the benefit of the people in the city's hinterland.

During the British period, the tertiary sector contributed significantly to urbanization, although the rate of urbanization was rather subdued. The district and tehsil headquarters emerged during this period as the main urban centres with the collector's or tehsildar's offices, the courts, post offices, police stations and other paraphernalia of British administration. These centres were further aided by the introduction of the railways; railway stations and their related tertiary services became important landmarks in a number of cities. Educational and medical institutions owe their origins to this period. The facilities offered at these institutions attracted people to cities and towns. In the 20th century, and in particular in the 1930s, Indian cities witnessed the introduction and spread of cinema houses, city bus transportation, and the city tram cars; electricity, piped water supply and sewerage were also introduced. While all cities and towns did not enjoy these services, those that had the benefit of them saw rapid growth. It was the tertiary sector that provided the basic stimulus to urbanization during the British period.

Furthermore, the British also contributed to Indian urbanization through the establishment, between 1840 and 1900, of a number of hill stations. These new urban centres provided facilities for health and the education of children. Though the primary function was that of a health resort, these centres also functioned as administrative and military headquarters. The hill station is essentially a product of tertiary urbanization. Both primary and secondary production were irrelevant to the hill station, at least during the British period. In the post-Independence period, some of the hill stations have become collecting and distributing centres for hill products.

The role of the tertiary sector in urbanization is no less important at the present time. The city and the countryside interact more closely today than ever before. This process of interaction is highlighted by the frequent visits of rural folk to cities and city folk to villages. The cultural gap between city and village is being narrowed. Tertiary services in the city are largely responsible for this closer interaction between the city and its hinterland. Rural people come to the city to visit the shops or the cinema, for the education of their children, for medical facilities, to settle legal disputes, to obtain agricultural inputs such as fertilizers and new varieties of seeds, and for the purchase or repair of tractors, pumpsets and other equipment. Thus, towns and cities today function as service stations for rural areas. The bicycle and the transistor set helped in a big way in the 1960s and 1970s to bring the villages closer to the city. The city has become an agent of rural change. People living in villages close to metropolitan cities have sought and obtained jobs in the city and have adapted to the ways of the city. There is a daily movement of people from village to city, from within a 10–15 kilometre radius around most cities. The city's business depends to a large extent on this daily inflow of people from the rural areas. Often a small town may have a large market place, whose size is not justified by the population of the town. This is particularly true in parts of the country where the Green Revolution has made its impact. In such areas, the towns and cities have an unusually large number of eating places, shops and cinema houses. The closer interaction between the city and its hinterland necessitates an increase in commercial establishments and institutions for educational and medical services. This, in turn, provides further employment in the city and attracts permanent settlers who increase the population. A process of tertiary urbanization is thus initiated.

The city and the town are centres of production, whether at the primary, secondary or tertiary level. They generate goods and services and provide employment. The economic activities sustain the city and generate further growth of population. The larger cities have a greater pool of labour; a process of cumulative causation attracts more capital and skills; and the cities tend to get bigger and bigger. Thus, economic forces accelerate the pace of urbanization, once the basic threshold for economic functions is attained.

URBANIZATION AS A GEOGRAPHICAL PROCESS

The proportion of a country's total population living in urban areas has generally been considered as a measure of the level of urbanization. Since the industrial revolution, which began in the latter half of the 18th century, all western countries have experienced rapid urbanization, in the sense that the proportion of urban population to total population has increased steadily from around 10 per cent to nearly 80 per cent. In India, the proportion of urban population to total population remained static at about 10 per cent over a long period until 1931; thereafter, it increased to 18 per cent in 1951 and was around 24 per cent in 1981. Since 1951, there has been a remarkable relative growth of larger cities (with a population of one lakh or more). Their contribution to the total urban population increased from 44 per cent in 1951 to 60 per cent in 1981. This means that there has been a major shift of population to larger cities, while the smaller towns have remained virtually stagnant.

Population growth in urban areas is partly a function of natural increase in population and partly the result of migration from rural areas and smaller towns. An increase in the level of urbanization, that is, an increase in the proportion of population living in urban areas, is possible only through migration of people from rural to urban areas. Hence, migration or change of location of residence of people is a basic mechanism of urbanization. This is essentially a geographical process, in the sense that it involves the movement of people from one place to another.

This spatial movement can occur in many ways, not all of which may lead to urbanization. For example, people in India do migrate from one village to another. Such rural to rural migrations constitute nearly two-thirds of all migrations in any time period. This migration is substantially explained by the permanent and temporary movement of agricultural labourers from densely populated areas to areas of increased agricultural activity. This type of migration does not concern us at all. On the other hand, there are three major types of spatial movements of people relevant to the urbanization process. These are (a) the migration of people from rural villages to towns and cities, (b) the migration of people from smaller towns and cities to larger cities and capitals, and (c) the spatial overflow of metropolitan population into the peripheral urban fringe villages. The first type leads to a general process of urbanization or macro-urbanization, while the second leads to metropolization, and the third to a process of suburbanization. These three processes are discussed in the following subsections.

Macro-urbanization

The level of urbanization was remarkably stable in India from about the 6th century BC to AD 1900. Throughout this long period the level of urbanization was never higher than 12 per cent, nor was it ever lower than 5 per cent of the total population. Since 1900, however, there has been a slow but steady upward trend in the level of urbanization. By 1981, India's urban population of 159 million people, perhaps the largest in the world, constituted about 24 per cent of the total population. The increase in the urban population is substantially due to migration from rural to urban areas. In 1961–71 itself about 24 million people migrated from rural to urban areas in India. Currently, every year, about 3 million rural people migrate to the cities, and this flow is also showing a steady increase.

Rural-urban migration was given exaggerated importance in the 1950s and this led to the fear of 'over-urbanization'. Over-urbanization refers to a level of rural-urban migration far in excess of what can be absorbed by the urban areas. It is true that, following the partition of the subcontinent, millions of people from East and West Pakistan flocked to the metropolitan cities of India, particularly Calcutta and Delhi. However, this was a temporary phenomenon. Subsequently, Sovani has shown that the concept of over-urbanization is actually a myth. The proportion of urban population in India did not rise to any significant extent between 1951 and 1971.

Rural people in India migrate to cities in small trickles rather than large waves. An important aspect in rural-urban migration is the 'push' factor, that is, the increasing pressure of population in rural areas and the consequent poverty of the people. However, the number of people below the poverty line is only marginally higher in rural, as compared to urban, areas. Nevertheless, the rural poor are attracted to the cities, where job opportunities as perceived by them are greater. In actual fact, the slow growth of modern industry and tertiary activities in Indian cities has been inadequate to provide jobs for all migrants. The result is that the rural poor eventually end up as the urban poor, a change of status that is empty of meaning. The causes of rural-urban migration and also its consequences are still not fully understood.

Not all rural-urban migrants are poor or illiterate. In fact, the rural rich migrate to the city in greater proportion to their numbers than the rural poor. There is a tendency for the better educated and skilled workers from the rural areas to migrate to the city. This drains the rural areas of their human resources and adds to the city's skilled manpower. Such migrants have contributed significantly to the urban economy and polity and some of them occupy positions of power and influence. It is not unusual to meet an influential urbanite who boasts of his rural background.

Interestingly, rural-urban migration has generated a 'parallel' society in urban areas, in which the *varna* and *jati* systems are perpetuated. The lower *jatis* from rural areas continue to dominate lower status jobs in the city, while the higher *jatis* tend to obtain higher status jobs. The status of the scheduled castes shows little difference between urban and rural areas.

Both the rich and the poor from rural areas who migrate to the city use family and social links to establish themselves there. In the city, people congregate in dwellings, on the basis of family, village and *jati* relationships. Thus the city, instead of contributing to the loosening of family and *jati* affiliations, often tends to increase them further.

Rural-urban migration occurs over short as well as long distances. The daily commutation and eventual migration of people from the urban fringe zone is an example of short distance migration. On the other hand, rural landless labourers have migrated long distances to metropolitan cities to seek employment as domestic

servants, or as unskilled workers in construction and other industries. There is no necessary correlation between distance of
migration and the socio-economic status of the migrant. Long distance migrants, however, show distinct regional concentrations.
The Marwaris of western Rajasthan have traditionally played an
important role in urban trade and commerce from Bombay to
Assam and Kashmir to Kanyakumari. Intellectuals and bureaucrats, as well as domestic servants, have migrated from Tamil Nadu
to Bombay, Delhi, Calcutta and numerous other cities. There are
fewer migrants from Bihar, Assam, Orissa or eastern Uttar
Pradesh. The inter-regional migration of people constitutes an
important aspect of national integration.

Rural-urban migration was an important feature in western
countries during the 19th and early 20th centuries. This movement, triggered by the industrial revolution, led to a high level of
urbanization, where about 80 per cent of the population lived in
urban areas. In India, industrialization has made only a marginal
impact on urbanization. Even in Maharashtra, the most industrialized state in India, urban places account for only 35 per cent
of the total population. In India, urbanization may not reach the
same high levels as in the west. In any case, such a high level of
urbanization will not be attained during the remaining period of
this century.

Metropolization

In the post-Independence period, India has witnessed a new form
of urban growth, namely, metropolization. The one-lakh cities
(numbering 219 in 1981) and the 12 one-million cities have shown
remarkable growth. They account for over 60 per cent of the urban
population today. At the same time, the small towns in India have
remained stagnant and their contribution to the total urban
population has declined.

The rapid growth of metropolitan cities has been brought about
by (a) the direct migration of rural folk to metropolitan cities, in
preference to smaller towns, and (b) the migration of people from
smaller towns to larger cities. Urban-urban migration in India
accounts for about 8 per cent of total migration and is not inconsiderable in relation to rural-urban migration which accounts for
about 15 per cent of the total. Further, urban-urban migration is
of the long distance type, where people move either between districts within the same state or between different states. On the

other hand, rural-urban migration tends to be largely of the short distance type, that is, within the same district.

Metropolization is essentially a product of the centralization of administrative, political and economic forces in the country at the national and state capitals. The million cities that are also state or national capitals have shown the highest growth rate. These cities have also witnessed remarkable industrial growth. The migration of people to these leading cities is, therefore, natural and inevitable.

Metropolization is also a product of intense interaction between cities, and the integration of the national economy and urban centres into a viable independent system. The metropolitan cities have a cosmopolitan population drawn from different regions and different states in India. They differ from their neighbouring towns in terms of their urban ethos and urban values. There is a greater degree of westernization in evidence here.

Suburbanization

The rapid growth of metropolitan cities has also brought about the spatial spread of urban areas. Cities have expanded into the adjoining rural areas in a haphazard and unplanned manner. There is a reverse flow of people from the city to the countryside. The agricultural lands of the peripheral villages are converted for industrial and residential use. To these newly developed areas, the city folk migrate in search of better and cheaper accommodation. These areas often do not have basic urban amenities such as piped water supply and sewerage. However, they are outside the ambit of municipal taxes and regulation, and this acts as an incentive for new housing construction. Urbanization of the metropolitan fringe is a recent phenomenon, only a couple of decades old. It is, essentially, an outgrowth of metropolization; but, nevertheless, different from it in terms of the nature of migration and its concomitant problems.

The processes of urbanization in India, relating to the past as well as the present, are highly varied and complex. A multiplicity of forces operate simultaneously. Predictions of future urbanization in India must highlight the positive aspects as well as the pitfalls.

SELECTED READING

Bogue, Donald J. and K. C. Zachariah: 'Urbanisation and Migration in India', in Turner, Roy, ed.: *India's Urban Future,* Oxford University Press, Bombay, 1962, pp. 27–54.

Bose, Ashish: *India's Urbanisation 1901–2001,* Tata McGraw Hill, New Delhi, 1980, pp. 3–29.

Dutta, Ashok and Allan G. Noble: 'Modernisation and Urbanisation: An Introduction', in Noble, Allan G. and Ashok Dutta, eds.: *Indian Urbanisation and Planning: Vehicles of Modernisation.* Tata McGraw Hill, New Delhi, 1977, pp. 1–10.

Peach, G. C. K.: 'Urbanisation in India', in Beckinsale, R. P. and J. M. Houston, eds.: *Urbanisation and Its Problems,* Basil Blackwell, Oxford, 1970, pp. 297–303.

Prakasa Rao, V. L. S.: *Urbanisation in India: Spatial Dimensions,* Concept, New Delhi, 1983, pp. 13–19 and 43–63.

Premi, M. K.: 'Role of Migration in the Urbanisation Process in the Third World Countries: A Case Study of India', *Social Action,* Vol. 31, 1981, pp. 291–310.

Roy, B. K.: 'Internal Migration in India: An Evaluation of 1971 Census Data', *Transactions, Institute of Indian Geographers,* Vol. 2, No. 1, 1980, pp. 33–57.

Sovani, N. V.: *Urbanisation and Urban India,* Asia Publishing House, Bombay, 1966, pp. 1–3.

Srinivas, M. N.: *Social Change in Modern India,* Allied Publishers, Bombay, 1966.

Sundaram, K. V.: *Urban and Regional Planning in India,* Vikas, New Delhi, 1977, pp. 190–8.

CHAPTER 4

Definition of Urban Places and Areas

What constitutes an urban place and how does it differ from a rural place? How does one define the boundary separating urban from rural areas? At the outset, these issues might appear trivial, particularly when they are posed immediately after an elaborate discussion of the history and processes of urbanization. In dealing with the past, the focus was essentially on the leading towns and cities such as Varanasi or Madurai, Pataliputra or Kancheepuram, and there was no doubt that these were indeed urban places. The smaller towns of medieval and ancient Indian history were rarely examined as to their urban character. While this macro approach may be justified in a historical context, spanning several centuries, it is not adequate in dealing with the contemporary urban scene. Here again, one has no difficulty in identifying the larger cities and capitals; the problem arises when one wants to identify the smaller towns and distinguish them from the larger villages. Further, in the case of the larger cities, such as Delhi, Bombay or Calcutta, the outer limits of the urbanized areas are not clear; for these cities have been expanding rapidly and what was once outside the city is now well within it. All this involves a micro-level approach and it is necessary to clarify the concepts and definitions at the outset.

An even more important reason why one should probe further into the issues of rural-urban differences relates to the fact that much of our knowledge about Indian cities today is based on quantitative information provided by the decennial Censuses. In obtaining this vast body of information, the Census organization is compelled to define urban and rural places and to delimit urban areas, so that their exact boundaries can be recognized on the ground. It is up to academics to accept or reject the Census definitions or to suggest improvements. In any case, if one wishes to use the Census data, one has to accept the constraints imposed by the Census definitions. This chapter examines these issues to provide a clearer perspective on the problems examined in the subsequent chapters.

IDENTIFICATION OF URBAN PLACES

Hamlets, villages, towns and cities constitute the basic structural elements of India's cultural landscape. Within the confines of these settlements, ancient and new, live nearly 700 million people. The question that is often asked is whether these settlements fall into two neat and mutually exclusive categories, namely, rural and urban. If such a distinction is indeed meaningful, what criteria may be employed to identify urban places? Alternatively, one may postulate that the settlements, small and large, form a continuum and that there is hardly any qualitative difference between them. As a prelude to the discussion of the substantive issues of rural-urban dichotomy or continuity and the criteria for identification of urban places, the nature of the settlement structure is first examined. The theoretical range of criteria for identification of urban places and the practical choice, as exemplified by the Census definitions of urban places, are then discussed.

Settlement Structure

Settlements consist of clusters of ten or more houses used as dwellings or residences by people. India has nearly a million such settlements. Their exact number is, however, not known. The number of administrative (revenue) villages and the number of towns, as recognized by the Census, are known. Revenue villages number around 5,76,000 and the number of recognized towns in 1981 was 3,245. Revenue villages, whose boundaries are legally defined, often consist of one or more settlements; often, there is a large central village, surrounded by a number of smaller hamlets. Occasionally, revenue villages have no settlement whatsoever; this is true of uninhabited villages, which numbered around 48,000 in 1981. In other cases, revenue villages are merely small hamlets with a population of less than 200 persons. At the other extreme are revenue villages with a population of 5,000 persons or more. There were over 9,000 such villages—if at all these could be so called—in 1981. Information on the number and size of settlements within revenue villages is not available, since no systematic survey of small settlements has ever been done. The topographical maps of the Survey of India do, however, show all settlements; but most topographical maps are based on field surveys carried out decades ago. In the future, satellite pictures may be used to obtain accurate and up-to-date information on Indian settlements. For the present, however, only rough estimates of the number of settlements can be made. According to one such estimate, India has 9.6 lakh settlements, which include the smallest hamlets as well as the largest cities.

TABLE 4.1
Settlement Structure in India, 1981

Population size	Number of settlements	Percentage of total	Population in millions	Percentage of total
Less than 200	1,18,798	21.43	12.01	1.82
200– 499	1,48,695	26.83	50.50	7.66
500– 999	1,34,213	24.21	95.88	14.55
1,000– 1,999	93,800	16.92	130.10	19.74
2,000– 4,999	46,729	8.43	136.93	20.78
5,000– 9,999	7,924	1.43	52.67	8.00
10,000– 19,999	2,881	0.52	46.02	6.98
20,000– 49,999	739	0.13	22.41	3.40
50,000– 99,999	270	0.05	18.19	2.76
1,00,000–9,99,999	204	0.05	52.27	7.93
One million or more	12	–	42.02	6.38
Total	5,54,265	100.00	659.00	100.00

NOTE: (a) The data are for 1981 and they exclude Assam and Jammu and Kashmir.
(b) The number of settlements is defined as the number of inhabited revenue villages plus number of urban agglomerations plus towns and cities not included in urban agglomerations.

SOURCE: *Census of India, 1981* (tables A–3 and A–4).

Mere numbers, obviously, are not adequate to give us a notion of the structure of settlements. Settlement structure refers to the distribution of settlements according to their population size. In the absence of information on settlements as such, the structure of settlements can be inferred from the available Census data. The Census uses administrative areas for purposes of data collection. In the context of settlements, the relevant administrative units are the revenue villages and the towns, recognized as such by the Local Bodies Acts of the state governments. There were nearly 5,55,000 such administrative units in 1981. The distribution of these surrogate settlements according to size is given in table 4.1.

Generalizations based on table 4.1 can only be approximate. Nevertheless, some useful insights into the settlement structure in India can be inferred from this table. Over 12,000 settlements in the country have a population of 5,000 or more persons and these settlements account for nearly a third of the total population. The largest settlements, namely, those with a population of one lakh or more have within them roughly 15 per cent of India's population. At the other extreme, the small hamlets with a population of 200 persons or less, account for only 2 per cent of the total population. In terms of numbers, however, these settlements present a pyramid-like structure, with a large number, in lakhs, at the lower levels and fewer at the higher levels. The million cities, that come at the very highest level, were only 12 in 1981.

Rural-urban Continuum versus Dichotomy

The fundamental generalization about settlements is that there is an inverse relationship between the number and the size of settlements in any region or country. On the other hand, we may ask whether the larger settlements differ in fundamental respects from the smaller ones and if so in what respects. One view is that all settlements, small and large, constitute centres of human activity, whether at the primary, secondary or tertiary level. Furthermore, in terms of social structure, there is hardly any difference between smaller and larger settlements. In India, even today villages as well as cities are socially stratified on the basis of religious, ethnic or linguistic origins, *jati* or *varna*. The size of families and the type of family system, that is, joint, nuclear or extended, are more or less the same in the city as well as the village. Social customs, particularly those relating to marriage, are governed by nearly the same rules, irrespective of the size of the settlement. The number of children per household or even the size of the household does not differ markedly between city and village. Piped water supply, sewage and garbage disposal are not available to a great majority of Indian city dwellers and in this respect they are, if anything, worse off than rural folk. Huts and fragile dwellings are as much a part of the Indian city as of the Indian village. Large parts of cities are occupied by hutted slums. The proportion of people below the

poverty line is nearly the same in the smaller, so-called rural settlements as in the larger urban settlements. Further, there is a
gradual and continuous increase in settlement size from hamlets
to million cities and there are no abrupt breaks in the frequency
distribution of settlements according to their size. Thus, according
to this view, dividing settlements into two categories, rural and
urban, is arbitary, as there is no sharp dividing line between the
two. On the contrary, it may be asserted that settlements fall along
a continuum without any distinct dividing line.

In the developed countries of the West, rural-urban contrasts
have all but vanished; over 80 per cent of their people now live in
urban areas and the remaining 20 per cent live in isolated farm
houses and hamlets. The majority of those who live in these 'rural'
habitations are not engaged in agriculture, for the labour force
engaged in farming is only about 5 per cent of the total labour
force. Moreover, even the isolated farm houses have all the modern amenities such as piped water supply, telephones, electricity,
and so on; besides, the automobile provides the people easy access
to the cities. In contrast, the absence of these facilities is common
to both urban and rural areas in India.

Despite the arguments and evidence presented above, supporting
the concept of a rural-urban continuum, it is almost conventional
to regard cities as different from rural villages. There is a strong
historical reason for this persistent convention. Cities emerged
around 5,000 years ago in response to changes in the human way
of life. At that time a majority of people were engaged in farming
and lived in small, compact settlements and produced surplus
food. On the other hand, a small minority of the population lived
in cities. These people were not involved in farming, but were
engaged in other productive activities such as crafts and industries,
various professions such as teaching, medicine and religion.
Others were soldiers, administrators or rulers. The urban centres
stood out as places with a different character in relation to their
rural counterparts. In course of time, the sheer size of these settlements introduced elements that visually differentiated the villages
from the city. The cities had large and imposing buildings, monumental structures, busy bazaars and a variety of institutions—
educational, religious, business, administrative, and so on. The
city population was segregated into residential quarters on the
basis of language, religion, ethnic origin or status in society. The
city population acquired a high degree of heterogenity with people

coming from different regions and countries to settle there. Such heterogeneity was not to be found in the villages. While in the village all the people knew each other, in the city people perhaps did not even know their neighbours. In the city the relationships between people were governed by a new set of rules. The urban value system governing social behaviour emphasized secular and liberal attitudes and there was greater concern with material objects and the accumulation of wealth. With the introduction of automobiles and railways, cities became even more different from villages. In particular, the cities grew in size and accommodated as many as several million people within a few square kilometres.

In India, the processes of Aryanization, Persianization, and westernization have brought about sharp differences in social behaviour as between rural and urban areas. This is particularly remarkable in the case of the latter. Westernization has influenced cities much more than villages; though villages have not been unaffected by it. The contrast in life-style becomes greater and more self-evident when large cities are compared with the smallest settlements. From this the rough contours of a rural-urban dichotomy emerge; the city and the village stand out as two distinct entities, deserving recognition as such.

Criteria for Identification of Urban Places

The acceptance of the existence of a rural-urban dichotomy does not in itself provide us with an adequate frame of reference for defining and identifying urban places. The focus now shifts from the extreme situations of city and village to the marginal cases of a small town or a large village, where there is a need for precise qualitative or quantitative yardsticks. It is generally taken for granted that a single criterion is not satisfactory, and the issue has to be decided on the basis of a set of suitable criteria. These criteria, in general, fall into five categories: (a) demographic, (b) economic, (c) social, (d) morphological and (e) functional. The criteria must have relevance to the Indian settlement situation, but should at the same time be applicable to different regions in the country, where the level and character of urbanization are significantly different.

The simplest and the most widely used criteria for distinguishing urban places from rural villages relate to the demographic dimension. In particular, the size of a settlement is used as a definite yardstick. However, there is no unanimity of opinion as to the cut-off point, in terms of population. The population of an urban place may be as low as 1,000 or as high 20,000 persons. Between these two extreme limits, any number of cut-off population values may be suggested. In India, a population of 5,000 is used as a cut-off point. There is no sanctity or magic behind this; its chief merit is its general acceptance by administrators and academics alike. A second important demographic variable is the density of population. Urban areas have a higher concentration of people within a small area; the density of population is higher in urban areas than in rural areas. Very high densities of population of 50,000 or more persons per square kilometre are possible only in urban areas. Ordinarily, the gross density of population in urban areas varies from 500 persons per square kilometre to over 10,000 persons per square kilometre, while the rural densities of population range from 200 persons per square kilometre to 1,000 persons per square kilometre. Densities of more than 1,000 persons per square kilometre are certainly indicative of an urban setting. Here again, it is very difficult to set up an objective cut-off point. The limit has by necessity to be arbitrary and subjective.

The economic criteria for identification of urban places tend to focus on the occupation of the working population. For this purpose, the workers are divided into two categories—those engaged in agriculture and those engaged in the tertiary and secondary sectors. The basic assumption here is that agriculture is a non-urban occupation and hence the absence of this occupation is an indication of the urban character of a place. This is a rather tenuous argument, but one which suits the general image of a rural area being essentially agricultural. The fact, however, is that even the smallest villages have a substantial number of people engaged in secondary and tertiary activities. After all, cottage industries employ more workers than the organized industrial sector. A variety of activities such as weaving, carpet making, metal work and the production of a range of household articles, are concentrated in rural areas. The tertiary sector is also well represented in rural areas: *dhobis*, barbers, carpenters, *mochis*, blacksmiths and goldsmiths form only a part of the wide range of services available in villages. In all, about 20 to 30 per cent of the village population is engaged in the tertiary sector. Consequently, the differentiation between rural and urban areas depends upon the relative importance of agricultural and non-agricultural occupations. Here again, we can only set up arbitrary limits in terms of the percentage of workers in agriculture or in secondary or tertiary activities. A simple and straightforward criterion would be to designate all places with 50 per cent or more workers in non-agricultural activities as urban, and to assume the rest to be rural.

The city, in any part of the world, is a place where salaried wage earners form the dominant social group. The self-employed are fewer in number, but perhaps more influential and economically more prosperous. In India, the self-employed in urban areas include both businessmen and people who perform a variety of services in the residential areas. Their number is often several times larger than that of the salaried class; nevertheless, the typical urbanite is a salaried person. It is, however, impossible in practice to use salaried employment as a criterion for identification of urban areas in view of the lack of information on this aspect.

Urban and rural societies differ in terms of their value systems and patterns of social behaviour. By and large, these aspects, though of great significance, cannot be measured with any degree of precision. As such, these cannot be used as criteria for identifying urban places, particularly in marginal cases such as small towns. In addition to the intangible aspects, rural and urban societies are also differentiated in terms of the degree of social heterogeneity. Urban areas have a substantial proportion of new migrants. Their population consists of people coming from different regions, speaking different languages and belonging to different faiths. In particular, Indian towns have a greater proportion of Muslims and Christians than the villages. In small towns, new migrants and strangers are few in number. However, data on this social dimension are rarely available for smaller places. Hence, in spite of the measurability of this criterion, it is not useful for purposes of identification of urban places.

Finally, the urban population in India has a greater proportion of literates and degree holders. Data on literacy is easily available for villages as well as towns and may be used as a yardstick. The basic problem here is that marked regional variations in literacy rates within the country, preclude a uniform cut-off point for the whole country. This factor, in effect, totally negates the value of literacy as a criterion for identifying urban places.

To the layman, urban places are different from rural areas in terms of their physical appearance. There are two aspects relating to this: the morphological aspect and the functional aspect. In terms of morphology, the urban areas are characterized by a core area with brick and mortar structures, with at least some of the structures having two or more storeys. The main street is often paved and carries heavy vehicular and pedestrian traffic. The public buildings, such as administrative offices, courts, schools and hospitals, stand out prominently in the urban landscape.

Buildings in urban areas also signify the different role that these areas play in relation to other settlements. This leads to a consideration of the functional aspect. Here again, the layman's perception of the city or town is essentially in terms of its commercial role. The clustering of shops within a bazaar or market area is a characteristic phenomenon of an urban place. Even the smallest urban places have 20 or more shops in a cluster, forming an important focal point of the settlement. The presence of a such a cluster may be used as a criterion for identifying urban places and differentiating urban from rural places. It should be remembered that even small villages have shops; but these are few in number and scattered within the settlement. The cluster of shops in an urban place shows variety. Apart from the tea shops and *pan* stalls, we have a number of grocery shops, cloth shops, tailor shops, and shops dealing in stationery, or electrical and other gadgets. These shops attract customers not only from within the settlement but also from nearby settlements. In this sense, an urban place is a focal point of a wider area and a larger number of smaller settlements.

Census Definition of Urban Places

From 1901 onwards, the Census organization in India has set up its own criteria for identifying urban places. The specific criteria used by the Census have changed from time to time; however, for 1971 and 1981 the Census has used the same criteria and this has brought about some measure of stability. The frequent changes in the criteria reflect the basic problems of identifying urban places, and the issue could not be settled on a permanent basis even in 1981. The Census is by far the most important source of information on urbanization in India and, therefore, an understanding of the Census definition of urban places is important to the student of urban geography.

The 1981 Census defined an urban place as:

(a) any place with a municipality, corporation, or cantonment or notified town area; or
(b) any other place which satisfied all the following criteria:
    (i) a minimum population of 5,000,

(ii) at least 75 per cent of the male working population non-agricultural, and

(iii) a population density of at least 400 per square kilometre (i.e. 1,000 persons per square mile).

The first part of the definition includes all places which have a legal/administrative status that is different from a revenue village—the smallest administrative unit in India. These legal/administrative urban places may not satisfy the criteria listed in the second part of the definition. In particular, a legal/administrative town may have a population of less than 5,000 persons. The number of such towns was approximately 230 in 1981. On the other hand, a large number of revenue villages satisfied the criteria listed in the second part, but were not legally/administratively recognized as towns. Their number runs into several hundreds. In fact the number of legal/administrative towns in India was around 1,500 in 1981, of a total of 3,245 towns recognized by the Census. Thus, if only the legal/administrative status were to be taken into consideration, the total number of towns as well as the total urban population would be considerably smaller.

In India urban areas are given different administrative status by different state governments. The conferring of this status depends on the state-level Municipal and Local Bodies Acts. The administrative status of an urban area varies from that of a municipal corporation, which has maximum powers, to that of a township committee or simply a sanitation board with very few powers. The town administration, however, is in contrast with the village administration which, since 1961, has come under the system of gram panchayats. In some states, there are also nagar panchayats, which have obtained an urban administrative status. However, in a number of cases, the conferment of town status by the government is not based on any precise criteria; but rather on the basis of judgement or discretion exercised by the administrators. In a country where the administration is historically oriented to the collection of land revenue, there is a distinct reluctance to recognize a place as an urban area. This is reflected in the smaller number of legal/administrative towns in relation to the total number of towns recognized by the Census.

The Census criteria are conservative as well as vague. Thus, from the very beginning, after specifying the criteria for the identification of urban places, the Census confers wide powers of discretion to its officers at the state level. As a footnote to the criteria outlined above, the Census notes that:

The Director of Census of each State/Union Territory was, however, given some discretion in respect of some marginal cases, in consultation with the State Government, to include some places that had other distinct urban characteristics and to exclude undeserving cases.

This, indeed, is a totally unscientific procedure. In actual fact, the state level officers do exercise their discretion in an arbitrary manner and the result is that comparisons of the number of towns and of the total urban population in different states can be misleading. This has also led to the phenomenon of sudden increase or decrease in the number of towns in different states from one Census to the next.

Apart from the problems of their application, the Census criteria themselves do not stand up to close scrutiny. The Census prescribes a lower population limit of 5,000 persons for an urban place. However, according to the Census there were over 12,000 places in India with a population of 5,000 or more, while again according to the Census only 3,245 of these places were fit to be recognized as urban. Here, the exceptions to this criteria outnumber the valid ones by 3:1—strange logic indeed. In actual fact, few other Census organizations in the world use as high a limit as 5,000 persons to define urban places. In most cases, the limit varies from 1,000 to 2,500. According to the Census again, there were nearly 1,850 places with 10,000 or more persons which were identified as rural. In an exceptional case a rural village had a population of nearly 50,000 persons. The Census obviously has not taken its own criteria seriously.

Another Census criterion relates to the density of population, with all places having a gross density of population of 400 persons or more per square kilometre qualifying as urban places. This is indeed an unrealistically low density value in the Indian context. The average density of population in India in 1981 was above 200 persons per square kilometre, and three large states—Kerala, West Bengal and Bihar—had densities of well over 400 persons per square kilometre. According to the Census criteria, all the three states ought be recognized as urban. A much higher value, of around 1,000 persons per square kilometre, would be more appropriate in the Indian situation.

A third criterion suggested by the Census organization would classify as urban all places having 75 per cent or more of their male working population engaged in non-agricultural activities. This criterion is based on the assumption that agricultural activity is unsuited to an urban environment. However, according to the Census data, at least 25 per cent of the Census towns have agriculture as the dominant (most common) activity. Further, female workers are excluded from the criterion and it is not very clear why this has been done. Females are engaged as agricultural labourers as much as males, and they are also engaged in a wide range of non-agricultural activities. In India, there has not been discrimination against females in the major primary, secondary and even tertiary occupations. Apart from this, one could take a broader view of urbanization and consider all activities—primary, secondary and tertiary—as legitimate urban activities. In reality, the farmers are no less skilled than the great mass of the urban labour force. The distinction made between rural and urban labour force is arbitrary and carries no special significance. The application of this criterion is, however, responsible for the exclusion of over 9,000 places, with populations of over 5,000, from the Census list of urban places.

The three Census criteria discussed are to be considered together; in other words, a place has to satisfy all three criteria in order to qualify as an urban place. This is a rather stringent requirement and, perhaps, no other Census in the world has as rigid a definition of an urban place. But on the other hand, the Census grants discretionary powers to its regional officers to recognize or de-recognize urban places. This reduces the rigidity of the criteria to a farce. What is given by the right hand is taken away by the left. On the whole the negative aspects of the Census definition outweigh its positive aspects.

A rather simple way out of this dilemma is to recognize urban places on the basis of: (a) a minimum population of 5,000 or more, and (b) the presence of a compact settlement within the limits of the revenue village. A compact settlement with a population of 5,000 or more persons is bound to have a commercial core to serve its own population and the population in the smaller settlements around it. Besides, the sheer size of such a settlement would make intimacy of social contact, so characteristic of village life, impossible. The larger size would also imply a greater degree of heterogeneity in its population. If we accept this simple definition of an urban place, the total number of urban places in India would increase from 3,245 (according to the Census) to 12,030, a threefold increase; while the urban population would increase by about 50 per cent.

Census Typology of Urban and Rural Places

The Census recognizes three categories of urban places: metro-politan areas, cities and towns. The Census typology of urban places is entirely based on the population criterion. Thus, the term 'metropolitan area' is applied to places with a population of a million or more, while the term 'city' is applied to all places with a population of one lakh or more. All other urban places with a population of less than one lakh are designated as towns. Towns are further subdivided into class II towns (with populations between 50,000 and 1,00,000), class III towns (20,000 to 50,000), class IV towns (10,000 to 20,000), class V towns (5,000 to 10,000), and class VI towns (less than 5,000). The cities form the class I category. This Census classification has found general acceptance and has been used consistently from 1901 onwards.

The Census, however, designates all rural places as villages. It does not distinguish between small and large villages. In a strictly administrative sense, all Census villages are in fact revenue villages. These villages may have one or more compact settlements. It is these compact settlements that actually constitute villages. When a compact settlement has a population of less than 500 it is usually designated as a hamlet; when the population size of a settlement is less than 50 and the number of dwellings less than ten, then it is really not a settlement at all, but an isolated cluster of dwellings. Compact settlements with a population of 500 persons or more, but less than 5,000 persons, constitute villages.

The typology of settlements, rural and urban, discussed above, is by and large arbitrary and has no specific theoretical or conceptual significance. Nevertheless, common usage has given the typology more than academic significance. Thus, however arbitrary these definitions, when applied consistently and uniformly, they are vital to any discussion on urban issues and problems.

SPATIAL LIMITS OF URBAN AREAS

The problem of defining urban areas goes far beyond the issue of distinguishing between rural and urban places. In particular, it involves the problem of determining the boundaries or spatial limits of an urban place. At the outset, it must be emphasized that the administrative boundaries of villages and towns do not accurately represent the actual or real-world limits of an urban place. Further, while the administrative boundary is rather static, the actual limits of an urban place change with time in response to the growth of the place. Thus, the physical spatial expansion of the cities, in particular, is a basic and vexing issue for which there is no fully satisfactory solution. However, approximations to the actual boundaries can and are frequently made. In this section, such approximations, as proposed by the Census organization, are examined. Before doing so, it is also pertinent to discuss the concept of the geographical city which represents the 'ideal' or 'conceptual' approximation of the real-world city.

The Geographical City

Just as a settlement comprises a collection of dwellings in close proximity to each other, an urban place encompasses contiguous built-up areas, with a few vacant or even agricultural plots here and there. In the case of small towns, the contiguous built-up area is often smaller than the administrative areas. Thus, the geographical town boundary lies entirely within the administrative boundary and is separated from the latter by extensive agricultural or vacant land. In the case of larger urban places, namely cities, the contiguous built-up area of the city may extend beyond the administrative limits and cover a much larger area, including, at times, dozens of revenue villages and other legal towns. For example, the geographical city of Delhi includes the administrative cities of New Delhi, Delhi Municipal Corporation, Delhi Cantonment, and in addition a very large number of villages. The limits of the geographical city are determined by the processes of city growth. While the construction of buildings for housing or other purposes within the municipal areas is governed by laws and regulations, construction in the non-municipal towns and the villages surrounding the municipal town is not governed by these laws. Further, even where laws and regulations are in force, these are often not implemented or enforced. The result is that new residential colonies, industrial and commercial establishments come up in an unauthorized and illegal manner. Thus, the physical expansion of Indian cities is more or less haphazard, unplanned and unregulated. Given this situation, it is natural that towns, in the process of growth, spill over the administrative boundaries into adjoining areas. These newly built areas, outside the city limits, however, remain as part of the city in functional terms, that is, in terms of employment and daily movement of people for work and other purposes.

The geographical city, therefore, includes all continuously built-up areas around a main settlement, irrespective of the administrative status of these areas. The limits of the geographical city change rapidly, depending on the rate of growth of a city. Its limits, at any given point in time, can be accurately determined with the help of an areal photograph of the city. However, such areal photographs are not always available, and in such a situation, detailed field-work using existing base maps of the city and the adjoining areas will become necessary. The degree of accuracy of the limits of the geographical city, would depend on the scale of the base maps and the depth of the field enquiry. Since such detailed field enquiries have rarely been carried out in India, the geographical city is essentially an idealized, abstract concept. However, all other definitions of the spatial limits of cities have to be evaluated in relation to the ideal, namely, the geographical city concept.

The Administrative City

The simplest solution to the problem of defining the limits of urban places and areas is provided by the administrative boundaries, which are clearly defined on the ground as well as on maps. In the case of municipalities, cantonments and township committees, the limits of these administrative areas are specified in the respective Acts of the state and central governments. In the case of towns that are not administratively recognized as urban places, the boundaries are given in cadastral maps of revenue villages. Such maps are readily available locally or at the state level. Thus, the administrative limits of all towns and cities, can be easily determined. By and large, the academic community and even the Census organization are compelled to accept the legal/administrative city limits for practical reasons. The legal city is, obviously, the only city that administrators take cognizance of.

The boundaries of urban areas as delimited by administrators, rarely correspond to the spatial limits of the geographical city. Two types of anomalies occur: (a) the administrative boundary of the city extends far beyond the limits of the geographical city, and in this case we have extensive non-urban areas, such as agricultural land, waste land or other negative areas such as water-bodies, within the legal limits, or (b) the built-up areas extend beyond the administrative boundaries into the adjoining villages. In this case, the administrative city is smaller than the geographical city and the problems of the expansion of the city lie beyond the jurisdiction of the city authorities.

The city of Calcutta is an example of an underbounded city, where the urban area extends far beyond the legal city limits to include a number of other contiguous legal cities such as Howrah, Dum Dum, Garden Reach and so on. On the other hand, Greater Bombay is an overbounded city, which includes large and as yet unbuilt-up areas of the Salsette Island. Greater Bombay's population of 8.2 million in 1981 includes the entire geographical city and more, while Calcutta's population of 3.3 million within the legal city, excludes much of the population of the geographical city of Calcutta, whose population was approximately 9.2 million in 1981.

The legal/administrative boundaries of urban areas may be changed from time to time by state governments under the rules prescribed in this regard in the state Local Bodies Acts. The procedure for annexation of adjoining villages is, however, lengthy and tedious. Further, the rural folk often resist annexation on the grounds that they would have to pay city taxes and be constrained by city building regulations. Despite this, city administrative boundaries are legally altered from time to time. As a result, the decennial Census data on the population of individual cities, are not strictly comparable.

Town Groups

Until 1951, the Census organization took note of only the legal/administrative towns. In that year and in the subsequent Census of 1961, a new definition of urban areas was used, namely the 'town group'. A town group, according to the Census is 'a group of towns which adjoined one another so closely as to form a single inhabited urban locality'. Further, the Census identified town groups only when the aggregate population of the towns in a group exceeded one lakh. In 1961, there were as many as 132 town groups out of a total of 2,700 urban places.

The town group in actual practice is a cluster of towns. The inclusion or exclusion of a town from a town group, obviously, poses some problems. The 1961 Census explained the rationale behind the town-group concept as follows:

> . . .in certain clusters the urban area is not really limited only to the notified boundary of any one or two places but embraces satellite towns and cities, industrial towns or settlements close

to this urban area, which may even be surrounded by rural areas. There was, therefore, an attempt from the very beginning to define well formed clusters and treat them as town groups, the main determinants being facility of road and rail transport, and interchange of population on account of business and work. These town groups emerged in two types: (a) town groups which were made up of a cluster of neighbouring municipalities only; and (b) town groups which were made up of municipal and non-municipal localities. In actual practice, in those cases where there was no clear articulation of extension, any town falling within a radius of 2 to 4 miles and sometimes 5 miles of the periphery of the main and the most populous city was empirically examined in respect of continuity of urban character-istics, communications, possibility of satisfactory communica-tions and economic interdependence of function, to determine whether the town should be incorporated in a town group. These town groups were devised with the intention of marking off areas of conglomerate growth which as a whole rather than the individual units should henceforth receive attention in matters of planning and development. Further, a town group also suggests the spatial directions of future growth.[1]

The town group idea was severely criticized by geographers in 1968 at the International Geographical Union Congress held in Delhi. The main arguments against it were:

(1) The town group is not a compact and contiguous area, but a scattered collection of towns, with intervening rural villages, which are left out of the town group.

(2) It is not possible to prepare city plans for such a discontiguous set of settlements, where, in the process of development, the inter-vening spaces are likely to be urbanized.

(3) In some cases (42 out of a total of 137 town groups), the town group consisted of an amalgam of towns of small size, with-out a large unifying city. In such cases, the town groups failed to convey a sense of cohesion as one unit. The Census definition becomes an artificial entity.

(4) A town group defined by the Census will have no stability over time and will thus create problems of comparability of data over time as well as lose its utility as a unit of city planning. With each decade, the town group cluster will grow with the addition of new towns into the cluster.

Census of India 1961, Vol. 1, Part-II-A (i), p. 52.

For the reasons outlined above, the town group definition was abandoned from the 1971 Census onwards and it was replaced by a new Census concept—the urban agglomeration.

Urban Agglomerations

The urban agglomeration concept, adopted by the Census in 1971 and continued further in 1981, represents a close approximation to the concept of the geographical city outlined earlier. Unlike the town group, the urban agglomeration constitutes a contiguous area. Included within the agglomeration are other municipal towns, Census towns, revenue villages and outgrowths—such as railway colonies, factory townships, and residential and commercial complexes, without a well-defined administrative status. According to the 1981 Census, there were 293 urban agglomerations, out of which around 150 had a core city with a population of one lakh or more. Again, unlike the town groups, no population limits were defined for the urban agglomerations. The smallest urban agglomeration in 1981 had a population of less than 5,000 and consisted of two small townships. In this respect, the Census had taken a retrograde step. The concept is reduced to the level of absurdity when the Dalhousie urban agglomeration in Himachal Pradesh having a total population of 4,178 (comprising the Dalhousie Municipal Committee area and the Dalhousie Cantonment Board area), is contrasted with the Calcutta urban agglomeration having a population of 9.16 million and having as many as 107 urban component units. It is like putting a mouse and an elephant in the same category. In actual fact, it would be appropriate to restrict the urban agglomeration to areas having a core city with a population of one lakh or more.

The Census rationale for defining urban agglomerations reads as follows:

In several areas, fairly large railway colonies, University campuses, port areas, military camps have come up around a core city or statutory town. Though these are outside the statutory limits of a corporation, municipality, or cantonment, they fall within the revenue boundary of the place by which the town itself is known. It may not be altogether realistic to treat such areas lying outside the statutory limits of a town as rural units; at the same time each such area by itself may not come up to the minimum population limit to be treated as an independent urban unit. Such areas deserve to be reckoned along with the main town and the continuous spread including such urban outgrowths would deserve to be treated as an integrated urban area which is being called 'urban agglomeration (UA) at the 1971 Census'. The following are the different situations in which urban agglomeration would be constituted:

(a) a city with a continuous outgrowth (part of the outgrowth being outside the statutory limits but falling within the boundaries of adjoining village or villages)

(b) one town with a similar outgrowth, or, two or more adjoining towns with their outgrowth as in (a)

(c) a city and one or more adjoining towns with their outgrowths, all of which formed a continuous spread.[2]

An important feature in the definition of urban agglomeration is the recognition of a new entity—the urban outgrowth. The 'outgrowth' is not a town or a revenue village, but simply a part of a revenue village having a special status. A railway colony is on railway land and neither a town nor a gram panchayat will have administrative jurisdiction over it. It is in fact administered by the Railways directly. This special status exists in a number of situations, such as university campuses and townships built by public sector undertakings. Secondly, unlike the town groups, even revenue villages which do not measure up to the criteria for identification of urban places are included within the urban agglomeration, to maintain contiguity.

It is also important to note that out of a total of 293 urban agglomerations in 1981, only about 150 had a core city with a population of one lakh or more. There were in fact 75 one-lakh cities which were not recognized as urban agglomerations since there was hardly any urban spread beyond their statutory limits. It is evident that the process of spatial spread beyond the statutory limits is characteristic of only a small fraction of Indian cities and towns. The urban agglomeration concept is, by and large, a useful concept, and reflects the actual limits of an urban place in a reasonably accurate manner.

In spite of its inherent positive advantages, the concept of urban agglomerations has certain disadvantages. Firstly, its outer spatial limits change from Census to Census, making comparisons over time difficult. For purposes of planning, the urban agglomeration is not useful, since much of the new growth is likely to occur outside its limits. However, no definition of an urban area can represent

---

[2] *Census of India, 1971*, General Population Tables, Series I—India, Part II-A (i).

its present as well as future limits. There is a need for an additional definition which takes into account possible future development around the urban fringe.

Standard Urban Area

The Standard Urban Area concept, introduced by the Census in 1971, is in many ways complementary to the concept of urban agglomerations. While the urban agglomeration is an approximation of the geographical city, the standard urban area covers not only the built-up city but also the adjoining rural belt which is likely to be urbanized in the future. In a sense, the name given to this concept is not appropriate, for the standard urban area in actual fact is substantially a rural area with an urban core. It extends far beyond the geographical city and includes what is generally known as the rural-urban fringe zone.

The Census defines the Standard Urban Area in the following terms:

(1) it should have a core town of a minimum population size of 50,000;

(2) the contiguous areas made up of other urban as well as rural administrative units should have close mutual socio-economic links with the core towns; and

(3) the probabilities are that this entire area will get fully urbanized in a period of two to three decades.[3]

Unlike urban agglomerations, the standard urban areas are not defined for all towns, but restricted to towns and cities with populations of 50,000 or more. The choice of the population limit could well have been one lakh, for the towns below this level have not shown any tendency towards rapid growth in the past few decades. The standard urban area concept will make sense only in the case of a rapidly growing city; otherwise, there ought to be no difference between the urban agglomeration area and the standard urban area. On the other hand, for rapidly growing towns and cities, the standard urban area provides a fixed spatial frame of reference for studying the process of growth within the urban area as well as at its periphery. Besides, it also provides a stable base area for purposes of perspective planning. In this way, the standard urban area concept is a useful spatial unit for urban research scholars as well as urban planners.

[3] *Census of India, 1971*, Monograph Series,Census Centenary Monograph No. 1: *India Censuses in Perspective*, pp 131–2.

The actual delimitation of the standard urban areas was done between 1969 and 1970, just prior to the 1971 Census. This was done in a hurry. While the Town and Country Planning Organization of the Government of India in Delhi provided the basic guidelines for defining the boundaries, the actual work was entrusted to the state agencies. As a result, neither uniform procedures nor uniform criteria were used in the delimitation of the standard urban areas in various states. The basic fault lay in the vagueness of the criteria suggested by the Census: for instance, the possibility of future urbanization was a well-intentioned but highly speculative criterion. Nor did the Census spell out the exact meaning of 'close mutual socio-economic links' between the core city and parts of the delimited area. The Town and Country Planning Organization, however, provided more specific guidelines. Accordingly, the general criteria to be kept in mind while delineating the boundary were:

(1) the present urban spread of the city;

(2) the physical and other constraints to contiguous expansion of the city;

(3) the pace, direction and pattern of expansion around the city;

(4) any urban land-use or fringe characteristics in the surrounding villages;

(5) the major developments envisaged during the next two decades or so, such as location of industries, opening of new transport and communication lines, housing developments and urbanizable limits envisaged in the master plan of the city.

In actual practice, wherever city master plans were prepared, the standard urban area boundary more or less coincided with the planning area specified in the master plans. In other cases, the delimitation of the boundaries involved a study of certain characteristics of villages within a radius of 8 kilometres around the main city. These characteristics included: (1) rate of growth of population, (2) density of population, (3) proportion of non-agricultural male workers to total workers, and (4) rate of increase in literacy among males and females. On the basis of the analysis of these variables, cut-off points were determined empirically and peripheral villages were either included or excluded from the standard urban area. In the final analysis, the definition of the boundaries of standard urban areas varied from one state to another. In all about 300 standard urban areas were defined during the 1971 Census.

The standard urban area is of tremendous value in the study of urban fringe characteristics. However, the publication of detailed data on standard urban areas began only in the second half of the 1970s, and as yet this enormous source of information has only scantily been examined. On the other hand, the preparation of city master plans and their implementation, for which the data on standard urban areas is most relevant, came to a virtual standstill by the late 1970s. This could partly account for the lack of interest in the standard urban areas on the part of the planners. Figure 4.1 gives a comparative view of the boundaries of the legal city, urban agglomeration and standard urban area.

Metropolitan Areas

Considerable urban growth has taken place around the million cities since 1951. The standard urban areas around the large metropolitan cities tend to merge with the adjoining standard urban areas of bigger towns and cities. Around Delhi, the standard urban areas of Faridabad, Ghaziabad and Gurgaon, for example, tend to form a contiguous geographical area. Such an area may be designated as a metropolitan area. Apart from Delhi, such metropolitan areas exist only in the case of a handful of million cities. Nevertheless, given the rapid growth of these cities, it is very likely that metropolitan areas will develop around more cities in the coming decades.

URBAN PLACES AND URBAN AREAS: A CRITIQUE

The identification of urban places from the settlement continuum and the delimitation of larger urban units constitute basic problems in urban studies, to which there are no ideal solutions. Whatever criteria we may employ, the end product will still remain less than satisfactory. In other words, there is an inherent error component in every definition of urban places, which can be reduced to a certain extent. An increase in the number of criteria would lead to a larger number of marginal cases, and also to a corresponding increase in the variability of their interpretation; in the Indian context, this would involve differences in actual definition from one state to another. Reduction in the number and complexity of criteria would, on the other hand, increase the uniformity of their interpretation in different states and thus contribute to greater comparability. In a vast country such as India, simplicity and comparability are far more important.

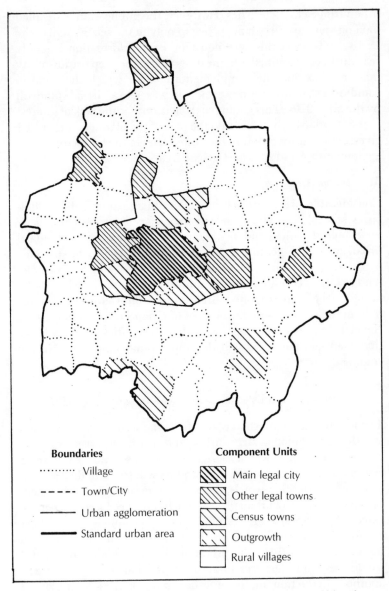

FIGURE 4.1. Administrative City, Urban Agglomeration and Standard Urban Area: a comparative view

Fortunately, the Indian spatial administrative framework enables one to define urban places and areas with some degree of accuracy. The Indian village is indeed very small in its spatial extent—5.5 square kilometres on an average. In other parts of the world the smallest administrative areas cover several times this area. The danger of including non-urban areas within urban units is therefore minimal in India. The use of the village as the smallest spatial unit and the use of only one or two criteria for identifying urban places and delimiting urban areas will go a long way in making the urban data more comparable and useful.

SELECTED READING

Chatterjee, M.: 'The Town-Village Dichotomy in India', *Man in India*, Vol. 48, July–September 1968, pp. 139–200.

Bose, Asish: *India's Urbanisation 1901–2001*, Tata McGraw Hill, New Delhi, 1980, pp. 33–47.

Srivastava, S. L.: *Indian Census in Perspective*, Office of the Registrar General, Ministry of Home Affairs, New Delhi, 1971, pp. 39–41 and 131–2.

Sundaram, K. V.: *Urban and Regional Planning in India*, Vikas, New Delhi, 1977, pp. 48–67 and 68–75.

CHAPTER 5

Patterns of Urbanization

Urbanization occurs unevenly over space. This chapter focuses on the urban landscape of India as it exists at present and highlights the spatial structure of urban settlements and the irregular spread of towns and cities in the country. Spatial structure is discussed entirely at the macro level, that is, taking the country as a whole. A micro-level analysis of spatial patterns will form the main thrust of chapters 7 and 8. The macro-level analysis presented in this chapter is not confined to the administrative framework alone, namely, the basic division of the country into states. The objective here is to uncover the national spatial patterns of urbanization within and outside the administrative framework.

The chapter focuses on three major aspects: levels of urbanization, spatial-structural patterns and macro-spatial patterns. The first two are discussed using the state as the basic spatial unit of analysis, while the third discusses patterns not revealed by the use of states as units of analysis. Furthermore, Census data for 1981 is used in the former, while the latter is based on an analysis of distribution maps of towns and cities.

LEVELS OF URBANIZATION

The level of urbanization of the country as a whole or of any state within it may be measured from data provided by the Census. A basic problem, at this stage, relates to the Census definition of an urban place. While this problem has been discussed at length in the previous chapter, the issue that concerns us here has to do with the variations from state to state in the actual implementation of the Census definition. Such state-level variations are indeed significant. For example, Uttar Pradesh had 659 Census towns in 1981, while it had only 325 in 1971; this stands in contrast with Tamil Nadu which had only 245 towns in 1981, while it had 400 in 1971. In one case the number of towns more than doubled, while in the other, the number of towns fell by 39 per cent in one decade. These rather unbelievable statistics are a product of the inherent weaknesses of the Census definition of urban places. The variations in the number of towns are entirely due to additions and subtractions from the list of small and mini towns in the states. If we use the Census data as they are, inter-state variations in the level of urbanization would in part be due to the variability of the Census definition. To eliminate this problem, the small and mini towns with a population of less than 20,000 are excluded from the analysis below. Further, there is a strong consensus of opinion that places with 20,000 or more persons are truly urban in character. The 20,000-plus towns account for 86.4 per cent of the total urban population as defined by the Census.

The level of urbanization in a state may be measured in a number of ways. The most common and best understood criterion is the percentage of urban population (however defined) in the total population. The level of urbanization defined in this way could vary from zero to one hundred. Nowhere in the world do these values attain either the minimum or the maximum. However, such a possibility exists for areal units smaller than a country. This criterion of urbanization attaches great value to the human and social aspects of urbanization, where the number of people constitutes a measure in itself. However, there are other and equally meaningful alternative measures of urbanization. Towns and cities perform a variety of roles in relation to the rural countryside. In India, towns serve as focal points of socio-economic change. The rural population served by a town can be regarded as an indication of its effectiveness. The larger the rural population served by each town, on an average, the lower the level of urbanization. When no rural population is served, urbanization is total and no further urbanization is possible. There is, however, no upper limit to the number of people that an urban centre may serve. In exceptional cases, there may be no urban centre in an area to serve its population. In this case, there is no urbanization in the area and hence the question of measurement of urbanization does not arise. The rural population of an area, divided by the number of recognized urban places may be used as a convenient measure of the level of urbanization of the area. Another alterna-

tive measure of urbanization has to do with the distance that rural
people have to travel to the nearest urban centre. The greater the
distance that they have to travel, the lower the level of urbanization, because such a situation indicates that urban centres are
spaced farther apart and are fewer in number. In rural India,
urban places are commonly visited on foot, by bicycle or by bul-
lock cart. In any case, distance is of paramount importance in
terms of the time and effort spent on reaching an urban place. In
a state with a well developed system of urban places, people will
have to go smaller distances.

The three measures of the level of urbanization suggested above
can individually reveal different aspects of urbanization. This is
explored in the following subsections. Further, an attempt is made
to combine all the three measures into a composite index of
urbanization in the final section.

Urban Population Ratio

People living in towns and urban agglomerations with a population
of 20,000 or more accounted for 20.5 per cent of India's total
population of 683 million in 1981. In relation to developed countries
this represents a low level of urbanization. While no country in the
world has the whole of its population in towns of 20,000 or more, a
number of countries have over 60 per cent of their population living
in such places. The percentage of population living in urban
centres in India is increasing at an annual rate of approximately
two per cent. In 1971, the percentage of population in 20,000-plus
towns was 16.1 and there was a 25 per cent increase during the
decade 1971–81. While the percentage will continue to increase in
the future, it may not reach the level prevalent in developed countries
for decades to come.

There are significant variations in the level of urbanization (as
measured by the percentage of urban population) between the
different states in India. Maharashtra and Tamil Nadu have more
than 30 per cent of their population living in towns; they are the
most urbanized states in India. Gujarat and West Bengal also
have a very high level of urbanization with just over 25 per cent of
their population in towns. The least urbanized state is Arunachal
Pradesh, which has no towns with a population of 20,000 or more.
This state and the union territories of Lakshadweep and Dadra
and Nagar Haveli are the least urbanized areas of the country. In
Himachal Pradesh only 2.6 per cent of the population lives in

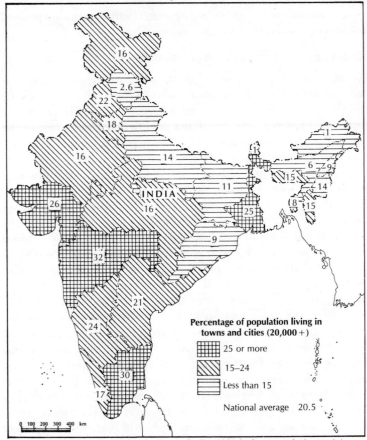

FIGURE 5.1. Level of Urbanization in India, 1981 (urban population ratio).

towns of 20,000 or more. Urbanization is at a lower level in the north-eastern region, including Assam, Nagaland, Tripura and Manipur; and in the area of the Ganga plains covering Uttar Pradesh and Bihar. Orissa has the lowest level of urbanization—9 per cent—among the bigger states in India. In general terms western and southern India are relatively highly urbanized while eastern and northern India are least urbanized (see figure 5.1).

The least urbanized states have the following characteristics: (a) they are hilly or mountainous, (b) they have a larger proportion of tribal population, and (c) they are generally inaccessible with respect to metropolitan cities and the main arterial railways connecting them. But the plains of Orissa and Bihar, where the three characteristics noted above are absent, stand out as unexplained pockets of low levels of urbanization.

Rural Population Served by Urban Centres

An aspect that is not covered by the measure discussed above is the number of towns in an urban system. Obviously, the larger the number of towns, the more urbanized an area. However, the number of towns has to be related to either the population or the area of the territorial units. The first aspect is discussed in this section. This measure of urbanization may be expressed as the number of towns per million population. In 1981, for India as a whole, there were 1.8 towns of 20,000 or more per million of total population. To avoid mentioning towns in terms of fractions, we use the concept of population served by each town, which is actually the reciprocal of the above figure. Further, we restrict the population served to the rural component only. Rural, in this context, is defined as the population living in places other than the 20,000-plus towns and cities. The reasons for this limitation are twofold: (a) If we include the urban component along with the rural, a highly urbanized area with a metropolitan city, as well as a less urbanized area with a small town, may both have a large population served by the respective centres. The distinction between the two will not, therefore, emerge. On the other hand, the *rural* population served by a town would reflect the level of urbanization. (b) In the context of socio-economic development, the main function of a town is to serve its surrounding rural areas. Further, the rural population served by a town may also be interpreted as the minimum population required—given the level of incomes and social development in an area—to support a town. This is known as the population threshold of a town, an important concept which will be explored in greater depth in chapter 7.

The population threshold of a town will depend on the level of urbanization—high levels of urbanization resulting in lower population thresholds and vice versa. Lower population thresholds are also, concomitantly, a product of higher per capita incomes and consequently higher levels of services rendered to the rural population.

In 1981, a town or city with a population of 20,000 or more served on an average 4.3 lakh rural people. Among the states, Tamil Nadu had the lowest population threshold of 2.82 lakhs, closely followed by Punjab and Sikkim. The whole of the western

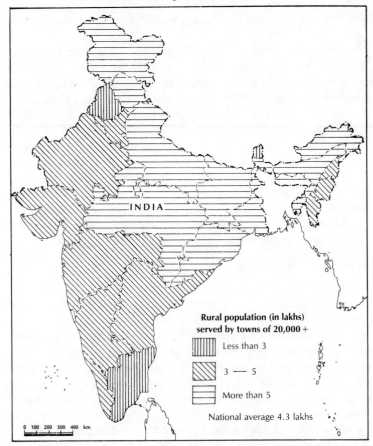

FIGURE 5.2. Level of Urbanization in India, 1981 (rural population served by towns).

region of India, extending from Punjab to Kerala, including all the southern states, Maharashtra, Gujarat and Rajasthan reflected a relatively higher level of urbanization. The entire northern and north-eastern region from Kashmir to Assam, Orissa and Madhya Pradesh, and the two most populous states of Uttar Pradesh and Bihar had lower levels of urbanization with high population thresholds of 6 lakh persons or more. Himachal had the highest population threshold of nearly 14 lakhs. West Bengal, which has a high proportion of urban population, had in fact a lower score in terms of the rural population dependent on towns. The extreme north-eastern states of Nagaland, Manipur and Mizoram have thresholds closely corresponding to the national average, thus reflecting a higher level of urbanization as compared to the northern states.

From the foregoing analysis, Tamil Nadu and Punjab emerge as the most urbanized states in India, along with Goa and the union territories of Sikkim, Pondicherry, Chandigarh and Andaman and Nicobar Islands. Himachal Pradesh, Assam and Jammu and Kashmir stand out as the least urbanized states in the country (see figure 5.2).

The poorly urbanized states in India belong to two opposite categories: (a) the more densely populated areas such as Uttar Pradesh and Bihar, and (b) the less densely populated areas, such as Himachal Pradesh, Assam and Meghalaya. In the case of the latter, high thresholds of population are further aggravated by the greater distances that people have to travel to the nearest town. This aspect is examined in the following section.

Distance to the Nearest Town

The number of towns could be related to the area of a state or any other territorial unit. The simplest approach is to measure the density of towns per unit area. Alternatively, we may use the reciprocal of density, namely, the area served by a town. The latter concept is in keeping with the tradition in urban geography, where urban centres are thought of as the foci of their rural hinterlands. The size of the hinterland is an indication of development: for towns with larger hinterlands, the town's services would be thinly spread over a larger area, while the converse would be true of towns with smaller hinterlands. In 1981, each 20,000-plus town served, on an average, an area of 2,691 sq. km; this is larger than the area of a tehsil and at least four times the size of a community development block. Thus, from the point of view of rural development, the towns in India are indeed too few in number. A much higher level of urbanization is necessary in order to support block-level rural development programmes.

The size of the hinterland also determines the maximum distance that rural folk have to travel to reach the nearest town. Distance to the nearest town and the area served by a town are indeed two sides of the same coin and measure the same phenomenon. Furthermore, the spacing of towns in the country is also a function of the area served by a town. Thus, the larger the area served by a town, the greater the distances that people have to travel to a town, and the greater the spacing between towns. The level of urbanization is inversely proportional to the area served by a town.

Rural people go to their nearest town for a variety of goods and services. Apart from consumer goods and inputs for agriculture, they also depend on the towns for education, medical facilities and entertainment. The level of interaction with the town is greater when the distance from village to town is less. Distance to the nearest town is an easily understood concept and is very meaningful as a measure of urbanization.

With these general considerations, we now go on to the specific analysis of distance to the nearest town in the states and union territories of India. As mentioned earlier, the average area served by a town in India in 1981 was 2,691 sq. km. In order to find the maximum distance to the nearest town, we assume that this hinterland is hexagonal in shape. The assumption of a hexagonal hinterland has advantages over other theoretical alternatives such as squares and circles, in that hexagons provide a better approximation of the real world situation. Given a regular hexagonal hinterland, the maximum distance to the town is equal to the length of the side of the hexagon. This distance may be computed using the formula:

$$D = \sqrt{A}/2.6$$

where D is the maximum distance to the nearest town, and A the area of the hinterland.

In 1981, the mean distance between towns of 20,000 plus was 56 km, and the maximum distance to the nearest town was 32 km, on an average. The distance to the nearest town was least in Kerala, only 15.3 km, followed by Tamil Nadu, Punjab, West Bengal, Goa and Haryana, which had mean distances of between 20 and 25 kilometres. These are the most urbanized states from the point of view of distance to the nearest town (figure 5.3).

The least urbanized states formed three contiguous regions: (a) a belt extending from Orissa in the east to Rajasthan in the west, (b) Kashmir and Himachal Pradesh in the extreme north, and (c) the north-eastern states of Meghalaya, Nagaland, Manipur, Assam, Tripura and Mizoram. Among these states, the distance to the nearest town varied from 40 to 238 km. The greatest distances to the nearest town occur in hilly or mountainous areas, desert areas, and sparsely populated areas.

Over the greater part of India, including the large states of Uttar Pradesh, Bihar, Maharashtra, Gujarat, Karnataka and

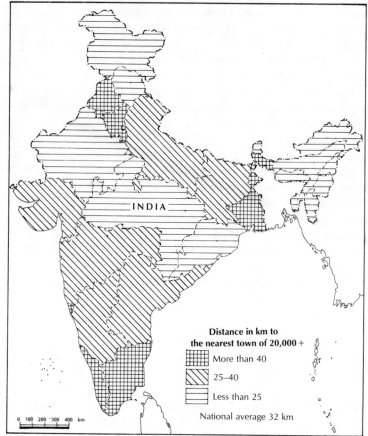

FIGURE 5.3. Level of Urbanization in India, 1981 (distance to the nearest town).

Andhra Pradesh, the distance to the nearest town varied within the limits of 27 to 31 km—revealing a remarkable uniformity in the spacing of towns over a very wide region.

Composite Index of Urbanization

The three criteria of urbanization discussed above reveal widely different macro-spatial patterns. States ranking high on one criterion do not necessarily rank high on the others. For example, Maharashtra which has the highest percentage of urban population among the states in India, occupies only a middle rank on the other two criteria. Tamil Nadu ranks uniformly high on all three criteria, while Punjab ranks high on two of the three criteria. On the other hand, a number of states show consistently low rankings, as for example, Orissa, Assam and Himachal Pradesh. In order to arrive at an overall picture, the three measures may be combined into a composite index of urbanization.

Developing this composite index poses a number of problems. To begin with, the relative importance of each criterion needs to be specified. In the absence of any theoretical or practical consideration to the contrary, we could assume that all the three criteria are of equal importance and as such assign them equal weightage in the composite index.

A second problem has to do with the units of measurement—the first criterion is measured in terms of percentages, the second in terms of population, and the third in terms of distance. These units are not comparable. In order to make them comparable the values of each of the criteria may be transformed into a standard form by using the statistical formula:

$$Z = \frac{X - \bar{X}}{S}$$

where Z is the standardized value, X the actual value, $\bar{X}$ the mean of the criterion being measured, and S its standard deviation. In order to eliminate the influence of extreme cases, only the values for major states, with populations of 10 million or more and for which data are available for 1981, are used for computing the means and standard deviations. The standard scores on each of the criteria have zero as their mean and unit standard deviation.

A third problem has to do with the fact that the percentage of urban population is inversely related to the other two criteria. To overcome this problem, the signs of the standard scores are corrected, so that the positive values indicate a high level of urbanization, while the negative values indicate a low level. The standard scores on all the three criteria are then added together to give a composite index of urbanization (table 5.1).

Apart from the union territories such as Chandigarh, Pondicherry, Goa[1] and Delhi, which have a high composite index, Tamil Nadu has the highest level of urbanization on the composite scale. It is closely followed by Kerala and Punjab; while Maharashtra and Gujarat also have relatively high scores. These, then, are the most

[1] Goa became a state on 30 May, 1987.

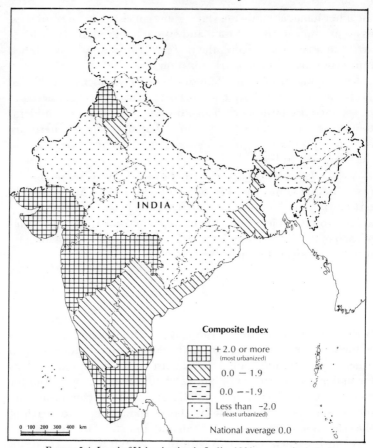

FIGURE 5.4. Level of Urbanization in India, 1981 (composite index).

urbanized states in India. The other two southern states, namely Karnataka and Andhra Pradesh, and the states of Haryana and West Bengal form a middle category of relatively high levels of urbanization. All these states have positive values on the composite index, ranging from zero to two. Low levels of urbanization are reflected in negative scores. Interestingly, there is a significant break-point between the states having positive values and those having negative values. There are no states where the composite index is between 0 and –2. The states with negative scores of 2 or more form a contiguous block covering most of central, northern and eastern India. Low levels of urbanization characterize the region extending from Orissa in the east to Rajasthan in the west and

TABLE 5.1
Levels of Urbanization in Different States in India, 1981

	State/Union Territory	Per cent Urban Population	Rural Population Served by an Urban Centre (in lakhs)	Maximum Distance (in km) to Nearest Urban Centre		Composite Index of Urbanization
1	Andhra Pradesh	21.1	3.07	27.7	+	1.48
2	Bihar	11.0	6.76	27.0	−	3.65
3	Gujarat	26.5	3.05	29.6	+	2.11
4	Haryana	18.1	3.66	24.2	+	1.18
5	Himachal Pradesh	2.6	13.67	84.7	−	10.90
6	Karnataka	24.0	3.05	28.3	+	1.96
7	Kerala	17.5	3.28	15.3	+	3.24
8	Madhya Pradesh	15.7	5.29	45.3	−	5.07
9	Maharashtra	32.2	3.37	30.6	+	2.54
10	Manipur	14.3	4.00	53.1	−	4.62
11	Meghalaya	15.4	5.50	105.6	−	6.27
12	Nagaland	8.8	3.50	55.5	−	5.37
13	Orissa	9.0	6.64	40.8	−	6.63
14	Punjab	22.1	2.95	20.9	+	3.22
15	Rajasthan	15.6	3.85	42.2	−	3.02
16	Sikkim	11.9	2.80	53.0	−	4.15
17	Tamil Nadu	29.8	2.82	20.4	+	4.73
18	Tripura	7.5	9.25	44.9	−	9.06
19	Uttar Pradesh	13.8	6.28	27.3	−	2.77
20	West Bengal	25.3	5.90	22.1	+	0.56
21	Assam	5.9	8.08	69.2	+	10.35
22	Jammu and Kashmir	15.8	7.74	238.0	−	8.44
23	Andaman and Nicobar	26.3	1.40	55.5	−	0.35
24	Chandigarh	93.3	0.30	6.2	+	11.70
25	Delhi	91.9	5.00	24.0	+	4.20
26	Goa, Daman and Diu	23.6	1.19	16.9	+	6.03
27	Mizoram	15.5	4.10	89.9	−	4.85
28	Pondicherry	48.8	1.55	9.8	+	10.45
	INDIA	20.5	4.27	32.2		00.00

Uttar Pradesh and Bihar in the north. The northern states of Himachal and Kashmir also have very low levels of urbanization (figure 5.4).

A notable feature of the analysis of levels of urbanization is the existence of a north-south urban divide which separates northern India with lower levels of urbanization from southern India which has relatively high levels of urbanization. The divide, however, lies along the traditional east-west Vindhyan axis. The comparatively high level of urban development south of the Vindhyas is partly due to the continuous history of urbanization there from around the 3rd century BC. In the south urbanization has been less affected by political upheavals; while in the north the ancient Aryan cities have all but been destroyed. By and large, urbanization in the south has taken place within the framework of Hindu traditions and culture, while in the north the Muslim culture and traditions are more prominent in the urban landscape. Tamil Nadu and Bihar both have a long urban tradition; nevertheless, the two are at opposite ends of the scale of urbanization today—they exemplify a historical urban paradox.

STRUCTURAL PATTERNS

An important aspect of urbanization all over the world is the uneven pattern of development of small towns and big cities within the system. Every urban system is characterized by the presence of a few large cities and a large number of small towns. The large cities account for a larger share of the total urban population, while the small towns, despite their numbers, account for a smaller share. This is true of the Indian urban system, and is brought out in table 5.2.

The million cities form the apex of the Indian urban system and account for over a quarter of India's urban population. They are followed closely by the one-lakh cities and the medium towns, each of which accounts for over a quarter of the urban population. Together these three categories add up to more than 85 per cent of the urban population. The small towns, which account for 55 per cent of the total number of towns, constitute only 13 per cent of the urban population. The mini towns have a trivial role in India's urban system. The distribution patterns of the major categories of cities and towns in the different states of India show remarkable unevenness (tables 5.3 and 5.4).

TABLE 5.2
Urban Structure in India, 1981

	Number	Percentage of total	Population (in millions)	Percentage of Total
Metropolises (Million cities)	12	0.4	42.0	26.9
Cities (Class I cities)	204	6.3	52.3	33.5
Medium Towns (Class II and III towns)	1,009	31.1	40.6	26.0
Small Towns (Class IV and V towns)	1,790	55.1	20.5	13.1
Mini Towns (Class VI towns)	230	7.1	0.8	0.5
Total	3,245	100.0	156.2	100.0

NOTE: The table does not include towns and cities in Assam and Jammu and Kashmir.

The Metropolis and the City

Of the 25 states in India, 17 have no million cities. None of the union territories, excepting Delhi, possesses a million city. While the smaller states and the union territories cannot be expected to have million cities, there are large states, in particular Bihar and Madhya Pradesh, which have no million cities. Both states ought to have these, considering the size of their population. However, they fall within the urban shadow of two leading metropolitan cities of India, namely Calcutta and Delhi. The four principal metropolitan cities account for the absence of million cities in a number of peripheral states and union territories. Thus, the state of Kerala comes under the shadow of Madras; Jammu and Kashmir, Punjab, Himachal Pradesh and Haryana come under the influence of Delhi, while Bihar, Orissa and the entire north-eastern area come under the shadow of Calcutta.

A number of states, however, have fully developed and independent urban systems with their own million cities at the apex. There were 8 such large states in India in 1981. Maharashtra had three cities with populations of a million or more, while Uttar Pradesh had two such cities in close proximity to each other. However, a major part of Uttar Pradesh comes directly under the influence of

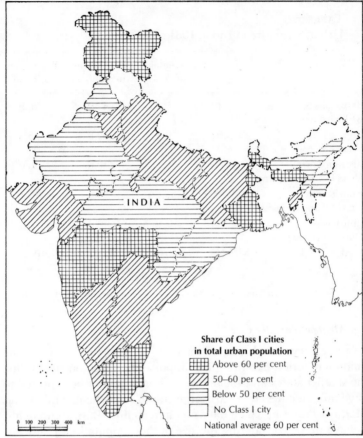

FIGURE 5.5. Urban Structure, 1981 (level of metropolization).

Delhi, the national capital. The other states where the urban system is dominated by one metropolitan city are the three southern states of Tamil Nadu, Karnataka and Andhra Pradesh, and the states of Gujarat, West Bengal and Rajasthan (figure 5.5).

At a lower level, the one-lakh cities play an important role in the Indian urban system. There were over 200 such cities in India in 1981. In spite of this, the entire states of Goa, Himachal Pradesh, Mizoram, Nagaland and Sikkim, and all Union Territories, excepting Delhi, Chandigarh and Pondicherry, had not even a single one-lakh city. In fact, all these territorial units are small in terms of their total population which is less than 5 million in each case. Several other states had urban systems with one city at the

TABLE 5.3
Number of Towns/Urban Agglomerations in Indian
States According to Size Classes, 1981

	State/Union Territory	Million Cities	Cities (I)	Medium Towns (II, III)	Small Towns (IV, V)	Mini Towns (VI)	Total
1	Andhra Pradesh	1	19	118	92	4	234
2	Bihar	–	16	76	82	5	179
3	Gujarat	1	12	69	129	9	220
4	Haryana	–	11	18	46	2	77
5	Himachal Pradesh	–	–	3	14	29	46
6	Karnataka	1	16	75	142	16	250
7	Kerala	–	8	56	21	–	85
8	Madhya Pradesh	–	14	69	217	3	303
9	Maharashtra	3	22	101	134	16	276
10	Manipur	–	1	2	13	16	32
11	Meghalaya	–	1	1	2	3	7
12	Nagaland	–	–	2	5	–	7
13	Orissa	–	6	30	64	3	103
14	Punjab	–	7	37	76	14	134
15	Rajasthan	1	10	63	120	1	195
16	Sikkim	–	–	1	–	7	8
17	Tamil Nadu	1	19	100	119	6	245
18	Tripura	–	1	1	6	2	10
19	Uttar Pradesh	2	28	122	425	82	659
20	West Bengal	1	11	57	54	7	130
21	Assam	–	1	16	54	9	80
22	Jammu and Kashmir	–	2	3	20	20	45
23	Andaman and Nicobar Islands	–	–	1	–	–	1
24	Arunachal Pradesh	–	–	–	5	1	6
25	Chandigarh	–	1	–	–	–	1
26	Delhi	1	–	–	5	–	6
27	Goa, Daman and Diu	–	–	5	8	4	17
28	Mizoram	–	–	1	5	–	6
29	Pondicherry	⋯	1	1	2	–	4
30	Other Union Territories	–	–	–	4	–	4
	INDIA	12	204	1,009	1,790	230	3,245

NOTE: (a) Data for Assam and Jammu and Kashmir refer to 1971.
　　　(b) Totals for India exclude Assam and Jammu and Kashmir.

TABLE 5.4

Relative Proportion of Towns and Urban Agglomerations in Different States in India, 1981

	State/Union Territory	Million Cities	Cities (I)	Medium Towns (II, III)	Small Towns (IV, V)	Mini Towns (VI)	Total No. of Towns
				(percentage of total)			
1	Andhra Pradesh	0.4	8.1	50.4	39.3	1.7	234
2	Bihar	–	8.9	42.5	45.8	2.8	179
3	Gujarat	0.5	5.5	31.4	58.6	4.1	220
4	Haryana	–	14.3	23.4	59.7	2.6	77
5	Himachal Pradesh	–	–	6.5	30.4	63.1	46
6	Karnataka	0.4	6.4	30.0	56.8	6.4	250
7	Kerala	–	9.4	65.9	24.7	–	85
8	Madhya Pradesh	–	4.6	22.8	71.6	1.0	303
9	Maharashtra	1.1	8.0	36.6	48.6	5.8	276
10	Manipur	–	3.2	6.3	40.6	50.0	32
11	Meghalaya	–	14.3	14.3	28.6	42.8	7
12	Nagaland	–	–	28.6	71.4	–	7
13	Orissa	–	5.8	29.1	62.1	2.9	103
14	Punjab	–	5.2	27.6	56.7	10.4	134
15	Rajasthan	0.5	5.1	32.3	61.5	0.5	195
16	Sikkim	–	–	12.5	–	87.5	8
17	Tamil Nadu	0.4	7.8	40.8	48.6	2.4	245
18	Tripura	–	10.0	10.0	60.0	20.0	10
19	Uttar Pradesh	0.3	4.2	18.5	64.5	12.4	659
20	West Bengal	0.8	8.5	43.8	41.5	5.4	130
21	Assam	–	1.3	20.0	67.5	11.3	80
22	Jammu and Kashmir	–	4.4	6.7	44.4	44.4	45
23	Andaman and Nicobar	–	–	100.0	–	–	1
24	Arunachal Pradesh	–	–	–	83.3	16.7	6
25	Chandigarh	–	100.0	–	–	–	1
26	Delhi	16.7	–	–	83.3	–	6
27	Goa, Daman and Diu	–	–	29.4	47.1	23.5	17
28	Mizoram	–	–	16.7	83.3	–	6
29	Pondicherry	–	25.0	25.0	50.0	–	4
30	Other Union Territories	–	–	–	100.0	–	4
	INDIA	0.4	6.3	31.1	55.2	7.1	3,245

NOTE: (a) Data for Assam and Jammu and Kashmir refer to 1971.
      (b) Totals for India exclude Assam and Jammu and Kashmir.

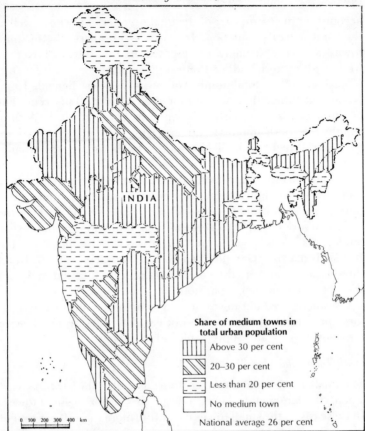

FIGURE 5.6. Urban Structure, 1981 (level of medium town development).

apex; they include Meghalaya, Manipur and Assam (1971). Each of the larger states, with a population of 10 million or more, had several one-lakh cities. Among these states, Haryana, Kerala, Bihar, West Bengal, Andhra Pradesh, Maharashtra and Tamil Nadu had a relatively higher proportion of one-lakh cities. One-lakh cities were deficient in Punjab, Uttar Pradesh, Rajasthan, Madhya Pradesh and Gujarat. These point to minor structural deficiencies in the urban systems of these states.

Medium Towns

The medium towns form an important link function within an urban system. They can serve to offset the deficiencies in the number of larger cities as well as of small towns. Medium towns account for over a quarter of the total number of towns as well as the total urban population. In terms of numbers, the medium towns are very strongly represented in the states of Kerala, Maharashtra and Andhra Pradesh, where they account for over 50 per cent of the total number of towns. In West Bengal, Tamil Nadu and Bihar, they account for slightly over 40 per cent. The medium towns are poorly developed in Uttar Pradesh, Assam, Madhya Pradesh among the larger states, and Himachal Pradesh, Manipur, Meghalaya, Sikkim and Tripura among the smaller states. Medium towns form the largest urban centres in the states of Himachal Pradesh, Sikkim and Nagaland (figure 5.6), where they are called upon to act as the state capitals: Simla (now Shimla), Gangtok and Kohima. These towns often do not have the infrastructure required to perform such a function. In the case of Simla, this is offset by the fact that it was the summer capital of British India, but Gangtok and Kohima are less well off. In all three cases, however, the constraints of hilly location and cold winters inhibit further expansion.

Elsewhere, medium towns are major market centres for agricultural produce and have a rural oriented tertiary sector. Few of these towns have any appreciable industrial base.

Small Towns and Mini Towns

The smaller states and union territories as well as the less urbanized among the larger states, have a larger proportion of small towns. In these cases, the small towns constitute more than 60 per cent of the total number of towns. Among the big states, Madhya Pradesh, Uttar Pradesh, Orissa, Rajasthan and Assam are notable for the high proportion of small towns. Kerala has a lower proportion of small towns (figure 5.7).

The mini towns, though not large in number, are an important component of the urban systems of Sikkim, Meghalaya, Manipur, Himachal Pradesh, Jammu and Kashmir, and Tripura. Among the largest states, Uttar Pradesh has as many as 82 mini towns: more than a third of the 230 mini towns in the country.

Mini towns are a characteristic feature of the hill areas, particularly in Himachal Pradesh, Manipur and Jammu and Kashmir. In these areas, the nature of the terrain accounts for the small size of both rural and urban settlements. Most of the mini towns of Uttar Pradesh also belong to the hill tracts of Kumaon and Gharwal districts. Those in the plains are actually project towns, collieries,

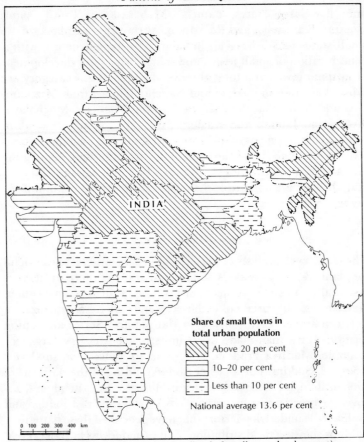

FIGURE 5.7. Urban Structure, 1981 (level of small town development).

or small industrial townships. By and large, most mini towns have clear and specific urban attributes.

The identification of small towns, on the other hand, poses a problem. Small towns have a population of 5,000 or more; however, the number of revenue villages with a population of 5,000 or more is roughly 10,800, and of these only 1,790 are recognized by the Census as small towns. The inter-state differences in the number and ratio of small towns are, at least in part, due to the Census definition of urban areas.

Summary

A balanced distribution of towns and cities of various size categories, roughly conforming to the national pattern, exists in only five large states, namely, Maharashtra, Tamil Nadu, Gujarat, Karnataka and Rajasthan. At the other extreme are the small states which have an imbalanced urban structure with a concentration of small towns and mini towns, poor development of medium towns and total absence of cities. In this category are Himachal Pradesh, Sikkim and Nagaland, apart from Mizoram, Goa and Arunachal Pradesh. In Tripura, Manipur, Meghalaya, Assam and Jammu and Kashmir, the urban system is weak in terms of development of medium towns, although all these states have at least one city at the head of the urban system. Among the larger states, Uttar Pradesh, Madhya Pradesh, Kerala, Haryana and Orissa have noticeable deficiencies of towns at the middle or higher level.

MACRO-SPATIAL PATTERNS

The state level analysis of patterns of urbanization is meaningful for planners, policy makers and administrators, as urban affairs is essentially a state subject under the Indian Constitution. Nevertheless, the variations in the levels and patterns of urbanization between states reveal only a partial picture. States and union territories are man-made areal units; some are very large, for example, Madhya Pradesh, and some are indeed too small, for example, Sikkim. For a better understanding of the patterns of urbanization, it is necessary to discard the state as an areal unit, uncover the broad macro-patterns of city location and distribution and evaluate the underlying factors that have generated these patterns.

Maps showing the distribution of cities and towns in India reveal three major macro-spatial patterns. There are: (a) urban corridors and axes (figures 5.8 and 5.9), (b) urban agglomerations and clusters (figure 5.10), and (c) urban dispersals (figure 5.11). Each one of these patterns has a number of variant sub-patterns. These are all examined below at the macro level.

National Urban Corridors and Axes

From very ancient times urban centres have developed in a linear fashion along rivers, along the coast or other waterfronts, or along major trade routes. This is one of the most fundamental patterns of urbanization all over the world. Why are urban centres located along linear axes? The answer, though simple, depends on the time period of their development and the socio-economic forces that act upon urbanization. It also depends on the nature of the axial development, whether the axes lie along rivers, transportation routes, or foothills of linear mountain ranges.

At this stage, it is also necessary to point out the difference between axial and corridor development. If towns and cities develop along a railway line or a river front, it is axial development; while the growth of towns in a river valley, but not necessarily on the banks of the river, is corridor development. In corridor development a long belt of territory, often of some width, occurs. Corridor development may occur along transportation routes, rivers or along the coast. In axial development on the other hand, towns and cities are located on a river, or railway line or road, or on the coast. In this case, the movement of goods and people between the towns is by the river, railway or road.

The linear pattern of location of urban centres in India falls into four neat categories: (a) foothill and mountain alignment, (b) river alignment, (c) coastal alignment, and (d) railway alignment.

The Foothill and Mountain Alignment. Although the linear development of cities and towns along foothills and mountains is not an important phenomenon in India today, it has its origin in very ancient times. The colonization of the Indus-Ganga plains by the Aryans proceeded in a linear fashion from west to east. The early settlements in the foothills of the Himalaya, and the earliest cities, belonging to the 3rd century BC or earlier, show a certain alignment: Kapilavastu, Kusinagara, Sravasthi, Achichatra and others are close to the mountains. In South India, early neolithic settlements were located on high ground; perhaps the reason for this is the difficulty of clearing forests in lower valley areas in the absence of iron tools. In medieval times, particularly in the Deccan and Rajasthan, a hilly location was preferred because this provided an ideal site for a fortified town. As a result, towns abounded in the foothills of linear mountain ranges. In the British period, towns of a new type—hill stations—were established at elevations of approximately 1,500 m in the middle Himalaya. The hill stations, from Dalhousie to Simla, Mussoorie and Nainital, reveal an overall linear aligment. Small townships also developed as adjuncts to the hill stations at the base of the mountains; they became railway terminals or road junctions. All such urban development has, on account of the terrain, been restricted to small towns; one-lakh cities are conspicuous by their absence.

River Alignment. Like the foothill settlements of the Himalayan region, the river settlements also have ancient origins. Apart from the Harappan cities, which were located along the Indus river, the Aryans also built cities along river valleys. However, this development took place in the Ganga plains after the introduction of iron tools in the later Vedic period. From the foothills of the Himalaya, the Aryan colonizers made their way along the valleys of the Yamuna, Ganga, Ghaghara and so on. The agricultural settlements avoided the flood plains or the *khader* belts and were located on the older alluvium or *bhangar*. Towns, however, were located nearer the rivers, on high ground wherever possible, to facilitate trade and transport. Cities such as Indraprastha, Hastinapur, Mathura, Prayag, Varanasi, Pataliputra, Kausambi and Ayodhya were all located in a linear fashion along the major rivers. The number of cities along the river front grew in course of time. Rivers provided the main highways for transport throughout history till the end of the Mughal period. They lost their importance with the introduction of railways in the latter half of the 19th century.

Fifteen one-lakh cities are today located on the banks of the rivers Ganga and Yamuna: this includes the three metropolitan cities of Calcutta, Delhi and Kanpur as well as a large number of major cities such as Patna, Varanasi, Allahabad, Agra and Mathura. Not many cities are located on major rivers in the South; the Narmada and Tapi have major port cities only at their estuaries, while the Godavari has only three major cities on it, namely, Nasik, Nanded and Rajahmundry. The Kaveri river supports four cities, while the Krishna has only two cities on its banks. The river alignment of cities is not observed in the south mainly because the rivers here are not useful as transport arteries in view of their low water levels. Cities are located near rivers mainly for reasons of water supply, strategic location, and command over the agricultural wealth in the river basin (figure 5.8).

Coastal Alignment. From very ancient times port cities on the west coast of India have carried on a flourishing trade with other parts of the world. Coastal port cities existed during the Harappan phase—Lothal, Bagatrav, and several other towns in Gujarat and on the Makran coast, had trade links with the Sumerians. In later periods, trade flourished through contact with the Arabs, Greeks and Romans. Port towns such as Musiri, Cranganore, Quilon, Calicut, Goa, Surat, Broach and Cambay testify to the role of trade over the high seas in the urbanization of the west coast of India. Ports on the east coast of India developed at the same time,

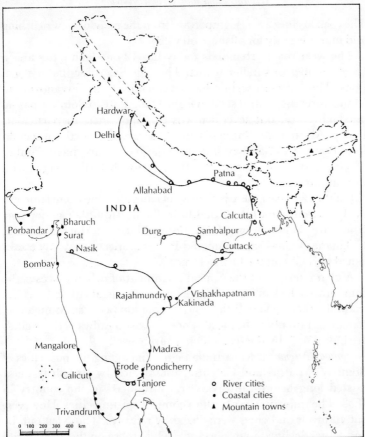

FIGURE 5.8. Corridor and Axial Development (river, coastal and mountain alignments).

particularly in southern India. Puhar or Kaveripatnam, Korkai, Pondicherry and Nagapattinam were the earliest ports on the east coast. Trade with South-east Asia attained great heights during the reign of the Pallava and Chola kings from the 4th to 12th century AD. The European traders, and later colonizers, strengthened the development of coastal port cities during the 17th, 18th and 19th centuries. They added new cities to the existing list—Bombay, Madras and Calcutta, in particular, have come to play a leading role in India's international trade. Thus, east coast and west coast urban axes have developed and flourished in India from prehistoric times. In all about 90 towns and cities are located along the coastline of India from Calcutta in the east to Kandla in the west.

The coastal cities are also important from the point of view of fishing and more recently for offshore oil wells.

The west coast urban axis today has 12 one-lakh cities and a large number of smaller towns. The axis has three distinct sections. The southern section has seven cities, from Trivandrum to Mangalore; the central section from Mangalore to Bombay has no one-lakh cities, but several towns of importance, in particular, Panaji, Marmagao, Ratnagiri and Karwar. The northern section from Bombay to Cambay and the Gujarat coast also has a number of cities, such as Surat, Bharuch (Broach), Bhavnagar and Porbandar.

On the east coast there is a string of cities all along from Tuticorin in the extreme south to Calcutta in the north. Other major port cities are Pondicherry, Cuddalore, Madras, Machilipatnam, Kakinada, Vishakhapatnam and Puri. Paradeep is a newly established port city on the Orissa coast.

A characteristic of the coastal alignment of urban places is the comparative lack of inter-linkage between coastal cities. Thus, for example, there is very little or no interaction between Mangalore, Panaji and Bombay. In the absence of coastal railways these cities are linked only by the sea, which is rarely used.

Railway Alignment. Most Indian cities (including the port cities of Bombay, Madras and Calcutta, established by British traders) existed long before railways were introduced in the country in 1853. The railways were built to connect existing cities. However, not all towns and cities were linked by railways. Those left out, by and large, declined in importance, while those on the arterial rail routes grew in size and importance. In this way, the railway network changed the relative importance of cities and in due course generated linear alignment of cities. It must, however, be remembered that the railways, in some cases at least, followed the existing trade routes; for example, the tracks closely follow the Grand Trunk Road and the Ganga river route, which had played an important role in medieval times. The railway lines linking Delhi to the west coast and southern India pass through the Malwa Plateau and Burhanpur, thus closely following the traditional trade routes of the Mughal period.

In one respect the railways made a significant departure from the earlier patterns. Bombay, Calcutta, Madras, and later Delhi, emerged as the foci of the railway network; thus raising these cities to pre-eminence in India's urban system. The towns and cities

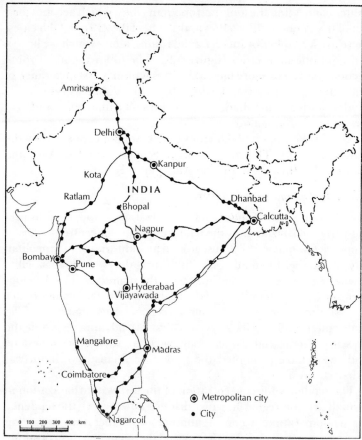

FIGURE 5.9. Corridor and Axial Development (railway alignment).

located on the major arterial routes connecting the four metropolitan cities naturally gained in importance. Further, a number of new industrial townships were established along some of the axial routes; for example, Jamshedpur, Asansol and Dhanbad. In the post-Independence period, a much larger number of industrial towns have been established and invariably these are located on existing railway lines. The Bombay-Calcutta axis has emerged as a major industrial urban corridor. This axis has India's leading steel towns—Jamshedpur, Rourkela and Bhilai; in addition, it has four one-million cities, and as many as 14 one-lakh cities. The Delhi-Calcutta axis has an even larger number of cities. This axis widens into a corridor in the Ganga plains, which have the highest density of railway lines in the country. Beyond the major axial routes connecting the four metropolitan cities, which account for 8 out of the 12 one-million cities and 50 out of the 219 one-lakh cities, there are a number of smaller axial routes, along which we have a string of one-lakh cities (figure 5.9). The following axial route sections have 5 or more one-lakh cities within a distance range of 500 km: (a) Amritsar-Delhi, (b) Ahmedabad-Navsari, (c) Hyderabad-Aurangabad, (d) Madras-Tirunelveli, and (e) Trivandrum-Mangalore.

Among the 219 one-lakh cities only 6 are not connected by the railway network. These are Srinagar, Shillong, Imphal, Agartala, Rewa in Madhya Pradesh, and Alleppey in Kerala.

Urban Agglomerations and Clusters

A distinct feature of industrial urbanization, as opposed to pre-industrial urbanization, is the tendency for urban centres to cluster around a few major foci. Thus, around an industrial or metropolitan city, a number of smaller satellite towns develop; these satellite towns have close economic links with the main city. The development of city clusters is also encouraged by the factors of greater accessibility to market, labour force, and raw materials. The major metropolitan cities have the first two advantages, while the presence of industrial raw materials, such as coal, iron ore, limestone and so on have prompted the growth of a cluster of industrial urban centres.

The tendency for concentration of the forces of urbanization in a small area or region has two distinct aspects: (a) the tendency for agglomeration, where a number of smaller towns develop around a major city, so that the city and the towns together constitute a contiguous urban area; and (b) the tendency of a number of cities to locate within a radius of 75 to 100 km from another major city, which acts as a focal point for all the cities. Sometimes the cluster of cities may not have a distinct focal point. This type of city location may be termed as an urban cluster, to distinguish it from the urban agglomeration.

Urban Agglomerations. The tendency for urban agglomeration in India was recognized by the Census in 1951 and the term 'town group' was used to denote such agglomeration. Since 1971, the term 'urban agglomeration' has been used in preference to the term 'town group'. While the Census recognizes nearly 300 urban agglomerations in India, out of a total of 3,245 urban places, a number of these are in fact small in size with a total population of

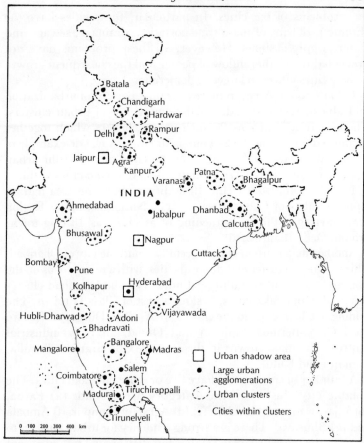

FIGURE 5.10. Urban Agglomerations and Clusters.

less than 1,00,000. In fact only 21 agglomerations are large, i.e.
with at least 10 or more component units making up the agglomeration. The largest urban agglomeration in India is found around
Calcutta, which contains as many as 107 urban units, of which 18
have a population of a lakh or more, and another 17 have a population between 50,000 and one lakh. The cities of Bangalore, Madras,
Delhi, Ahmedabad are the other major urban agglomerations in
India. The tendency for the development of an urban agglomeration
is strongest among the million cities, the industrial cities, and the
half-million cities. In a sense, the larger a city, the greater its
tendency to expand into an urban agglomeration (fig 5.10).

The growth of large urban agglomerations in India has aggravated the problems of big cities. In particular, these cities have the chronic problems of mass transportation, drainage, sewage and water supply systems. However, all these problems have not prevented the further inflow of people and the consequent growth of these cities into even larger agglomerations.

Urban Clusters. An even more revealing pattern of urbanization in India in recent decades is the emergence of urban clusters. There were as many as 26 such urban clusters which together accounted for 112 of the 219 one-lakh cities. A classic example of an urban cluster is that of Delhi. Outside of the Delhi urban agglomeration, there were as many as 11 one-lakh cities within a radius of 75 km from Delhi. In addition, the same area had an equal number of Class II towns. The National Capital Region Plan envisaged the strengthening of as many as 18 ring towns around Delhi (figure 5.10).

Another major urban cluster occurs around the city of Dhanbad. This is really a cluster of industrial cities, with a major focus on the iron and steel and metallurgical industry. The Dhanbad cluster has in all 8 one-lakh cities, besides a host of Class II towns. The leading one-lakh cities in the cluster are Asansol, Durgapur, Bokaro Steel City, Bermo, Raniganj and Ondal; all truly industrial centres. The major towns in the area are Chittaranjan, Purulia, Bankura and Kulti.

A number of city clusters have five or more one-lakh cities. The notable city clusters of this category are around: (a) Patna, (b) Vijayawada, (c) Coimbatore, (d) Agra, (e) Rampur, (f) Ambala and (g) Bhusaval. There is a strong tendency for urban clusters to occur in the more urbanized states, but they are not totally absent from less urbanized states such as Bihar and Orissa (figure 5.10).

The factors that have led to the emergence of urban clusters are not fully understood and there is clearly a need for further research in this area.

Urban Shadows. The antithesis of an urban cluster is an urban shadow. The main feature of an urban shadow is the absence of cities and towns within a radius of 75 km from a large city. Hyderabad, Nagpur and Jaipur have cast distinct urban shadows around themselves. Here the growth of the city somehow tends to inhibit further urbanization of its hinterland. Bombay has an urban shadow effect in South Raigad District. Indeed, a common feature of the hinterlands of these cities is their low level of socio-

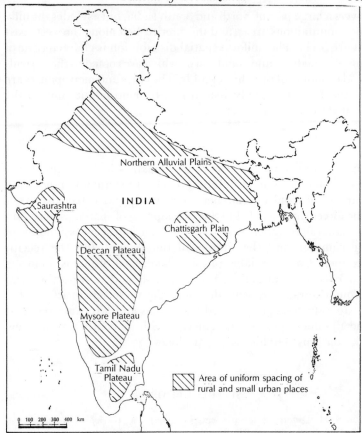

FIGURE 5.11. Urban Dispersals.

economic development. The cities stand out as islands of urban exuberance within a sea of poverty and underdevelopment.

Urban Dispersals

The vast expanse of productive agricultural areas support urban centres at a rather subdued level. Such areas may be found in the plains of the Punjab, Uttar Pradesh and Bihar, as well as in the undulating surface of the peninsular plateau region extending from Malwa, through Vidarbha, to the Mysore Plateau and beyond. In all these areas there are nucleated village settlements at regular intervals. Between the villages we have an even distribution of small and medium towns. These two together constitute a typical landscape feature. This pattern of dispersed urban centres covers a large part of North and South India, but excludes the hilly and mountainous areas, and the lateritic belt along the west coast (figure 5.11). The uniform spatial distribution is characteristic of only the medium and small towns which are rooted to the agricultural economy of their hinterlands. The cities and metropolises are by and large unequally spaced and bear no relationship to the rural agricultural economy.

OVERVIEW

The macro-spatial patterns of urbanization in India reveal the spatial overlapping of different levels of urbanization with the patterns of axial development, clustering and urban dispersal. The forces that have led to this overlapping of spatial patterns are not as yet fully understood. The Indian urban scene is a mosaic of the complex and the simple, of the ancient and the recent, juxtaposed on a variable physical landscape of plains, plateaus and hills. Coastal and riverine channels and transport arteries through urban nodes divide and unite these territories. As the urban kaleidoscope is turned new facets and forms are revealed and the underlying reality emerges with its contradictions, new relationships, and historical paradoxes.

SELECTED READING

Alam, S. M. 'Distortions in Settlement System of India', *Geographical Review of India*, Vol. 42, No. 4, 1980, pp. 305–22.

Lall, A. and R. Thirtha: 'Spatial Analysis of Urbanisation in India', *Tijdschrift voor Econ. en Soc. Geografie*, Vol. 62, 1971, pp. 234–48.

Mitchell, Nora: *The Indian Hill Station—Kodaikanal*, The University of Chicago Department of Geography Research Paper No. 141, Chicago, 1972, pp. 56–90.

Mookerjee, Debnath: 'Urbanisation Pattern in India—1951–61', *Professional Geographer*, Vol. 21, 1969, pp. 308–14.

Pathak, C.R.: 'Spatial Variation in Urban Industrial Growth in India', *Indian Journal of Regional Science*, Vol. 7, No. 1, pp. 1–10.

Datta, Kusum L.: 'Urban Zones of India', *The National Geographical Journal of India*, Vol. 13, 1967, pp. 97–109.

Prakasa Rao, V. L. S.: *Urbanisation in India: Spatial Dimensions*, Concept, New Delhi, 1983, pp. 24–43.

Raza, Moonis, *et al.*: 'Spatial Organisation and Urbanisation in India: A Case Study of Underdevelopment', in Misra, R. P. and K. V. Sundaram (eds.): *Rural Area Development: Perspectives and Approaches*, Sterling, New Delhi, 1979, pp. 333–77.

Roy, B. K. (Direction): *Census Atlas: National Volume*, Census of India, 1971, plates 35–45.

Sita, K. and V. S. Phadke: 'Declining Towns of India—1971', *Transactions, Institute of Indian Geographers*, Vol. 2, No. 2, 1980, pp. 1–7.

CHAPTER 6

Classification of Urban Places

The classification of India's urban places poses several major problems. First and foremost, the number of urban places in India is indeed very large, as many as 3,245 in 1981. This is at least three times as large as the number of towns in the United States, which has a total urban population nearly equal to that of India. Second, the data on various characteristics of cities available in the Indian Census are rather meagre compared to the range of data available for cities in the United States. With the detailed information at their disposal, American geographers in the 1950s and 1960s were able to develop a number of schemes of classification of towns and cities. Third, unlike towns and cities in the United States, most Indian cities have a long urban history, and are far more complex in terms of their economic, social and cultural structure. As a result, few attempts have been made by Indian geographers to classify urban places taking the country as a whole. Apart from the simple classification on the basis of population, for which the Indian Census terminology is now widely accepted, there are only three major studies on the classification of Indian cities. These will be reviewed later in this chapter. For the present, we shall confine ourselves to a discussion of the need for a scientific or rational classification of Indian's urban places and suggest certain lines along which this may be attempted.

THE NEED FOR CLASSIFICATION

Towns and cities are too numerous and too varied in their characteristics to be understood without meaningful categorization. Such grouping has been attempted since very ancient times in India; this is clearly brought out in the Pali texts dating back to the 3rd and 2nd centuries BC. The *Arthasastra* of Kautilya, *Kamasutra* of Vatsayana, the *Mahabhasya* of Patanjali and the Buddhist texts *Manasara* and *Devyavandana* all divide cities and towns into different categories. The common types of cities of this period were the *rajadhaniya nagara, kevala nagara, sthaniya nagara, kharvata, pattana, nigama* and *dronamukha*. Thus, cities were classified according to their politico-administrative status, port and trade functions, and their role as defence outposts. The motive that prompted Kautilya and others to classify towns is still valid today. In simple terms, the purpose is to aquire a better understanding of the importance of a town or city for the local community and for the nation.

Indian towns and cities have seen much change since Kautilya's days. There are many more cities today, and many more types of cities. The social, cultural and economic characteristics of towns have greatly changed. However, while we cannot use the classifications made by ancient scholars, neither can we ignore the past completely. Indian cities have a history of 2,500 years, in the course of which they have successively been transformed by distinct cultural influences from near and far. Essentially, a first classification of Indian cities must have a temporal or historical focus. Further, the same cities have played different roles in different periods and the present role of a city may be quite contrary to its past function. Take for example the role of hill stations in India during and after British rule. During the British raj they were essentially European cultural and ethnic enclaves; they are at present places of tourist attraction, more Indian than European. We need to look at both the past and the present roles of cities in order to put them into meaningful categories.

Qualitative and Quantitative Classification

Urban areas may be classified on the basis of a qualitative assessment of their characteristics and roles, or alternatively, on a quantitative analysis of the people and their occupations. The ancient city classifications, mentioned above, are of the qualitative type. In fact, until the 1950s, qualitative classification of urban places was the only mode of classification attempted all over the world. Since 1950, American and European geographers have increasingly relied on quantitative methods. This trend reached its climax in the 1960s, and studies based on quantitative methods flooded the professional journals. Thereafter, these methods have been all but abandoned in the West. This represents a reaction against sterile and mechanical classifications, which go against common sense and intuitive knowledge. We are back on the track of qualitative classification, but perhaps on a more scientific and rational plane than before.

The Bases of City Classifications

The classification of urban places may be attempted either on a limited contextual basis or on a comprehensive scale. Most classifications have a limited scope; they focus on geographical, social, political, historical or economic aspects of urban places. Comprehensive classifications based on the totality of all the aspects mentioned above have become possible, using computers and advanced statistical methods. Though they have achieved very little success so far, such attempts should continue. On the other hand, classifications based on a few aspects of urban places are easy to undertake and, further, are easily understood. Cities may be easily classified according to their political or administrative status: national capital, state capitals, district headquarters, tehsil headquarters and so on. Classifying cities on the basis of historical, social or economic attributes is not as simple, and such classifications do not find wide acceptance by scholars and laymen. They are, nevertheless, important from an academic point of view.

In this chapter we shall explore four bases of classification of India's urban places. In most cases, a complete classification of all urban places in India is not possible. The focus is more specially on the one-lakh cities. The four bases of classification are: (1) physical, (2) historical, (3) social and cultural and (4) economic or functional.

CLASSIFICATION BASED ON PHYSICAL CHARACTERISTICS

The geographical setting of a town is of great importance in determining the quality of the urban environment, stimulating its further growth, and occasionally threatening its very survival. The physical attributes of a town influence its attractiveness to residents and outsiders alike. Much of the beauty of a town is inherent in its location and surroundings, and it is for this reason that planners take care in selecting a proper site for a new town. A city with hills and a rolling terrain has greater charm than a flat city; further, a city having features of scenic beauty like a lake, a river, a beach or a good view of magnificent snow-covered mountains has natural charm. On the other hand, the geographical setting of a city may pose a serious threat to its survival. Many cities of the world have been destroyed by floods, earthquakes and other natural calamities. Cities located on flood plains obviously face a threat. Often flash floods on smaller rivers are far more devastating than the flooding on larger rivers.

Apart from the site characteristics, the climate of a city is also equally important to its residents. In India climatic variations are relatively small; whatever variation there is, is due to elevations above sea level and distance from the sea. At higher elevations, the summer heat is considerably reduced, and nearness to the sea, while increasing humidity, also tends to reduce the oppressive heat of the summer months.

Thus, in very general terms, the geographical setting of a city has two impotant aspects: (a) the physiographical aspect of the site and (b) the climatic aspect, determined by relief and distance from the sea.

Classification Based on Site Characteristics

The location of a city on a lake front, sea shore or rolling plateau provides both tangible and intangible satisfaction and benefits to the people of the city. The wide sandy beaches of Madras city, the view of the Arabian sea from Malabar Hill in Bombay, the presence of the lakes in Srinagar or Udaipur, all provide intangible, but nevertheless highly valued enjoyment to people. On the tangible side, a river front location ensures an adequate water supply; hardy base rocks permit the construction of tall buildings and a rolling terrain facilitates proper drainage. Often both tangible and intangible aspects are generated by the same physiographical elements—a river or lake ensures recreational opportunities as well as an adequate water supply. On the basis of site characteristics Indian cities may be classified into five locational categories as follows: (a) sea front location, (b) river front location, (c) lake front location, (d) hill location and (e) flat land location.

The categories mentioned above are not necessarily mutually exclusive. A sea front location may occur either with flat land or hill location. In the case of sea front location, this very aspect is far more important than the flat land or hilly character of the site. Nevertheless, for a more detailed classification, combinations of the five basic characteristics may be considered. We do not have sufficient information on all Indian cities and towns with reference to their site characteristics to attempt a detailed and comprehensive classification (see table 6.1 for a partial list of cities), and what follows is an analysis of site characteristics with reference to representative towns and cities in India.

Sea Front Location. Nearly 90 towns out of the total of 3,245 in India have a sea front location. Of these 20 are one-lakh cities, 12 along the west coast and 8 on the east coast. Not all port cities are on the sea front, for example, Calcutta is a major port, but it is located on the Hooghly river, approximately 50 km from the sea. In the same way, some of the sea front towns and cities are not port cities. The primary characteristic of the sea front city is the access to a view of the sea. In many cases, these cities boast of beaches, which provide relaxation and recreation to the city's population. The most developed and easily the longest and widest beach occurs in the city of Madras. Here the beach extends almost continuously for a distance of 12 km. Greater Bombay has two beach sections which are well known landmarks of the city—the Chowpatty and Juhu beaches. Many other cities have beautiful beach sections, particularly along the west coast; examples are Trivandrum, Quilon, Alleppey and Calicut.

The beach is not the only attraction of a sea front city. Some cities, such as Vishakhapatnam and Mangalore, have rocky shorelines which are of great scenic beauty. Residential areas having a view of the sea are highly valued.

The terrain of a sea front city may be either low lying flat land or a hilly surface. Along the shorelines, cities are often located on parallel sand dunes; in between the dunes, there are elongated patches of low lying land, only a few metres above sea level, which are likely to get flooded during the rainy season. While offshore bars are rare along the Indian coast, lagoons occur in several areas, notably near Cochin, Alleppey and Madras. The lagoons offer good recreational avenues; however, given the lack of means of transportation, these water bodies are rarely used for recreational purposes.

Flat land cities on the sea front may suffer from a lack of potable ground water. The cities of Alleppey and Madras face such a problem. While there is saline water all around, there is a scarcity of drinking water.

Along the west coast, most cities are located along a submerged shore line. Here, the lateritic hills extend right up to the shoreline, which is characterized by cliffs, caves and wave-cut platforms. The

TABLE 6.1
Site Characteristics of Selected Indian Cities

I SEA FRONT LOCATION		
A. *Hilly Terrain*	B. *Flat Terrain*	
1. Calicut	1. Alleppey	8. Patan
2. Cannanore	2. Cochin	9. Porbandar
3. Greater Bombay	3. Cuddalore	10. Pondicherry
4. Mangalore	4. Jamnagar	11. Puri
5. Trivandrum	5. Kakinada	12. Quilon
6. Vishakhapatnam	6. Machilipatnam	13. Tuticorin
	7. Madras	

II RIVER FRONT LOCATION		
A. *Hilly Terrain*	B. *Flat Terrain*	
1. Burhanpur, M.P.	1. Agra	8. Lucknow
2. Delhi	2. Allahabad	9. Mathura
3. Guwahati	3. Bharuch	10. Nellore
4. Hardwar	4. Calcutta	11. Patna
5. Kota	5. Faizabad	12. Surat
6. Kurnool	6. Gorakhpur	13. Varanasi
7. Nasik	7. Kanpur	
8. Vijayawada		

III LAKE FRONT LOCATION		
1. Ajmer	4. Hyderabad	7. Srinagar
2. Bhopal	5. Hospet	8. Udaipur
3. Chandigarh	6. Shillong	9. Sagar

IV HILLY LOCATION		
1. Ahmadnagar	5. Hubli-Dharwad	9. Kolhapur
2. Alwar	6. Jaipur	10. Tirupati
3. Coimbatore	7. Jodhpur	11. Valparai
4. Gwalior	8. Junagadh	12. Warangal

V FLAT LAND LOCATION		
1. Aligarh	5. Bijapur	9. Hisar
2. Ambala	6. Bikaner	10. Kancheepuram
3. Amritsar	7. Gadag-Betgeri	11. Ludhiana
4. Bellary	8. Gulbarga	12. Madurai

cities on such shorelines have a hilly terrain, which while offering ideal drainage conditions, somewhat restricts the availability of land for residential and other urban uses. The notable examples of west coast cities with a hilly terrain are Trivandrum, Calicut and Mangalore.

River Front Location. Urban settlements have been located on the banks of major perennial rivers from time immemorial. The prehistoric cities of Harappa and Mohenjodaro were located on the Indus and its tributaries; while the historic cities of Varanasi, Pataliputra, Mathura and Prayag were located on the banks of the Ganga or the Yamuna. In South India, Madurai is located on the river Vaigai, Nasik on the Godavari, Nagarjunakonda on the Krishna, and Uraiyur and Tanjore on the Kaveri. Several factors led to the selection of the river bank as the site for a major city. The river was a source of water for the city; it functioned, in northern India, as an arterial highway for trade; it provided security against invasion—both the Red Fort in Delhi and Agra Fort are located on the bank of the Yamuna. Srirangapatnam was located on an island along the Kaveri river essentially for reasons of security. These historical considerations are no longer of any importance. Nevertheless, the river front location of cities is characteristic of the Indian urban scene. Approximately 20 per cent of the one-lakh cities have a river front location. This includes the leading million cities of Calcutta, Delhi, Kanpur and Lucknow and a host of half-million cities.

Many rivers are considered sacred in India and have special significance for Hindus. India's major temples are located on river banks. A dip in the river, particularly in the Ganga, is part of the daily ritual of a devout Hindu. On ceremonial occasions, thousands and even lakhs of people take a bath in the Ganga; or in areas far removed from it, in any major river such as the Narmada, Krishna or Kaveri. The dead are cremated on river banks and the ashes are thrown into the river. Every city on a river bank invariably has a bathing *ghat*, a *dhobi ghat* where clothes are washed, and cremation grounds along the water front, in addition to temples.

The river front as an area of recreation is not well entrenched in the Indian mind. While the western view of a river front location emphasizes the scenic, recreational and transport aspects, these have no special significance in India.

River front cities are often located on clay banks by the river side. These clay banks, constitute the river levees (narrow high ground on either side of a river). Most river front cities, therefore, have a linear elongated shape; classic examples are Varanasi and Patna. The expansion of these cities is restricted by the presence of the river on one side and the existence of low lying flat lands beyond the levee. These lands may have swamps and are subject to annual flooding. Occasionally, however, they can be converted into lakes, thus offering alternative recreational areas for the city. The river is the main source of water for the city as well as its main drainage and sewage channel. The use of the river for the disposal of sewage conflicts with its other uses such as water supply, bathing and recreation.

Apart from its utility, the river is also a source of danger. Floods are not uncommon in India. Many cities are protected by embankments and alternative drainage channels for the removal of the flood waters. In spite of this, floods occur in every river front city. The major flood of 1980 in Patna completely isolated the city and caused heavy damage to property and life. The city also faces another type of danger in the form of erosion of the river banks and the shifting of the river channel. The Taj in Agra is threatened by erosion, while the Red Fort in Delhi, which was built by the river channel in the 17th century, is now at least a kilometre away from it. Varanasi, however, remains on the main channel—a position that has remained unaltered for over 2,500 years. The shifting of the river channel can produce features such as oxbow lakes and swamps, which are often the breeding grounds of mosquites. These areas, in view of the lack of proper drainage, are unsuitable for city expansion. A classic example of such a situation occurs in Gorakhpur in Uttar Pradesh. The river front location, in summary, has both good and bad points.

Not every river front city is located on a levee or a flat flood plain. Many cities are located on high ground near a river, with rocky outcrops in the form of hills. This is the case in Delhi, Vijayawada, and most cities in peninsular India. In such locations, the negative aspects of river front location are minimized, while the city benefits from the presence of the river as a reliable source of water supply and as a source of recreation for the people of the city.

Lake Front Location. Cities and towns with lake front locations are rare in India. Nevertheless, there are a few good examples. Srinagar in Kashmir, Ajmer in Rajasthan, Nainital in Uttar Pradesh, and Kodaikanal in Tamil Nadu are known for their lakes which form, perhaps, the main attraction of these cities for tourists. Udaipur is a classic example of a city of lakes; however, these are man-made rather than natural. There are few natural lakes in India. In a number of cases, artificial lakes have been created near cities, either for city water supply or for purposes of irrigation and hydel power development. The lakes in Hyderabad, Chandigarh and

Trivandrum, for example, are essentially sources of water and only incidentally places for recreation. Lakes near large cities are used for boating and often the lake front provides a suitable location for the city parks and playgrounds. Except for tourist cities such as Srinagar and Udaipur and hill stations with lakes such as Nainital, Kodaikanal and Ooty, lakes are not fully used or developed in India for recreational purposes. In South India, where tank irrigation is widespread, many cities obtain part of their water supply from tanks, which are indeed small lakes. However, these tanks have not been developed for recreational uses, except in rare cases.

Since Independence, a number of major irrigation and hydel projects have been completed and in some cases the reservoirs of these schemes lie close to a city. Sambalpur in Orissa, Kota in Rajasthan, and Vijayawada in Andhra Pradesh are good examples of such cities.

Hill Location. In the context of city site characteristics, hill location refers to the presence of prominent hills within the developed area of the city. Hills give a distinctive character to a city, and in South India, many temple towns have developed around them. The Golden Rock temple in Tiruchirappalli, the temple on Palni hill and Sri Venkateswara temple at Tirupati are all examples of hill temples, with a town or city at the base of the hill. There is thus a distinct tendency in South India to locate temples, and concomitantly towns, near a prominent hill. Again, in ancient times a hilly location was preferred for cities from the point of view of security. Rajgir in Bihar is a classic example of such a town. In medieval times hill slopes provided good sites for forts. Hills and the associated forts and their ramparts form a characteristic landscape feature of a number of towns and cities in Maharashtra and Madhya Pradesh. The city of Golconda was a fort city on the slope of a hill. Gwalior, Jaipur and Jodhpur are well known for their hill forts and palaces.

Apart from this, many cities have prominent hills which are not developed for any specific purpose, but which nevertheless form an important aspect of the city's landscape. In western countries hill slopes are valued for high quality residential development, mainly on account of the panoramic view which they offer of the city or the surrounding areas. In India, such development is rare, though Malabar Hill in Bombay is a good example of a western type, high quality residential development. In many cases hill slopes within the Indian city shelter squatter slums; a good example of such a development is found in the city of Vijayawada in

Andhra Pradesh. Hills are often considered an obstruction to city development in India; they impede direct access between localities in a city and are not considered suitable for residential development in view of the difficulty and high cost of providing water supply and sewerage. In hill stations, particularly in the Himalayan region, the steep slopes provide a rather unstable foundation for buildings. In Simla, the weight of the buildings has caused a slow down-slope movement. Further, there is an acute scarcity of residential land in such cities.

Flat Land Location. Most towns and cities, whether in the Ganga plains or peninsular India are located on flat terrain with very little or no relief. By and large, these cities have unlimited scope for spatial expansion. The concept of geometrical layout of streets, and the development of core and periphery along established lines, becomes possible in such cities. In Rajasthan, the cities such as Bikaner, Jaisalmer, Jaipur and the towns and cities of the Ganga canal region have regular rectangular road lattices. While such planned layouts are rare among other flat land cities in India, recent urban developments tend to follow such a pattern. Flat land location minimizes the costs of construction of roads, water and sewage lines and provision of city amenties. However, there is the problem of drainage, particularly storm water drainage. Low lying areas within such cities are likely to be flooded during the rainy season, causing dislocation of traffic. Calcutta and Bombay are examples of cities which face such a problem.

Flat land location is most characteristic of cities in the Ganga plains. In the plateau region of peninsular India, most cities are located on a gently sloping or undulating plain, where there are few, if any, problems of drainage. The negative aspects of flat land location are restricted to the coastal cities and the alluvial plain cities.

Classification Based on Climate

Climates differ in a number of ways among Indian cities. At one extreme, we have the hill stations, where summers are cool and pleasant and winters are cold and unpleasant. Coastal cities have hot and humid summers and relatively warm winters as well. Cities in Northern India have very hot and often dry summers, followed by a hot and humid monsoon season. These cities, however, do have rather pleasant cool winters. The cities with near ideal climate are found in the Mysore and Deccan plateau region. These cities, in view of their elevation above sea level, have milder summers and very pleasant winters.

Indian cities could be classified on the basis of their daily

TABLE 6.2

Climatic Norms of Comfort and Discomfort for Indian Cities

Period	Description of Weather	Degree of Comfort or Discomfort	Climatic Norms
DAY TIME	(a) Very Pleasant	PLEASANT WEATHER	Daily maximum temperature below 25° C but above 20° C.
	(b) Pleasant under fan	Comfortable to moderately comfortable	Daily maximum temperature below 35° C with daily minimum humidity less than 50 per cent OR Daily maximum temperature between 25° C and 30° C with humidity at any level.
	(c) Very hot	UN-PLEASANT WEATHER	Daily maximum temperature above 35° C
	(d) Hot and humid	Moderate to high discomfort	Daily maximum temperature above 30° C but below 35° C. Daily minimum relative humidity above 50 per cent.
	(e) Cold	"	Daily maximum temperature below 20° C.
NIGHT TIME	(a) Very pleasant	PLEASANT WEATHER	Daily minimum temperature above 10° C but below 20° C.
	(b) Pleasant under fan	Comfortable to moderately comfortable	Daily minimum temperature above 20° C but below 25° C.
	(c) Hot and dry	UN-PLEASANT WEATHER	Daily minimum temperature above 25° C but maximum relative humidity less than 50 per cent.
	(d) Hot and humid	Moderate to high discomfort	Daily minimum temperature above 25° C and maximum relative humidity above 50 per cent
	(e) Cold	"	Daily minimum temperature less than 10° C.

Note: Climatic norms based on author's own observations and daily weather data provided in newspapers.

maximum and minimum temperature conditions as well as data on daily maximum and minimum humidity. Such data are available at monthly and five-day (pentad) intervals for 134 of the 218 one-lakh cities in India. However, climatic data on temperature and humidity are available for a small fraction (roughly ten per cent) of India's 3,200-odd towns. Further, there are hardly any studies on climate and aspects of human comfort for work and for rest or relaxation. What constitutes pleasant or unpleasant weather in a city environment?' On the basis of available climatic data, a tentative scheme of identifying pleasant and unpleasant weather has been prepared (table 6.2). However, the lack of data for a large number of towns and cities, precludes a comprehensive classification of India's urban places on the basis of climatic data.

TABLE 6.3
Classification of Cities According to Climatic Types

Location	Climatic type	Number of One-lakh Cities
1. Hill stations (above 1,000 m)	Cool summers and cold winters	3
2. Plateau cities (elevation 500–1,000 m)	Mild summers and cool winters	30
3. Coastal cities (elevation less than 500 m and within 50 km of the shoreline)	Humid, hot summers and warm winters	34
4. Northern inland cities (elevation below 500 m, beyond 50 km from shoreline and north of the Vindhyas)	Hot, dry summers, humid and hot monsoon season, followed by cool winters	93
5. Southern inland cities (elevation below 500 m, beyond 50 km from the shoreline and south of the Vindhyas)	Hot summers and warm winters	54
6. Desert towns and cities (elevation less than 500 m, inland location with rainfall less than 50 cm per annum)	Hot, dry summers and cool, dry winters	5

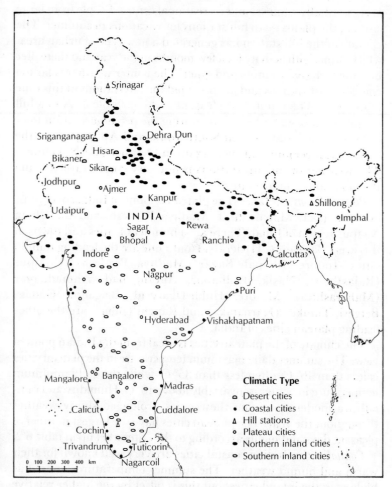

FIGURE 6.1. Climatic Classification of Indian Cities.

The climate of Indian towns and cities can, however, be easily inferred from their elevation above sea level and their distance from the sea. By treating these surrogate climatic variables, we could classify Indian cities into six types (table 6.3 and figure 6.1). The significance of climate to the urban way of life merits further elaboration in relation to each of the six climatic types in India.

Hill Stations. Although they are not numerous, hill stations have come to occupy an important position in India's urban system. Climate—a cool summer—is the main attraction of the hill station.

It is essentially a tourist and recreational centre. People from large cities in the plains go to hill stations for vacations in summer. The climate of the hill station has generated a new type of urban area, which brims with activity for a few months in the year and thereafter becomes relatively empty and quiet. The winter weather is far too cold for most Indians and people avoid the hill stations at this time of the year. The number of pleasant and enjoyable days in a hill station are indeed few; these are during the pre-monsoon summer months, April and May in South India and April–June in the Himalayan region; and then again in October and November. The weather of the hill stations is not very comfortable during the monsoons and in winter.

Plateau Towns and Cities. The plateau regions of India cover most of Karnataka, Maharashtra, Madhya Pradesh, and the Chota Nagpur region of Bihar. There are a number of cities and towns in this area: Bangalore, Hyderabad and Pune are the leading million cities. Indore, Bhopal, Sagar (Madhya Pradesh), Udaipur (Rajasthan), Nasik, Kolhapur, Aurangabad, Ahmadnagar (Maharashtra), Mysore, Hubli-Dharwad, Belgaum, Gadag-Betgeri, Tumkur (Karnataka) and Ranchi (Bihar) are the other leading plateau cities of India.

The climate of the plateau cities is ideal from the Indian point of view. The summer daily maximum temperature in the plateau cities is less than 40° C, often less than 35° C, while the daily minimum temperature in winter is invariably above 10° C. Humidity and rainfall are moderate, giving these cities prolonged sunny weather throughout the year. The plateau cities have the largest number of pleasant days and nights according to the criteria set up in table 6.2.

Coastal Cities. Indian coastal cities are very well known for their warm and humid weather. The summer temperatures are not as high as in the inland cities, but this is offset by the higher relative humidity. The coastal cities, however, have the advantage of land and sea breezes. In Madras city, the sea breeze invariably sets in at about two o'clock in the afternoon and continues through the greater of part of the night. The sea breeze provides welcome relief to the people of the city suffering from heat and humidity. An east-west orientation of houses—of windows and doors—is most desirable in these cities as it permits the maximum flow of fresh air from the sea. The breeze does reduce air pollution from factories and automobiles; on the other hand, the salt particles in the air tend to corrode all metallic objects and furniture. Salt also increases the stickiness of the weather.

Coastal towns and cities often face the full impact of cyclonic storms in the Bay of Bengal and the Arabian Sea. The city people face dislocation of their daily activities during such storms; these may last up to a week and occur in October–December along the east coast and in June–September along the west coast.

With the exception of Calcutta, coastal cities do not have a winter season. Warm clothing is not required at any time of the year. The winter months, however, have longer spells of pleasant weather, both during the day and at night.

Northern Inland Cities. This category includes the largest number of cities and towns. All inland towns and cities from West Bengal to Punjab, Orissa, Gujarat and the northern parts of Rajasthan and Madhya Pradesh belong to this category. The cities of the northern plains differ from the southern inland cities mainly on account of their cooler or even cold winters. The winters are most severe in Punjab and western Uttar Pradesh and milder in West Bengal and Gujarat. Winter minimum temperatures in Delhi are less than 10°C, and occasionally night temperatures may approach freezing point. The northern cities have a three-month winter season from December to February. Warm clothing is a must in these cities. Poor people in the northern cities suffer much hardship on account of the cold and the illnesses associated with exposure to cold. On the other hand, winter is generally considered as pleasant for work and for rest. The sunny but cool winter days are ideal for outdoor activities.

The northern plains cities are also characterized by rather severe summers, when the daily maximum temperatures are above 40°C. The extreme heat is accentuated by dusty hot winds during the day. Dustiness, actually, is a distinguishing characteristic of these cities, where the fine clayey soils of the alluvial plains are blown away by hot, dry winds from the west. In summer, particularly in May and June, the temperature drops rapidly at night, although it remains far above 25°C. People sleep in courtyards and other open spaces to escape the heat radiated from cement concrete buildings. However, housing in northern cities is characterized by compactness, with little or no ventilation. The lack of ventilation assures protection from extreme cold in winter and from hot and dusty winds in summer.

Southern Inland Cities. In South India there are comparatively fewer inland plains cities, because almost the whole of Maharashtra and Karnataka, and parts of Andhra Pradesh, are on a high plateau. Inland plains are all but non-existent in Kerala. Only Tamil Nadu and Andhra Pradesh have extensive inland areas at an elevation of less than 500 m. The major inland plains cities in the South are Madurai, Coimbatore and Salem in Tamil Nadu; Kurnool, Cuddapah and Anantapur in Andhra Pradesh; Raichur, Bellary and Gulbarga in Karnataka; and Nagpur, Gondia and Chandrapur in Maharashtra. Some, at least, of these cities are at an elevation of more than 400 m, where the effects of altitude are appreciable. Thus Coimbatore has distinctly mild summers and has a climate very similar to that of a plateau town.

Towns in the southern inland plains have no winter season. The winter daily minimum temperatures are invariably between 15°C and 20°C; nights are particularly pleasant. The daytime, even in winter, is warm, if not hot, with maximum temperatures in the range of 25–30°C. The summer conditions vary somewhat, depending on elevation above sea level and distance from the sea. Nagpur has extremely hot, dry summers; but there are no dust storms or dusty hot winds. There is rapid radiation cooling during the night, with the result that it is tolerably pleasant outdoors; however, few people in southern India sleep outdoors by choice.

The Desert Cities and Towns. The western half of Rajasthan, Marwad, is the only desert area in India. This region has a number of beautiful cities and towns which are well planned and have a grid iron pattern of roads. The houses are well maintained and artistically decorated. The Marwaris, or the trading class, are well known all over India for their enterprise; but even more important is the fact that Marwaris preserve their links with their home towns and take every care to maintain their ancestoral property. The towns and cities in Marwad, therefore, have certain unique features.

In desert towns water is scarce. The towns and cities are located in carefully chosen areas that are richer in ground water resources. Summers are hot and dry, while winters are cool and dry. The winter weather in desert towns is very pleasant. On the other hand, the severity of the summer is extreme with maximum daily temperatures far above 40°C. Dust storms may last for days on end, and visibility becomes very poor. Prolonged dustiness causes the choking of lungs and high fever. Outdoor space plays an important role both in summer and in winter: in summer, the evenings and nights are spent outdoors, and in winter people enjoy the warmth of the sun and do all their chores outdoors. In fact, many houses in desert towns do not have kitchens, since the cooking is done outdoors both in summer and in winter.

Bikaner, Jodhpur, Ganganagar, Hisar and Sikar are the principal cities of the desert region. Jaisalmer is perhaps the most beautiful desert town. Towns and cities are few in number as the overall density of population in this region is relatively low. Villages and towns are spaced farther apart. There is a lack of greenery and the houses are built of mud or, rarely, with burned bricks. Desert towns, therefore, have a distinctive appearance and form.

HISTORICAL CLASSIFICATION

The past coexists with the present in Indian cities. Relics of the past are conspicuous landscape features and focal points of historical cities. The Red Fort and Jama Masjid in Delhi, the palaces of Jaipur, Udaipur, Jodhpur and Mysore, the temples of Madurai, Tanjore and Kancheepuram, the Victoria Memorial and Dalhousie Square in Calcutta, all testify to the role of the past in the present landscape of the Indian city. Not all cities have monumental vestiges of the past; Varanasi, perhaps the oldest among Indian cities, does not have even a single structure older than 300 years. Nevertheless, the past exists in an intangible form in the minds of people and in the atmosphere of the city, and affects life in the city. The past, therefore, is as important as the present in determining the character and role of a city. In chapter 2 the historical origins of Indian towns and cities were reviewed. Here an attempt is made to classify the 219 one-lakh cities along historical lines. Our concern is with historical influence on the present landscape, rather than the mere fact of historical origin. Keeping this in view, four classes of cities may be identified: (a) ancient cities, (b) medieval cities, (c) British Indian cities, and (d) post-Independence cities (figure 6.2 and Appendix).

Ancient Cities

Forty-five of the 219 one-lakh cities of present-day India have existed continuously for about a thousand years or more. Among these, the southern cities have significant landmarks in the form of temples

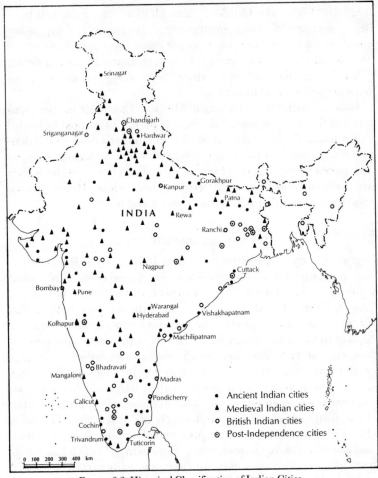

FIGURE 6.2. Historical Classification of Indian Cities.

that date to the period before AD 1200. Most of the temples of
southern cities were constructed during the period from the 5th to
12th century AD. The temple cities of the South have a typical
pattern of streets which form squares centred around the temple.
The temples continue to perform their funtions today as in the
past, and are the main focal points of the cities. Other than the
temples and the street layout, there is not much architectural
evidence of the past.

   In northern India, particularly in the Ganga plains, there are
hardly any major architectural relics of the ancient period. The

small town of Rajgir in Bihar which served as the capital of the early Magadhan kingdoms, has a number of relics. Patna and Varanasi have no structures dating to the ancient period. The cities of Allahabad, Mathura, Faizabad (Ayodhya), all have ancient histories; nevertheless the architectural evidence is unimpressive. In a social and cultural sense, however, these cities continue to play an important role.

The Medieval Cities

The medieval cities are more numerous than the ancient cities and their number is 101; approximately 40 per cent of today's one-lakh cities originated in the medieval period. The most important of these are Delhi, Hyderabad, Jaipur, Lucknow, Agra, Ahmedabad, Nagpur and Pune. These cities had already grown to a substantial size before AD 1800. An important and conspicuous landscape feature of medieval cities, both in the North and in the Deccan, is the fort with its associated features. The fortified towns and cities in India number several hundreds. An adequate macro-study of such urban places has not been attempted so far.

Shahjahanabad in Delhi, Hyderabad and Jaipur, are well planned cities belonging to this period. While each of these cities has seen much growth in the British and post-Independence periods, much of the old city is still present and forms a conspicuous central area. Segments of concentric walls representing the periphery of the medieval city are still in evidence; the fort, the mosque and the traditional market centre or the chowk still continue to dominate the city landscape. The older city areas are now overcrowded; nevertheless, the old medieval *mohallas* or localities still continue to hold on to their special ethnic, linguistic, social and occupational characteristics. The city of old is very much in evidence in the modern city.

British Indian Cities

The leading metropolises of India—Calcutta, Bombay and Madras—belong to this period. In addition, as many as 56 one-lakh cities originated during the 150 years of British rule. The hill stations, although more numerous, have rarely grown to the size of one-lakh cities. Medieval and ancient Indian cities were also considerably modified during this period, but British influence is most visible in the cities that originated in this period. European systems of architecture are best represented in the principal metropolitan cities of Calcutta, Bombay and Madras. Madras, however, has a number of temples belonging to a much earlier time period—the temples at Triplicane and Mylapore are still important focal points, reflecting strongly Indian traditions. The British period also saw the emergence of truly industrial cities such as Jamshedpur, Bhadravati, Dhanbad and Asansol, for example. These cities have no links with the past and have in fact very little by way of architecture or monuments. Except in the capital city of New Delhi which was built in the 1920s, the architectural relics of the British period are not very impressive.

Post-Independence Cities

Eighteen one-lakh cities have come up in India since 1947. This number is large in relation to the short time period. With a few exceptions like Chandigarh, which is a well-planned city, most post-Independence cities have grown around industrial or residential townships. Urban growth around the original nucleus has been neither foreseen nor planned. As a result, these cities are a hotch-potch of urban units, some planned and some unplanned. The administrative status of these one-lakh cities, for example, Bokaro Steel City, is yet undefined. These cities exemplify the chaotic character of urban growth in the post-Independence period.

CLASSIFICATION BASED ON SOCIO-CULTURAL CHARACTERISTICS

The population of most Indian cities is heterogenous. Cities have peoples who speak different languages and profess different religions; further, there are differences in terms of *jati* and *varna*, apart from differences in the regions and states from which people have migrated to the cities. The population mix of a city is a measure of its cosmopolitan character. From the viewpoint of western concepts of modernization and secularization, a cosmopolitan character is considered a desirable attribute. In general, it is observed that the bigger the city the more cosmopolitan it is. Thus, Bombay and other metropolitan cities are more cosmopolitan than smaller one-lakh cities such as Ahmadnagar or Tiruchirappalli. The medium and small towns have hardly any cosmopolitan characteristics.

The measurement of cosmopolitanism and the classification of cities on the basis of their composite social structure is a complex task and has not been attempted in India even by sociologists. However, individual aspects of the social and cultural milieux of cities can be measured and understood more readily. Thus, cities may be classified on the basis of the dominant language or languages used in social interaction, or the religious composition of the population. Aspects of literacy, age structure, proportion of new migrants, male-female ratio, number of households or persons per house, or the size of the families are other attributes of social structure for which data are provided by the Census.[1] But for a large range of social attributes related to family types, patterns of kinship and social interaction, *jati* and *varna* and their ramifications in urban social behaviour, data are not available for all cities in India. Given the limited nature of the database, only a partial classification of Indian cities on the basis of social-cultural criteria can be attempted. More specifically, two major attributes of urban social life—language and religion—may be used for this purpose.

Linguistic Classification

Language is a major social parameter that lends a distinct personality to a city. Twelve languages figure prominently in the Indian urban scene; within each linguistic framework, most cities show a high degree of homogeneity. The least degree of homogeneity is seen in metropolitan cities. Bombay is easily the city with the highest degree of linguistic diversity, with 48 per cent of its population speaking Marāthi, 21 per cent Gujarati, 18 per cent Hindi/Urdu and the remaining 13 per cent represented by Tamil, Telugu, Kannada, Malayalam and Punjabi, each accounting for 1–3 per cent of the total population. In Calcutta 65 per cent of the population speak Bengali, 20 per cent Hindi and 9 per cent Oriya, with a sprinkling of other languages. Delhi is even more linguistically homogenous with 76 per cent of its population speaking Hindi, 13 per cent Punjabi, and 6 per cent Urdu. Madras has a similar pattern with 72 per cent of its population speaking Tamil, 14 per cent Telugu, 6 per cent Urdu and 3 per cent Malayalam. English, though not claimed as a mother tongue by a significant number of people, is widely used in all the metropolitan cities.

In relation to the premier metropolitan cities, other one-lakh

[1] A casual analysis of Census data on these variables reveals a strong differentiation between northern and southern cities. Northern cities generally have lower sex ratios (fewer females), lower literacy rates, larger proportions of scheduled caste people and smaller proportions of migrants into the city than southern cities.

cities are overwhelmingly dominated by a single language. The linguistic homogeneity varies inversely with the size of the city or town. Small towns are almost entirely unilingual. Given the dominance of a single language in Indian cities and towns, it is possible to classify India's urban places on the basis of dominant language used in social interaction within the city.

On the basis of dominant language, India's one-lakh cities fall into twelve groups. The most common linguistic type is, understandably, the Hindi city, which constitutes 39 per cent of the 219 cities in India. The Marathi city accounts for slightly over 10 per cent; this is closely followed by Tamil, Telugu, Kannada, Gujarati and Bengali groups, each of which makes up 5 to 10 per cent of the

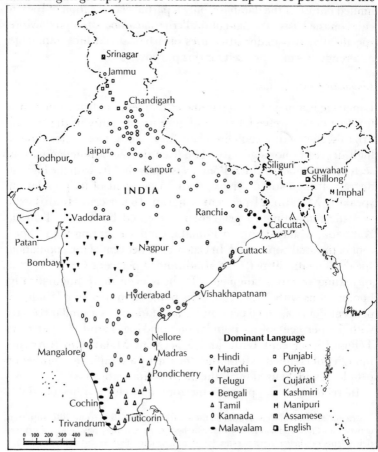

FIGURE 6.3. Linguistic Classification of Indian Cities.

total number of cities in India. Assamese, Kashmiri and Manipuri
are represented by one city each, while Shillong does not have a
dominant recognized language other than English. English, however, is the official language of Meghalaya, of which Shillong is the
capital (figure 6.3).

The linguistic pattern of cities closely follows the administrative
pattern, in view of the fact that since 1956 the states in India have
been organized along linguistic lines. The very obvious nature of
this classification of cities, however, does not in any way diminish
its significance in relation to the other city classifications.

Classification Based on Religion and Ethnicity

Indian cities vary in the religious composition of their population.
Of the nation's urban population as a whole, 77 per cent are Hindus, 16 per cent Muslims, about 13 per cent Christians and 2 per
cent Sikhs. The Jains, Buddhists and Parsis constitute numeri-
cally very small, but nevertheless locally important, sections of the
urban population of India. In fact, except for the Sikhs, religious
minorities show a distinct tendency towards concentration in urban
places. Parsis and Bohra Muslims are concentrated in the west
coast port cities of Bombay, Bharuch and Surat. Jains are found in
almost all urban areas in India, but with a relative concentration
in western India and, in particular, Rajasthan and Madhya
Pradesh. There is an extraordinarily high concentration of Buddhists in the cities of Maharashtra, explained by the mass conversion
of the scheduled caste followers of Dr B. R. Ambedkar (table 6.4).

While the vast majority of India's 219 cities have a predominantly
Hindu population (50 per cent or more), six cities have a Muslim
majority. However, a simple majority is not necessarily a satisfactory
criterion for determining the social fabric of a city. The presence of
religious minorities has enriched the culture of many Indian cities
which have acquired a distinct social character as a result. The
Muslims constitute by far the most important religious minority
in urban areas, contributing approximately 16 per cent of the
urban population. It may be reasonably argued that when the
population of Muslims in any city equals or exceeds 20 per cent of
the city's population, they add a new dimension to the city's
socio-cultural milieu. We may in fact apply the same yardstick to
other religious minorities in cities. On the basis of this criterion,
three types of cities may be identified: (a) Muslim cities, (b) Sikh

cities and (c) Christian cities. This is in addition to the cities which have a predominantly Hindu population with only an insignificant proportion of religious minorities.

TABLE 6.4

Sikhs, Christians, Buddhists and Jains in Indian Cities

City	State	Contribution of Religious Group in Total Population (per cent)
A SIKHS		
1. Patiala	Punjab	41.2
2. Amritsar	"	40.1
3. Ludhiana	"	34.4
4. Bathinda	"	33.1
5. Batala	"	29.4
6. Jalandhar	"	23.0
7. Chandigarh	Union Territory	19.8
8. Ambala M. C.	Haryana	16.1
9. Yamunanagar	"	14.3
10. Jammu	Jammu and Kashmir	11.8
11. Pathankot	Punjab	10.9
12. Karnal	Haryana	10.6
B CHRISTIANS		
1. Trichur	Kerala	41.2
2. Shillong	Meghalaya	41.1
3. Cochin	Kerala	36.3
4. Alleppey	"	27.1
5. Nagarcoil	Tamil Nadu	24.4
6. Tuticorin	" "	23.9
7. Quilon	Kerala	22.6
8. Kolar G. F.	Karnataka	18.8
9. Valparai	Tamil Nadu	18.3
10. Mangalore	Karnataka	17.0
11. Trivandrum	Kerala	16.5
12. Dindigul	Tamil Nadu	15.2
13. Pondicherry	Union Territory	13.9
14. Tiruchirappalli	Tamil Nadu	11.2
C BUDDHISTS		
1. Nagpur	Maharashtra	14.9
2. Aurangabad	"	13.9
3. Nanded	"	13.1

City	State	Contribution of Religious Group in Total Population (per cent)
4. Chandrapur	Maharashtra	12.1
5. Akola	”	9.8
6. Parbani	”	9.2
7. Bhusaval	”	8.3
8. Latur	”	7.1
9. Gondia	”	7.0
10. Pune	”	6.9
11. Bombay	”	5.7
12. Amravati	”	5.7

D JAINS

City	State	Contribution of Religious Group in Total Population (per cent)
1. Udaipur	Rajasthan	9.4
2. Ratlam	Madhya Pradesh	8.3
3. Sagar	” ”	6.3
4. Bhilwara	Rajasthan	5.7
5. Ichalkaranji	Maharashtra	5.0

SOURCE: *Census of India, 1981:* Series-1, Paper 4 of 1984: 'Household Population by Religion of Head of Household (Up to District, U. A. & City Level)'.

TABLE 6.5
Muslims in Indian Cities, 1981

City	State	Muslim Population as a Percentage of Total
1. Srinagar	Jammu and Kashmir	92.4
2. Rampur	Uttar Pradesh	72.2
3. Sambal	” ”	71.3
4. Amroha	” ”	68.1
5. Malegaon	Maharashtra	67.5
6. Bhiwandi	”	52.2
7. Moradabad	Uttar Pradesh	47.5
8. Burhanpur	Madhya Pradesh	46.0
9. Shahjahanpur	Uttar Pradesh	42.0
10. Cuddapah	Andhra Pradesh	41.5
11. Sikar	Rajasthan	40.7
12. Bihar	Bihar	38.4
13. Parbani	Maharashtra	37.6
14. Calicut	Kerala	37.2

City	State	Muslim Population as a Percentage of Total
15. Firozabad	Uttar Pradesh	35.6
16. Cannanore	Kerala	35.4
·17. Aligarh	Uttar Pradesh	34.6
18. Raichur	Karnataka	34.4
19. Gulbarga	”	34.4
20. Meerut	Uttar Pradesh	33.9
21. Hyderabad	Andhra Pradesh	33.5
22. Nanded	Maharashtra	33.5
23. Bareilly	Uttar Pradesh	33.0
24. Bijapur	Karnataka	32.7
25. Kurnool	Andhra Pradesh	32.0
26. Jaunpur	Uttar Pradesh	31.4
27. Aurangabad	Maharashtra	31.3
28. Saharanpur	Uttar Pradesh	31.2
29. Nizamabad	Andhra Pradesh	31.0
30. Etawah	Uttar Pradesh	30.4
31. Bulandshahr	” ”	30.1
32. Muzaffarnagar	” ”	29.6
33. Bhagalpur	Bihar	28.8
34. Sitapur	Uttar Pradesh	28.7
35. Bellary	Karnataka	28.4
36. Bhopal	Madhya Pradesh	27.9
37. Adoni	Andhra Pradesh	27.8
38. Lucknow	Uttar Pradesh	27.8
39. Bharuch	Gujarat	27.4
40. Patan	”	26.7
41. Jalna	Maharashtra	26.2
42. Khandwa	”	26.1
43. Darbhanga	Bihar	26.1
44. Tumkur	Karnataka	25.7
45. Hapur	Uttar Pradesh	25.2
46. Ananthapur	Andhra Pradesh	25.0
47. Prodattur	” ”	24.8
48. Varanasi	Uttar Pradesh	24.2
49. Gorakhpur	” ”	24.1
50. Latur	Maharashtra	24.1
51. Hubli-Dharwad	Karnataka	24.1
52. Palghat	Kerala	23.7
53. Akola	Maharashtra	23.6
54. Alleppey	Kerala	23.5
55. Hospet	Karnataka	23.5
56. Davanagere	”	23.4

City	State	Muslim Population as a Percentage of Total
57. Dhule	Maharashtra	23.2
58. Shimoga	Karnataka	22.4
59. Allahabad	Uttar Pradesh	21.7
60. Gadag-Betgeri	Karnataka	21.4
61. Ratlam	Maharashtra	21.2
62. Agra	Uttar Pradesh	21.1
63. Gaya	Bihar	21.0
64. Purnia	"	20.9
65. Asansol	West Bengal	20.8
66. Jamnagar	Gujarat	20.5
67. Kanpur	Uttar Pradesh	20.4
68. Faizabad(Ayodhya)	" "	20.3
69. Muzaffarpur	Bihar	20.3
70. Junagadh	Gujarat	20.0
71. Mysore	Karnataka	20.0

SOURCE: *Census of India, 1981:* Series-1 India, Paper 4 of 1984: 'Household Population by Religion of Head of Household (Up to District, U.A. & City Level)'.

Among the 219 cities in India, 71 cities have a significant (i.e. 20 per cent or more) representation of Muslims; Christians are present in significant measure in 7 cities, while Sikhs are well represented in 6 cities, all in Punjab. In all, 83 cities, representing 37 per cent of the total number of cities in India, have a significant religious minority representation. Religious minorities are also present in a large number of other Indian cities (as is indicated by table 6.4), though their contribution to the population may be far less than 20 per cent.

The spatial distribution of religious minority cities reveals the importance of minorities in all parts of India. This is especially true of Muslims. Of the one-lakh cities, Srinagar in Kashmir, Rampur, Amroha and Sambal in Uttar Pradesh, and Malegaon and Bhiwandi in Maharashtra have a predominantly Muslim population. Uttar Pradesh has the largest number of cities where Muslims constitute 20 per cent or more of the population; it is followed by Karnataka, Maharashtra, Bihar and Andhra Pradesh.

Kerala, Madhya Pradesh and Gujarat also have a few cities with a significant Muslim population (table 6.5). The distribution of cities with significant proportion of Muslims covers almost all the states in India. The only states where such cities do not exist are Punjab, Haryana, Orissa and the north-eastern states.

Unlike the Muslim population, Sikhs and Christians are concentrated in certain areas of the country. There are no cities in India which have a majority (50 per cent or more) of persons belonging to the Sikh or Christian religion. Although the Sikhs form a majority in Punjab as a whole, in only two cities is the percentage of Sikhs over 40 per cent—Amritsar and Patiala. Other cities with 20 to 40 per cent Sikh population are: Ludhiana, Bathinda, Batala and Jalandhar. In Chandigarh Sikhs form slightly less than 20 per cent of the population. Sikhs are well represented in another six cities mainly in Punjab, Haryana and Jammu. The absence of predominantly Sikh cities is explained by the fact that Sikhs are primarily engaged in farming, while services, trade and industry are dominated by Hindus. The Hindus in Punjab are mainly found in urban areas.

The cities with significant—20 per cent or more—Christian population are found mainly in three states: Kerala, Tamil Nadu and Meghalaya. Only Shillong in Meghalaya and Trichur in Kerala have slightly over 40 per cent Christian population. The other cities with a significant percentage of Christian population are: Cochin, Alleppey and Quilon in Kerala and Nagarcoil and Tuticorin in Tamil Nadu. In seven other cities, mainly in Tamil Nadu, Kerala and Karnataka, the Christian population constitutes 10 to 20 per cent of the total (table 6.4). In the north-eastern states of Meghalaya, Nagaland and Mizoram, Christians form a sizeable part if not a majority, of the total population. Shillong is the only one-lakh city, but there are many smaller towns in these states where Christians form a majority. The cities and towns in these states may also be designated as tribal towns and cities, as all the people are recognized as scheduled tribes. In Goa, Christians form about 30 per cent of the total population, and although there are no one-lakh cities here, Christians form a sizeable part of the population in most towns.

Leh in Ladakh is essentially a Buddhist town, but it may also be characterized as a tribal town. Among tribal towns, Jagdalpur and Koraput in Orissa, and Itanagar in Arunachal Pradesh are the well known and prominent urban centres representing different tribal areas. There is, however, a basic built-in contradiction in the use of the term 'tribal town'. A tribal society is pre-literate and rural by definition, and as such a tribal town is a cultural impossibility; yet the tribals in India, even after becoming literate, have successfully maintained their own separate identity. The use of the term 'tribal town' has to be understood in this context.

ECONOMIC OR FUNCTIONAL CLASSIFICATION

Cities may be classified on the basis of the types of economic activity carried on within the city. Certain economic activities have acquired greater significance than others. The presence of an iron and steel industry or textile industry lends a certain name and character to the city. Some cities are known for their administrative status as state or district capitals, others for their educational institutions, and yet others for trade or transport activities. In addition, there are mining towns and even fishing and forestry towns. The range of economic activities in a city covers the entire spectrum of primary, secondary and tertiary activities. Nevertheless, there is a tendency among scholars to exclude primary economic activities such as mining, agriculture or fishing from urban economic activities. We have in chapter 3 argued against this proposition. In the Indian context, primary activities are very much a part of the urban scene, as nearly a third of India's urban places have agriculture as relatively the most dominant economic activity. However, employment in agriculture is significant only in small towns, while in one-lakh cities there is a distinct emphasis on secondary and tertiary economic activities. In general, tertiary activities are by far the most important, followed by secondary activities including household industry and organized modern industry. Primary activities form the third and relatively less important part of economic activity in urban places.

The classification of cities based on the relative importance of primary, secondary and tertiary activities is by itself not very meaningful. Cities show a remarkable degree of specialization in one or more specific activities, such as trade, transport, household industry, modern industry, public administration and so on. It is, therefore, more meaningful to classify cities on the basis of detailed categories of primary, secondary and tertiary activities.

The Database

Data on economic activities in urban places are rather meagre. The main source of information on this aspect is the Indian Census. In the 1961 and 1971 Censuses, data for all towns and cities are provided for nine industrial categories of workers. This classification of workers closely corresponds to the Standard Industrial Classification of workers at the first digit level. The categories are:

I   Cultivation
II   Agricultural labour
III   Forestry, fishing, plantations, mining and quarrying, etc.
IV   Household industry
V   Manufacturing other than household industry
VI   Construction
VII   Trade and commerce
VIII   Transport, storage and communication
IX   Services

The industrial categories of workers include primary, secondary and tertiary economic activities. The first three categories represent primary activities, categories IV and V represent the secondary sector, while categories VI, VII, VIII and IX represent tertiary services. The first two categories relate to agriculture, which is not considered as an urban economic activity by most scholars. The third category has a mix of urban and non-urban activities. Mining, particularly of coal, iron ore, gold, petroleum and so on, represents the organized industrial sector and has a definite urban connotation. Similarly, plantation settlements also have an urban character, while most fishing and forestry settlements are rural in character. Categories IV to IX have a definite association with urban areas. Nevertheless, household industry, construction, trade and commerce, and services are all represented in rural areas as well. In fact, nearly a fourth of rural workers are engaged in secondary and tertiary economic activities. This is true in even the most inaccessible villages. Urban areas, however, have a larger proportion of workers in the secondary and tertiary sectors. It is this aspect that is relevant to the economic classification of India's urban places. But, the number of industrial categories for which data are provided in the Census is far too small for any in-depth classification of towns and cities. The US Census provided data for 36 categories of workers, which explains the pioneering role of American geographers in the functional classification of cities.

Concept of Dominant Function

The Census industrial categories form the basis for a functional classification of urban places. The term 'function' in fact refers to an economic activity in a town, whether at the primary, secondary or tertiary level. In chapter 7, a much more restricted definition of 'function' will be used, wherein the primary and secondary sectors are totally excluded, while only a restricted range of tertiary activities are included. For purposes of city classification such a restricted interpretation of the term is not desirable.

While every town and city has some workers engaged in each of the industrial categories, the proportion or percentage of workers in one industrial category may be greater than in others. This category represents the dominant function of a town or city. In the early 1950s, it was considered appropriate to classify urban places on the basis of their dominant function. This approach is, however, far too simple and tends to ignore the presence of other activities in the city. Further, the number of workers is not always the best measure of the importance of an economic activity. Trade and commerce may involve fewer workers, nevertheless, they play an important role in linking the city with its hinterland. The dominant function approach would not fully reveal the role of the city within the economy of the region of which it is the focal point.

The dominant function approach, therefore, has all but been abandoned in the functional classification of cities and has been replaced by the multiple function approach. In this approach, a town or a city could specialize in one or more functions; the degree of specialization is determined by the number of workers in a city in relation to some norm which is set for an average city.

India's cities were first classified in terms of functional categories by Amrit Lal using the 1951 Census data. This study included 67 one-lakh cities. The classification, however, suffers from a number of methodological deficiencies, and in fact does not even list the 67 cities according to the functional groups into which they have been divided. Asok Mitra has attempted a classification of all towns and cities common to the 1961 and 1971 Censuses. Of the two methods employed by Asok Mitra, the earlier method is more satisfactory and is discussed in the following section. His second classification employs a rather complicated quantitative procedure of factor and cluster analysis, but the end product is less satisfactory than his original simpler classification. The factor analytical method and various grouping procedures were also adopted by Qazi Ahmed for classifying the one-lakh cities of India in 1961. The major defect in Ahmed's classification is that he used in all 63 variables, most of which are neither relevant or meaningful to the classification of Indian cities. The irrelevance of the variables was reflected in the classification, which made little sense. Asok Mitra's application of the factor method is more judicious; but given only six functional categories, there is hardly any justification for the use of factor analysis, whose basic function is to discover underlying dimensions given a very broad range of characteristics. Thus the reason why Asok Mitra's use of factor analysis is defective is just the opposite of the reason for the failure of Qazi Ahmed's use of the same technique. Qazi Ahmed used too many variables with no selectivity while Asok Mitra used too few variables representing only the economic or functional aspect.

Functional Classification by Asok Mitra

A thorough classification of all urban places in India was attempted by Asok Mitra, a former Registrar General of the Census and a noted authority on population statistics in India. As a first step in his classification, he grouped the seven industrial categories of workers (excluding the first two categories representing the agricultural sector) into three broad groups to derive three major functional types:

A. *Manufacturing town* : Where the percentage of workers in the industrial categories of III, IV, V and VI put together is greater than the percentage of workers in categories VII and VIII put together or the percentage of workers in category IX.

B. *Trade and transport town* : Where the percentage of workers in categories VII and VIII together is greater than in category IX or in categories III, IV, V and VI put together.

C. *Service town* : Where the percentage of workers in category IX is greater than the total percentage of workers in categories III, IV, V and VI or the total percentage of workers in categories VII and VIII.

The manufacturing towns and trade and transport towns were further subclassified as follows:

1. Mining and quarrying, livestock, forestry, fishing or plantation town: Where the percentage of workers in category III is greater than in IV, V or VI considered individually.

2. Artisan town: Where the percentage of workers in IV is greater

than that in III, V or VI.

3. Manufacturing town: Where the percentage of workers in V is greater than in III, IV or VI.

4. Construction town: Where the percentage of workers in VI is greater than in III, IV or V.

5. Trade town: Where the percentage of workers in VII is greater than in VIII.

6. Transport town: Where the percentage of workers in VIII is greater than in VII.

Triangular Method. In all, seven types of towns were recognized. The degree of specialization in each of the three basic groups was identified on the basis of a triangular method. In this method, the number of workers in each of the three groups is expressed as a percentage of the total; thus the values for all three groups would add up to 100. The values for the three groups are then plotted on a triangular graph, represented by an equilateral triangle. Thus,

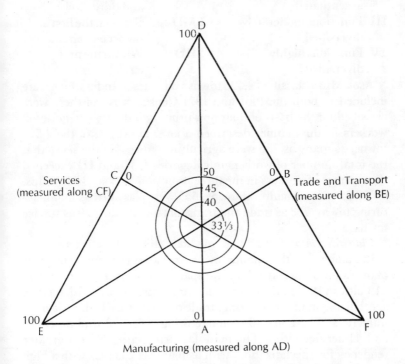

FIGURE 6.4. Asok Mitra's Triangular Method for Measurement of Degree of Specialization in Functions.

each town or city may be plotted as a point within the equilateral triangle, where the perpendiculars drawn to each of the three sides of the triangle are directly proportional to the percentage of workers in each of the three groups (figure 6.4).

The incentre of the equilateral triangle represents a town in which the percentage of workers in each of the three groups is exactly 33⅓. Such a town has obviously no functional specialization. Towns located farther away from the incentre show increasing tendency for specialization. Asok Mitra drew three circles at distances of 6⅔, 11⅓ and 16⅔ units from the incentre to differentiate four levels of specialization. He designated the degrees of specialization as follows:

Degree of Specialization	Code	Location in triangle
I Predominant function highly accentuated	PEHA	Outside the outer circle (third circle)
II Predominant function accentuated	PFA	Between the second and third circles
III Functions moderately diversified	FMD	Between the first and the second circles
IV Functions highly diversified	FHD	Within the first circle

Asok Mitra classified 2,528 towns and cities in India which were included in both the 1961 and 1971 Censuses. All of these were classified on the basis of their non-primary industry categories of workers in the manner described above. However, of the 2,528 towns, as many as 736 were agricultural towns, in the sense that the total number of workers in categories I, II and III exceeded the number of workers in the three basic non-agricultural groups. Of 1,792 non-agricultural towns, 655 were classified as manufacturing towns, 708 as trade and transport towns, and 429 as service towns.

Classification of Cities. The one-lakh cities, classified by Asok Mitra along with the smaller towns, are easier to examine in terms of the range of specialization and spatial patterns (figure 6.5). The 219 cities (1981) fall into seven categories; among which cities specializing in manufacturing, trade or service are by far the most numerous. There are 80 manufacturing cities, 78 trading cities, and 41 service cities. The manufacturing cities have a greater tendency for specialization, with as many as 26 cities with a high degree of specialization. Only 3 trading cities and 6 service cities show such a high level of specialization (table 6.6).

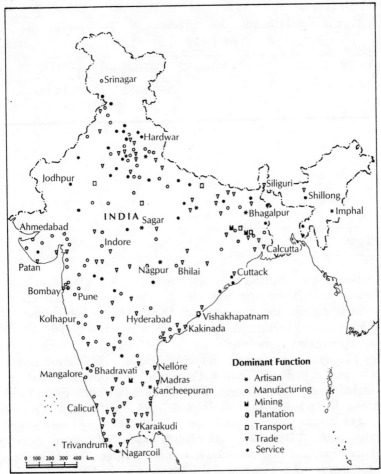

FIGURE 6.5. Functional Classification of Indian Cities (based on Asok Mitra's 1971 classification).

The leading manufacturing cities which show clear specialization are Ahmedabad, Surat, Jamshedpur, Ulhasnagar, Ludhiana, Salem and Solapur. Manufacturing cities are distributed widely all over the country—from Tamil Nadu in the south to Bihar and Uttar Pradesh in the north and Maharashtra and Gujarat in the west. Kerala and Assam, however, are not represented.

The three cities which have a high degree of specialization in trade are Vijayawada in Andhra Pradesh, Siliguri in West Bengal and Katihar in Bihar. The trade cities show a lower level of speciali-

TABLE 6.6
Functional Classification of Indian Cities
(based on Asok Mitra)

City Type	Code	Degree of Specialization				Total Number of Cities
		FHD	FMD	PFA	PFHA	
		Number of Cities				
1. Manufacturing	MMt	17	28	9	26	80
2. Artisan	MA	2	2	2	2	8
3. Mining	MMg	—	—	1	1	2
4. Plantation	MP	—	—	—	1	1
5. Trading	TTg	22	35	18	3	78
6. Transport	TTt	—	1	3	5	9
7. Service	SS	8	15	12	6	41
Total		49	81	45	44	219

zation and are distributed widely over all the states in India. The service cities, like the trading cities, are also ubiquitous in terms of spatial distribution. Chandigarh, Dehra Dun, Bhubaneshwar, Shillong and Agartala are the only cities that have a high degree of specialization in services.

The artisan cities are few in number, eight in all. Of these, Kancheepuram in Tamil Nadu and Sagar in Madhya Pradesh have a high degree of specialization. Other cities in this category are Varanasi, Bhagalpur, Nagarcoil, Imphal, Sambal and Gondia. Transportation is a major specialization of the cities in the coal mining area, namely, Dhanbad, Asansol and Ondal. The railway cities of Kharagpur and Bhusawal also have a high degree of specialization in transportation. Valparai in the Anamalai Hills of Tamil Nadu is the only city with a specialization in the plantation (tea) industry, while Kolar Gold Fields in Karnataka and Bermo in Bihar have specialization in mining activities.

Summary. Asok Mitra's classification, on the whole, does bring out the major categories on the basis of their broad economic activities. In particular, it succeeds in differentiating the manufacturing, trading and service (administration) cities. The vast majority of Indian cities, however, have no clear specialization in any one economic activity and in fact have a diversified economic base. Specialization appears, on the whole, as the exception rather than the rule. Nevertheless, manufacturing cities do appear as a major subtype among Indian cities, and stand in contrast to the general run of diversified cities. Specialization in trade, service, mining or transport occurs only in a handful of cities. Though these are important deviant or exceptional cases, their numbers are too insignificant. The diversified city with multiple functions including manufacturing, trade and service constitutes the most common and representative type of city. The Indian urban system is indeed basically a system of diversified cities.

CLASSIFICATION: A CRITIQUE

Classification in itself represents a basic form of measurement— nominal scale measurement. Measurement, in turn, is a basic scientific procedure. The classification of urban places, as such, is a fundamental first step in scientific enquiry into the character of urban places. At the nominal scale of measurement, classification of urban places presents few, if any, problems. Thus, towns and cities may be classified on the basis of their site characteristics as sea front, lake front, river front, flat land or hilly cities; or they may be classified on the basis of their social attributes as Hindu cities, Muslim cities, Christian cities or Sikh cities. One could develop an almost infinite number of such elementary classifications. They have only a limited utility value; nevertheless, they are useful and meaningful in specific situations. A slightly higher order of classification becomes possible when an ordinal scale of measurement is made. For example, urban places may be classified on the basis of their administrative status as national capital, state capitals, district or tehsil headquarters. These categories are discrete (there is no ambiguity about a city's status), and they form a hierarchy with decreasing status or importance. Cities are ranked on the basis of status, either deliberately assigned by the bureaucracy, or resulting from the presence of organizations of a cultural or business character. There is no such thing as a natural hierarchy of urban places; hierarchy is invariably man-made.

Problems in urban classification arise mainly when the level of measurement of urban characteristics is raised to the interval scale. Here urban places are differentiated on the basis of single or multiple criteria or variables. Population size is a basic criterion for urban classification. However, the frequency distribution of urban places on the basis of their population, would yield a moderately skewed distribution curve, which is continuous and has hardly any break-points. The vast majority of city characteristics, such as employment in manufacturing, trade or commerce, follow the same pattern. Classification of cities on the basis of interval scale measurement, involving continuity of values, has by necessity to be arbitrary. The Census classifies Indian urban places into six categories. By varying the class limits and intervals one could develop an infinite number of classifications of cities on the basis of population. None of these classifications is inherently superior or inferior to the others. The general acceptance of the Census classification is simply a matter of convention and convenience. Thus, interval scale measurement of urban characteristics cannot lead us to any unique scientific classification. Further, all urban classifications based on interval scale measurement are arbitrary.

It has been argued, but not established, that urban places tend to form clusters within a linear interval scale measurement. Thus, one may expect clusters of cities in a linear unidimensional variable such as percentage employment in manufacturing. If such clusters exist then there is a logical and scientific basis for the classification of urban places. So far, the existence of such clusters has not been proved beyond doubt. Therefore, a rational, logical or scientific classification of urban places on the basis of quantitative measurement, is still an illusion rather than a reality.

The problems of classification using one critierion or variable at a time are formidable enough. Nevertheless, scholars have attempted to combine several criteria or variables into a classification scheme. Most often, such attempts have generated more confusion than clarity. Thus, the factor analytical method used for classification of India's urban places by Asok Mitra and Qazi Ahmed, have generated more doubts and ambiguities and fewer new insights into the basic characteristics of Indian cities. A holistic or comprehensive approach to urban classification is neither feasible nor even desirable or meaningful. How can one synthesize the historical, environmental, social and economic attributes of urban places into an understandable set of categories? Classification, whether of the qualitative or quantitative variety, is an exercise in simple logic. The utility and meaningfulness of the outcome is the only criterion for judging the value of a classification.

SELECTED READING

Ahmed, Qazi: *Indian Cities: Characteristics and Correlates,* The Department of Geography Monograph Series, University of Chicago, 1965.

Ananthapadmanabhan, N.: 'Functional Classification of Urban Centres in Madras State', *Bombay Geographical Magazine,* Vol. 13, 1965.

Krishna, Prabha: *Towns: A Structural Analysis—A Case Study of Punjab,* Inter-India Publications, Delhi, 1979.

Lal, Amrit: 'Some Aspects of Functional Classification of Cities and a Proposed Scheme for Classifying Indian Cities', *The National Geographical Journal of India,* 1959, Vol. 5, Part 2, pp. 12–24.

Mitra, Asok: *Functional Classification of India's Towns,* Institute of Economic Growth, Delhi, 1973.

————, et al.: *Functional Classification of India's Urban Areas by Factor Cluster Method 1961–1971,* An ICSSR/JNU Study, Abhinav Publications, New Delhi, 1981.

Rafiullah, S. M.: 'A New Approach to Functional Classification of Towns', *The Geographer,* Vol. 12, 1965, pp. 40–53.

Singh, K. N.: 'Functions and Functional Classification of Towns in Uttar Pradesh', *The National Geographical Journal of India,* Vol. 5, 1959, pp. 121–48.

Verma, N. R. and Gopal Krishan: 'Site Analysis of Hill Towns', *Transactions, Institute of Indian Geographers,* Vol. 2, No. 1, 1980, pp. 101–9.

CHAPTER 7

Settlement Systems

Hamlets, villages, towns and cities are mutually dependent on each other and they coexist as a unified system of settlements in any region, state or nation. The notion of interdependence between settlements of different sizes and categories, is of fundamental importance in urban geography. The nature of interdependence may be economic, political, social or cultural; often, the economic aspect is emphasized more than the others. It is the notion of economic interdependence between settlements that makes it possible to develop theories of settlement spacing and location. The theory of settlement location, in turn, helps us to understand the existing inter-relationships between settlements and to discover deviations from the 'ideal' or 'normal' situation. This chapter focuses on the theoretical aspects of settlement systems in India and its constituent states.

In chapter 6, urban places were considered as discrete objects and were classified into different categories on the basis of their economic, social and physical attributes. This chapter will focus on the population and economic characteristics of settlements in relation to the role that each settlement plays within the overall system of settlements. Furthermore, as the theoretical considerations are unfolded, the distinction between urban and rural places becomes irrelevant. This chapter, therefore, is concerned with all settlements, whether small or large, rural or urban.

BEHAVIOURAL AND NORMATIVE SETTLEMENT SYSTEMS

Theories of settlement systems may be (a) behavioural or (b) normative. A behavioural theory of settlements attempts to explain the existing pattern of settlement in a region. The normative settlement theory, on the other hand, is not concerned with the existing pattern of settlements but attempts to define an ideal system of settlements. The 'ideal' is based on notions of efficiency which are spelt out at the very outset. A normative theory is concerned with how settlements ought to be organized rather than how they are organized in the real world. This chapter will explore both behavioural and normative theories of settlement location with reference to India.

Behavioural settlement theories are based on empirical similarities in settlement systems in different countries in the world. Thus, Zipf's rank-size rule emphasizes the regularity in city size distributions, while the primate city concept emphasizes the abnormally large size of the premier city in different regions or nations of the world. On the basis of the empirical observations a theory is developed to explain the regular pattern which emerges in different parts of the world. The normative theory of settlement, namely, the central place theory, focuses on the tertiary services provided by larger settlements to smaller settlements and develops a theory of settlement location based on considerations of economic efficiency. When differences between these sets of theories are viewed using a systems approach, the nature of the dynamics of settlement systems is revealed.

PRIMATE CITY SETTLEMENT SYSTEM

In the period of the emergence of the earliest cities in the world, the settlement consisted of a city surrounded by hundreds of villages and hamlets. Such a system of settlements was prevelant in India around the 6th century BC. In the first phase of Aryan urbanization, the *janapada* consisted of a capital city surrounded by villages. With the spread of urbanization, the number of towns and cities increased; nevertheless, the largest city, representing the capital of a kingdom or empire, became dominant within the system of towns and cities. Such a dominant city is known as the primate city and an urban system characterized by the presence of a dominant city is designated as a primate city settlement system.

In modern times primacy is said to exist when the largest city in a nation or a region is exceptionally large in relation to the second largest city. In many countries of the world, such as the United Kingdom, France, Netherlands, Thailand and the Philippines, the largest city accounts for as much as one-fifth of the country's population; further, the largest city is 5 to 10 times larger than the second biggest city. The possible reasons for the emergence of primate cities was explained by Mark Jefferson in 1939. His theory of primate cities focuses on the forces of agglomeration and cumulative effects of agglomeration in the growth of large cities. Once a town or city attains a premier position in a nation or region it tends to retain that position and in actual fact, grows faster than other towns and cities. Eventually, it tends to overshadow all other cities or even retard their growth.

Agglomeration Effects and Primacy

The agglomeration effect on the growth of cities is a world-wide phenomenon. It has operated in the past and continues to operate today. All over the world, the leading cities tend to attract the best of human talent and skills. Entrepreneurs are attracted to these cities and with them comes the capital needed for investment in industry. The premier city is perceived as providing the greatest opportunity for employment. The effect of concentration of skills and capital in the leading city is seen in its rapid growth; on the other hand, this also leads to the draining away of skills and capital from the smaller cities and towns. These stagnate and even decline; they find it difficult to compete with the premier city, and as a result the gap between the primate city and the second largest city tends to widen through time.

The primate city, in course of time, becomes the dominant economic, social, cultural and political nerve centre of a country. The presence of people from all parts of the country makes the primate city a mini country in itself. Furthermore, since it has the best talent in the country, it symbolizes national achievement. The primate city is, therefore, much more than a premier city—it is, in effect, a symbol of the nation and its achievement in all fields. The existence of a primate city signifies strong forces that unify a nation. These forces may be cultural, political or economic, or all of these together.

Primacy at the National Level

There is no primate city in India at present. The absence of a primate city is partly explained by the large size of the country, its colonial heritage, and weaknesses in the forces of nationalism in the country. No city in India exercises dominance over the entire nation. Throughout much of the 19th century and the first half of the 20th century, Calcutta was India's leading metropolis. Even in 1981, Delhi, the national capital, occupied third position, after Calcutta and Bombay, among the country's leading metropolitan cities.

However, Delhi has been growing rapidly since 1947 and it is very likely that it will outstrip Calcutta and Bombay in the coming decades.

The absence of a primate city has its roots in Indian history. India was never a politically unified nation until 1947. During the Mughal period, Delhi and Agra functioned alternately as the capital of the empire, which covered only northern India up to Burhanpur in the Malwa Plateau. Subsequently, the British established their empire which covered all parts of the country excepting the motley collection of 500-odd princely states. Calcutta was the capital of India throughout the 19th century and up to 1911, when the capital was shifted to Delhi. This accounts for the rise of Calcutta as India's leading city in modern times. Furthermore, during the British period Calcutta and its citizens led the way for the entire nation. Most of India's eminent reformers, scholars and scientists were associated with the city of Calcutta. Calcutta also became the country's leading port city and industrial centre. After 1911 Calcutta lost some of its importance, and since Independence it has lost ground to Delhi which has emerged as the country's most 'prestigious' metropolitan city. Nevertheless, the process of Delhi's rise as the premier city is not yet complete; hence the absence of a primate city in India.

Primate city development is essentially a politically directed process and it takes time to assert itself under conditions of political stability. Further, primate city development at the national level is characteristic of unitary states with strong central governments. India has had a strong central government in the post-Independence period and this has enhanced the status of Delhi. However, India is not a unitary state, nor is it a full fledged federal state; the Constitution of India envisages a partially federal political set-up with the states and the Union sharing power. This permits the development of national as well as state level primate cities.

Primacy at the State Level

India is a very large country with a considerable degree of diversity in terms of language and culture. The federal framework of the Indian Union and the states has emerged within this background of cultural diversity. The twenty-five states that form the Union today are, by and large, new political entities, although in cultural terms they may have a long historical background. Language was recognized as the fundamental basis for the reorganization of states in 1956. Each state, at present, is a unilingual entity with distinctive cultural roots. Given the political and cultural unity within the states, there has been a distinct tendency for primate city formation at the state level (table 7.1).

Among the 25 states in India, 13 have primate cities. Several large states, such as West Bengal, Karnataka, Tamil Nadu, Maharashtra, Andhra Pradesh and Gujarat, have primate cities which have a population that is at least three times the population of the second ranking city. Among the smaller states, Sikkim, Manipur, Tripura, Meghalaya and Mizoram show a distinct tendency towards city primacy. Among these states, Nagaland is the only one where primacy does not occur. Primate city characteristics are absent in the northern states, from Orissa and Bihar in the east to Rajasthan and Punjab in the west.

West Bengal is an example *par excellence* of primacy at the state level (table 7.1). The Calcutta urban agglomeration accounts for nearly a fifth of West Bengal's population; a situation that is comparable to that of the United Kingdom or other countries with primate city characteristics. West Bengal's second largest city, Asansol, is indeed very small in relation to Calcutta; it is $^1/_{25}$ the size of Calcutta. Apart from size, Calcutta is indeed Bengal in a cultural and economic sense. It is most unlikely that Calcutta's present pre-eminent position will be altered in the foreseeable future.

Like Calcutta, Madras and Bombay also dominate the urban landscape of their states, though to a smaller extent. In all three cases, however, primacy appears to be essentially a product of the colonial heritage. In Karnataka, Andhra Pradesh and Gujarat, the primate cities are of medieval origin. Nevertheless, the present state boundaries are of the post-Independence period. In the smaller states such as Tripura, Manipur, Sikkim and so on, primacy has developed over the past few decades. These states have witnessed considerable changes in population with the influx of refugees and migrants.

Northern India, including the most populous states of Uttar Pradesh and Bihar, has not shown any tendency for primate city formation. Several factors account for the absence of primate cities in this region. In the case of Bihar and Orissa, their location peripheral to Calcutta accounts for the absence of dominant cities; similarly, in the case of Uttar Pradesh, Haryana and Punjab, their nearness to Delhi tends to inhibit the development of primate

TABLE 7.1
Primacy and Urban Systems in Different States in India, 1981

State	First Ranking City	Second Ranking City	Third Ranking City	Index of Primacy
1. West Bengal	Calcutta (9,165,680)	Asansol (365,371)	Durgapur (305,838)	25.08
2. Sikkim	Gangtok (36,768)	Singtam (4,042)	Jorethang (3,922)	9.10
3. Manipur	Imphal (155,639)	Kakching (21,145)	Churachandpur (20,970)	7.36
4. Tripura	Agartala (131,513)	Dharmanagar (20,802)	Udaipur (16,301)	6.32
5. Karnataka	Bangalore (2,913,537)	Hubli (526,493)	Mysore (476,446)	5.53
6. Meghalaya	Shillong (173,062)	Tura (35,131)	Jowai (12,908)	4.92
7. Maharashtra	Bombay (8,227,332)	Pune (1,685,300)	Nagpur (1,297,977)	4.88
8. Tamil Nadu	Madras (4,276,635)	Coimbatore (917,155)	Madurai (904,362)	4.66
9. Mizoram	Aizawl (75,971)	Lunglei (17,773)	Kolosib (8,256)	4.27
10. Andhra Pradesh	Hyderabad (2,528,198)	Vishakhapatnam (594,259)	Vijayawada (544,958)	4.25
11. Himachal Pradesh	Simla (70,479)	Sundernagar (20,774)	Nahan (20,085)	3.39

Urbanization and Urban Systems

State	First Ranking City	Second Ranking City	Third Ranking City	Index of Primacy
12. Gujarat	Ahmedabad (2,515,115)	Surat (912,568)	Vadodara (744,043)	2.75
13. Jammu and Kashmir	Srinagar (586,038)	Jammu (214,759)	Anantnag (33,978)	2.73
14. Rajasthan	Jaipur (1,004,669)	Jodhpur (493,809)	Ajmer (374,350)	2.03
15. Haryana	Faridabad (326,968)	Rohtak (166,631)	Yamunanagar (160,154)	1.96
16. Uttar Pradesh	Kanpur (1,688,242)	Lucknow (1,006,538)	Varanasi (793,542)	1.68
17. Assam	Guwahati (123,783)	Dibrugarh (80,348)	Nowgong (56,537)	1.54
18. Bihar	Patna (916,102)	Dhanbad (676,731)	Jamshedpur (699,984)	1.35
19. Kerala	Cochin (685,686)	Calicut (546,060)	Trivandrum (519,766)	1.25
20. Arunachal Pradesh	Pasighat (9,125)	Old Itanagar (7,656)	Along (6,498)	1.19
21. INDIA	Calcutta (9,165,680)	Bombay (8,227,332)	Delhi (5,713,581)	1.11
22. Goa	Panaji (76,839)	Marmagao (69,517)	Margao (64,820)	1.11

State	First Ranking City	Second Ranking City	Third Ranking City	Index of Primacy
23. Nagaland	Kohima (36,014)	Dimapur (32,315)	Mokokchung (18,423)	1.11
24. Madhya Pradesh	Indore (827,071)	Jabalpur (757,726)	Bhopal (672,329)	1.09
25. Punjab	Ludhiana (606,250)	Amritsar (589,229)	Jalandhar (405,209)	1.03
26. Orissa	Cuttack (326,468)	Rourkela (321,326)	Bhubaneshwar (219,419)	1.02

NOTE: (a) City populations given in parentheses refer to urban agglomerations or legal cities as given in the Census.
(b) For Assam, the data are for 1971.
(c) Index of primacy = population of the largest city ÷ population of the second largest city.

cities in these states. In Punjab and Haryana, the state capital lies outside the states in the union territory of Chandigarh. The development of primate cities in these states is further precluded by the peculiar circumstances of their location. Madhya Pradesh and Rajasthan before Independence were composed of a number of princely states, each having a leading primate city. Since the formation of these states, the new state capitals Bhopal and Jaipur have grown rapidly, but have not yet assumed a dominant position. In southern India, Kerala is the only state which does not have a primate city. This state has three major half-million cities, each of which exercises regional rather than state level dominance.

In the post-Independence period, there has been a distinct tendency towards the concentration of investment in industries and provision of urban amenities and social infrastructure in state capitals. Educational and medical institutions, research laboratories, and a multitude of administrative bodies have been set up in capital cities. Much of this centralization is due to the attitudes of the ruling elites and the concentration of political activities in the capital cities. Decentralization, an important component of Gandhian philosophy, has received considerable vocal but insubstantive material support. No decentralization has in fact occurred in the post-Independence period. Thus, the state capitals and the national capital have received greater attention in relation to other cities and they have grown more rapidly than others. Primate city development at the national and state levels is a product of our political framework and there is every likelihood that this process would continue to operate in the future as well.

Primate City System: A Critique

Two basic issues have generally been debated with reference to primate city urban systems. The first has to do with the universal applicability of the primate city concept. The second issue concerns the desirability of having a primate city urban system. In both cases the debate is inconclusive. Nevertheless, primate city urban systems do occur in several countries in the world and in several states in India. The theory underlying primate city development cannot be totally disregarded by the urban geographer.

In India, the primate city concept is not at present relevant at the national level; nevertheless, the emergence of Delhi as the national primate city in the decades to come cannot be ruled out. At the state and, in some cases, regional levels, the primate city systems are indeed relevant. Almost all of India's peripheral states, outside the Hindi-speaking belt, have primate cities. Further, state capitals are assuming greater importance in political and economic spheres and their role in the generation of primate cities needs to be recognized.

It is commonly asserted, but not convincingly substantiated, that primate cities contribute to an imbalanced and, therefore, undesirable urban system. Further, the development of primate cities is often attributed to low levels of socio-economic development and urbanization. While the first argument may have some merit, the second is totally false. In India primate city characteristics occur in the more urbanized and more developed states as well as in the ones less urbanized and less developed. There is no inherent relationship between primacy and socio-economic development. Primacy, therefore, is neither desirable nor undesirable; it is essentially a fact in some states and regions of India. The forces that have brought about this situation are multiple and a universal explanation is not yet possible.

SETTLEMENT SYSTEMS AND THE RANK SIZE RULE

The character of the leading city does not adequately describe the settlement system as a whole, though the leading city does have a greater role in the system than other cities and towns. It is necessary, therefore, to develop a theory that explains the role of the leading city as well as all other settlements within a region. It is a well known fact that in any country or region there are always a few large settlements (cities) and a large number of smaller settlements (towns and villages). In other words, the number of settlements in any region is inversely proportional to the size of the settlements. This empirical generalization requires no elaborate proof; it becomes self-evident if one examines any table giving the number of settlements according to their size. However, two important questions emerge from this generalization. First, why are there fewer settlements of large size and more settlements of smaller size? Secondly, what is the exact nature of the relationship between size and number of settlements? The answers to both the questions have been given by G. K. Zipf, a sociologist, and they merit a more detailed discussion.

Forces of Diversification and Unification

Zipf postulates that the size and number of settlements in any nation are governed by two sets of forces—the forces of diversification and the forces of unification. The balance between the two forces results in the regularity of settlement size and number.

The forces of diversification produce a large number of settlements which are small in size. In the extreme case, these settlements would tend to be autarkic communities, like the idealized village communities of India. The location of these small settlements would be determined by nearness to the source of raw materials. In such a situation, where primary economic activities predominate, land becomes the basic raw material or resource. Land is tilled by farmers to produce food and other basic necessities of life. A peasant society rooted to the land emerges, with a large number of village settlements within walking distance of each other. Similarly, apart from agriculture, other primary activities such as mining, fishing and forestry also generate dispersed settlements of small size at regular intervals of distance. As society advances, secondary production makes it possible to locate settlements at greater distances from the sources of raw materials. Thus, the settlements specializing in secondary production can be located farther apart, and may also be larger in terms of population. Nevertheless, a wide range of secondary economic activities must be located near the sources of raw materials so that the costs of transportation can be minimized. Secondary economic activites generate settlements of larger size and greater distances apart as compared to primary activities.

In contrast with the forces of diversification, the forces of unification result in the emergence of a few large settlements. Here the focus is on tertiary economic activities. Nearness to the market rather than the sources of raw materials is the determining factor in the location of settlements. The size of the market is measured by the population of the settlement itself. Thus, a large settlement in itself constitutes a large market. Tertiary activities, such as education, health and administration, are all consumer oriented and tend to be concentrated in large cities. In recent times, a wide range of secondary activities have acquired a market orientation (for example, electronic and engineeering goods industries); these secondary economic activities also tend to concentrate on large metropolitan cities. These forces lead to the emergence of a few, very large cities.

The forces of unification and diversification operate simultaneously in any region or nation. The balance between these forces, at a given technological scale, determines the relationship between size and number of settlements.

Rank Size Rule

Zipf further postulated that the relationship between size and number of settlements could be expressed in the following mathematical form:

$$P_r = \frac{P_1}{r^q}$$

where P_r is the population of the rth ranking city, P_1 the population of the first ranking city and q is an exponent which can take on any value. The value of q is often assumed to be unity, representing equality of the forces of unification and diversification. Under this condition an integrated and stable system of settlements is supposed to exist.

The exponent q in the rank size equation cannot, however, assume negative values, for, in that case, the second ranking city will have a population greater than the first. When the values of q range between zero and one, the decline in population with rank is gradual; values greater than unity for q indicate a very rapid decline in the size of settlements with their rank. The former indicates the dominant role of the forces of diversification, while the latter exists when the forces of unification are stronger than the forces of diversification.

Zipf's rank size rule is rather rigid and rarely would one expect to find an exact empirical fit. Further, as in the case of the primate city concept, the rank size rule also attaches great importance to the population size of the largest city in a region or nation. The population size of every other settlement depends on the size of the largest city. Thus, according to the rank size rule (assuming $q=1$), the second largest city has half of the population size of the largest city, the third ranking city has one-third, and so on. On the other hand, if this rigid arithmetical relationship is relaxed, the rank size rule becomes a truism; the populations of cities would by definition decline with their rank, and a high degree of correlation may be expected between the population of settlements and their rank in the system. In this case, the rank size rule would explain practically nothing.

Rank Size Relationships at the National Level

It has been asserted by Qazi Ahmed that rank size relationships hold good in the case of one-lakh cities in India for 1951 and 1961. Qazi Ahmed came to this conclusion on the basis of a visual interpretation of a double logarithmic graph in which population of Indian cities is plotted against rank. Ahmed's conclusion is not justified on a closer examination of the data. Not only has the second largest city in India, Bombay, nearly the same population as the largest city, Calcutta, but even the fifth ranking city has more than a million people in excess of its population as indicated by the rank size rule. In fact, all Class I cities, according to the 1981 Census of India data, have populations much larger than would be justified under the rank size rule. And this is not the only way by which we can examine deviations from the rank size rule. We could, for example, reverse the process and estimate the population of the largest city given the population of the nth ranking city. Such an analysis would lead to a similar conclusion: that Indian cities do not conform to the rank size rule.

The most important implication of the absence of rank size relationships at the national level in India is, perhaps, that we do not have an integrated system of settlements at the national level. In a large and diverse country such as India this is to be expected. Nevertheless, it is also important to note that the rank size rule, in itself, has a weak theoretical basis and unless it is supported by other evidence, it can not lead us to any firm conclusions.

Rank Size Relationships at the State Level

The absence of rank size relationships at the national level is further supported by the fact that the urban settlements in a great majority of states in India also do not conform to the rank size rule. As already noted, primacy exists in at least 13 out of the 25 states; that is, the population of the premier city is at least three times larger than that of the second city. It is obvious that rank size relationships are not valid in these states. In another eight states, the leading city is only just larger than the second city. This is the case in Bihar, Kerala, Madhya Pradesh, Punjab, Orissa, Goa, Arunachal Pradesh and Nagaland. In Kerala, the three cities of Cochin, Calicut and Trivandrum have nearly the same population size; this is also the case with the cities of Indore, Jabalpur and Bhopal in Madhya Pradesh, and Ludhiana, Amritsar and Jalandhar in Punjab. In the case of Bihar and Orissa, the leading industrial cities such as Dhanbad, Jamshedpur and Rourkela have brought about major distortions in the settlement structure. Rank size relationships thus appear more as exceptions than as a general rule.

Rank size relationships appear to hold good in three states in India: Rajasthan, Haryana and Uttar Pradesh. Among these Rajasthan alone has a near ideal fit to the rank size rule. In Haryana and Uttar Pradesh the approximation to the rank size rule is perhaps a statistical accident, for, in both cases, Delhi is very close by and does exert an overwhelming influence on their urban systems. Further, in Uttar Pradesh, the two largest cities, Kanpur and Lucknow, are located close to each other, forming a twin city cluster. Uttar Pradesh, however, has a longer history, both as a province of British India and later as a state in the Indian Union. On the other hand, Haryana was formed in 1971 and Rajasthan in 1966. In all three cases, therefore, the existence of rank size relationships does not indicate any specific property which is unique to the urban systems of these states.

Rank Size Relationships: An Assessment

The rank size rule and the primate city concept are empirical constructs and their objective is to explain the real world structure of settlement systems. Although the rank size rule covers the entire settlement system, while the primate city concept focuses only on the leading city, the rank size rule has less empirical validity. In the Indian context, rank size relationships are an exception, while primate city characteristics appear to be important in a majority of Indian states. The rank size rule is essentially an economic, rather than a sociological, theory of settlement structure. It attempts to explain the size of settlements in relation to economic activities. Primary activities are associated with smaller settlements, while secondary activities are associated with middle order settlements, and the largest settlements are associated with tertiary activities, which are market oriented. Zipf even went so far as to examine the size of the market areas commanded by the large settlements and he came up with the concept of the domain of goods. In other words, tertiary activities may be distinguished on the basis of the size of the market area (domain) they command. The size of a settlement increases with the domain of the goods produced there. However, Zipf's theoretical formulation is incomplete and unsatisfactory. Even before Zipf had formulated his rank size rule,

Christaller, a German geographer, had come up with a deductive economic theory of settlement size and location. His theory, known as the central place theory, is a more complete theory of settlement location and structure, which emphasizes the role of tertiary activities in settlements.

CENTRAL PLACE SETTLEMENT SYSTEMS

The central place theory envisages a hierarchical structure of settlements with seven or more levels in a meso-region. This settlement system has a metropolitan city at its apex. In this respect, it is comparable to both the primate city and rank size settlement systems. However, at lower levels, there is a plurality of settlements of the same hierarchical level; further, the number of settlements at a level increases inversely with its status in the hierarchy. Thus, the central place theory, like the rank size rule, envisages an inverse relationship between settlement numbers and their size. However, the central place system differs markedly from the rank size system, in that it rejects the idea of a settlement continuum; but, instead, introduces the idea of a discrete hierarchy of settlements. Furthermore, the central place theory is essentially a normative deduction theory and in this respect it differs from both the primate city concept as well as the rank size rule, both of which are rooted in the empirical inductive approach.

The central place theory focuses entirely on tertiary economic activities in settlements; both secondary and primary economic activities are excluded from its consideration. It is necessary to emphasize this point because the central place theory is not a comprehensive theory of settlements. Nevertheless, it does encompass the vast majority of settlements in any region and has, therefore, considerable value. In particular, this theory identifies the role of settlements at different hierarchical levels in providing goods and services to settlements lower in the hierarchy. It is a theory of the inter-relationships between settlements of varying size classes.

Tertiary activities form an important aspect of the economy of settlements at all levels in India—from the small village to the large metropolitan city. In fact, there are no settlements, except the smallest hamlets, where tertiary activities are totally absent. This is true of agricultural villages as well as manufacturing or industrial cities. Apart from the presence of tertiary activity in a settlement, the central place theory emphasizes the periodic movements of people from one place to another to obtain services and goods. In India, village people go to the nearby towns to obtain medical help, for education, to purchase a variety of consumer products such as clothes or tobacco, and for other services such as the repair of agricultural equipment and so on. By any reckoning, Indian villages are no longer self-sufficient, isolated communities. Daily movement of people from the village to town, town to city, or even city to metropolis is a common occurrence. It underlies a fundamental functional relationship between settlements. The central place theory explores this relationship in a deductive manner and in the process establishes the basic characteristics of an ideal tertiary settlement structure.

The central place theory is a deductive theory and it is necessary to present it as such. Its empirical aspects can be discussed at a later stage. We therefore start with the fundamental concepts underlying the theory, the derivative concept and later the major postulates, before examining the text of the theory, that is, its translation into empirical reality.

Fundamental Concepts

Fundamental concepts are those notions that have meaning and applicability beyond the domain of a theory. The central place theory is concerned with settlement structure, but the fundamental concepts on which this theory is based are applicable to a wider range of phenomena, from the structure of biological organisms to that of the solar system. The fundamental concepts on which the central place theory is based are: (a) the principle of centralization, and (b) the principle of hierarchy. These principles govern the structure of all phenomena, including settlements.

The Principle of Centralization. All matter in the universe, whether organic or inorganic, has a core or focal point and a periphery. The sun is located at the centre of the solar system, the neutron at the centre of the atom; the human cell has a nucleus with protoplasm around it. Similarly, regions have core and peripheral areas. The village has its focal point in the temple, mosque, church or the *chaupal* (meeting place). The bazaar is located at the centre of a city and serves as a focal point of the city and its region. Further, the smaller settlements are organized around a larger settlement which serves as a focal point for all the settlements around it. In other words, small towns serve as focal points for a number of villages and hamlets. It is not, however, necessary that the focal point has to be at the geometric centre of the settlements. Thus, centralization is not a geometrical concept; it is a concept concerning the relationship between a central settlement and peripheral settlements.

The Principle of Hierarchy. Underlying the ordering of phenomena is the second principle of hierarchy. Most phenomena are arranged in a hierarchical fashion; for example, the sun, the planets and the moons form a three-tier hierarchy in the solar system. Humans, apes and monkeys form a hierarchy among the primates. In human affairs, hierarchy exists both as a natural or spontaneous characteristic and as an element deliberately introduced by man. The hierarchy formed by successive generations within a family is natural and spontaneous. On the other hand, the hierarchy formed by nobles, common people and slaves in a feudal system is not natural, but a deliberate act of man.

Man-made hierarchies change through time, according to changes in the way of life. Nevertheless, most socio-economic phenomena have a hierarchical organization. Thus, we have everywhere an administrative hierarchy, a military hierarchy, and every institution has its concomitant hierarchical order. Finally, hierarchy manifests itself in terms of territorial divisions and places. Thus, the state, district and tehsil form an administrative territorial hierarchy, which is complemented by the place hierarchy of state capitals, district headquarters and tehsil headquarters. Territoriality is not confined to the administrative framework alone; it exists within large business organizations, which have national, regional and subregional offices and corresponding territorial operational areas. The hierarchy of territories and hierarchy of places complement each other.

Derivative Concepts

The principles of centralization and hierarchy, which have universal validity, lend themselves to specific interpretations in the context of settlement systems. Some of these interpretations involve the mechanisms by which centralization and hierarchy are generated within settlements. There are six major derivative concepts ingrained in the theory of central places: the concept of a central place, the concept of a complementary area, the concept of central goods and services; the concept of range of good, the concept of thresholds, and finally the concept of centrality.

Concept of a Central Place. A simple and direct derivative of the principle of centralization is the concept of central place. A central place is a settlement which serves as a focal point for a number of other settlements which are dependent on it. The concept of a central place implies a lasting and regular influence. It is not a transient state. For example, a place where a festival is held once a year is not a central place, though it may influence a number of other settlements. Nor are weekly markets in rural areas central places. These markets come to life once a week, but do not necessarily involve a permanent settlement or permanent establishments such as shops. A central place can be a village or even a hamlet; it may be a rural place or an urban place. All urban places are not necessarily central places. A manufacturing town or mining town is not a central place, unless it has some tertiary activities catering to the needs of the surrounding villages. To be a central place, a settlement must offer some service of a very regular nature, with daily periodicity, to the settlements around it. A settlement becomes a central place when people from the surrounding area visit it for some service or good.

The Concept of Complementary Area. The area for which a central place is the focal point is the complementary area of that place. As the very term implies, the complementary area is an adjunct to the concept of central place. The size of the complementary area and the importance of a central place are directly related to each other: the complementary area would be larger for bigger and more important central places and smaller for the less important ones. The complementary area, furthermore, is really a cluster of settlements. Some of these settlements are central places of lesser importance, and others (small villages and hamlets) are non-central places. The complementary area, in a theoretical sense, is a collection of settlements of lesser importance.

The limits of the complementary area are to be determined with respect to the complementary areas of adjoining central places of equal importance. In the real world, this boundary is a vague rather than a definite, recognizable limit.

Central Goods and Services. The offering of goods and services in a place constitutes the primary function of a central place. It is in this context that central place functions are considered as synonymous with central place goods and services. Central place functions are essentially the tertiary economic activities carried on within a place. But not all tertiary activities are included within the framework of central place functions. City bus transport is a tertiary activity but not a central place function. This is because, in order to be recognized as a central place function, the particular good or service offered must attract customers from the complementary area. However, it is not always necessary that people should come to the central place to obtain a good or service. Newspapers published from a central place find their way through a network of distributors and sales agents to the actual consumers in the complementary area. Nevertheless, the provision of newspapers represents a service to the people of the complementary area and it is, therefore, a central place function. Using the same argument we can say that radio and television broadcasting also constitute central place functions. In all such cases, it may be noted that the central place has certain physical establishments, such as newspaper offices and presses, or television and radio broadcasting stations, which offer the service or good.

The goods offered by central places may range from ordinary consumption items of daily use to expensive equipment, clothing or jewellery. The items of ordinary consumption offered in retail shops in central places include items such as cloth, footwear, stationery items, electrical goods and grocery items. Services such as repair of cycles, repair of farm equipment including tractors, banking services, schools, dispensaries and post offices are available in small central places. Larger central places offer, in addition, goods and services that are less frequently required and which cost more, such as expensive clothing, jewellery, radio and television sets, higher education and so on. Thus, the goods and services offered in central places differ in terms of importance, cost and frequency of use.

Goods and services offered by itinerant traders to villages and homes do not constitute central place functions. In India there is a large informal sector, consisting of weekly markets and individual traders who move from one place to another. This form of offering goods and services is not part of the central place system of settlements, but exists independent of it.

Range of a Good. While goods and services are offered at central places, the consumers in the complementary area have to travel a certain distance to the central place to obtain these. Looking at this from a consumer's angle, one could compare the constraints of distance in terms of time and money with the advantage to be gained by obtaining the good. Weighing both the aspects, the consumer will be willing to travel only a certain distance to buy a good. For example, one would not like to travel too far to buy a pack of cigarettes; but in order to buy a bicycle one would be willing to travel a much longer distance. The maximum distance that a consumer is willing to travel in order to buy a specific good is the range of that good. Each good has its characteristic range which may vary from a fraction of a kilometre for some goods to a hundred kilometres or more for others. For basic necessities one would not ordinarily walk more than a kilometre, but for luxury items one might be willing to travel a hundred kilometres or more to a big city.

The range of a good may also be viewed from the point of view of the establishment offering the good in a central place. This establishment would, naturally, attract customers from near and far. If we map the distribution of the customers of an establishment, we would notice a large proportion of customers coming from nearby areas and fewer from farther away. The number of customers would in fact decrease with distance from the central place. The rate at which this decline occurs will vary from one good to another. For basic needs the rate of decline would be very steep, while for costly and infrequently needed items the rate of decline would be gradual. However, in each case, customers would cease to come beyond a certain distance. This distance is the range of that good. The range, in this sense, defines the maximum distance and maximum area from where the clientele of an establishment may come. The total population of this area determines the maximum potential demand for the good.

Threshold. In order that a good be offered in central place, the establishment offering it must have a sufficient number of customers to make it profitable. This minimum number of customers required is the threshold for the good or service. However, the minimum number of customers is often translated in terms of population or distance. Thus, the population threshold for a good or service is the population required in a central place and its complementary area together to provide the minimum number of customers. Unless this threshold population exists within the complementary area, the good or service will not be offered there. If the population of the complementary area is larger, there would be surplus profits, which would eventually attract more establishments offering the same good.

The distance threshold is related to the area served by the establishment with minimum threshold population. The distance

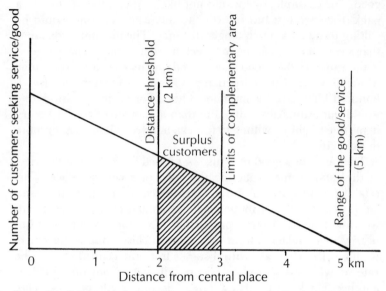

FIGURE 7.1. Relationship between Threshold and Range of a Good within the Complementary Area.

threshold, the limits of the complementary area, and the range of the good occur in a sequence, the threshold being the nearest and the range of the good being the farthest in the sequence (figure 7.1).

The threshold and range vary from one good to another, but the limits of the complementary area are the same for all. All goods and services having thresholds lower than the limits of the complementary area will be offered in a central place. At the same time, the range of all the goods and services offered in a place should be greater than the limits of the complementary area. If this condition is not fulfilled, then parts of the complementary area will remain unserved by the central place. In reality, the cluster of goods and services offered in a central place usually have similar threshold and range characteristics. Goods and services having greater threshold and range will be offered in central places of a higher rank. These central places would, naturally, be spaced farther apart and would have larger complementary areas as well.

The Concept of Centrality. The concept of a central place implies in itself the importance of a centre as a focal point. This importance is generated by the offering of goods and services, the size of the complementary area, and the number of people coming to the central place. All three are interrelated and each exists because of the others. The importance of a place would increase with the number and hierarchical order of the goods offered. It would also vary with the size of the complementary area. Central places serve the people living within the central place as well as those living outside it but within the complementary area. Establishments and goods offered exclusively for the people of the central place will not, in theory, contribute to the centrality of the place. Every central place, by definition, has a surplus of goods and services that are offered to the people of the complementary area. It is this 'surplus' that constitutes the centrality of a place.

The Propositions of the Theory

The substantive part of the central place theory consists of a set of propositions that explain the nature of relationships between central places, their complementary areas, and the hierarchical systems of settlements. The propositions are normative in nature and are based on a number of efficiency and optimality criteria. These propositions are discussed below under five headings: uniformity of the settlement landscape, the shape of the complementary areas, the number of central places, the hierarchical levels and the patterns of nesting.

The Uniformity of the Settlement Landscape. In a normative theory, it is customary to start with a simplified real world situation. The complexities of the world are then unravelled at a later stage. The central place theory assumes that the landscape of settlements is uniform with respect to terrain, resources, distribution of population, and income levels of people. In other words, the landscape is assumed to be an isotropic plane. It must be remembered that the theory is dealing with an ideal situation. However, this point of view is helpful in understanding to what extent the reality departs from the ideal. Further, in some parts of India, in particular the Ganga plains and parts of the peninsular plateau region, the condition of uniformity is by and large satisfied over extensive areas. The assumption of landscape uniformity is not, therefore, unrealistic in any way.

The Shape of the Complementary Area. The entire landscape of settlements is to be fully served by a set of uniformly spaced central places, wherein no part of the area is left unserved by a centre and no area is served by more than one centre. This requires a partitioning of the region into a number of complementary areas with clear

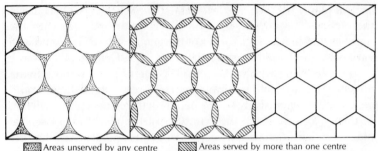

Areas unserved by any centre   Areas served by more than one centre

FIGURE 7.2. Circular and Hexagonal Complementary Areas.

boundaries. Hexagonal complementary areas satisfy the optimality conditions specified above. In addition, the hexagonal shape corresponds closely to that of a circular area around a centre. While circular complementary areas are ideal, they do not satisfy the basic optimality conditions set out earlier. Circular complementary areas would either result in leaving several areas unserved by any centre, or they would overlap, thus generating wasteful competition between the centres (figure 7.2). Hexagonal complementary areas would, on the other hand, cover the entire landscape without any gaps or overlaps.

Number of Central Places. The optimality of central places is seen from the point of view of efficient distribution of goods and services to the population of the region. The cost of distribution is minimized in this system by having a minimum number of central places; hexagonal complementary areas ensure a minimization of centres. But this covers only one aspect of the problem. It is also necessary that a central place serves the maximum number of people. This, however, will depend on the range of the good. In other words, the complementary area limits should be as close to the range of the good as possible. Given a cluster of goods, the limits of the complementary area will correspond to the range of the good only in an approximate manner. The number of centres may also be minimized by another mechanism, namely, the offering of a maximum number of goods and services in the same place. This enables the consumer to buy a variety of goods in one trip, thus saving both time and cost. The more facilities offered in a place, the more efficient it becomes. However, all goods and services cannot be offered in one place. This is so because the offering of a good or service is constrained by (a) the threshold and (b) the range, as discussed earlier. Goods and services which cannot be accommodated in smaller central places will be offered at other hierarchical levels.

Hierarchical Levels. The great variety of goods and services required by people necessitates their availability at a number of hierarchical levels of central places. Again, from the point of view of minimization of the number of central places, the number of hierarchical levels also has to be a minimum, to make the system fully efficient. The number of hierarchical levels of centres is minimized by accommodating the maximum number of functions at each hierarchical level. Further, higher order central places should also function as lower order centres; this will again tend to reduce the total number of central places in a region. The actual number of hierarchical levels would depend upon: (a) the size of the region, and (b) its degree of development. Intuitively one should assert that the larger the size of a region, the greater would be the number of hierarchical levels. The size of a region would determine the presence or absence of higher order centres. A small region would not have the threshold population to support higher order centres. While at the national level one would expect six or seven hierarchical levels, there may be only three or four hierarchical levels of centres at the district level. In developed areas, the people have higher incomes and demand a greater variety of goods and services, therefore the number of hierarchical levels may be more. In backward areas, the number of hierarchical levels of centres would be less. The number of hierarchical levels, in reality, is also influenced by the spacing of the lowest order centres and the manner in which the complementary areas of lower and higher order centres are meshed together. The spacing of the lowest order centres, in turn, is influenced by the mode of transportation used and other related factors. The problem is indeed very complex, but can be partly unravelled by an examination of the pattern of nesting of central place hierarchies.

The Pattern of Nesting. For each hierarchical level of central places, there is a corresponding network of hexagonal complementary areas. The lower order hexagonal networks nest within the higher order network, since they all cover the same territory. The geometrical pattern of nesting is again determined by certain optimality considerations. Christaller envisages three such criteria. They are: (a) the marketing principle, (b) the transportation principle, and (c) the administrative principle.

The marketing principle assumes that the number of central

places of lower order would be the minimum required in relation to the number of places of immediate higher order. This arises from the dynamics of central places, which will be discussed in a later section. At this stage, we may note that with the growth of population or incomes, goods earlier offered only in higher order places will now be offered in the next lower order centres as well. In such a situation, if the number of lower order centres within each higher order centre is the minimum, then it would add to the efficiency or optimality of the system. The exact geometry of nesting on the basis of the marketing principle follows the rule of three. The k factor, which in the marketing principle is equal to 3, determines the relative spacing of centres of lower order and immediate higher orders, as also the relative number of lower and higher order centres, and the geometrical system in which the hexagons of different hierarchical levels fit into one another (figure 7.3).

Under the marketing principle, lower order centres are located at the vertices of the hexagonal complementary area of the next higher order centre. Thus, the areas farthest away from a higher order central place are served by a lower order central place, thus compensating for the disadvantages of their location. This factor contributes to the greater accessibility of the system of central places to the general population.

The transportation principle involves the minimization of the length of roads connecting central places at all hierarchical levels. In this system of nesting, the lower order centres are all located along the roads linking the higher order centres. This alignment of places along a road leads to minimization of road length. However, for each higher order centre, there are now four centres of immediate lower order, as opposed to three centres under the marketing principle.

The administrative principle emphasizes the notion that complementary areas of lower order centres should lie entirely within the limits of the complementary area of the next higher order centre. Such a principle is inherent in any administrative territorial system. In India, all outer tehsil boundaries coincide with the district boundary; likewise, all district boundaries are enclosed by the state boundary. This is an administrative necessity. A hexagonal system of complementary areas with a k factor of 7 gives a network that approximates to this principle. However, the geometrical fit here is not exact and the shapes of the complementary areas need to be modified to give an exact fit (figure 7.3).

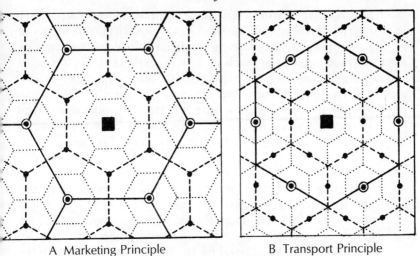

A Marketing Principle B Transport Principle

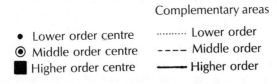

C Administrative Principle

Complementary areas

- Lower order centre   ·········· Lower order
- ⊙ Middle order centre   - - - - Middle order
- ■ Higher order centre   —— Higher order

Figure 7.3. The Patterns of Nesting of Complementary Areas.

The real world pattern of nesting of central places would depend on the historical processes at work in a region. In particular, one of the three principles may have a dominant influence in a given area. One could empirically examine the reasons for existing patterns of nesting. Alternatively, Christaller's three networks may be considered as ideal systems. One could, in this context, evaluate the efficiency of the real world nesting patterns in relation to one of the three nesting principles and thus gain insight into the working of existing, but none too efficient, systems of central places.

The Dynamics of Central Places

The system of central places is not a static arrangement, but responds to changes occurring in society and economy. These changes are of several kinds. For example, one can visualize an increase in population, an increase in the income levels of people, or an increase in the demand for specific goods, either due to the above factors, or due to changes in consumption patterns in society. An example of change in social attitudes is seen in the increase in the number of patients in hospitals and dispensaries. The opposite trend, namely, a decline in population, incomes and so on, is also possible, although less common. Nevertheless, changes in technology and the production of goods and services can reduce demand for traditional goods and even make them obsolete. Changes in the mode of transportation—from walking to bicycles and later to local buses—can also change the demand for goods and services in a central place. Broadly speaking, there are two basic situations: (a) an increase in demand in the complementary area for certain goods or services, and (b) a decrease in demand for one or more goods. Each of the two possibilities needs to be considered separately.

Increase in Demand for Goods. When the demand for a good increases within the complementary area, one of three alternative responses, or a combination of all three, would take place. These are: (a) the establishment or establishments offering the good may expand and reap more profits, (b) the number of establishments offering the good may increase in the central place; thus, more shops or more doctors would offer their services from the same place, or (c) new establishments would emerge in the lower order centres. If there is no lower order centre, then a new one would emerge at the periphery of the existing complementary area.

The new lower order central places would tend to be located at vantage points. For example, new centres may emerge at the midpoints of the roads connecting existing central places. In this type of location, the shift in location may be purely temporary or experimental. Often the owner of the establishment continues to make his permanent residence at one of the two central places and commutes to the new location daily, since it is easily accessible. In any case, this pattern of location will lead to a $k = 4$ network of settlements. A second possibility is that a new establishment may locate itself at the point in the complementary area which is farthest away from the existing central place. This is often a permanent movement, as the new location is often less easily accesssible and daily commuting to the new location from the existing central place becomes difficult. The new location, however, is the least efficiently served by the existing centres, and as a result the new centre will have a definite competitive advantage. This pattern of growth of new centres will lead to a $k = 3$ network of settlements, which is efficient from the point of view of the marketing principle.

In any growth process, there are both gains and losses. What is a loss for the higher order central place is a gain for the lower order centre. The gains and losses, however, tend to generate cumulative and multiplier effects. The loss of one function tends to take away other functions, while the gain of one function may result in the gain of more. This is due to the fact that people prefer to buy more than one good at a time. The multi-purpose nature of visits to central places plays an important role in the clustering of functions, as well as in generating a multiplier effect when a function is added or deleted. As a result, the emergence of new central places can be very rapid and even dramatic.

Decrease in Demand for Goods. The second situation is one in which there is a decline in demand. This is often due to changes in the consumption patterns of the people. For example, hurricane lamps are no longer needed in the majority of villages in India today. On the other hand, rural electrification has brought about a demand for a new good—the electric bulb. The elimination of some goods and the introduction of new ones will have no effect if both changes occur at the same hierarchical level of centres. In this case, the changes are structural, that is, one set of shops is replaced by another set of shops, or a shop may make changes in goods that it usually trades in. However, this is not always the case. The new goods, such as electrical gadgets, radios and television sets, are higher order goods and will, therefore, be sold or serviced in higher order central places. In this situation, the importance of the lower order centres will decline and people may go to the bigger places to buy even the lower order goods.

Another way in which a decline in demand for goods in the lower order centres is brought about is through changes in the mode of transportation. The construction of new roads, the increasing use of bicycles, buses and railways all bring about greater spatial mobility. The effects of distance are reduced to a considerable extent and, concomitantly, the range of goods and services may also increase. Under these circumstances, people prefer to go to higher order centres, thus causing a decline of the lower order centres. The goods and services offered in the lower order centres will no longer be offered there but would be available only in higher order centres. These lower order centres may become stagnant or even decline. In rare cases, they might even disappear. The decline of the small towns in India during the past decade or two, strongly indicates that socio-economic development is generating significant readjustments in the system of central places in India. These aspects have not been adequately studied as yet.

Central Place Systems in India

The key elements of the central place system of settlements are: (a) the hierarchical ordering of settlements, and (b) the even spacing of settlements of different levels under ideal conditions of near homogeneity. The theory, it must again be emphasized, is normative in character and as such it is not correct to ask whether the theory is empirically valid at the national or regional level in India. On the other hand, it is pertinent to ask whether the settlement systems in India, at the national or regional level, approximate to the ideal central place system. No real world settlement system can be expected to conform to all the propositions of the central place theory. There are bound to be deviations. Nevertheless, comparisons (however fragile) are possible, and can give us newer insights into our national and regional settlement systems.

India has a six-level hierarchy of settlements from the point of view of administration. This hierarchy of places and areas has practical relevance and meaning in the everyday life of people in India. Thus, we have the national capital, 24 state capitals, about 400 district headquarter cities, over 2,500 tehsil towns, and finally slightly over 5,000 block development centres. In addition, there are nearly 2,00,000 gram panchayat centres, which provide some services to the adjoining clusters of hamlets and smaller villages. The national and state capitals are in reality important metropolitan cities; most, if not all, headquarters of districts and even tehsils are recognized urban places. At the block level, however, though a majority of the block headquarters are large villages, sometimes with a population of 5,000 persons or more, most of them are not recognized urban places. Gram panchayats are, by definition, rural in character; but as they also provide a variety of services to the neighbouring hamlets, they are central places of the lowest order.

The administrative hierarchy of settlements in India, however, appears to differ considerably from the central place system under the administrative principle as postulated by Christaller. Theoretically, one would expect a ratio of 1:7 between the number of settlements of higher and lower orders. In India, the ratio of districts to states is almost 1:19, while there are as many as 40 gram panchayats per community development block. The number of tehsils per district is slightly over six and this corresponds to the administrative principle fairly closely. Again, from the theoretical point of view, the spacing between settlements of lower and higher orders should increase by a factor of 2.6; in most cases, in India, this ratio is much larger (table 7.2). Here again, the spacing of tehsil and district level centres conforms to the theory. Thus, the limited

TABLE 7.2
Administrative Hierarchy of Settlements in India

Hierarchical Level	Number of Settlements	Spacing between Settlements (km)	Population Served (in lakhs)	Area Served (sq. km)
National capital	1	—	6,840	32,80,543
State capitals	25	428	311	1,49,116
District headquarters	412	100	17	7,962
Tehsil headquarters	2,500	40	2.8	1,250
Block headquarters	5,026	30	1.4	652
Gram panchayats	2,00,000	5	0.04	20

NOTE: A gram panchayat may include one or more revenue villages. In some cases, tehsils and blocks are one and the same unit. However, in a majority of cases, there are two or three blocks in a tehsil. The data on number of tehsils and gram panchayats is approximate.

evidence available to us provides a mixed bag of agreements and disagreements between theory and reality. Nevertheless, an administrative hierarchy of places does exist, though the number and spacing of the different hierarchical levels of places is far from the ideal.

The administrative hierarchy of settlements is, however, only one aspect of the settlement system. We could also look at the hierarchy of places from other angles. A system of hierarchy of places commonly recognized in India is based on the Census of population. The Census organization has, for the past several decades, consistently recognized ten categories of settlements. These range from the million cities to revenue villages with a population less than 500, which in India are in fact hamlets. This categorization of settlements is based only on population size and has an element of arbitrariness in that the population limits of various categories are not based on any specific rationale. Nevertheless, categories of places, such as million cities, one-lakh cities, medium towns, small towns and so on are fairly widely accepted and have some significance in reality. In other words, the population size of a settlement bears some relation, even if approximately, to the centrality of a place. It is remarkable that, in spite of the various constraints noted above, the settlements in India bear a close similarity to the theoretical central places system based on the marketing principle (table 7.3). In this system, the ratio of spacing of higher order centres to the immediate lower order centres is 1:1.72. The actual ratios of spacing of settlements in India vary from 1.41 to 1.83, barring two exceptions (table 7.3). The major exception relates to the million cities, which appear to stand apart as primate cities. A second exception distinguishes between the level of settlements with a population of 5,000 or more and the level below it. This is in the nature of a rural-urban demographic divide. It does appear from the foregoing that a rough approximation to the central place settlement system does obtain at the lower levels of the settlement hierarchy in India.

The evidence that we have examined here cannot be taken as conclusive proof of the existence of an ideal central place system of settlements in India. In fact, this is far from the truth. However, the usefulness of central place theory will become more apparent when we take up the study of settlement systems at the empirical level. Since this involves a wide range of issues it will be considered in depth in the following chapter. The central place theory, it may again be emphasized, cannot be rejected entirely on the basis of empirical evidence, nor can it be accepted without any reservations.

TABLE 7.3

Demographic Hierarchy of Settlements in India

Hierarchical Level (based on population)	Number of Settlements	Population Served by Each Settlement	Area Served by Each Settlement (sq. km)	Spacing between Settlements (km)	Ratio of Spacing
Metropolitan Cities (1 million or more)	12	54,916,000	248,000	535	4.25
One-lakh Cities (1 lakh to 1 million)	204	3,051,000	13,800	126	1.50
Intermediate Towns (50,000–99,999)	270	1,356,000	6,140	84	1.58
Medium Towns (20,000–49,999)	739	538,000	2,440	53	1.83
Towns (10,000–19,999)	2.881	160,000	727	29	1.71
Small Towns (5,000–9,999)	7,924	55,000	248	17	2.21
Large Villages (2,000–4,999)	46,729	11,215	51	7.7	1.60
Villages (1,000–1,999)	93,800	4,320	20	4.8	1.41
Small Villages (500–999)	1,34,213	2,298	10	3.4	1.42
Hamlets (less than 500)	2,67,493	1,189	5	2.4	—

NOTE: (a) The data above are for 1981 and exclude Assam and Jammu and Kashmir; source for population data: *Census of India, 1981*–Series 1, India, tables A-3 and A-4.

(b) Population served by each settlement = Population of India (659 million) ÷ Number of settlements in each size class or above

(c) Area served by each settlement (A) = Area of India ÷ Number of settlements of each size class or above

(d) Spacing between settlements (S) = 1.075 $\sqrt{A}$.

(e) Ratio of spacing (R) = Spacing of settlements in size class ÷ Spacing of settlements in the immediate lower size class.

THE SETTLEMENT SYSTEM: A CRITIQUE

In the foregoing sections we have examined three alternative theories of settlement systems and their relevance to conditions in India. The primate city system appears to be particularly relevant at both state and regional levels, while at the national level we may, in fact, be progressing towards such a system. The primate city system is the product of political and administrative over-centralization, which is a characteristic feature of post-Independence India. The rank size rule and the central place theory are relevant only in a regional or even local context. They do not appear to have any significance at the national or even at the state level. Nevertheless, the three theories of settlement systems have certain complementary features and a comparative study of the three systems is important to the proper understanding of settlement systems.

A Systems View of Settlement Systems

It has generally been argued that the three theories of settlement systems—primate city, rank size and central place systems—are mutually exclusive and contradictory in nature. The rank size distribution of settlements is a negation of the concept of hierarchy and in effect, what we have here is a settlement continuum. The primate city concept and the central place theory both imply the existence of a hierarchy of settlements. The primate city concept has very little to say about settlements other than the primate city. Therefore, at the lower levels, there is no contradiction between the primate city system and the other two systems. The primate city concept, however, identifies the crucial role of the forces of agglomeration and centralization in the process of metropolitan urbanization, which is missed out in the other two theories.

A more fundamental correlation of the theories of settlements can be made from a 'systems' viewpoint. A system is a set of interacting and interdependent elements. A settlement system fits this definition. However, it must be understood that it is not a 'settlement' but its attributes that constitute the elements of the system. The attributes of a settlement are its population, its location, aspects of spacing between settlements, the number of services offered, and so on. The system of settlements in the nation or in a region is an 'open' system and is influenced from outside the system, for example by changes in the technology and mode of transportation, changes in agriculture and industry, and even by social change. Society and economy act as the 'environment' within which the settlement system operates and changes in the environment will generate a suitable response from the settlement system.

Christaller's central place system is an ideal (normative) 'closed' system of settlements, while the primate city concept and the rank size rule describe the state of the real world 'open' system at a given point in time. The latter can be thought of as derivatives of the former, given the imperfections of the real world. Thus, in the central place system of settlements, we have a fully 'organized' system with complete 'information'. This means that this system can be predicted. Given the location of one settlement and its hierarchical level, the locations, hierarchical levels, and functional characteristics of all other settlements can be predicted with certainty. An organized system, such as the one above, tends to disorganize itself spontaneously, given sufficient time. This means that even if we plan and build a central place system in a pioneer area, the system will begin to break down with time and will become a mere shadow of its former well organized and planned self. In fact, such a phenomenon has been observed in the Polders area of Netherlands, where a system of new settlements was established after reclaiming the land from the sea. In the long run, the completely organized system of settlements will turn into a completely disorganized system, with all elements of the system being randomly determined. Thus, a random spatial distribution of settlements is indicative of total disorganization of the settlement system. However, this will occur only in a closed system. The real world settlement systems are not closed systems and hence they are never totally disorganized.

The real world settlement systems, therefore, lie somewhere between the state of total disorganization and the state of complete organization. The level of disorganization in systems theory is known as entropy and this level can be measured mathematically. In open systems, there is a tendency for systems to attain a state which remains more or less stationary. Such a state is known as an 'equilibrium' state. The rank size rule, in the opinion of some scholars, represents an equilibrium state in an open system of settlements, while the primate city system represents a second type of equilibrium. The rank size distribution is a product of a homostatic system, which is a system that resists change and brings about counteracting forces to balance the external stimuli. In a dynamic system, there is constant change. There is increasing disequilibrium between settlements, characterized by such processes as metropolization. The ultimate state of this dynamic system is a one city region without any other settlements. This is, however, only a theoretical possibility. The primate city system represents, perhaps, an intermediate stage in a dynamic system of settlements.

Settlement Systems in a Developing Economy

The Indian settlement system is influenced by the processes of socio-economic development initiated since 1947. Industrialization, the Green Revolution in agriculture, social change as seen in the adoption of western values in Indian society, are all contributing to urbanization, and more specifically to the process of metropolization. The political system and the methods of centralized planning have contributed to the increasing concentration of decision making at the national and state capitals. One major effect of all these developments is the rapid growth of larger cities and metropolises. Indian settlement systems, both at the regional and national levels are contributing to the emergence of primate cities.

In the literature on third world urbanization, primate cities are described as a major characteristic of underdeveloped areas and they are often viewed as agents retarding the socio-economic development of their surrounding areas. However, this is not entirely true. Primate cities exist even in the most developed countries. The primacy of Tokyo in Japan has been on the increase in recent times, and Japan is neither an underdeveloped country nor is its economy stagnant. As mentioned earlier, primate cities in themselves are neither good nor bad. They are the objective reality in both developed and developing countries. It is true that large cities generate problems of overcrowding, squalor and transportation bottlenecks. Nevertheless, in countries with scarce financial resources, it is more efficient to concentrate investment in a few large cities. It is commonly found that such concentration of investment leads to rapid growth. Primate city development may thus have at least short term benefits for developing countries. It is legitimate, however, to question the long term gains and losses of the primate city settlement system. This is an issue of major importance in any discussion of a national urbanization policy.

SELECTED READING

Ahmed, Qazi: *Indian Cities: Characteristics and Correlates,* University of Chicago Press, Chicago, 1965.

Bhatia, S. S.: 'A Reconsideration of the Concept of the Primate City', *Indian Geographical Journal,* Vol. 37, 1962, pp. 23–4.

Christaller, Walter: *Central Places in Southern Germany,* translated by C. W. Baskin, Prentice Hall, 1966.

Farmer, B. H.: 'Christaller Revisited: Description versus Prescription', in Sundaram, K. V., ed.: *Geography and Planning: Essays in Honour of V. L. S. Prakasa Rao,* Concept, New Delhi, 1985, pp. 136–53.

Gupta, Vinod K.: 'The System of Cities in Relation to Economic Development in India', in NCAER: *Market Towns and Spatial Development,* New Delhi, 1972, pp. 104–12.

Jefferson, Mark: 'The Law of the Primate City', *Geographical Review,* Vol. 29, 1939, pp. 226–32.

Mayfield, Robert C.: 'A Central Place Hierarchy in Northern India', in Garrisson and Marble, eds.: *Quantitative Geography, Part I: Economic and Cultural Topics,* Department of Geography, Northwestern University, Evanston, Illinois, 1967, pp. 120–66.

Prakasa Rao, V. L. S.: *Towns of Mysore State,* Asia Publishing House, Bombay, 1964.

———: 'Central Place Theory in Retrospect and Prospect', *Annals of the National Association of Geographers of India,* Vol. 1, No. 2, 1981, pp. 39–50.

———: *Urbanisation in India: Spatial Dimensions,* Concept, New Delhi, 1983, pp. 113–25.

Sen, L. K., *et al.: Growth Centres in Raichur: An Integrated Area Development Plan for a District in Karnataka,* National Institute of Community Development, Hyderabad, 1975, pp. 10–58.

Singh, K. N.: 'Spatial Pattern of Central Places in the Middle Ganga Valley, India', *National Geographical Journal of India,* Vol. 12, 1966, pp. 218–26.

Singh, B. L.: 'Rank-Size Relationship in the Central Place System of Mithila Plain, North Bihar,' *The National Geographical Journal of India,* Vol. 31, Part 2, 1985, pp. 129–46.

Wanmali, S.: *Periodic Markets and Rural Development in India,* B. R. Publications, Delhi, 1981.

Zipf, G. K.: *Human Behaviour and the Principle of Least Effort,* Addison Wesley Press, Massachusetts, 1949.

CHAPTER 8

Empirical Studies on Settlement Systems

Nearly a million settlements in India, big and small, generate a varied matrix of interactions that on closer examination reveal a more manageable set of inter-relationships between settlements. These insights provide a better understanding of settlement systems in India at the regional and local levels. Empirical studies on the location, spacing and spatial interaction between settlements form the basis for inductive theorization of settlement systems; on the other hand, empirical verification is often considered to be a necessary part of a deductive settlement theory. Geographers have always had a special attachment to field investigation and it is, therefore, not surprising, that considerable energy has been devoted to an empirical understanding of settlement systems in India at the regional level. It is not the objective of this chapter to review the vast body of literature on settlement systems in India; on the other hand, an attempt is made here to explain the methodology of field studies, noting both their utility and limitations. Every methodology does, however, relate directly or indirectly to a theory of settlement systems. By and large, empirical studies on settlement systems in India have tended to rely heavily on the major concepts of the central place theory. Empirical studies have also experimented with concepts borrowed from biological and physical sciences, but to a lesser extent.

The methodology of empirical work on settlement systems in India may be examined under eight main areas: (a) settlement spacing, (b) entropy of settlement systems, (c) identification of central place functions, (d) measurement of range of a good, (e) measurement of thresholds, (f) measurement of centrality, (g) identification of settlement hierarchies, and (h) rural-urban travel behaviour. This list is obviously not exhaustive. However, the object here is to focus on the most common and recurring concerns of geographical field studies on settlement systems in India.

The spatial distribution of settlements in an area is a central theme in any geographical study of settlements. In a uniform area, for example a plain or plateau surface, nucleated village settlements tend to be distributed at regular intervals. The distance between settlements varies from region to region, depending on a host of factors that also influence the density of population. It is a common practice to look at the topographical maps of the Survey of India to understand and to correlate the spatial patterns of settlements in any given area. This practice is still valid, even though the topographical maps represent ground conditions that existed a few decades ago. Areal photographs and satellite imageries are, of course, of more recent origin. In these cases, however, there is a significant measure of scale distortion, and consequently they should be used with caution. Maps and photographs provide the basis for visual observations; they can also be used for rigorous quantitative analysis of spatial patterns. This can be done by the measurement of direction and distance between neighbouring settlements. It is in this respect that a new analytical tool, the nearest neighbour technique, has been widely used by geographers. Before we discuss this technique, it is necessary to briefly describe the major theoretical spatial patterns.

Theoretical Spatial Patterns

In theory, there are three basic spatial patterns of settlement: (a) uniform distribution, (b) random distribution, and (c) clustered distribution (figure 8.1). In a uniform spatial distribution, settle-

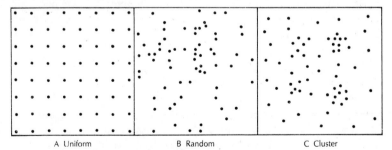

A Uniform   B Random   C Cluster

FIGURE 8.1. Theoretical Patterns of Settlement Distribution.

ments are spaced equal intervals apart, the distance between a settlement and its nearest neighbour being exactly the same for all settlements. In addition, the settlements are all located along straight lines, which together may form a square grid or a lattice of parallelograms. Geometrical shapes such as triangles, squares, rectangles and hexagons can be discerned in this point pattern. Such a uniform distribution of settlements is indeed a very rare, if not an abstract, phenomenon. In the central place theory, such a distribution pattern is conceived as an ideal or normative pattern of settlements. From this point of view, it becomes relevant to test to what extent the real world distribution pattern differs from the ideal.

A random spatial pattern, which in a theoretical sense is the opposite of a uniform distribution, is produced in a two dimensional surface, when both the coordinates of location are randomly determined. For any given area, it is easy to generate a random spatial point distribution. This is done by taking pairs of random numbers from a random number table. The number of points to be located within the area can be changed depending on the density of settlements in the given area. However, it should be remembered that, for a given number of point locations, there is not one but an infinite number of random spatial distributions. Consequently, a random pattern is not a unique spatial pattern, but only a sample from a set of random distributions. This point forms the fundamental basis for the adoption of inferential statistical procedures for testing the randomness of spatial patterns. Surprisingly, random or near random settlement patterns are fairly frequently met with in the real world. However, the random spatial pattern represents a chaotic situation, where a multiplicity of factors influence settlement location. For this reason, it is futile to look for specific explanations of a random spatial distribution. From a systems theory point of view, a random spatial point pattern is a condition of maximum entropy, a condition in which the settlement system is in a state of total disorganization.

A third theoretical pattern of settlements is a clustered spatial distribution. In this pattern, some settlements are located close together, while others are spaced far apart. A clustered distribution, in the real world, can occur due to differences in terrain, quality of agricultural land, availability of irrigation facilities, and social differences, such as the presence of tribal and non-tribal settlements in the same region. Clustered distribution of settlements can also occur near metropolitan cities. This form of clustering owes its origin to the effects of agglomeration and the economies of scale of urban productive activities. A pseudo-clustered pattern of settlements occurs when substantial parts of a region are negative areas, such as swamps, hilly areas with steep slopes, or areas covered by lakes or other water bodies, all of which are unsuitable for settlement location. Nevertheless, a truly clustered pattern of settlements is also commonly met with in the real world; it represents an intermediate stage between a uniform and a random spatial distribution. It represents a state of equilibrium in the settlement system.

Nearest Neighbour Technique

A technique for identifying uniform, random and clustered settlement patterns on the basis of measurements of actual nearest neighbour distances between settlements has been adapted from the biological sciences (Clark and Evans 1956). In this analysis, settlements of a given hierarchical level are taken into account, and for each settlement its nearest neighbour is identified. The distance to the nearest neighbour is measured on a map using the direct distance. When a nearest neighbour settlement lies outside the area of study, the distance to this settlement is still taken into account, ignoring the boundary of the study area. The nearest neighbour distances of all settlements in the study area may be used to compute the arithmetic mean $(\bar{r}_a)$.

In a theoretical random distribution of settlements, it has been shown that distance to nearest neighbour is distributed statistically in the form of a normal curve with mean $(\bar{r}_e) = \dfrac{0.5}{\sqrt{D}}$, where D is density of settlements in the study area. This rather simple looking equation, has a fairly complicated mathematical proof, which is based on the Poisson probability distribution, which in turn represents a random process in space. The actual mathematical proof is given by Clark and Evans.

The actual mean nearest neighbour distance between settlements in the study area may be compared with the theoretical or expected mean nearest neighbour distance. It may be noted that the expected mean nearest neighbour distance depends only on one factor, namely, the density of settlements in the study area. While comparing the mean nearest neighbour distances three possibilities exist. The actual mean nearest neighbour distance may be greater than, equal to, or less than the expected mean nearest neighbour distance. If, for example, in the study area $\bar{r}_a$ is greater than $\bar{r}_e$, it would indicate that the existing settlements are more uniformly spaced than a random distribution of settlements. If, on the other hand, $\bar{r}_a$ is equal to $\bar{r}_e$, we have a random spatial pattern of settlements in the study area. When $\bar{r}_a$ is less than $\bar{r}_e$ the settlements are more closely spaced than in the random situation, and the actual distribution of settlements is of a clustered type.

The ratio of $\bar{r}_a$ to $\bar{r}_e$ is known as the nearest neighbour statistic R, which varies from zero to 2.15. Values less than unity indicate a clustered distribution, a value of unity represents a random distribution, and values greater than one indicate a uniform distribution. When settlements are located at the centre of hexagons of uniform size, the spacing between settlements is maximum. In this theoretical pattern of settlements, the nearest neighbour statistic assumes its highest value, that is 2.15.

Application of the Nearest Neighbour Technique

The nearest neighbour technique is commonly used to test to what extent a specific regional distribution of settlements is random.[1] Wherever the settlement pattern is found to be more clustered than random, a bias of some kind may have influenced the result and, therefore, the results of statistical testing have doubtful validity. In fact, the validity of the nearest neighbour technique depends upon: (a) whether the study area has been properly defined (if there are large segments of negative areas, then the technique should not be applied at all); (b) whether the study area has significant spatial differences in terrain, population density, and so on (in areas where these spatial differences exist, the technique again has no value); and (c) whether in the study area there are strong linear alignments of settlements, as in coastal areas and along rivers and major roads (here again, the technique should not be applied). In some cases of linear alignment of settlements, a unidimensional nearest neighbour technique may be used to test for randomness of linear distribution.

---

[1] Tests of hypotheses relating to the randomness or otherwise of settlement distribution can be made using the sampling distribution of $\bar{r}_e$. The test statistic in this case is $Z = \dfrac{\bar{r}_a - \bar{r}_e}{\sigma_{\bar{r}_e}}$, where $\sigma_{\bar{r}_e} = \dfrac{0.261}{\sqrt{ND}}$ (N is the number, and D the density of settlement in the study area).

The application of nearest neighbour technique in the study of settlements in various parts of the country has shown that generally settlements in India are not randomly distributed. There is a tendency, according to the findings of a number of studies, for settlements to be distributed in a clustered rather than random manner. None of the studies has produced evidence of a uniform distribution of settlements in any part of India. It should, however, be pointed out that most studies suffer from inadequate appreciation of the limitations in the use of the technique.

ENTROPY OF SETTLEMENT SYSTEMS

Settlements considered as interacting and interdependent parts, together constituting a system, have a tendency to decay in course of time. This tendency is a universal characteristic of all systems and it applies to individual settlements as well. The central place theory describes a well organized and orderly system of settlements, where the characteristics of these settlements and their location can easily be predicted. In reality, settlements are never so well organized. On the other hand, there is the theory that, given sufficient time, a closed system tends to be totally disorganized. This is the ultimate state of inert uniformity, or a state of entropy, where all characteristics and locations of settlements are totally haphazard or random. This is also an extreme situation, rarely (if ever) encountered in the real world. The nearest neighbour technique offers one method of measuring randomness in a settlement system. This method, however, cannot give us a measure of the degree of entropy or disorganization in the system. The entropy method offers a more viable way of measuring the random component in the location of settlements.

The entropy method was originally developed by Medvedkov and has since been applied in India by geographers. The actual use of this technique involves the superimposition of a square grid on the study area, the sides of the squares being greater than the average spacing of settlements in the area. The number of settlements (n) in each grid cell is counted. A frequency distribution of cells having the same number of settlements is then prepared. From this, the relative frequency in each size class is calculated by means of the formula:

$$p_i = \frac{f_i}{\sum\limits_i f_i}$$

where p_i is the probability of finding i settlements in a cell, and f_i is the number of cells having i settlements each. The entropy of the settlement system is then defined as:

$$H_s = p_i \; \Sigma \; \log_2 \; p_i$$

If we apply this formula to Christaller's central place system, where settlements are uniformly distributed, the entropy value will be zero, while for a random spatial point pattern, the entropy would be maximum.

The measure of entropy defined above suffers from a number of deficiencies: (a) Entropy is measured purely on the basis of location of settlements, and other characteristics of settlements, which are in fact equally important, are not taken into account. These characteristics include functions, hierarchical level, size of complementary area, and so on. (b) The measurement of entropy depends on the quadrat size, which is often selected in an arbitrary manner. (c) Uniformity of the study area in terms of density of settlements is assumed in the method, but this condition is often not fully satisfied in any study region. Often differences in terrain, density of population, etc. exist within the study area and in such a situation the method can lead to faulty conclusions.

The entropy method was used by Thakur to study the system of settlements in the following regions: (a) Bihar plains, (b) lower Ganga plains, (c) Chota Nagpur plateau, (d) Utkal coastal plain, and (e) the Orissa highland region. His studies indicated an increase in entropy over time in all the regions from 1872 to 1971. While this conclusion is consistent with the systems theory, there is, however, some doubt regarding its validity. The measure of entropy, as noted earlier, is dependent on the density of population. Population density increased in all the regions from 1872 to 1971, and the increase in entropy may have actually been a result of that increase. This example illustrates the complexity of the problem and the difficulty in isolating the disturbing factors. However sophisticated a technique may be, its usefulness is constrained by the complex variations in the real world situation.

IDENTIFICATION OF CENTRAL PLACE FUNCTIONS

Goods and services offered at any place reflect the socio-cultural and economic conditions in the area of study. There are significant differences in the type and variety of goods and services offered, not only among the countries of the world, but in some cases even among different parts of the same country. Goods and services offered in Indian cities and towns do differ markedly from those in western cities. For example, the clothes worn in India (saris, dhotis and so on) are worn hardly anywhere else in the world. Similarly, food articles and other consumer goods offered in Indian towns differ from those in the West or in Japan. Each country has its own unique mosaic of mass consumption goods and this, in a way, contributes to the distinctiveness of the central place systems in each country. Furthermore, even within a vast country such as India, there are significant variations from one region to another in the variety of goods offered in towns and cities. For example, woollen garments are an important item sold in the cities of North India, while they have no relevance to cities in Kerala. The types of goods and services also differ from one hierarchical level of centres to another. At the same time, towns and cities in various parts of the country (and in other countries of the world) have much in common. It is therefore necessary to make a thorough study of central place functions offered at various levels, from the small town to the metropolitan city, before we can hope to understand the settlement system.

As mentioned earlier, a central place function, to be recognized as such, must satisfy the following criteria: (a) It must be offered on a regular basis, preferably on a daily basis throughout the year. Seasonal functions, such as tourism and recreation, regulated agricultural markets or *mandis*, are not central place functions. (b) It must be offered in a shop or built structure of a permanent or semi-permanent nature. Pavement hawkers, mobile trolley vendors, foot vendors and so on are not considered as establishments offering central place goods or services. (c) Establishments offering a variety of goods, such as for example, electrical goods, stationery goods, grocery items, are considered as offering a single good. (d) The goods or services offered must cater not only to customers within the central place, but also to those from outside it. In fact, it is the latter who make a function a central place function.

Town amenities such as electricity, street lighting, piped water supply, fire service, sewage facility, town milk supply, town bus services, railway stations, airports, telephone exchanges, parks, playgrounds, and so on are not considered as central place functions. All the above may be related to the importance of the town or city or to the quality of the urban way of life. Most Indian cities and towns do not have the full range of amenities listed above, and it is a common practice to judge the importance of a place from the amenities available there. While such an assessment is legitimate in itself, it tells us nothing about the city's relationship with its surrounding area. It is obvious that people in the surrounding areas derive no benefits from the city amenities, and these would not cause them to come to the city.

Some periodic activities in a town or even in a city may attract large gatherings of people from surrounding areas. These activities are often conducted in public parks, playgrounds or other open spaces, often with the express permission of the municipal authorities. Such activities include weekly markets, circus shows or temporary cinema houses, religious fairs and festivals associated with temples, churches or mosques, the flow of tourists on a seasonal basis in places such as hill stations on account of sports facilities or recreational facilities, and so on. However, wherever such flow of people occurs on a regular basis, as in Varanasi, Hardwar and Rameswaram, for example, the activities tend to assume the role of central place functions.

In a country where agriculture and other primary activities provide occupation for over 70 per cent of the population, seasonal activities play an important role. Regulated wholesale markets for agricultural and other primary produce constitute an important function in many medium and small towns. These markets are invariably housed in permanent structures and involve a large number of wholesale establishments. The presence of the wholesale market is an important support for many other central place functions in the town; farmers who come to the town would also like to take advantage of other services.

A wide range of central place functions is provided by the government and its various departments and agencies. The level of services differs, depending on the administrative hierarchy of the place. Schools and other educational institutions constitute an important service. While primary schools would attract students from outside only in rare cases, as in a small village, secondary schools, junior colleges and other higher educational institutions, and institutions for specialized vocational training, attract students from a wider area. Dispensaries and hospitals form another important category of government services. The direct administrative services include the land revenue and land record offices at the tehsil level, the block level offices of the rural development department, and the courts at various levels.

The central place functions performed by places at various hierarchical levels can be ascertained by field survey. A number of studies have been carried out in India along these lines. By and large, five hierarchical levels of central places have been distinguished. They are: village, small town, town, city and metropolitan city. At each level, certain functions and services appear for the first time and they constitute the distinctive cluster of functions at that level. Several studies have attempted an identification of the characteristic functions and services at different hierarchical levels. A summary of the findings is given in table 8.1. The identification of central place functions at various levels has a wide range of applications in field studies, particularly for the measurement of range of goods, thresholds, and centrality of places.

The services and goods listed in table 8.1 do not include the informal commercial sector. Village weekly markets, itinerant traders selling all kinds of goods from village to village, agents of wholesale merchants of agricultural products visiting villages to collect grain or other produce, village money lenders, astrologers, gypsies, the magic man, the village midwife, and the village priest all provide services of sorts to people in rural areas. Some of these people are residents of small towns, others live in the larger villages. In both cases, their clients are spread over an area which is easily accessible. There are also two types of movements involved here. In the first case, the seller of goods, who lives in a small town, goes to different villages periodically to sell his ware. In the second case, the villagers come to the money lender, priest or astrologer to seek his services. Weekly markets involve both types of movement. The buyers come mainly from the surrounding villages, while the professional sellers move from one weekly market to another. Weekly markets, unlike wholesale markets, are almost invariably held in open spaces with no permanent buildings or shops. Regional weekly markets, such as the one at Hapur in Uttar Pradesh, or Pollachi in Tamil Nadu, are markets of great importance and attract farmers and merchants from several districts. In addition to these, there are specialized cattle markets and markets where tribal people and nomadic herdsmen exchange goods with the plains people and traders. All these services are not exactly rooted to a place, in the sense of permanent buildings, shops, etc. They do not constitute an urban activity in themselves. They do, however, help in the process of urban growth in some cases.

TABLE 8.1
Central Place Functions in Five Levels of Centres in India

Hierarchical Level	Select List of Functions
I. Village	1. Tea shops
	2. Pan shops (betel leaf, beedi etc.)
	3. Tailor shops
	4. Grocery stores
	5. Fair price shops
	6. Flour mills
	7. Gram panchayat offices
	8. Post offices
	9. Primary schools (government)
	10. Middle schools (government)
II. Small Town	1. Restaurants
	2. Temporary cinema houses
	3. Banks
	4. Pawn shops
	5. Cloth stores
	6. Goldsmith/silversmith shops
	7. Hardware/paint shops
	8. Stationery shops
	9. Bookshops (school books)
	10. Cycle rental/repair shops
	11. Ayurvedic/Unani drugs shops
	12. Country liquor shops
	13. Tractor/implements repair shops
	14. Utensils shops (aluminium, brass)
	15. Allopathic doctors
	16. Govt. dispensaries
	17. Junior colleges/senior schools
	18. Aided primary and secondary schools
	19. Block offices
	20. Tehsil offices
	21. Tehsil courts
III. Town	1. Agricultural wholesale markets/regulated markets
	2. Hotels/lodging places
	3. Permanent cinema houses
	4. Optician (shops)
	5. Dentists
	6. Dry cleaners
	7. English wine shops
	8. Clothing—sari shops
	9. Retail outlets of DCM, Bombay Dyeing, etc.

Hierarchical Level	Select List of Functions
	10. Bata, BSC shoe shops
	11. Barber shops
	12. Photographers/studios
	13. Allopathic drug stores
	14. Petrol pumps
	15. Bakeries
	16. Electrical shops (selling fans)
	17. Watch repair shops
	18. Cycle sales outlets
	19. Radio/transistor sales outlets
	20. Auto repair shops
	21. Sewing machine sales outlets
	22. Stainless steel utensils shops
	23. Crockery shops
	24. District level government offices
	25. District courts
	26. Degree colleges
	27. Typing/commercial institutes
	28. District hospitals (100 beds)
	29. Printers
IV. City	1. Woollen textile shops
	2. Silk saris and other expensive clothing shops
	3. Furniture shops (sofa, dining table, etc.)
	4. Steel furniture shops
	5. College level bookshops
	6. Post-graduate colleges, universities
	7. Ladies' beauticians
	8. Car/scooter sales outlets
	9. Electrical goods (refrigerators, etc.) outlets
	10. Homoeopathic drug stores
	11. *Barat ghar/kalyana mandapam*/public halls
	12. Wrist-watch sales outlets
	13. Sports goods shops
	14. Language newspaper/magazine offices (publishing)
	15. Radio stations
	16. Luggage shops (trunks, suitcases, briefcases)
	17. Public English medium schools
	18. High courts
	19. State capital functions
	20. Hospitals (privately run)
	21. Private nursing homes

Hierarchical Level	Select List of Functions
	22. Medical specialists: eye, ENT, orthopaedic, gynaecologist
	23. Public libraries
	24. Timber markets (plywood and special wood panelling)
V. Metropolitan City	1. Stock exchanges
	2. Five star hotels
	3. Head offices of major business houses
	4. Head offices of national associations doing public service
	5. Head offices of public sector corporations
	6. Head offices of banks/insurance companies
	7. Specialized private hospitals
	8. Shops for specialized equipment—medical, engineering, electronic goods
	9. Industrial tools and equipment sales outlets
	10. Heavy vehicles sales outlets
	11. Luxury goods, carpets, interior decorators
	12. Jewellery shops for diamonds, pearls, precious stones
	13. Florists
	14. Pet animal shops/hospitals
	15. Electronic gadgets, computers, colour TV sales outlets
	16. Seat of national/state government
	17. High courts/Supreme Court
	18. National institutes of research; laboratories
	19. National sports organizations
	20. National book publishers
	21. English language newspaper offices
	22. TV stations with studios
	23. Airconditioned cinema houses
	24. Reserve Bank offices
	25. Embassies/Consulates
	26. Museums and zoos
	27. National libraries

The informal sector is of great importance in both rural and urban areas in India. Even the metropolitan cities have a large informal commercial sector. Nevertheless, the informal sector plays a complementary rather than competing role in relation to the formal commercial sector. While the informal sector cannot be included within the framework of central place functions, still it cannot be ignored altogether.

The identification of central place functions and rural-urban linkages provided by the informal sector show significant variations from one part of the country to another. These regional differences, however, are not adequately understood. It is only through systematic field observations that we can gain further insight into the variety of services that link the towns and cities with the villages and hamlets in India.

MEASUREMENT OF RANGE OF A GOOD

The range of a good has to do with distances travelled by people in order to obtain goods and services. Rural people go to the towns to watch movies, buy clothing, consult doctors, and many other purposes. Table 8.1 gives a list of purposes for which people go to places of varying importance, such as the small town, the city or the metropolis. While the more important places offer all the goods and services offered in the smaller centres, it is important to note that the measurement of the range of goods should not be confined to the most important centre alone. In fact, it is appropriate to measure the range of goods only in relation to functions at the corresponding hierarchical level of places. Thus, the range for a dentist or an optician, for example, may be at the level of a town, while the range for a bicycle rental or repair shop may be studied at the level of a small town. The range of lower order goods cannot be correctly measured using higher order centres as the location for field investigation. In such a situation, the measured range would tend to be higher than the actual range, because of the influence of multipurpose visits involving both lower and higher order services.

Choice of Methods of Measurement

The range of a good may be determined by three different methods: (a) using official data sources, (b) interviewing customers who go to an establishment in a city or town, and (c) interviewing people in the surrounding area of a city or town. The choice of the method would depend upon the characteristics of the service or good and the time and effort that one is willing to spend.

Official Data Sources. This method is easy and fairly accurate, but can be applied only to a rather restricted number of functions. In the case of educational institutions, it is not difficult to get a list of students enrolled and also their residential addresses. With this information, it is possible to measure distance travelled by students daily to attend classes, using maps of the area, if necessary. Places like dispensaries, private nursing homes, hospitals and so on also maintain records of patients with their addresses. Banks, particularly in small towns, attract customers from rural areas. The names and addresses of all persons having accounts at a bank can be used to prepare a frequency table of distances travelled by people to the bank. Strictly speaking, the range of a good is the maximum distance travelled by a person to obtain it. However, in practice, in order to avoid exceptional cases, the extreme values are ignored and the 95th percentile value is regarded as the actual range.

Interview of Customers at Establishments. A more direct and common method for measurement of range is to obtain information directly from actual customers at an establishment. Interviews for this purpose may be conducted in front of cinema houses, major shops, or other establishments offering goods and services to people from outside the centre. The main disadvantage is that people do not have the time for long interviews at such locations, but if the interviewer asks brief and pertinent questions, useful information can be gathered. From the investigator's point of view, this method saves a lot of time and effort and one is able to meet people from far and near at one place. A very large number of interviews can also be completed within a short period of time. Nevertheless, a number of precautions regarding the choice of establishments, the coverage of all establishments performing the same functions, the selection of people for interview without bias, and the timing of the interviews during the course of the day, have to be taken so that the data collected accurately reflects the actual situation. Neglect of any one aspect during the interviews can lead to erroneous results. Above all, in no case should the total number of interviews be less than a hundred.

Interview of People in the Surrounding Area. This method is rather difficult and has a number of pitfalls that can invalidate the data. The method involves interviewing people in villages and hamlets surrounding a town or city. Alternatively, a number of sample villages may be taken from a wider region in which central places, large and small, are located. The selection of villages can pose a major problem, but one could use the list given in the District Census Handbooks. However, many Census villages consist of not one but several settlements; in such a situation all the settlements within a village will have to be taken into account in the second stage. After the selection of sample villages, one would require a second level sampling of individuals for actual interview. This process again can be highly laborious if one wishes to attain a high level of accuracy. Voters lists may be of some value here. The third stage consists of the actual interview. The questions would naturally focus on places to which the person being interviewed ordinarily goes for obtaining various services and goods. One advantage of this method is that one could obtain information on a wide range of services simultaneously. Since the individuals are interviewed at their homes, time is not a major constraint. Interviews can also be done in a more relaxed atmosphere which would contribute to a better response from the person being interviewed.

The method, however, has several disadvantages. Perhaps the foremost problem is how to make an unbiased and random selection of villages and individuals. While this sounds easy in theory, in practice it is indeed difficult. Even in a very careful and rigorous study, biases can occur. The second problem is that for any given village where the interviews are conducted, the choice of places where the people can go for services is limited and this leads to similar if not the same responses in most interviews. However, differences in the choice of places and in the use of goods and services exist among the different communities in a village. A large sample is still necesary to cover the whole social spectrum in a village. The method also requires a large sample in terms of number of villages covered. The minimum sample size for villages should be 30, while the minimum for personal interview would have to be at least 500. A survey on such a scale would ordinarily be beyond the capacity of a single investigator. Mayfield, however, used this method in Ludhiana and Jalandhar districts of Punjab to measure the range of common white cloth. He interviewed 182 persons in all, from 35 villages. Mayfield found the range of common cloth to be approximately 15 km in Punjab.

Distance Decay and Range of a Good

Distances travelled by people to obtain a specific good or service may be plotted on a frequency graph in which the y-axis represents the number of customers, while the distance from the establishment to the place of residence of the customer is measured on the x-axis. Examples of such graphs for selected functions are given in figure 8.2. These graphs generally indicate a non-linear decline of number of customers with distance. It is possible to fit a mathematical function of the form $F = aD^{-b}$, which is known as a Pareto function, to this data. The parameters a and b of the Pareto function may be determined by taking logarithms on both sides of the equation; thus, converting the non-linear function into linear form as below:

$$\log F = \log a - b \log D$$

This is a linear regression function in variables $\log F$ and $\log D$, which then makes it possible to estimate a and b by computing the regression equation from the observed data.

It may be observed from the graphs in figure 8.2 that the distance decay function tends to taper off gently with distance. By convention, the tail of the graph is truncated at the 95 per cent level to give us the range of a good. However, it is not absolutely necessary to fit a Pareto function to arrive at the range.

The value of fitting a Pareto function to the data lies mainly in the fact that it makes generalizations and comparisons easier. For example, we could compare the slope of the curve, as measured by the parameter b, for a set of central place functions. The parameter b measures the rate of decline of interaction with distance. One

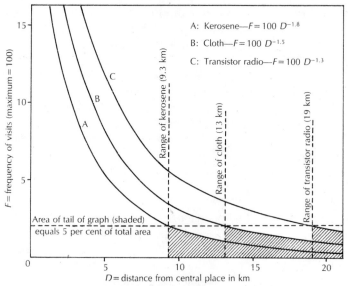

FIGURE 8.2. Distance Decay and Range of a Good.

would expect high values of *b* for lower order functions and lower values of *b* for higher order functions. One could also make comparisons of *b* values for the same goods in different parts of the country. Such differences in *b* values may indicate differences in relative levels of economic development, density of population, and other factors. The Pareto function can also be used as a generalized estimator function for predicting the demand for goods and services in central places. Unfortunately, none of these possibilities has been explored empirically in India.

The distance decay effect and the concept of range of a good can be used by planners to determine distance norms for various services. For example, in the minimum needs programme in the sixth five year plan, distance norms were mentioned for location of primary schools, sources of drinking water supply to villages and so on. Such norms could be more realistically determined by empirical studies for a variety of services, such as dispensaries, hospitals and technical training institutes, but such studies have been rare so far.

MEASUREMENT OF THRESHOLDS

Threshold is an important concept in that it determines the population level at which a particular good or service will be offered in a place. In a developing country, where new services are being introduced for the benefit of rural and even urban people, the threshold concept has an important utility value from the point view of spatial planning. Population norms are often prescribed by government organizations. For example, the Reserve Bank of India stipulates a minimum population of 20,000 for granting of licence to establish a bank in any place. Hospitals, dispensaries, schools, colleges and other services have corresponding thresholds of population prescribed by local bodies or the state governments. Here we are not concerned with the prescribed or normative thresholds for various goods and services, but with the threshold determined by demand for a good or service at any point in time. The actual thresholds differ not only from the prescribed norms, but also from region to region and from one point in time to another.

Every establishment performing a given function has to have a minimum number of clients to sustain it. Some, at least, of the clients come from the settlement itself, while others may come from outside. In the context of central place theory, the focus is on establishments that attract customers from outside the settlement. This rather important aspect is often neglected or ignored in determining thresholds of various functions. A related aspect that may be noted here is that when thresholds are measured in terms of population, they should include not only the population of the settlement where the establishment is located, but also the population of the area served by the establishment. Again, one encounters situations where only the population of the central place is taken into account. This is often necessitated by lack of data on area served by a place.

The measurement of threshold population also involves a number of other conceptual and practical problems. In some cases, the definition of population threshold itself has been modified to overcome some of the problems. One such modified definition identifies the threshold as the entry point, in terms of population of a settlement, at which a good or service is offered in an establishment. In other words, the threshold is the population of the smallest place at which the function makes its first appearance. The presence of more than one establishment with the same function indicates that the threshold has been overtaken. Consequently, the measurement of threshold should, in fact, focus on places that have only one establishment performing the function. While this rule is sound in theory, it is often difficult to follow in practice. A variety of approaches and definitions have been used in the measurement of thresholds. These approaches may be classified as direct or indirect.

Direct Approach to the Measurement of Thresholds

The direct method involves interviewing managers of establishments, such as owners of shops, managers of banks or cinema houses, doctors, lawyers or other professionals, or wholesale merchants. However, it is assumed here that the establishment is the only one of its kind in the place where the study is made. If there are two or more establishments, the smallest of the lot should be chosen; the threshold concept is concerned with the smallest number of customers. The actual interviews may elicit information on the number of customers or clients, their distribution, socio-economic background, and the economics of the establishment. The threshold, in an economic sense, is the minimum turnover that (in the perception of the manager) makes it worthwhile to run the establishment. However, questions involving sensitive monetary issues can be difficult, unless the interviewer has personal rapport with the manager. Therefore, a case study approach, rather than sample survey, is more appropriate. After the data have been collected, the threshold, measured in terms of number of customers or in monetary terms, may be translated in terms of population of the settlements where the service is offered. The problem is rather simple if there is only one establishment in each of the places where the interviews are held. In such a case, the threshold population may be defined as the average population of the places where the interviews are held. In other cases, a more elaborate method will have to be employed. The method offers direct and more in-depth information on the manner in which new functions are introduced in the smaller centres.

Indirect Approaches to the Measurement of Threshold

The direct method of measurement of thresholds involves much time and effort, and the accuracy of the information depends entirely on the competence of the interviewer and the rapport that he is able to establish with the person interviewed. As opposed to this, indirect methods are less time consuming and can be employed for a wide variety of functions. Direct methods are of no use for establishments and functions that are non-profit-making, such as hospitals, post offices, schools and so on. Indirect methods can be used irrespective of whether the services are managed by private entrepreneurs or government or charitable organizations.

Indirect methods are based on a survey of the functions existing in a number of centres and the number of establishments performing each function in each centre. Thus, a survey may be made of the number of establishments for each of the functions listed in table 8.1 in all centres in a given region. Such a survey will provide sufficient data for estimating the threshold population for each function. The centres surveyed should include both the smallest as well as the largest in the region. While the largest centres are easily identified, the lowest order centres are not so easy to identify, not only because they are too numerous, but also because their presence may not be obvious from the secondary sources of information. On the other hand, the survey of establishments and functions in small centres is easy, since they are fewer in number in such centres. In the larger centres such as one-lakh cities, it may be impossible to cover all establishments in the city. In such cases, only the functions and establishments in the main market area are surveyed; the assumption here is that the establishments in other parts of the city cater to the city population only and not to those living outside it.

The functions performed by centres are basically of two types: (a) functions for which there can be more than one establishment, for example, cloth shops, electrical goods shops, cinemas, banks, and so on; and (b) those that are performed by one establishment in a place, for example, tehsil offices, courts and the offices of various government agencies. The former is a variable type function, while the latter is an attribute type function. In the case of attribute type functions, there are only two possibilities—either a function is present in a place or it is not. The methods of estimation of threshold differ depending on whether a function is of the variable type or attribute type.

Thresholds of Variable Type Functions. For this type of function, it is necessary to obtain information on the number of establishments for each function in all the centres in a region. These data may be plotted on a graph as in figure 8.3. In such a graph the number of establishments is measured on the x-axis and the population of the centres on the y-axis. The population data is invariably taken from the Census Handbooks. The relationship between the number of establishments and the population of the centre is not linear, for the following reasons: (a) The *number* of establishments does not increase in proportion to the population, since an establishment can expand and accommodate more customers. This, however, can happen only up to a point; beyond that competition will appear on the scene. (b) In large centres, establishments sell goods with lower profit margins, partly due to the economies of scale and partly due to competition. (c) The establishments in a town also serve the surrounding area. The population of the surrounding area increases in a non-linear fashion with increase in the size of the town. The mathematical relationship between the number of establishments performing a particular function and the population of the centre may be expressed in the form:

$$P = ab^N$$

where P is the population of the centre, and N the number of establishments for the function at a centre. The non-linear function may again be transformed into a linear function by taking logarithms as follows:

$$\log P = \log a + N \log b$$

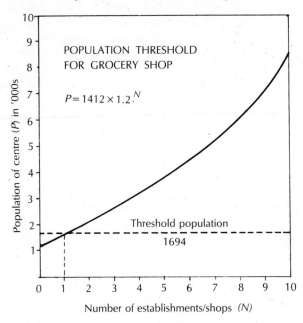

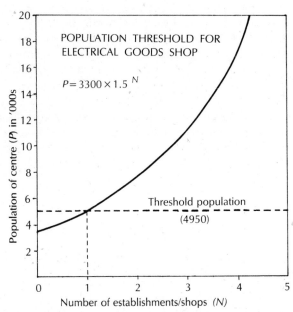

FIGURE 8.3. Population Thresholds for Variable Type Functions.

Again the parameters *a* and *b* in the equation above may be determined by the least squares method. Once the values of the parameters for a given function are known, the threshold population is obtained from the equation by assuming that the number of establishments equals one.

In actual fact, the parameter *a* in the mathematical function represents the threshold population for the function, while the parameter *b* represents the scale factor of the establishments. The value of *b* can vary from 1 to 3; when $b=1$, the establishments are all of the same size, irrespective of the population of the settlement. When $b>1$, the average size of establishments increases with the number of establishments in a centre. This is realistic, as big towns have bigger shops with large turnovers. For example, a cloth shop in a small town is likely to be far smaller than a cloth shop in a big city. The ratio of their sales can vary from 1:10 to 1:1000. The *b* factor identifies this scale. However, the scale varies from one function to another and from one region to another.

Thresholds of Attribute Type Functions. Attribute type functions are performed mainly by government agencies. In India, the government makes its presence felt from the level of the gram panchayat to the national capital. Foremost among the government related functions are the administrative capitals at the state, district, tehsil, and block levels. There is a parallel set-up of courts at these centres. In addition, the government plays a vital role in communication; thus, post offices, telegraph offices, telephone exchanges, and radio and television centres come under various government departments. The police department makes its appearance in all but the smallest settlements. Besides, educational institutions, hospitals and dispensaries, particularly those serving the rural population, are by and large run by state governments or local bodies. Some of these services are on the borderline between attribute type and variable type functions. For example, while some metropolitan cities like Delhi, Calcutta or Hyderabad may have more than one university, in most cases, there is only one university in a city. Similarly, hospitals with facilities for major surgery perform an attribute type function, in that most towns have only one government hospital serving the people of surrounding areas. In actual practice, for reasons of convenience, some of the variable type functions, particularly the borderline ones, are often treated as attribute type functions.

A biological assay method is commonly used for determining

the population thresholds of attribute type functions. For the application of this method, information on the presence or absence of a given function in all the central places in a region is required, along with data on the population of all the centres. The centres for which data are collected should invariably include the complete range of places from the very smallest to the very largest. This in practice means that all the larger villages should also be taken into account.

From the above information, it is possible to identify the settlement with the lowest population in which the function is present. Similarly we can also identify the settlement with the largest population in which the same function is absent. The population values of the two settlements identified above give us the population limits within which the particular function makes its appearance. In other words, these provide the threshold zone for the function. Settlements within the threshold zone may or may not have the function; settlements with population values above the zonal limits will invariably have the function, while settlements below the lower limit will not have the function. The actual threshold, however, is the median population of all the settlements in the threshold zone.

TABLE 8.2
Population Thresholds of Selected Services in India

Selected Services	Population Thresholds
Daily newspapers	55,000
District headquarters	52,000
Colleges	25,000
Tehsil headquarters	15,000
Cinema houses (permanent)	10,500
Banks	8,000
Secondary schools	5,000
Dispensaries (allopathic)	5,000
Cloth shops	1,700
Tea shops	1,100
Grocery shops	750
Tailor shops	750
Barber shops	750
Primary schools	500

NOTE: (1) Population thresholds refer to the population of the centre in which they are offered.
(2) The estimates of thresholds are based on author's field studies.

The simplest procedure is to arrange all the settlements in this zone in ascending or descending order and find the population of the median settlement. This is the threshold population for that function. This method has been widely used in India. Threshold populations for a selected range of functions are given in table 8.2. It may be emphasized here that these populations refer to the population of the centre where the service is offered, rather than the combined population of the centre and the area served by it.

The Threshold Concept and Planning

The population threshold concept for various services is widely adopted in India by planners as well as administrators. However, in most cases, threshold norms are based on intuitive reasoning rather than on actual field surveys or other empirical evidence. Thus, for example, the Reserve Bank's stipulation of a population level of 20,000 for the establishment of a bank in a place, is based on subjective judgement. This is not to denigrate a subjective approach; on the contrary, intuitive judgement has a lot of merit. But the responsibility for providing a more objective and rational method lies with the academic community. In this area, considerable work has been done by Indian geographers in the recent past. The work of Wanmali is particularly notable in this respect.

The concept of population thresholds can also be used to develop models of services and functions that ought to be available at the tehsil, district or block level. It would then be possible to develop appropriate physical land-use models for these centres, which in turn can serve as models for the preparation of master plans for small towns.

MEASUREMENT OF CENTRALITY

Centrality is a measure of the importance of a central place. Conceptually, the importance of a place has two components. The first component includes services and goods offered in the place for the convenience of its own population. The second component has to do with services and goods offered at the place for the people of the complementary area. From a theoretical point of view, the second is more important, but in actual practice it is difficult, if not impossible, to separate the two components, for most establishments in a town cater to both the people of the town as well as people from outside. When both components are taken together, we have the absolute importance of the place. The services and goods offered to the people of the surrounding area alone are a measure of the relative importance of a place. However, it is easier to measure the absolute importance of a place than the relative importance.

Three different approaches have been used to measure centrality. The first approach involves an assessment of existing services in a central place. The second approach involves the measurement of the area served by a central place. The third approach attempts to circumvent the problems of primary data collection and uses available published information as a surrogate for measurement of centrality. The third approach is, obviously, a short-cut method and therefore theoretically unsatisfactory. The first and the third approaches have been more commonly used than the second which involves field survey on an elaborate scale.

Centrality Based on Survey of Services in a Place

The importance of a place, in the framework of the central place theory, depends on the number of functions offered in a place, the degree of importance of the various functions and the number of establishments engaged in each function. Naturally, the first step in the measurement of centrality is to obtain information on all the above aspects for all central places in the given region. This can be done only through a detailed field enumeration of establishments and services in each place. Such a survey is practicable in the case of medium and small towns, but rather difficult in the case of one-lakh cities. In metropolitan cities only the higher order functions can be surveyed. As a result, the measurement of centrality has generally tended to focus on the smaller centres. Such studies are by and large feasible at the district level or lower.

Once the survey has been completed, the data need to be put together to arrive at an acceptable measure of centrality. The first major problem here has to do with the relative importance of various functions offered in a place. For example, a cloth shop cannot, in normal sense, be compared to a bank, nor can we legitimately assert that they are of equal importance. In terms of the central place theory, the importance of any function may be measured by its threshold population. The higher the threshold population, the more important the function. Thus, a bank is obviously more important than a cloth shop, as the threshold population for a bank is around 8,000 while that for a cloth shop is only around

1,700. Functions may therefore be weighted in terms of their threshold populations.

A second problem relates to the presence of more than one establishment in a place. In some functions, there may be many establishments while in others there may be only one establishment. The problem, however, is normally solved by adding together the number of establishments for each function, after multiplying them by their corresponding functional weightage. Nevertheless, some additional problems still exist. It is commonly observed that establishments vary in size. For example, in the same town we may have a number of small as well as large clothing stores. Although this fact is obvious, it is often empirically difficult to measure the size of an establishment, in view of the difficulty in obtaining data on sales, number of employees and so on. The problem, however, has generally been ignored in most studies, as these relate to small towns where the differences in the size of establishments are relatively small.

The centrality of a place is then measured by using a formula of the following type:

$$C_k = \sum_{i=1}^{n} N_{ik} \cdot W_i \qquad (1)$$

where

$$W_i = \frac{nP_i}{\sum\limits_{i=1}^{n} P_i} \qquad (2)$$

C_k is the centrality index of place k, while N_{ik} is the number of establishments for function i in place k and W_i is the weight for function i. W_i is determined by the threshold population divided by the mean of the thresholds for all functions. It is possible to vary the formula for W_i without affecting the mathematical properties of the centrality index.

Centrality Based on Area Served by a Centre

All towns and central places in India are surrounded by a number of villages and hamlets. The data on area of revenue villages and their population is available in the District Census Handbooks. Nevertheless, to find the actual area served by a centre, it is necessary to go to all the villages around not just one central place, but a cluster of central places of the same level, and obtain information from each of the villages regarding the places that people in the village ordinarily visit for a specified set of services and goods. In western countries, information of this kind may be obtained by sending a questionnaire to the village schoolmaster or some other functionary. In India this approach is not feasible. Questionnaires hardly ever get an adequate response. The only alternative is to go to the villages, and this can be done only by a team of investigators. Such an approach, however, has been adopted by Wanmali in his study of the Miryalguda taluk in Andhra Pradesh. This pioneering study covered 150 villages and two small towns. But even this study had some unavoidable deficiencies. For example, central places in the taluk may also serve villages lying outside its boundaries; likewise, central places outside the taluk may serve some of the villages within the taluk. The latter aspect can easily be taken care of, while the former can be solved only by expanding the boundaries of the study area. Again, expanding the study area will lead to further problems, as additional centres will be brought into the picture. Thus, in order to measure the size of the complementary areas of one or more centres, one is compelled to cover a much wider area, which may be as much as two to three times the area served by the centres under study.

In the approach adopted above, the centrality indices can be developed for all central places whose complementary areas fall entirely within the area covered in the study. The places which are only partially covered must be excluded from the analysis. This also applies to villages in the study area which are served by centres outside the area of study. The centrality index for each place will depend on the number of villages that are dependent on it for each set of functions for which information has been collected. There is, however, no need to weight the functions here; the unit of measurement is a village, a unit which remains constant for all the functions. However, it would be more appropriate to use the population of the village and add all the populations together. This will eliminate the problem of variations in the size of the villages in the area. Further, we could also find the average population served by a centre by dividing the population totals by the number of functions. The formula for centrality index in this method will take the form:

$$C_k = \frac{\displaystyle\sum_{i \equiv 1}^{n} \sum_{j=1}^{N_{ik}} P_j}{n}$$

C_k is the centrality index for the place k, n is the number of services and goods for which data have been collected, N_{ik} is the number of villages served by place k for function i, and P_j is the population of the village j.

The centrality index is expressed here in terms of population. It connotes the average population served by a centre, taking into account a cluster of functions. However, if this cluster of functions includes those services that are appropriate to a still lower order centre, then the centrality index worked out by this method will not give us the correct picture. In fact, it will result in an under-estimation of the actual population served by the centre. Hence great care must be taken in selecting the functions. Theoretically, this measure of centrality is perhaps the best; it has an intrinsic meaning and at the same time is comparable from one study to another and from one region to another.

Surrogate Methods

The methods discussed above for measurement of centrality involve field-work and are both time consuming and expensive. The centrality of a number of places may be measured in an approximate and indirect way. Christaller in his original work on southern Germany used data on telephones for measurement of centrality. In India, the telephone service is still in its infancy; smaller towns and villages are rarely connected by telephone. On the other hand, medium towns and one-lakh cities are invariably served by telephone exchanges. The number of telephone connections in a place, for which data are available, may be used as a surrogate measure of centrality. In India, telephones are primarily used by government departments, commercial houses, and small and large industries. Residential lines serve the elite of the town or city. The number of telephone connections in a town or city, therefore, is a reasonably good surrogate measure of its centrality. Although the telephone index reflects the general importance of a town, it may overestimate the role of major industrial cities as central places providing services to the surrounding area.

Other surrogate variables that may be used to measure centrality of places in India are: (a) data on buses, trains and other modes of travel, and (b) published data on government, or quasi-government services such as post offices, police stations, courts, administrative offices at various levels, the presence or absence of colleges, hospitals, and so on. The use of transport data is based on the assumption that the various modes of travel link the towns and cities with the surrounding areas. Train services are useful only in the case of metropolitan cities, while the frequency of bus services is relevant in all but the smallest towns. One could generate a centrality index by finding the total number of daily bus services originating from a place to other places of lower importance. In some cases, even the transit bus services may be taken into account, provided these are assigned a lower weightage. Data on bus services are normally available at the offices of the Regional Transport Authority, at each district headquarters.

The published information on the presence or absence of various services only partially reflects the actual importance of places. There are many one-lakh cities in India which do not perform the various administrative and related services appropriate to their size, while smaller centres are sometimes called upon to perform the functions of state capitals. The published data, which are heavily weighted in favour of government functions, will not adequately reflect all aspects of the importance of a place.

It is often observed that, in addition to government services, data on civic amenities are also used to measure the centrality of places. These data may include the following: the availability of piped water supply, sewage facility, the status in terms of municipal administrative set-up, street lighting, presence of pavements in small towns, the number or area of parks and playgrounds, presence of airports, regulated or wholesale markets, and so on. The presence of civic amenities is not relevant to the central place theory; nevertheless, in India, their presence or absence is a valid measure of the importance of a place. Working out a centrality index based on such criteria would pose problems similar to those noted earlier with respect to the measurement of centrality through an assessment of services and goods offered at a centre. These problems can be resolved using the methods described earlier.

IDENTIFICATION OF SETTLEMENT HIERARCHIES

In central place theory, the hierarchy of central places is essentially a product of the hierarchy of functions. The hierarchy of functions, in turn, is determined by threshold and range of goods and services. In table 8.1 an attempt was made to identify the hierarchy of functions in relation to a five-level hierarchy of places in India. The hierarchical levels identified in the table are both subjective as well as tentative. The question has often been asked, but not adequately answered, whether it is possible to establish a hierarchy of places on an objective basis. Attempts in this direction have involved the use of new principles and techniques which are examined briefly below.

In a few cases, hierarchies of settlements can be identified easily and without any ambiguity. These hierarchies are evidently man-made and can be altered at will. Thus, a hierarchy of places from the gram panchayat to the district, state and national capital is self-evident. A number of other functions also follow the administrative hierarchy, for example courts, banks, government hospitals and so forth. Even private industrial houses have a hierarchy of offices that closely reflect the administrative model. The administrative hierarchy of places, therefore, may be accepted as an objective reality.

There are, however, a host of functions for which hierarchy is not self-evident. Each function has a threshold population, which distinguishes it from other functions. Functions with similar thresholds tend to be offered in the same place. The concepts of thresholds and number of establishments are used in the computation of the centrality index, which in effect measures the functional importance of a place. The centrality index, therefore, offers a conceptually sound and objective basis for the identification of central place hierarchy.

Centrality is a unidimensional continuous variable. Places may rank from very low to very high on this scale. Such a distribution of centrality scores does not necessarily imply a hierarchy of places. A hierarchy of places can be said to exist only if the centrality values cluster to form discrete groups, where each group of places stands distinct from others. The first step in demonstrating that a hierarchy of places exists is to establish the clustering of centrality values. This can be done by applying the nearest neighbour technique for one dimension. If the scores are found to be distributed in a more clustered than random fashion, then we may conclude that a hierarchy of places does indeed exist in the area. The actual cluster of places at each hierarchical level may be determined from the centrality values using the criterion of nearness to a group.

The alternative to the nearest neighbour technique is a simple visual graphical interpretation. The frequency graph of centrality values may be closely observed for distinct 'breaks', which would indicate discrete clusters of places. There is, obviously, an element of subjectivity in this approach and the method is by no means sacrosanct. In the social sciences, one often has to settle for the second best.

RURAL-URBAN TRAVEL BEHAVIOUR

The movement of people from rural to urban areas for goods and services may be considered from the point of view of the villages. In the past, there has been undue emphasis on central place theory which focuses mainly on the large settlements, while the complementary areas receive only indirect attention. In reality, however, no village in India is tied to the apron strings of any one central place; instead people from each village visit five to ten central places around them for goods and services. Furthermore, even for a single purchase or service, rural people have a choice of places and in actual fact they may go to more than one place for the same purpose at different points in time.

It must also be recognized that the movement of people from their villages to places around is motivated not so much by economic and commercial objectives as by social needs. A holistic approach is, therefore, necessary in understanding the relationship of a village with the surrounding towns and cities.

The range of economic and social purposes for which village folk go to places outside the village has been listed in table 8.3. This is obviously not intended to be comprehensive, but merely indicative. The major objectives of movement out of the village or hamlet fall into the following categories: (a) purchase of consumer goods, durable goods, farm inputs and construction materials; (b) repair of equipment, general services, administrative services and public facilities; (c) sale of farm products; (d) credit; (e) education; (f) medical services; (g) entertainment; and (h) social needs. In addition to the above, three other basic aspects of movement need to be examined: the number of centres visited and distances travelled for different purposes, the mode of transport used and the frequency of movement outside the village. Empirical data on all these aspects are indeed meagre; nevertheless, some tentative generalizations can be made about the movements of people outside of their hamlets and villages and more often directed towards urban places, small or large.[2]

The Distance Range of Movements

The movement of people from villages in India may cover distances which range, in ordinary circumstances, to a maximum of 150 km; 80 per cent of the visits are to places within a range of 15 km. With the maximum range of 150 km from a village, there may be as many as 40 centres offering various services and goods. However, most of these are smaller centres offering the same goods and services as available at other nearby places. On an average, people visit anything from four to a maximum of ten centres for various purposes. People who visit more than ten different places are indeed very few, accounting for less than one per cent of the total. The socio-economic differences among the village population are reflected in the choice of centres. The richer people prefer to visit the large centres, which are farther away, at a distance of 15–30 km, while the poorer sections restrict their visits to centres that are nearby, that is, within 15 km. This dichotomous pattern of visits holds true for all parts of India and is a significant aspect of the movement patterns of rural people in India.

TABLE 8.3
List of Services and Goods for which
Rural People Visit Towns and Cities in India

I. Consumer Goods
   1. Kerosene
   2. Beedi/cigarette/tobacco
   3. Tea powder
   4. Soap (washing/toilet)
   5. Footwear (leather/plástic)
   6. Cotton cloth (dhotis/saris)
   7. Books (notebooks/texts)
   8. Electrical goods (bulbs, battery, torch)
   9. Medicine (ayurvedic/allopathic)
   10. Woollen clothing (blankets, sweaters)
   11. Grocery items (sugar, salt, edible oils, dal)
   12. Tea and snacks

II. Durable Consumer Goods
   1. Radios/transistors/TV

---

[2] This section is based on the author's study of 12 villages in Meerut District.

List of Services and Goods for which
Rural People Visit Towns and Cities in India

2. Bicycles
3. Furniture (cots/chairs/tables)
4. Utensils (aluminium, brass, copper, bronze)
5. Jewellery (silver, gold)
6. Hardware

III. Farm Inputs
 1. Seeds
 2. Fertilizers
 3. Pesticides/insecticides
 4. Farm implements (diesel oil/petrol)
 5. Farm machinery (pumpsets, diesel engines, tractors)

IV. Construction Materials
 1. Cement
 2. Wood
 3. Bricks and tiles
 4. Steel rods and fabricated structures

V. Repair of Equipment
 1. Tractor repair
 2. Pump and motor repair
 3. Diesel engine repair
 4. Cycle repair
 5. Radio repair
 6. Watch repair

VI. Education
 1. Primary school
 2. Middle school
 3. Secondary school
 4. Senior school/junior college
 5. College/technical training institute
 6. University

VII. Medical Services
 1. Government dispensary
 2. Government hospital (in-patient treatment)
 3. Private allopathic doctor
 4. Maternity centre
 5. Veterinary services

List of Services and Goods for which
Rural People Visit Towns and Cities in India

VIII. Public Services
   1. Courts (tehsil/district)
   2. Tehsildar's office
   3. District Commissioner's office
   4. Block level offices
   5. Patwari/village muncif
   6. Gram panchayat office/meeting place
   7. Post office
   8. Telegraph office

IX. Sale of Farm Products
   1. Grain
   2. Cash crops (variable)
   3. Vegetables
   4. Milk/ghee

X. Credit
   1. Primary credit societies
   2. Land mortgage banks
   3. Scheduled banks
   4. Co-operative banks
   5. Money lenders

XI. Entertainment
   1. Cinemas
   2. Fairs
   3. Festivals

XII. General Services
   1. Carpenters
   2. Blacksmiths
   3. Goldsmiths
   4. Tailors
   5. Cobblers
   6. Barbers
   7. Priests
   8. Astrologers

XIII. Social Needs
   1. Marriages and related affairs
   2. Friends/relatives

List of Services and Goods for which
Rural People Visit Towns and Cities in India

3. Social gatherings/functions
4. Religious gatherings/functions
5. Pilgrimage
6. Caste panchayats

Modes of Transportation

Various modes of transportation are used by the rural people. These include travel on foot or bicycle, in ox-or horse-drawn vehicles, tractors, buses and trains. The first two modes are by far the most important. In particular, bicycles are making rapid progress in rural areas; in most parts of India, and particularly in the Ganga plains, bicycles can be used throughout the year even in the most inaccessible areas which have no roads. Bus services have also grown at a rapid rate in the past few decades and very large numbers of rural people use this mode of transport. The railways play an important role in long distance movements. However, railways are now commonly used by rural people living near major cities and metropolitan areas to visit the city. The range of travel on foot in India is about 10 km each way, and by bicycle, about 20 km, while travel by bus extends ordinarily to a distance of about 100 km. Thus, the mode of transport and distance travelled are related to each other.

Frequency of Movement

Every day people move out of their villages to some place or other. It has been observed that rural people make as many as 50 to 100 visits in a year to places outside their own hamlet or village. This, however, does not take into account the daily movement to and from work within or outside the village. The frequency of movement is, naturally, much greater among adult males than adult females; likewise, the richer people, particularly land-owning peasants, go out more often than the poorer people, namely landless labourers and artisans. Some among the artisan group travel more often than the non-artisan group, mainly for purposes of their trade. In some villages there is a class of people who are engaged in transport and they naturally travel a lot more frequently than others.

There is strong evidence of habitual movement from village to the nearest small town. This daily movement is not necessarily motivated by any specific purpose except that of spending some time in the town and meeting friends. Among the purposeful trips, the most frequent movements occur for the purchase of consumer goods and services, and less for medical, entertainment and religious purposes. Some of the movements, such as for farm inputs or sale of farm products are seasonal in character, and others are in fact of very infrequent occurrence. Visits to places of pilgrimage, for example, may take place only a few times in an individual's life.

The movements of people from village to city are also notable for their daily rhythm. Visits to larger centres start early in the morning and terminate in the evening. On the other hand, visits to the nearest town are more commonly undertaken in the late afternoon. In most small towns and even cities in India, the peak period of pedestrian traffic is invariably in the late afternoon. This period also shows maximum traffic on all the roads leading to the city from the countryside. The rural-urban movement of people on a daily basis is an important and interesting part of the rural-urban scene in India.

SELECTED READING

Bhat, L. S.: *Micro Level Planning: A Case Study of Karnal Area, Haryana, India*. K. B. Publications, New Delhi, 1976.

Clark, P. J. and F. C. Evans: 'Distance to Nearest Neighbour as a Measure of Spatial Relationships in Populations', *Ecology*, Vol. 35, 1954, pp. 445–53.

Kulkarni, Gopal S. and Vincent P. Miller: 'Lower Level Service Areas and the Hierarchy: A Heuristic Appraisal', in K. V. Sundaram (ed.): *Geography and Planning: Essays in Honour of V. L. S. Prakasa Rao*, Concept, New Delhi, 1985, pp. 169–88.

Mayfield, R. C.: 'An Urban Research Study in Northern India', *Urban Systems and Economic Development*, University of Oregon. 1962, pp. 45–52.

————: 'The Range of a Central Good in the Indian Punjab', *Annals of the Association of American Geographers*, 1963, Vol. 53, pp. 38–49.

Medvedkov, Y. V.: 'The Concept of Entropy in Settlement Pattern Analysis', *Papers of the Regional Service Association*, Vol. 28, 1966, pp. 165–8.

Prakasa Rao, V. L. S.: *Urbanization in India: Spatial Dimensions*, Concept, New Delhi, 1983, pp. 68–110 and 153–70.

————: *Development Strategy for an Agricultural Region*, Institute of Development Studies, University of Mysore, 1976, pp. 140–75.

Ramachandran, R. and V. L. S. Prakasa Rao: 'Mobility and Choice of Central Places', *Analytical Geography*, Vol. 1, No. 1. pp. 17–32.

Ramachandran, R.: 'Identification of Growth Centres and Growth Points in the Southeast Resources Region', *The National Geographical Journal of India*, Vol. 22, 1976, pp. 15–24.

Reddy, N. B. K.: 'Refinement of the Nearest Neighbour and Reflexive Neighbour Analysis', *The Indian Geographical Journal*, Vol. 48, 1973, pp. 1–9.

Reed L. J. and H. Muench: 'A Simple Method for Estimating Fifty Percent End Points', *American Journal of Hygiene*, Vol. 27, 1938, pp. 493–7.

Sen, Lalit, *et al.*: *Planning Rural Growth Centres for Integrated Area Development: A Study in Miryalguda Taluk*, National Institute of Community Development, Hyderabad, 1971.

Thakur, Baleshwar: *Urban Settlements in Eastern India*, Concept, New Delhi, 1980.

Wanmali, S.: *Service Provision and Rural Development in India: A Study of Miryalguda Taluka*, Research Report No. 37, International Food Policy Research Institute, Washington, D. C., 1983.

————: *Service Centres in Rural India: Policy, Theory and Practice*, B. R. Publishing Corporation, New Delhi, 1983.

————: 'Service Provision and Service Centres: Lessons from Miryalguda', in K. V. Sundaram (ed.): *Geography and Planning: Essays in Honour of V. L. S. Prakasa Rao*, Concept, New Delhi, 1985, pp. 189–219.

CHAPTER 9

City and Region

Cities form focal points for a number of smaller settlements (including smaller urban places) around them. Together, the city and the dependent settlements constitute a functional region. All settlements within the city region interact with the city in many ways and this forms the basis of their inter-relationships. The study of a city would be incomplete without an understanding of the nature of its complex relationships with the settlements around it.

THE NATURE OF CITY-REGION RELATIONSHIPS

The city is usually looked upon as an entity dependent on its surroundings, and less often as an independent unit. What is not so commonly understood is the fact that the city and the countryside are mutually interdependent and this relationship covers a wide range of physical, social and economic interactions. Further, the degree of interaction between the city and the neighbouring settlements tends to decrease with distance; this general spatial phenomenon is known as distance decay, and has wide-ranging implications. Closely related to the above is the role of the city in the socio-economic development of the region. While a city may either retard or promote growth in its surrounding region, in the post-colonial world, the city is often seen as a centre of development. All these issues deserve a more detailed and careful examination.

Dependence versus Independence

It is often asserted that cities are somehow or other dependent on their surrounding regions for their existence and growth. In ancient times, a city emerged as a result of the surplus production of food and other basic necessities of life in the area. The city had a class of citizens, engaged in tertiary activities, who were dependent on the countryside for food. The city, therefore, could not exist without the countryside. In the modern world, cities still depend on the countryside to a considerable extent for the supply of vegetables, milk and even grain. In some cities in India these items come, not from the immediate neighbourhood, but from hundreds of miles away. The modern industrial city also depends on the countryside for raw materials of mineral or agricultural origin. Not all industries, however, are dependent for their raw materials on the countryside, and the dependence of the modern Indian city on the surrounding region is generally declining in importance.

On the other hand, one might say that it is the region that is dependent on the city. The city in India today is the centre for a wide range of tertiary services, and the countryside depends on the city for these services. Rural people come to the city daily for medical or educational facilities, for entertainment or for shopping. The city is the focal point for the distribution of a wide range of consumer goods—from clothing and footwear to electronic gadgets. The countryside is trapped in the process of modernization and is, thereby, very dependent on the city for goods and services.

If we proceed a step further, we could even say that some industrial cities of post-Independence India exist as independent and isolated urban centres, surrounded by socially and economically backward rural areas. The modern city is a centre of secondary and tertiary production, and for this it may not depend on the countryside at all. An industrial city may have no meaningful relationship with its surrounding areas. In the post-Independence period a number of such industrial cities and townships have emerged in different parts of India—the best examples being Rourkela in Orissa, Bhilai in Madhya Pradesh and Bokaro Steel City in Bihar. In course of time, however, the interaction of industrial townships with the adjoining villages and towns does develop, in terms of employment of unskilled labour, the supply of milk and other perishable items and the supply of cheap housing for the low-paid employees of the city's industrial establishments. When industrial cities are located in tribal areas, the city and the countryside exist independently of each other. The tribal population cannot meaningfully interact with the industrial city without the basic features of the tribal way of life being destroyed, at least in part. During the British period, the hill stations provided another example of towns totally isolated from and independent of their surroundings. However, over time, hill stations such as Simla, Mussoorie and Ootakamund have developed close relationships with the adjoining hill settlements. Complete independence of a city from its countryside is, therefore, a rare and temporary phenomenon.

A more realistic and certainly the most common situation is one in which city and region are mutually interdependent. The city depends on the region for perishable items of food, for industrial raw materials, and as a market for its industrial products and tertiary services. The countryside depends on the city for non-agricultural employment, for sale of agricultural products and for various services and goods. It is pointless to argue about whether the city is more dependent on the countryside or vice versa.

Distance Decay Effect

The intensity of the interaction between a city and its neighbouring towns and villages declines rapidly with distance from the city. Thus, people from nearby villages, within a distance of four to five kilometres, may commute daily to the city for work, shopping, education or entertainment. Farther away, we will notice a decline in the number of people commuting to the city (in both absolute and relative terms) as well as in the frequency of movement of individuals to the city. Beyond a certain distance, which varies from city to city and is dependent on modes of transportation, daily movements are replaced by weekly or even irregular movements, until ultimately such movements to the city become rare or absent.

It should, however, be remembered that there are always some villages near the city which remain isolated, from where there is hardly any movement to the city. The number of such villages near the city tends to be small, and increases with distance. The law of distance decay operates irresistibly, even in a negative sense.

The distance decay effect may be seen in a variety of situations. Apart from the effect on daily or periodic commuting to the city, the effect is also seen in the distribution of goods and services from the city to the surrounding villages. Similarly, the quantum of milk, vegetables, flowers and so on, coming to the city from the villages is also subject to distance decay. If we examine lists of hospital patients or students attending schools or colleges a similar effect will be noticed. The distance decay effect extends from the city to the outer limits of the city region. At this point the quantum of interaction becomes insignificant.

The form of distance decay can, in fact, be mathematically

specified as a negative exponential curve (figure 8.2). This may be expressed as follows:

$$F = a\, D^{-b} \qquad (1)$$
$$\text{or } F = e^{-(a+bD)} \qquad (2)$$

where F stands for frequency of interaction and D is distance from the city, while a and b are parameters. The rate of decline with distance from the city is determined by the parameter b. This rate varies within narrow limits, depending on the different purposes of interaction within a region, as well as between city regions, and reflecting differences in the modes of transportation used.

The City and Regional Development

In recent times the role of the city in bringing about socio-economic development in the city region has been given due recognition. However, not all cities perform this role. In the past, when cities were centres of alien domination, they had hardly any role in the growth or development of the rural areas. Conflict, both socio-cultural and economic, has been a characteristic and continuing feature of the Indian rural-urban scene from early medieval times. The rural areas were in fact exploited by the city folk throughout this period. Even in the post-Independence period the bigger cities have acquired a distinct cultural identity of their own. Though the social distance between urban and rural elite is substantial, Indian cities today play a major role in changing the social and economic environment of villages. There is greater interaction between the city and the village than before, and the interaction continues to increase.

The city today serves as a focal point for development in education and health and even for rural development. The spread of banking from the cities to the rural areas was a remarkable achievement of the 1970s. In the process, rural wealth has been mobilized for development. The role of the cities and small towns in bringing about the Green Revolution cannot be denied. The city is seen as a key element in regional development planning in India today.

THE STRUCTURE OF CITY REGIONS

The city region is an area around the city over which the city exercises a dominant influence in relation to other neighbouring cities of equal importance. This rather simplified definition of the city region raises a number of conceptual problems which need

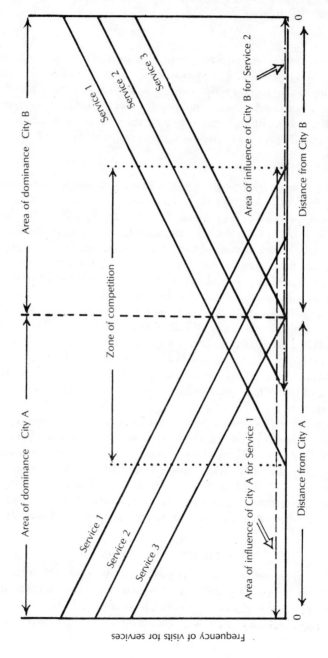

FIGURE 9.1. Area of Influence, Area of Dominance, and Zone of Competition between Cities of Equal Importance.

further elaboration. To begin with one should be clear about the concepts of influence and dominance and how these relate to the hierarchy of cities. When we talk about the city region we make comparisons with adjoining cities of equal importance; this necessarily implies that there are cities and towns of lesser importance within the city region, and, corresponding to these lower order cities, there are smaller city regions. Thus the structure of a city region is complex. It consists of a series of areas of influence and areas of dominance, apart from sets of smaller city regions which nest within it. It is pertinent at this stage to examine three basic notions in relation to the structure of the city region: (a) the concept of area of city influence, (b) the concept of area of city dominance, and (c) the concept of the city region.

The Concept of Area of City Influence

The areas of city influence are contiguous areas around a city from where people commute to the city to obtain certain goods or services. A cinema hall in a city may attract patrons from several villages around the city. The continuous area encompassing all these villages is the area of influence of the city with respect to entertainment through the cinema. Likewise, various institutions in the city such as hospitals, colleges, schools and so on have their corresponding areas of influence. The areas of influence for different services and goods may cover smaller or larger areas around the city and their shapes may also differ. Thus it is possible to visualize a large number of service areas around a city.

The Concept of Area of City Dominance

In any landscape one would expect to find a number of cities of the same or similar importance, and the areas in between these cities are often served by more than one city. In other words, the areas of influence of neighbouring cities tend to overlap; thus generating a zone of competition in between (Figure 9.1). In the middle of the zone of competition one can define a boundary which separates the areas of dominance of the competing cities. Within this boundary, the city exercises a dominant influence—its influence there is greater than the influence of any other city. The area of dominance of a city is an exclusive area and is, therefore, of great significance in terms of territorial or regional divisions. Further, the dominant area in reality is dominant not only with respect to one or two services, but with respect to all services of equal importance. Thus the area of dominance is a multifunctional area, while the area of influence is essentially an unifunctional area. The relationship between area of influence, areas of dominance, and zone of competition are illustrated in figure 9.1.

The Concept of City Region

The areas of city influence and dominance are further complicated by the existence of a hierarchy of cities and urban places which give rise to sets of areas of influence and dominance, one within the other. The city region may be defined as the area of dominance of a city corresponding to its hierarchical level. However, the same city also performs functions of a lower hierarchical order. As a result, each city may have more than one area of dominance. In fact, several areas of dominance fall within the city region in a concentric form. Similarly, for each hierarchical level we have a set of areas of influence representing each service or function. The city region is the largest of the several areas of dominance around a city (figure 9.2).

THE AREAS OF CITY INFLUENCE

Around every city it is possible empirically to demarcate areas that are dependent on it for some service or other. In the case of small towns, such services are few in number and these relate to goods and services of ordinary use. The area of influence for small towns (population 5,000 to 20,000) may, for example, be delimited on the basis of data on: (a) addresses of account holders of a local bank; (b) addresses of patients coming to a private allopathic doctor or government dispensary; (c) place of residence of customers visiting a local cloth store on selected days; (d) place of residence of customers coming for cycle repairs or cycle rentals; (e) villages from which farmers bring their tractors to the local tractor mechanic; (f) villages from which students come to the local secondary school or junior college; or (g) village of origin of persons coming to the cinema house in town.

However, if we wish to delimit the area of influence of a city (population 1,00,000 or more) these criteria would prove to be unsuitable. The city will provide all of the services rendered by the small town and the area of influence of the city for these services can be delimited in the same way as for a small town. However, this is not adequate. The city certainly will provide a wider range of services than a small town. It is necessary to select services that

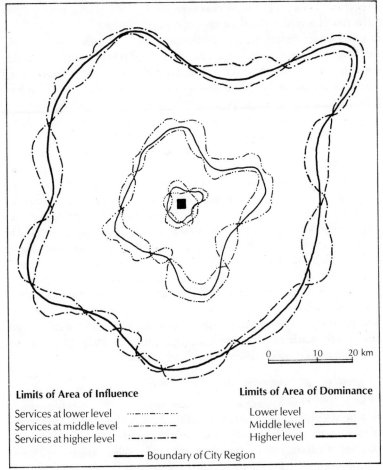

Limits of Area of Influence

Services at lower level	·····—··—·—···
Services at middle level	··—·—·—·—·
Services at higher level	·—··—·—·—·

Limits of Area of Dominance

Lower level	————
Middle level	————
Higher level	▬▬▬▬

———— Boundary of City Region

FIGURE 9.2. The Structure of a City Region with a Simplified Three-level Hierarchy.

correspond to the hierarchical level of the city. Such services in the Indian context may include: (a) treatment by a specialist in a major hospital, (b) college or university education, (c) purchase of high value agricultural equipment such as tractors, (d) purchase of expensive clothing for a special occasion, and so on.

The criteria used to delimit the areas of influence of a city should not only depend on the hierarchical level of the city, but also on the nature of the city's functional specialization. For example, for an agricultural marketing centre, the criteria would focus on the catchment area of specific agricultural products for which the city region is known. For a recreational centre, the places of origin of the tourists would be more appropriate.

For a city or town, any number of areas of influence may be delimited. However, in actual practice their number would ordinarily range from five to ten. In the studies on Indian cities, R. L. Singh's study of Varanasi stands out as a unique and pioneering effort. For Varanasi, Singh used six criteria: (a) vegetable supply, (b) milk supply, (c) supply of grain, (d) bus service, (e) newspaper circulation and (f) administrative area boundaries.

It may be noted that of the six criteria used, four do not constitute central place functions. The vegetable zone, the milk supply zone and the grain supply area represent areas on which the city is dependent, while the newspaper circulation area and the administrative areas depend on the city for these services. The bus service area, however, delimits the area with which the city interacts both ways. The bus service area is an appropriate surrogate for a number of central place services and is a useful criteria for delimiting area of influence of cities with a population of one lakh or more.

Mansur Alam, in his study of Hyderabad city, used the catchment area of students at the Osmania University, and also newspaper circulation. These studies indicate the range of criteria that have been commonly used by Indian geographers to delimit the area of influence of comparatively large cities.

Methods of Delimitation of Areas of Influence

The selection of appropriate services represent but the first stage in the delimitation of areas of influence around cities. However, different methods may be adopted in the delimitation process. Under Indian conditions four methods have generally been employed: (a) the use of published or unpublished secondary information, (b) the use of primary information through interview of customers or managers of establishments in the city or town, and (c) the use of primary information obtained from field interviews of persons from a number of villages in the area surrounding the town.

Use of Secondary Information. In a number of situations it is possible to use secondary sources of information to delimit the areas of influence of a city. This is easier than using primary data, and saves both cost and time. Schools and other educational institutions generally maintain records of students which include the residential addresses of their parents. From this information it is possible to locate the villages or towns from where the students come to the school. The actual location of the villages may be obtained from the Survey of India topographical maps of the area. In some cases local enquiry may become necessary to locate the villages. Hospitals maintain similar records of their patients, and banks have even more precise data on the residential addresses of persons who maintain accounts with them. The exact area served by a bank can easily be defined. Newspaper offices are invariably in a position to provide a list of their sales agents in the hinterland of the city. In addition, one could also obtain data on the number of copies of the daily being distributed by each sales agent. Newspaper data has been effectively used by R.L. Singh and Mansur Alam to delimit areas of influence of Varanasi and Hyderabad respectively.

An overview of studies on the delimitation of areas of influence of Indian towns and cities (of which there are many examples) reveals certain basic weaknesses in application of methodology. In every study in India, the boundary of the area of influence has been defined by a notional line enclosing all villages and towns to which the service is provided by the city. However, we know that the level of services is much higher near the city, than away from it. Secondly, the service is provided only in isolated spots at the periphery of the area of influence, where only a handful of villages may actually be using the service. Further, there are always exceptional cases where the service is provided although the village may lie very far away; it is necessary to exclude such cases. It is also useful, given the depth of the information, to provide a quantitative description of the area of influence. A series of isolines may be drawn around the city for each service to show the intensity of the service. Unfortunately, this has not been attempted so far.

Use of Data from Field Enquiry in the City. Areas of influence of a city may be delimited on the basis of data obtained from interviews of persons in the city itself. There are several ways in which these interviews may be carried out. The interviews may be confined to a few persons such as wholesale dealers, who are then requested to give names and locations of their retail clients. The customers themselves may be interviewed briefly in front of shops, cinemas, dispensaries, hospitals, or other institutions and establishments serving the area around the city. These interviews may include only a few specific questions relating to the location of the village or town of origin of the person, the frequency of past visits to the town, the purposes for which the trips are made, and the socio-economic status of the person. In some rare cases, such as the supply of vegetables and milk to the city, the persons bringing these goods into the city from the surrounding villages may be interviewed. This is often done in the early morning hours at the entry points on all the roads leading into the city. This method has been successfully employed by geographers in India and its utility has been fully established. However, this method can be employed only in the one-lakh cities, and not in the case of million cities. In metropolitan cities milk and vegetables are now supplied by trucks and other motor vehicles. In all field enquiries familiarity with village names and locations is necessary. Adequate preparatory work and reference maps must be prepared for this purpose.

Use of Data from Field Surveys in the City Region. Field surveys in the surrounding region of a city may be used both to determine the nature of the dependence of villages and hamlets upon the city and to identify the competing cities in the region. There are, however, a number of problems in this approach. First, the number of villages and hamlets around a city is indeed very large. Even in the case of a small town (population 5,000–20,000) the number of villages in the surrounding region can be as many as 250; for medium towns (population 20,000–50,000) such villages will number around 700; and for one-lakh cities, this number will go up to 2,000 or more. It is obvious that, even for small towns, it will not be possible for an individual investigator to carry out a survey of all the villages; for medium towns and cities, a sample survey of villages would become a necessity. The second problem has to do with the fact that villagers may depend on a number of centres for some, at least, of the services. In other words, villagers may go to more than one town or city for the same service. The choice of the centre may depend on the socio-economic status of the person; the poor tend to go to the nearest town, while the rich go to bigger towns and cities, where the quality of the service is better. The third problem in field surveys in the city region has to do with the actual collection of data on each village or hamlet. The general practice is to interview the village *pradhan* or *sarpanch*, the village school master, the secretary of the panchayat, the *patwari* or the village accountant, or even the *gram sevak*. The information obtained from these individuals is subject to personal prejudice and bias and it is always necessary to corroborate information from at least three independent interviews in the same village.

In view of the difficulties involved in field surveys in the city region, this approach has rarely been used in India. A notable exception is the study of Miryalguda taluk in Andhra Pradesh by Wanmali. In this study, all the villages in the taluk were surveyed by a team of investigators who enquired into the dependence of the villages on central places for a wide range of goods and services. Though the study is concerned with the concept of area of dominance of a central place rather than the area of influence of a centre, it is a major step forward in the development of an accurate methodology for the delimitation of the area served by centres at lower hierarchical levels.

Characteristics of Area of Influence

After the pioneering work of R. L. Singh, a number of studies of areas of influence of Indian cities were completed. While some of these are available in published form, others remain as unpublished theses and dissertations. Further, these studies have, by and large, focused on large cities with a population of several lakhs. Some of the cities for which studies are available in published form are Varanasi, Bangalore, Hyderabad, Pune, Agra, Allahabad, Baroda, Jamshedpur, Meerut, Howrah, Modinagar, Dehra Dun, and Chandigarh. In this list there are four one-million cities and one medium town; the rest are one-lakh cities.

The coverage of cities is comparatively more comprehensive in the plains of northern India, while such studies are rare in most of the southern, western, and even eastern parts of India. Most studies follow a set pattern, the model being the work of R. L. Singh on Varanasi. As a result, most studies do not go beyond the six criteria, listed earlier in this chapter, set by R. L. Singh. The studies also incorporate the same methodology. There is an excessive dependence on secondary data and less on actual field enquiry. Despite their limitations these studies do provide some insight into the characteristics of areas of influence of Indian cities.

One of the striking characteristics of areas of influence of Indian cities is the near uniformity in terms of actual size of area served for each of the six criteria mentioned earlier. There is, obviously, some variation from one service to another. Thus, in the case of the supply of milk and vegetables, the area of influence covers about 200 sq. km around a city; this increases to around 10,000 sq. km for the bus service zone, and 50,000 sq. km in the case of newspaper circulation. These areal units correspond to a radius of 8 km for milk and vegetables, 100 km for bus services, and 200 km for newspaper circulation. These figures, however, apply only to one-lakh cities in India.

The shape of the area of influence for all services tends to be rather regular and almost circular in most cities (figure 9.3). This regularity is, however, a reflection of the inexactness of the methods used in their delimitation. Most studies are rather vague about their sources of information and the exact methodology used. No study has ever attempted to set quantitative limits to areas of influence nor indicate quantitatively the gradational nature of these areas. In most studies, however, allowance has been made for the direction of major roads, the sea, or hills that act as barriers to the continuation of the area of influence in certain directions from the city. In almost all cases, the presence of competing cities and their effect on the area of influence of the city has been completely ignored. From this it is obvious that the delimitation of areas of influence around Indian cities is still at an exploratory stage. We certainly need more rigorous and thorough studies in this field.

Implications for Planning

The delimitation of areas of influence of individual cities has a number of uses. To begin with, the exercise in itself provides an understanding of the spatial form and extent of the city's influence with respect to one or more criteria. If the criteria are chosen with clear planning objectives in mind, then they become even more important. As an illustration, let us take a modern health facility such as a hospital equipped for the treatment of common diseases. The area of influence as defined from the hospital data on in-patients would surely indicate that some areas—villages—are not served by the hospital. It would then be possible to investigate why this is so. Such an investigation would provide the basis for a new strategy for the expansion of health facilities. A similar argument can be advanced for most social services, such as education at various levels, crop insurance, banking services, and so on. The methodology used in the study of area of influence of a city can also be used for examining the spatial extension of programmes and schemes for rural development. Most programmes for rural development originate from cities. Thus, schemes for family welfare and planning, health, agricultural extension, rural credit and marketing can be evaluated and better organized by the application of methods of geographical field enquiry.

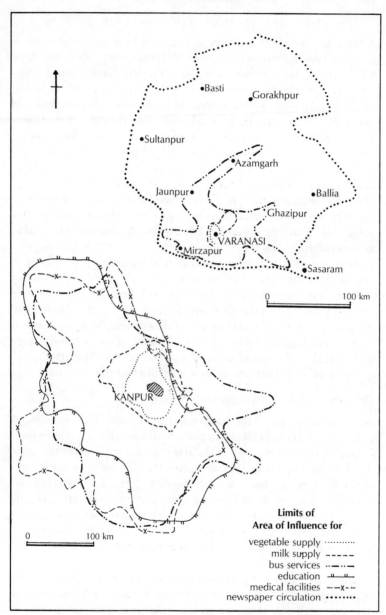

FIGURE 9.3. Area of Influence of Varanasi and Kanpur.

THE AREAS OF CITY DOMINANCE

A town or city tends to exert a dominant influence over a small area in its immediate neighbourhood. It may be recalled that there are several areas of dominance around a city. Each of these areas represents a specific hierarchical level. Thus, for one-lakh cities, we may have three levels of areas of dominance. For example, in his study of Varanasi, R. L. Singh points out the existence of three levels which are designated as: (a) primary, (b) secondary and (c) tertiary umlands (areas of dominance). Mansur Alam, designates such areas for Hyderabad city as: (a) areas of metropolitan dominance, (b) areas of metropolitan prominence and (c) areas of metropolitan association. The largest of these areas of dominance corresponds to the actual hierarchical level of the city and for this we use the term 'city region', while the smaller ones are referred to as areas of dominance.

The area of city dominance is almost by definition smaller in extent than the area of influence of any one service or group of services of the same hierarchical level. This is so because the city's areas of influence tend to flow over its own area of dominance and trespass upon the domain of competing cities. As noted earlier, such an overlap inevitably occurs in the zone of competition (figure 9.1). The delimitation of areas of dominance of a city is, therefore, far more difficult than the delimitation of areas of influence.

Delimitation of Area of Dominance

An understanding of the basic concept is essential in evolving a suitable methodology for the delimitation of areas of city dominance. Likewise, the delimitation of the city region also involves the same set of problems, because by definition the city region is the largest of all the areas of dominance of the city. Three basic conceptual issues involved in the delimitation of the areas of dominance are: (a) the concept of dominance, (b) the concept of cluster of services and (c) the hierarchical level of the city, and the number of hierarchical levels below it. The dominance of a city in any place is relative to other cities.

The comparison of relative influence will also depend on the criteria used. Thus, if we are to delimit the area of dominance for hospital facilities, then we should take into account all places around the city where hospital facilities are available. We can then repeat the procedure for a cluster of functions. While selecting the functions in a cluster one should be careful to ensure that all of the services included in the cluster belong to the same hierarchical level. The rationale here is that, at a given hierarchical level, the presence of one service tends to attract other services of similar threshold and range. The presence of one service in a cluster, in effect, ensures the presence of all other services.

The limits of the area of dominance of a city cannot be determined in isolation, but have to be determined in a wider geographical setting, where the influence of competing centres are also taken into account. In practice, however, this precondition is often violated. Thus, the umlands of Varanasi, Kanpur and Hyderabad have been delimited without reference to other centres of comparable size and importance. Often the city region is delimited on the basis of a single criterion; for example, the umland of Varanasi was delimited on the basis of newspaper circulation area alone. The criterion of newspaper circulation has been particularly preferred by several scholars. Nevertheless, this method is most unsatisfactory, not only because it does not take into account the influence of competing centres, but also because it relies heavily on a single factor, when in reality the city region is a multifactor region.

In some studies, the boundaries of areas of influence of a set of services are superimposed on one another and then the limits of the city region or the areas of dominance are determined by drawing a median boundary or a simple notional mid-line of the set of boundaries. It is important to note that even this procedure is not fully satisfactory, since the influence of the competing centres has not been taken into account. The precise delimitation of areas of dominance and the city region has remained largely unattainable and elusive.

There are, however, a few practical and theoretical alternatives for solving the problem of delimiting the areas of dominance. These are: (a) the use of legal and administrative boundaries and (b) the use of the method of thesian polygons and its variants.

Use of Legal and Administrative Boundaries. The administrative and legal functions of a city extend over an area that is fixed by the government. For example, a tehsil town performs a variety of functions such as collection of land revenue, registration of sale of land, dispersement of loans by government agencies, and distribution of benefits from a number of government sponsored schemes and programmes. All these services are available to people living within the tehsil limits, but not beyond. Nor would anyone living in the tehsil area receive these services from an adjoining tehsil centre. In other words, the tehsil boundary represents the actual limits of the area of influence as well as the area of dominance. In this case, there is no zone of competition. The boundary of the area of dominance is thus determined by law.

The tehsil boundary is a multifunctional boundary. It represents the outer limit of a cluster of services related to administration at the tehsil level. In addition to this, the tehsil limits often coincide with the limits of jurisdiction of the local courts and the limits of police circles.

In a similar way, the district boundary also constitutes the boundary of the area of dominance of the district headquarters. In this case, the district headquarters also functions as a tehsil centre and as a result, it will have two areas of dominance, corresponding to the two hierarchical levels of tehsil and district. As in the case of the tehsil boundary, the district boundary also defines the area of dominance for a cluster of services and functions. In fact, the list of services performed by the district centre is even larger, for the district is a far more important unit of administration in India. All the departments of the state government are represented here, particularly those that provide services to the rural areas, such as health, education, agriculture, social welfare and rural development departments.

Administrative areas of a smaller or larger extent than a district are also carved out by a number of government, quasi government and even private institutions providing services to the people. Territorial units and their focal centres are defined by these institutions and agencies. This phenomenon can be clearly seen in the case of postal, electricity and telephone services. Universities, for example, have legal jurisdiction over a specified number of districts mentioned in the respective acts of the state governments. The universities cannot affiliate colleges outside their legal area. However, students can enroll from outside this area; although in recent times restrictions on such admissions have been commonly imposed.

Private business houses, distributing consumer goods, often divide the country into zones and regions for purposes of distribution of their products. Each such territorial division has a headquarter city and a clearly defined area of influence, determined by the company. Most often, the boundaries defined by private business houses follow the administrative boundaries, for example a state boundary or the boundary of a group of districts. The boundaries so defined constitute areas of dominance for a specific function.

While legal and administrative boundaries are useful for delimiting areas of dominance, they should not be used as exclusive criteria. The limits of a city's dominance, particularly the city region, often go beyond the administrative boundaries. This is so, because cities perform a variety of other functions, mainly economic, that do not rigidly follow the legal boundaries.

Use of Proximal Boundaries. A very simple and straightforward method for the delimitation of the areas of dominance, as also the city region, is the proximal method. In this case the only prerequisites are a map showing the location of all places and information on the hierarchical level of each place shown on the map. To delimit the areas of dominance, only places at the given hierarchical level and places of higher rank are taken into account. Places of higher rank are included because they perform the functions of the lower rank as well. The proximal method involves the use of midpoints between a given city and all its nearest neighbours in all directions. Perpendicular bisectors are then drawn through all the midpoints. These bisectors are joined together to form a polygon around the city (figure 9.4). This procedure may be repeated for each of the hierarchical levels, starting from the lowest. The result is a series of polygonal areas representing the areas of dominance of the city at different levels. The largest of these, equalling the hierarchical level of the city, represents the boundary of the city region (figure 9.4).

The basic assumption in the proximal method is that places of equal hierarchical rank would have similar distance decay effects. As a result, the midpoint between two cities would have an equal degree of influence from either city. Each city will exercise dominant influence over places up to the midpoint, where its influence will be greater than that of the competing city.

Simple straight line distances between cities, however, do not wholly reflect the reality. The alignment of transportation lines, the presence of rivers or other physical barriers, and differences in the nature of specialization of the cities would tend to alter the actual boundary of the area of dominance. The proximal method is in effect an approximate method, which is easy to apply.

The proximal method may be used as a starting point for the delimitation of areas of dominance. Refinements may be attempted either on the basis of secondary information on transportation and

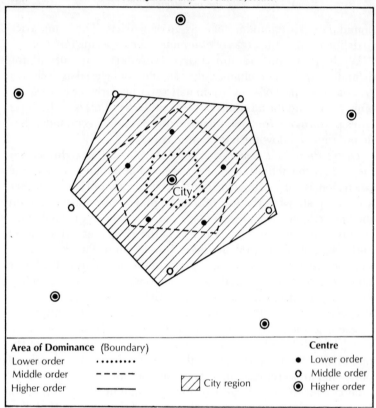

Area of Dominance (Boundary)

Lower order ·········
Middle order – – – – –
Higher order ————

City region

Centre

• Lower order
o Middle order
◉ Higher order

FIGURE 9.4. Areas of Dominance as Defined by the Proximal Method.

physical features or on a detailed field enquiry focusing on a narrow zone around the boundary arrived at by the proximal method. Such surveys may involve a study of selected villages in the boundary zone to determine the actual intensity of influence of the competing cities. This, obviously, would require considerable time and effort.

A variant of the proximal method is the use of the gravity concept in spatial interaction. Here, the assumption is that there are marginal yet significant differences in importance between cities of the same hierarchical rank. These differences may be measured on the basis of the evaluation of services and goods offered in each city or simply on the basis of population. The degree of interaction between the city and other places is then assumed to vary in direct proportion to its population and in inverse proportion to the square of the distance between the two places. It is possible to locate the boundary of the area of dominance between a pair of cities using the gravity approach. However, this will require a considerable amount of computation. The net outcome of such an exercise is often not worth the effort involved.

Significance of the Area of Dominance

The area of dominance has a number of applications in the process of regionalization, particularly, with reference to planning. It is possible to subdivide the whole country, an individual state or a meso-region into a finite number of areas of city dominance. It is also possible to arrive at a hierarchy of regions based on empirical urban hierarchy. In doing this, however, one should ignore the administrative and legal role of cities; failure to do this would involve circular reasoning. The area of dominance is a multifunctional nodal region with a clearly defined focal point or nucleus. From the point of view of planning and its implementation, it has definite advantages over other types of regions. In addition, the city or town which forms the focal point of the area of dominance is also the point of minimum aggregate travel distance within the area. This provides maximum accessibility to all in the region. It is often asserted that the delimitation of areas of dominance is a necessary first step in regional planning for development.

CITY REGIONS IN INDIA

Conceptually, the city region is but a logical extension of the concept of the area of dominance, and thefore the methodology for delimiting the city regions is the same as for the area of dominance of a city. However, for any city there may be several areas of dominance but only one city region. The delimitation of the city region is therefore, important from both the conceptual and the planning point of view.

The city region concept provides an ideal framework for regionalization of the country into a set of hierarchical territorial divisions having definite boundaries. But such an exercise is possible only if we can postulate a clear-cut hierarchy of urban places. While it is difficult to identify the hierarchical level of every urban place in India, the task is less difficult in the case of the more important urban places, such as the one-lakh cities and the million cities.

Numerous studies on the Indian economy have revealed the existence of four primary metropolitan cities and regions. Since Independence, the dominance of the primary metropolitan cities has been successfully challenged by newer and more rapidly growing cities, such as Jaipur, Ahmedabad, Bangalore and Hyderabad for example. This has resulted in the emergence of secondary metropolitan areas. At a still lower level, the one-lakh cities also show definite signs of dynamic growth. The number of such cities in 1981 was well over 200. At the level of the medium and small towns, which number over 2,000, there have been no appreciable signs of growth. As a result, the city regions and metropolitan regions have tended to shape the process of regional economic development. It is, therefore, pertinent to briefly examine the salient features of both the metropolitan and one-lakh city regions of India.

Metropolitan Regions

The colonial cities of Calcutta, Bombay and Madras have dominated India's economic organization since the early 19th century. To this list one should add Delhi, which became the national capital in 1911. Delhi's importance in economic and regional development has seen spectacular increase since Independence, and at present Delhi overshadows the colonial cities in the national spatial economy. The four metropolitan cities between them account for over 80 per cent of the richest people in the nation. They also attract the greatest volume of traffic in terms of goods and people. Their area of dominance includes several states. Attempts have been made to delimit the four primary metropolitan regions of India using data on: (a) air travel, (b) railway passenger and commodity flows, and (c) long distance telephone calls. In addition, the proximal and gravity methods have also been used. In deciding on proximity, rail distance has been considered rather than the straight line map distance. Further refinements are made on the basis of the alignment of the state boundaries and the major rail and road linkages that cut across these boundaries. From all these exercises a clear configuration of metropolitan regions emerges (figure 9.5).

The Delhi metropolitan region covers the northern states of Jammu and Kashmir, Himachal Pradesh, Punjab, Haryana and Rajasthan. The western part of Uttar Pradesh and most parts of Madhya Pradesh, excluding its extreme south-eastern and south-western parts, also form part of the Delhi region. The Calcutta region includes all the north-eastern states of Assam, Meghalaya, Nagaland, Tripura, Manipur, Arunachal Pradesh and Mizoram. Bihar, Orissa and Sikkim also form part of this region. The eastern part of Uttar Pradesh including the city of Varanasi, and the eastern

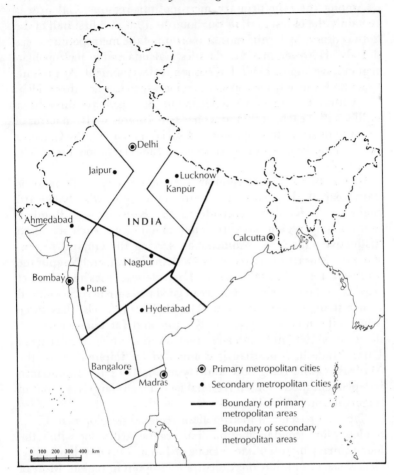

FIGURE 9.5. Metropolitan Regions in India.

part of Madhya Pradesh up to and including Raipur and Bilaspur, form the western fringe of the Calcutta region. The Bombay metropolitan region encompasses the two major states of Maharashtra and Gujarat, besides Goa and the union territory of Daman and Diu. In addition, it includes the south-western portion of Madhya Pradesh, including the city of Indore in the Malwa region. The Madras metropolitan region includes the four southern states of Tamil Nadu, Kerala, Andhra Pradesh and Karnataka and the southernmost part of Orissa and Madhya Pradesh—the area linked by the Vizag-Jagdalpur railway line.

Among the four primary metropolitan regions, Calcutta is certainly the oldest and, throughout the 19th and first half of the 20th century, by far the most important of the metropolitan areas of India. However, in recent decades, Calcutta and its metropolitan region have lagged behind in economic development. At present, Calcutta is the only metropolitan region which has no other million city within its borders, while Delhi and Bombay have three other million cities each, and Madras has two. Interestingly, in terms of urban industrial development and social indicators, the Calcutta metropolitan region is the least developed among the four metropolitan regions.

In the Bombay metropolitan region, the city of Bombay is paradoxically located in the centre of an otherwise backward region—the Konkan. Outside of the Konkan, the Bombay metropolitan region has three one-million cities, each serving a distinctive subregion—Ahmedabad serving the Gujarat region, Pune the Maratha country of the Deccan plateau, and Nagpur the Vidharba region of Maharashtra. Each of these cities have distinct regions, and owe their dominance in good measure to socio-cultural rather than economic factors. The Delhi region also has three other million cities. Of these, Kanpur and Lucknow, within a distance of 100 km from each other, form the bifocal nucleus of Uttar Pradesh. Rajasthan is dominated by Jaipur city. In the Madras region, Bangalore and Hyderabad are developing into independent metropolitan regional foci. This is largely a result of linguistic and political factors.

The major trend in metropolitan regional development is the tendency for secondary metropolitan regions to develop within the four primary metropolitan regions of India. This development is clearly seen in all but the Calcutta metropolitan region. Most of the secondary metropolitan regions seem to owe their origin to the formation of linguistic states in India in 1956. This process is likely to accelerate in future and many more secondary metropolitan centres, coinciding with state capitals, are likely to emerge in the coming decades. In spite of this phenomenon, however, the four primary metropolitan cities will continue to occupy pre-eminent positions in the near future. Delhi's importance, in particular, is likely to increase disproportionately, in view of its status as the national capital.

City Regions

India had 219 one-lakh cities in 1981, which also includes the twelve one-million cities. The million cities perform all of the functions of the one-lakh cities and therefore have to be included in the delimitation of city regions. The delimitation of city regions in India is far more difficult than the delimitation of metropolitan regions, not only because the number of places involved is larger, but also because of other inherent problems. The two major problems in city region delimitation for the entire country are: (a) the clustering of one-lakh cities, a phenomenon that has been discussed in chapter 5, and (b) the absence of one-lakh cities over vast areas in certain parts of the country. In a number of cases, entire states have no one-lakh cities. The problem merits a more detailed examination.

There is a distinct tendency in several parts of the country for clusters of three or more cities to occur within a radius of 75 km. Such clustering is very noticeable around some metropolitan cities, such as Delhi, or around industrial areas, such as the Dhanbad region. In the first case, there is a clear focal point for the entire cluster of cities and it is easier here to conceptualize a large city region, including all the cities in the cluster and with a metropolis at the centre. Other examples of city clusters with a distinct focal point are found around Coimbatore, Patna, Agra and Vijayawada. In the case of industrial areas, such a focal point may not be very obvious. Nevertheless, the cities within the industrial area are not only close together, but also have close economic linkages. Here again, it would make more sense to define a single city region for all the cities in the cluster, rather than individual city regions. However, there is a third and more common kind of city cluster, for which there is no clear focal point or central city. A parallel may be drawn here with the case of the twin million cities of Lucknow and Kanpur. It is futile to argue that one of these is more important than the other. In such cases, the clustering of cities has aspects of complementarity and competition. There is some justification in merging all the city regions in the cluster and treating them as one region. Examples of city clusters with no clear focal point are the Rampur cluster of cities in Uttar Pradesh, the Ambala cluster of cities in Haryana, and the Bhusaval cluster of cities in Maharashtra. There are in all 26 such clusters of cities in India and they account for 112 out of the 219 one-lakh cities. In other words, if

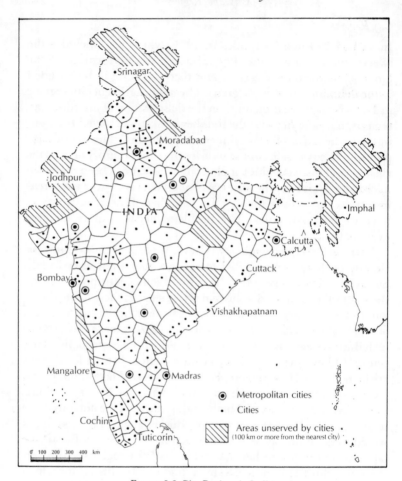

FIGURE 9.6. City Regions in India.

we combine the city regions for each cluster of cities, the total number of city regions in India would be reduced from 219 to 133.

The city regions in India, by and large, are much larger than an average district; in fact, in most cases, the city regions cover two or three districts. In the more urbanized states of Tamil Nadu, Maharashtra and Gujarat, the majority of the districts have a city within their territorial limits, while in northern and eastern India, the city regions encompass several districts (figure 9.6). The size of the city region, therefore, bears an inverse relationship with the level of urbanization.

In several states in India, such as Himachal Pradesh, Sikkim and Nagaland, there are no cities at all. Further, the hilly and mountainous areas of the country have few urban places, and one-lakh cities are more or less absent. The problem is most pronounced in the Himalayan region as well as in north-eastern India. In addition, large areas in the periphery of some states such as Gujarat, Uttar Pradesh and Madhya Pradesh are hilly and densely forested. These areas are also poorly served by cities. In Gujarat, such a region extends as an arc from the Rann of Kachchh towards the east. In Uttar Pradesh, the Uttarakhand region is not adequately served by one-lakh cities. Extensive areas in Madhya Pradesh, western Rajasthan and Orissa also lie outside the area of dominance of cities. Thus, the physiographic conditions and the sparseness of population together account for the absence of large cities in some areas.

Some, at least, of the one-lakh cities, have assumed the role of primate cities in their respective meso-regions. Srinagar in the Kashmir valley, Shillong in Meghalaya, Agartala in Tripura, and Imphal in Manipur are all primate cities in their own way. In other hilly areas, medium towns and even small towns have assumed the role of one-lakh cities. Simla in Himachal Pradesh, Gangtok in Sikkim, Kohima in Nagaland, Aizawl in Mizoram, and Leh in Ladakh are the premier cities of their respective areas and perform a role that is far more important than their population size would indicate.

No attempt has so far been made to divide the country into a set of city regions. This would be a difficult task. Nevertheless, approximate boundaries of city regions may be drawn using the proximal method. This can be done either mechanically by hand or by a computer. The proximal city region boundaries will have to take into account the twin aspects of (a) city clusters in the plain areas and (b) the absence of cities in the hilly areas. Apart from this, it will also be necessary to make some adjustments to administrative boundaries, as in an underdeveloped economy the government plays a vital role in providing services to the rural population. Another factor that may be taken into account is transportation, particularly by rail and road. Maps showing railways and roads may be used for this purpose. The approximate boundaries of city regions in India (based on the proximal method) are shown in figure 9.6. It must, however, be emphasized that an accurate map of city regions cannot be prepared without actual field surveys along the boundary lines to examine the relative pull of competing cities. This task would be a gigantic one at the national level, but can be undertaken at the state or meso-regional level.

The city region has often been recommended as a territorial unit for regional development planning. The recommendation is based on the comparative merits of the city region in relation to other types of regions, such as river valleys or homogeneous or formal regions. The city region as a unit of regional planning should, however, not be confused with the concept of 'city planning area'. The latter covers a much smaller area around a city or metropolis; although occasionally the city planning area is also mentioned as the city planning region. Nevertheless, the city region and city planning area are fundamentally different concepts; they are not only different in size, but the planning objectives, methods of planning and plan strategies for each also differ significantly. A clear understanding of these differences will eliminate the common misconceptions about the spatial framework of regional and city planning.

Regional Planning

The city region has a number of inherent advantages as a spatial unit for regional development planning. The city, being the only focal point, has easy access to all places within the region. Even at the initial stage, its influence in terms of tertiary services extends to all parts of the region. Economic and social planning can take advantage of the existing links between the city and the countryside. Development, it is commonly asserted, occurs in an uneven manner, with cities becoming the initial nuclei of development. Cities play an important role in bringing about changes in agriculture, rural education and health. In recent times, cities have become the new centres of modern industry. In some cases, the leading manufacturing units in the city attract ancillary industries, thus paving the way for self-sustaining growth. The forces of urban and industrial agglomeration not only contribute to the growth of the city, but also lead to the industrialization of the countryside. These notions have generated the concept of cities acting as growth points and growth centres. The promotion of a hierarchy of such centres is one of the major strategies of regional development planning at present. The city region provides a convenient and sound spatial framework for such an approach to regional planning.

City Planning

From the third five year plan period (1961–6), master plans have been prepared for well over 400 towns and cities in India. These cover all the one-lakh cities and the million cities, in addition to a selected number of medium towns. The city master plans generously use the terms City Planning Area, City Planning Region or Metropolitan Planning Region. In addition, several other terms connoting smaller areas are used, for example, the Delhi Master Plan used the term 'urbanizable limits' to connote the area proposed to be developed for urban land-use in the master plan period. The term 'green belt' is also used to designate areas around the city which the planners hope to retain for agricultural uses. The National Capital Region, however, is much larger than the Delhi Master Plan Area, and is actually a unit area for regional planning. The city master plans are invariably concerned only with city planning and have nothing to do with regional planning.

The city planning area has to do with all the settlements around a city which interact with it on a daily basis. In this zone people go to the city for employment and education. Often the area around the city has a transitional character; it is neither urban nor rural, but a mixture of both. This zone is known as the rural-urban fringe, which we shall study in depth in the following chapter. The rural-urban fringe is also an area into which the city is physically expanding. The city planners are, naturally, concerned with the manner in which the fringe area is urbanized, and it is the purpose of the city master plans to specify the nature of changes that are to take place in this area, so that the city expands in a regulated or planned manner. The city planning area ideally should include the entire rural fringe and the green belt. While the green belt is by definition rural, it is necessary to include it in the planning area to provide a legal base for prevention of urban growth within the zone. The concepts of rural fringe and green belt need further explanation; but this comes within the purview of the following chapter.

SELECTED READING

Alam, S. M.: *Hyderabad-Secunderabad (Twin Cities): A Study in Urban Geography*, Allied Publishers, Bombay, 1965.

————: *India: Metropolitan Systems and Their Structure*, Technical Bulletin No. 1, Centre for Urban Research, Osmania University, Hyderabad, 1980.

———— and W. Khan: *Metropolitan Hyderabad and Its Region—A Strategy for Development*, Asia Publishing House, New Delhi, 1972.

Bradnock, R. W.: 'The Hinterlands of Bangalore and Madras', *The Indian Geographical Journal*, Vol. 49, 1974, pp. 10–16.

Dikshit, K. R. and S. B. Sawant: 'Hinterland as a Region: Its Type, Hierarchy, Demarcation, and Characteristics—Illustrated in Case Study of the Hinterland of Poona', *The National Geographical Journal of India*, 1968, Vol. 14, pp. 1–22.

Dwivedi, R. L.: 'Delimiting the Umland of Allahabad', *The Indian Geographical Journal*, Vol. 39, 1964, pp. 123–39.

Ellefsen, Richard A.: 'City-Hinterland Relationships in India', in Roy Turner (ed.): *India's Urban Future*, Oxford University Press, Bombay, 1962, pp. 94–116.

Krishan, Gopal: 'Spatial Analysis of Vegetable Supply of a Planned City: Chandigarh', *The Indian Geographical Journal*, Vol. 38, 1963, pp. 1–15.

Nath, V.: 'The Concept of Umland and Its Delimitation', *Deccan Geographer*, Vol. 1, 1962.

Prakasa Rao, V. L. S.: *Urbanisation in India: Spatial Dimensions*, Concept, New Delhi, 1983, pp. 131–52 and 212–22.

Singh, Harihar: *Kanpur: A Study in Urban Geography*, Indrani Devi, Varanasi, 1972.

Singh, L.: 'The Umland of Agra Based on Bus Services', *The National Geographical Journal of India*, Vol. 2, 1956, pp. 149–53.

Singh, R. L.: *Banaras: A Study in Urban Geography*, Nand Kishore & Bros., Banaras, 1955.

————: 'The Concept of Umland', in ICSSR: *A Survey of Research in Geography*, Popular Prakashan, Bombay, 1972, Chapter 15, pp. 226–33.

Singh, U.: 'Umland of Allahabad', *The National Geographical Journal of India*, Vol. 7, 1961, pp. 37–51.

Wanmali, S.: 'Service Provision and Service Centres: Lessons from Miryalguda', in K. V. Sundaram (ed.): *Geography and Planning: Essays in Honour of V. L. S. Prakasa Rao*, Concept, New Delhi, 1985, pp. 189–219.

CHAPTER 10

The Rural-Urban Fringe

The walled cities of ancient and medieval India stood apart from the surrounding rural areas. The limits of the physical city were then clearly defined by the walls, the moats, and other protective structures around the city. The gates, few in number, provided the only regulated points of entry to and exit from the city. Inside the walled city lived an urban class of people engaged in non-agricultural occupations, and in the villages outside the city, there lived rural people who were primarily engaged in agriculture and animal husbandry. The city and countryside were clearly divided by a discernible and conspicuous boundary—the city wall. Even where walls were absent, the boundary between the traditional Indian city and the rural villages was abrupt and clearly defined.

Even today, the boundaries of all towns, large and small, and some one-lakh cities as well, are clearly demarcated. Even a casual observer in these places would notice the point where the urban area abruptly gives way to areas of rural land-use. The situation is very different in the case of metropolitan cities and some of the larger one-lakh cities. Around these major urban centres, the physical expansion of built-up areas beyond their municipal boundaries has been very conspicuous. Much of this development has occurred in a spontaneous, haphazard and unplanned manner. What were essentially rural villages beyond the municipal limits have now been unmistakably transformed by the location of urban residential, commercial and industrial complexes. The city has penetrated, in some cases deeply, into rural areas to a distance of 10–15 km. As one moves out of a major city along one of the arterial roads, one observes new residential colonies, a considerable amount of vacant land, partially developed residential plots, a few factories, commercial squatters on either side of the road, and further away from the city, warehouses, cold storage plants, timber yards and brick kilns. These features symbolize the physical expansion of the city. The term rural-urban fringe has been used to designate such areas where we have a mixture of rural and urban land-uses.

ORIGINS OF THE PHENOMENON

The occurrence of the rural-urban fringe is a rather recent phenomenon around Indian cities, though its occurrence around western cities was observed long ago. It has been aserted that the rural-urban fringe was non-existent even around the largest metropolitan cities in India before 1950. The main reason for the absence of the rural-urban fringe was the very slow growth of cities in that period. Any small increase in the population of a city is generally absorbed within the existing residential areas. It is only with the flow of new migrants into the city, that the city's residential areas are no longer able to absorb the growth, and the city begins to expand physically, first through the development of vacant land within the city itself and later by the slow encroachment on land in areas lying outside the city limits. Sometimes the new migrants, particularly the poorer sections, stay in the villages around the city and commute to the city for work. Even in this case, the character of the peripheral villages undergoes significant change.

During the British period, a number of villages around existing towns and cities were totally relocated or in some cases dislocated in order to obtain space for the construction of new cantonments and civil lines. This process continued throughout the 19th century and in some cases even up to the period of the Second World War. During the 19th century there was no real need for the physical expansion of towns and cities, given a stagnant or even declining urban population, and in the first half of the 20th century the increase in urban population was still marginal, and found adequate room within civil lines and cantonment areas, which had a very low density of population to begin with. City and town expansion throughout the British period was invariably confined to the development of new cantonments and civil lines. Otherwise, the towns and cities during this period showed no evidence of growth, and all remained within the city limits. The 'native' towns within the city area were often overcrowded, but were not allowed to expand beyond the city limits.

The post-Independence period has witnessed a radical transformation of the urban scene. In particular, during this period, the one-lakh cities and million cities began to grow rapidly; in many cases the population of these cities increased by more than fifty per cent in a decade. This rapid rate of growth of cities could not be entirely accommodated within the limits of the existing cities. Rapid growth of residential and other urban land-uses occurred in a haphazard manner, for neither did the municipal administrations anticipate, nor were they in any way prepared to cope with this problem. Private land developers interested in making quick profits, industrial entrepreneurs and businessmen played a key role in bringing about the physical expansion of the city. The villages in the periphery of the city, which had hardly any administrative or political clout, were an easy target for the manipulative tactics of the new urbanites, both rich and poor. Unlike their western counterparts, the majority of rural people in India are totally helpless against the money power of the new industrial and commercial elite. In fact, they often voluntarily succumb to monetary inducements. The net result is the conspicuous presence of urban land-uses within the rural areas surrounding the rapidly growing cities.

The physical expansion of the city inevitably brings in concomitant changes in the social aspects of life in the fringe villages. The growth of industry, commerce, administration, and institutions of learning, arts and health generate jobs for the rural population. Jobs, even if of an unskilled nature with low salaries, are invariably welcomed by the rural community, who in the past have had to depend on an uncertain and precarious living by farming. For those who want to continue with farming, the rapidly growing city provides an expanding market for vegetables, fruits, milk, and so on. These market forces produce significant changes in rural land-uses and even in the attitudes and values of the traditional rural people. In effect, the rural people change their life-style imperceptibly but significantly over a period of time and adopt a quasi-urban way of life. Thus we have the emergence of a semi-urban society—a transitional phase between the rural and urban societies.

The peripheral areas around Indian cities show remarkable changes in physical and morphological as well as in economic and cultural terms. An understanding of the processes involved is vital to city planning in India. Before various aspects of the problem are examined, it is pertinent to attempt a clear definition of the concept of the rural-urban fringe.

DEFINITION OF THE RURAL-URBAN FRINGE

The rural-urban fringe is not just an Indian phenomenon; it has its counterparts in the West. It is, therefore, useful to examine western notions and definitions of the rural-urban fringe. Wehrwein, an American land economist, was the first social scientist to define the rural-urban fringe. According to him, this is 'the area of transition between well recognised urban landuses and the area devoted to agriculture'. This definition has, perhaps, universal validity and is clearly applicable to the situation in India. However, it is rather vague and does not lend itself to a meaningful exercise in the delimitation of the rural-urban fringe around cities.

Blizzard and Anderson have attempted a more specific definition, and according to them 'the rural-urban fringe is that area of mixed urban and rural landuses between the point where full city services cease to be available and the point where agricultural landuses predominate'. This definition may be used to define the inner (city ward) and outer (rural) boundaries of the rural-urban fringe. The inner boundary is defined on the basis of the availability of city services. In the Indian context this criterion does not, however, make much sense. It is well known that within Indian cities civic services are generally very poor. For example, piped water supply and sewage, are not available in some parts of the city, or may even be totally absent, particularly in the poorer residential areas. Slums in Indian cities have hardly any amenities. If we apply Blizzard and Anderson's criterion here, there will be no inner boundary at all, and almost the entire city will have to be included within the fringe zone. The outer limits suggested by them place overwhelming emphasis on land-use. Again, while land-use is an important aspect, the human factor is even more important, particularly in India, where the rural people have a distinct culture. There is, therefore, a need to have a fresh definition of the rural-urban fringe from the point of view of Indian cities and villages.

The area surrounding an Indian city comprises revenue villages with clearly defined boundaries. Near the city, the revenue villages exhibit urban characteristics along with some rural features. Beyond a certain distance from the city, the urban characteristics disappear and the villages become distinctly rural. The problem of defining and delimiting the rural-urban fringe, therefore, involves the identification of villages having mixed rural and urban characteristics and then setting them apart from their purely rural counterparts. This, however, involves a clear definition of urban characteristics that one would normally encounter in the zone. This is not an easy task, for the types of urban land-use in this zone are indeed very diverse. Nevertheless, before proceeding to an in-depth analysis of the problem, a tentative definition of the rural-urban fringe in India may be attempted:

> The rural-urban fringe is an area of mixed rural and urban populations and land-uses, which begins at the point where agricultural land-uses appear near the city and extends up to the point where villages have distinct urban land-uses or where some persons, at least, from the village community commute to the city daily for work or other purposes.

The definition of the rural-urban fringe given above incorporates a number of important features. First, agricultural land-uses are considered as a distinct rural feature. This is in line with the western viewpoint, but in India the presence of agricultural land-uses is used to define the inner (city ward) boundary of the rural-urban fringe. Thus, if agricultural land-use occurs within the municipal limits, the fringe begins inside the city limits. This phenomenon is common in many Indian cities whose limits have deliberately been defined to include some agricultural land. A good example of such a city is Greater Bombay. On the other hand, a revenue village just outside the municipal limit, in which land-use is entirely urban, with no agricultural land whatsoever, would be deemed as part of the city. A revenue village in which land-use is partly agricultural and partly urban will be considered as part of the fringe zone. It is possible to argue, however, that those parts of a revenue village which are contiguous to the city and which have been entirely built-up with new residential colonies ought to be considered as part of the city. While this argument has some merit, it is much more convenient to consider the revenue village as a unit in itself, for the following reasons: (a) it is a legal and administrative area, (b) the Census and other data exist for the revenue village as a whole, (c) the revenue village ordinarily covers an area of only 1–3 sq. km, and this is very small in relation to the area of the city, and (d) the built-up area of the village and the agricultural land near it are functionally inter-related and should not be separated from each other. If, for example, in any given situation, the built-up area of a village is considered as part of a city, while its agricultural land is included in the fringe zone, this would create an artificial barrier between the farmers living in the built-up area and the lands that they have been cultivating for decades.

The inner boundary of the rural-urban fringe should not be confused with either the legal limits of the city or the outer boundary of the urban agglomeration as defined by the Census. The inner boundary of the fringe zone can lie within the city limits and also within the boundary of the urban agglomeration. More commonly, however, the inner boundary of the rural-urban fringe will lie outside the city limits but within the boundary of the urban agglomeration.

Away from the city, the distinct urban land-uses within the revenue villages become fewer, and in some cases there may be no urban land-use at all. Even in the latter type of village, the influence of the city may be seen in: (a) the type of crops grown (the presence of vegetable gardens, flower gardens, and dairies producing milk for the city, indicate strong linkages with the city) and (b) the employment pattern in the village (at least some adults in the village work in the city and commute to the city on a daily basis). The villages where these distinct urban influences are seen form part of the rural-urban fringe. Villages that satisfy the following three criteria: (a) absence of distinct urban land-use, (b) absence of city influence in farming and animal husbandry, and (c) absence of daily commutation to the city for work, lie outside the rural-urban fringe zone.

The identification of the rural-urban fringe zone, from the definition above, also involves a close scrutiny of the meaning of the term urban land-use. The presence of the following may be taken as indicative of urban linked land-uses in the fringe zone: (a) small or large factories using power located either at the village site or within the village boundary, (b) land developed for residential use by people who come from outside the village and more frequently from the city itself, (c) land used for warehouses, airports, bus and truck repair services, timber yards, or brick kilns, (d) rows of shops on either side of the road from the village leading to the city, (e) institutions such as colleges, dispensaries or hospitals, and (f) water works, sewage plants, cremation or burial grounds and slaughter houses.

A distinct feature of the Indian rural-urban fringe is the presence of both rural and urban people in the revenue villages around the city. This dichotomy is not directly revealed in the Census data, but may be indirectly inferred from it through a study of the literacy and occupational characteristics of the village population. At the village site, the original inhabitants of the village continue to reside and carry on their occupations. The peripheral parts of the village, near a main road, perhaps, may be developed into residential colonies, which brings into the village urban people whose socio-cultural background may differ significantly from those residing at the village site. Here, we have a cultural juxtaposition of the rural and the urban within the boundaries of the village, although social contact between the two communities is often minimal. In most cases, the poorer sections of the original population provide certain services such as domestic work, washing of clothes, supply of milk and vegetables, and so on. The dominant castes in the village often feel hostility to the newcomers.

DELIMITATION OF THE RURAL-URBAN FRINGE

In the light of the definition of the rural-urban fringe given above, it is possible to study and evaluate the problem of the actual determination of the inner and outer boundaries of the fringe zone around Indian cities. Ideally, the delimitation of the fringe zone ought to be based on a field survey of all the villages within a radius of 10–20 km from a city. This area would include as many as 100–200 villages. It is also worth noting that most, if not all, villages in the fringe zone are connected to the city by road and are easily accessible by bicycle. Furthermore, most fringe villages are also connected by the city bus service system. In view of all this, it is most surprising that detailed field surveys of fringe villages have not so far been attempted by geographers in India. It must, however, be reiterated that for a proper demarcation of the inner and outer boundaries of the rural-urban fringe, a field survey of all the villages is a necessity. A sample survey of the villages is not adequate.

The delimitation of the rural-urban fringe has been attempted for a number of major metropolitan cities in India. Among these, the studies on Delhi, Bangalore and Hyderabad are notable. None of these studies, however, is based on actual field survey of villages in the fringe zone. Instead, without exception, they all depend on secondary data on revenue villages, particularly from the Census of India, for the delimitation of the rural-urban fringe. The studies also suffer from an inadequate and ambiguous conceptual framework for the delimitation of the fringe zone. The city limits are invariably used as the inner limits of the fringe zone, and the city here is defined in a way as to include all the contiguous legal urban places. More attention is given to the outer boundary. It is illuminating to examine the variables used to determine the outer boundary of the rural-urban fringe zone. The Delhi and Bangalore studies use the following variables: (a) density of population—400 persons per sq. km or more; (b) population growth in the preceding decade—40 per cent or more; (c) females per thousand males—800 or less; (d) proportion of workers in non-agricultural activities—50 per cent or more; and (e) the outer limit of city bus services or local train services.

The rural-urban fringe may be delimited by joining the outer limits of all the five boundaries mentioned above. All the boundaries, except the last, are based on Census data and hence the unit of study is the revenue village. An alternative method of finding the outer limits of the fringe zone is to use the median of the five variable boundaries. In either case, the basic approach used above has its own limitations. All the five criteria are not in fact satisfactory from a conceptual angle. For example, there are significant regional variations in population density, the sex ratio and the rate of population growth. In high density areas such as West Bengal, the limit of 400 persons per sq. km is unrealistic, when the population density for the state as a whole is far higher. In Kerala, where there are more more females than males, the use of the sex ratio for delimiting the fringe may not have any validity at all. The rate of population growth is generally higher in less urbanized than in urbanized areas. What needs to be measured is the reverse movement of people from the metropolitan city to the fringe villages as a result of the development of new residential areas there. This, the Census data can hardly reveal. The city bus service area is useful in some cases, but even here movement by bicycle is far more important than movement by bus or train. The delimitation of the rural-urban fringe using the Census data can give us only approximate results which certainly need to be supplemented by actual field studies.

The use of indirect methods based on secondary data for the delimitation of the fringe zone have shown that the fringe zone extends from a minimum of 8 to a maximum of 16 km around Delhi. In Bangalore the outer limits of the fringe extend up to a distance of 20 km from the centre of the city. The fringe zone includes as many as 190 villages around Delhi and over 200 villages around Bangalore.

Another alternative to the method described above is the use of the limits of the standard urban areas as the outer boundary of the rural-urban fringe. The standard urban areas were first defined in the 1971 Census and they include all villages around an urban place with a population of 50,000 or more, which are expected to become part of the city in a period of two to three decades. Conceptually, this definition of the standard urban area is consistent with that of the rural-urban fringe; although the standard urban area concept has more to do with planning than with the process of urbanization. Further, in actual practice, the criteria and methodology used to define standard urban areas vary from one state to another, and occasionally even within a state. This lack of uniformity tends to reduce the value of standard urban areas as units for the study of the rural-urban fringe. It must, however, be noted that no serious evaluation of the standard urban area concept and definition has so far been undertaken.

THE STRUCTURE OF THE RURAL-URBAN FRINGE

The city and surrounding areas consist essentially of two types of administrative areas: (a) the municipal towns or nagar panchayats, and (b) revenue villages or gram panchayats. The municipal towns differ in terms of their distance from the main city. Close to the main city, the smaller municipal towns in particular tend to lose their identity and are indeed part of the geographical city. In these towns the level of municipal services is nearly as good (or as bad) as in the main city. Away from the main city, the municipal towns have their own distinct identity and a distinct set of problems relating to urban amenities and transportation. The provision of amenities in these towns tends to be unrelated to that in the main city and of very poor quality. The non-municipal areas around the city, namely the revenue villages or gram panchayats, show complex variety. Some are completely urbanized with much, if not all, of the agricultural land converted for present or potential urban residential or industrial use. Others are only partially affected; in yet others land-use is entirely rural, the only link with the city being the daily commuters. As a result, the rural-urban fringe has a complex structure. The major structural, conceptual and administrative units and their main characteristics are listed in table 10.1, and their spatial distribution for a hypothetical city is shown in figure 10.1.

The rural-urban fringe zone may begin within the city limits, but this is not a common feature, especially not in metropolitan

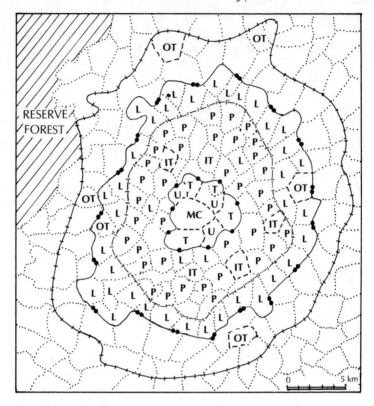

MC   Main city (municipal corporation)

T   Municipal and census towns contiguous to the city

U   Villages substantially urbanized

IT   Municipal and Census towns away from the city—inner ring towns

P   Villages with urban land-uses— partially urbanized

L   Villages having no urban land-uses but having other linkages with the city

OT   Municipal and Census towns outside the rural-urban fringe—outer ring towns

⋯⋯ Rural villages with no urban land-uses and no linkage with the city

⋯⋯⋯ Revenue village boundary

– – – Municipal town boundary

Geographical city boundary—

–•– Inner boundary of the rural-urban fringe

–••– Outer boundary of the rural-urban fringe

–ı–ı Inner boundary of the green belt

+–+ Outer boundary of the green belt

FIGURE 10.1: The Structure of the Rural-Urban Fringe

TABLE 10.1

The Stuctural Composition of the Rural-Urban Fringe

Concentric Structural Units	Conceptual Areas	Administrative Units and their Characteristics
I. The central city (1)	URBAN AREA (1–4)	1. The main city, usually a muncipal corporation
II. The urban fringe (2–4)		2. Other municipal towns contiguous to the above
	THE RURAL-URBAN FRINGE (3–9) / THE METROPOLITAN PLANNING AREA (1–10)	3. Non-municipal Census towns contiguous to the main city
		4. Revenue villages, fully urbanized and contiguous to the main city
III. The rural fringe (5–9)		5. Municipal towns away from the main city (inner ring towns)
		6. Non-municipal Census towns away from the main city (inner ring towns)
		7. Revenue villlages, partially urbanized, near or away from the main city
		8. Villages with no urban land-uses but having linkages with the main city
		9. Revenue villages that are wholly rural, but enclosed by other types noted above (the pseudo green belt)
IV. The rural area (within the metropolitan planning area) (10)		10. Rural revenue villages, with no urban land-uses and no linkage with the city (the green belt)
		11. Towns (municipal and non-municipal) having linkages with the main city, but surrounded by rural villages (outer ring towns)

cities. In Greater Bombay, which is a legal administrative city, the rural-urban fringe does begin within the city limits, and in fact a substantial portion of the fringe is within the legal city. This has happened because the boundaries of the municipal corporation of Bombay have been extended to cover almost the entire fringe zone. In Calcutta, Madras and Delhi, the fringe begins well beyond the city limits. The area lying just outside the municipal limits is an important area of new residential, industrial and commercial development, representing the outward physical expansion of the city. Around the metropolitan cities, this rather uncontrolled urban sprawl is necessitated by the rapid growth of the city's population, and the widening range of economic activities. The area beyond the city limits but contiguous to it, having other municipal towns, Census towns or fully urbanized villages, constitutes the so-called urban fringe part of the rural-urban fringe zone.

The urban fringe has all the appearances of the city proper with residential and commercial centres, but it often lacks proper city services such as, in particular, piped water supply, sewerage and garbage disposal facilities. Buildings are constructed without proper plans; industrial, commercial and residential uses occur within the same building. Plot sizes and shapes are haphazard. Streets are often narrow, winding and poorly maintained. There is a profusion of squatter slums in this area. The original village settlements, now detached from their agricultural land, remain as relics of a bygone age, and are gradually deformed into slums of decay and disorder. Occasionally the urban fringe is well organized in parts, with posh residential colonies or industrial townships, whose access roads are well maintained. These areas have all the urban amenities which are usually managed by a private body or industrial house. Such areas are exceptions rather than the general rule.

Beyond the urban fringe, we have the rural fringe consisting of villages only partly affected by urbanization. The degree of urban impact may vary greatly. Some are least affected; all their agricultural lands are intact, and the farmers in the village go about their daily chores as usual. Other villages have isolated blocks of urban land-use, as seen in the development of residential plots in patches along the main roads, and scattered industrial establishments outside the village site. Occasionally, portions of the agricultural land in a village are acquired by real estate agents for speculative purposes; these lands remain vacant for long periods of time. The changes taking place in the fringe villages are often forced on the people by a set of circumstances over which they have no control, and as a result fringe villages and the people of the villages are compelled by circumstances to go through a sequence of changes in which they become passive and at times unwilling participants.

The rural fringe may occasionally contain a small town or a number of well established townships. These are often designated as inner ring towns. The term suburb is also used in this context, although its usage is by and large confined to the three colonial cities of Bombay, Calcutta and Madras. Between the towns and the partially urbanized villages, there are generally a few less accessible villages which are unaffected by the expanding city. These villages are often ignored for one reason or another. Sometimes, they appear as a discontinuous belt around the city, which one is tempted to designate as the green belt. Actually this is a pseudo green belt, as it is essentially a product of fortuitous circumstances and not a feature of deliberate planning.

The rural villages surround the entire rural fringe zone. In this belt, the villages are unaffected by the presence of the city mainly because of the greater distances separating them from the city centre. In the master plans for city development, this area is often shown as the green belt. However, few master plans have actually been given administrative and legal approval, and so in most cases the 'green belt' exists only on paper and there is no machinery to protect it from future urban encroachment. Within the rural green belt area, one may also find a few towns with industrial establishments. Some of these towns are fully developed industrial townships with residential areas, schools, hospitals and markets. These places are often designated by planners as outer ring towns or as satellite towns. These towns maintain strong economic linkages with the city. People often commute from the city to the satellite town for work. The green belt and the satellite towns may extend to a distance of about 30 km from the city centre.

THE RURAL-URBAN FRINGE: SOME CONCEPTUAL NOTIONS

The complex variety of structural components existing in the rural-urban fringe zone has led to the recognition of a few major empirical and normative conceptual notions. Among these, the following merit special consideration in view of their importance to the planned development of the rural-urban fringe area and beyond: (a) urban corridors, (b) satellites and suburbs, (c) green belts and (d) new towns and urban countermagnets. Urban cor-

ridors and suburbs fall within the rural-urban fringe zone, while
satellites, green belts, new towns and countermagnets lie outside
the zone of the rural-urban fringe. Nevertheless, all four conceptual
notions are relevant from the point of view of planning the future
growth of the city and its contiguous areas.

Urban Corridors

The rural-urban fringe may extend in a linear fashion along the
arterial roads and railways, sometimes to a distance of over 30 km
from the city centre. Near the city the corridor is a part of the rural-
urban fringe, while some distance away it becomes very discontiguous with long stretches of rural land-use separating areas of
urban land-use. These discontiguous portions of the corridor lie
outside the rural-urban fringe zone. Most corridor developments
near metropolitan cities are easily identified. For example, there
are seven corridors around Delhi. These are: (a) the Delhi-
Ghaziabad-Modinagar corridor, (b) the Delhi-Ghaziabad-Hapur
corridor, (c) the Delhi-Ghaziabad-Bulandshahr corridor, (d) the
Delhi-Sonepat-Panipat corridor, (e) the Delhi-Najafgarh-
Bahadurgarh corridor, (f) the Delhi-Gurgaon-Riwari corridor
and (g) the Delhi-Faridabad-Ballabgarh corridor. Most, if not all,
of the above, are industrial corridors with a number of large scale
industries located on either side of the road leading to Delhi. In
theory, urban corridors are of two types: urban industrial corridors
and urban residential corridors. Urban residential corridors lie entirely within the rural-urban fringe area, while industrial corridors
may extend beyond the fringe in a discontiguous manner. Examples
of both types of corridors can be found near the metropolitan
cities. Corridor development, in general, is mainly confined to the
metropolitan periphery and is by and large absent in the area
around one-lakh cities. In particular, the four metropolitan cities
of Bombay, Calcutta, Delhi and Madras have very conspicuous
and fully developed corridors. The suburban electric railway network has greatly contributed to the growth of corridors near
Bombay, Madras and Calcutta. In Bombay and Madras, a string
of residential suburbs along the main railway lines have contributed,
to some extent, to the decentralization and decongestion of the
inner areas of the cities. Nevertheless, urban corridor development
is often considered as an undesirable development, which may
contribute in the long run to traffic congestion and clogging of the
main arterial roads leading to the metropolitan city.

Suburbs and Satellites

The term suburb, as currently used in India, implies merely a location near the periphery of a metropolitan city. The major metropolitan cities of Bombay, Calcutta and Madras are served by suburban railway lines which pass through a number of stations. These places are perhaps the best known suburbs in India. Not all suburban places are legal towns. Some of them, in fact, are not even recognized as urban places in the Census. However, to be designated as a suburb, a place need not be a legal town or a recognized administrative area. Very often suburbs develop as residential colonies within the villages in the metropolitan periphery. These colonies often have high sounding modern names. In actual fact, however, these places do not have a separate administrative identity but merely form part of a traditionally named revenue village. The people living in the residential suburbs, however, identify themselves with the metropolitan city and even claim to be living within the city. Further, the postal and telephone departments consider the suburbs as part of the metropolitan city and treat them in the same way as central areas of the city. These suburbs, however, do not receive the benefits of any of the metropolitan city services, nor do they pay taxes to the city.

Most suburbs are purely residential in character. People living in these suburbs commute to the city for work and are in fact dependent upon the city for most services such as higher education, health and shopping. There are, nevertheless, a few suburbs where large and medium scale industries provide employment locally. In addition, in some cases, the industrial establishments themselves provide housing for their employees. In this case, we have a self-contained township. Such townships with residential, commercial and institutional areas are often designated as satellite townships. Conceptually, satellite towns differ from suburbs mainly on account of the presence of industrial and other establishments which provide an employment base in the settlement itself. A good example of a satellite town is Faridabad, located about 40 km south of Delhi. In many cases, satellite towns generate reverse commuting from the city to the satellite town.

The term 'satellite town' is at times used to designate a place that is at a distance from the city, but linked to it through the daily commuting of people. In this case, the difference between suburbs and satellites is merely one of distance from the city centre. Suburbs are closer to the city while satellites are located farther away.

Satellites and suburbs, in this latter sense, may have a residential as well as an employment base. However, satellites in this case are located outside the rural-urban fringe, while suburbs are an integral part of the rural-urban fringe zone.

Suburbs and satellites are also labelled as ring towns, particularly by town planners. Around Delhi, the National Capital Region plan recognizes two categories of ring towns—the inner ring towns and the outer ring towns. These correspond to the terms suburbs and satellites discussed above. There are, however, some minor differences. The ring towns are in fact recognized urban places, while suburbs include both recognized and unrecognized urban places. The ring town concept is used by planners primarily as a strategy to stem the tide of immigration and overcrowding in the inner city. Towards this end, planners often suggest the strengthening of infrastructural facilities in the ring towns to attract more people there. In practice, the ring towns have not received the attention they deserve and in most cases, the infra-structural facilities, such as water supply and sewerage, remain woefully inadequate.

The Green Belt

The green belt represents yet another planning concept that aims to control the physical expansion of large cities. The green belt is an integral and absolutely necessary component of any city master plan. Ideally, a green belt of 2–5 km in width should encircle the entire city. The green belt is basically a western concept, and more particularly, a British innovation in city and country planning. The fundamental arguments in favour of the green belt are: (a) a green belt, where the existing rural land-uses are frozen permanently, acts as a barrier, preventing further physical expansion of the city, (b) a green belt preserves and enhances the quality of the environment around the city, (c) a green belt will have picnic spots, parks and other recreational areas, where the city people can spend their leisure time, and (d) the original agricultural uses of land will be permitted to continue, thus ensuring the supply of fresh vegetables, milk, flowers and other primary products to the city. The green belt concept is a very attractive planning proposition and, in fact, all city master plans prepared in India since 1960 have included the green belt in their physical land-use plans. Unfortunately, most if not all of the master plans for Indian cities and towns have not been implemented. As such, the green belt exists only in the master plan documents. Even where master plans have been implemented, as in Delhi, the green belt exists only partially on the ground. Some areas initially designated as part of the green belt of Delhi have later been used for urban residential development. Furthermore, after twenty years of implementation, the green belt around Delhi exists neither as a green area nor as a continuous belt around the city. Such failures at the implementation level need not be construed as an empirical rejection of the concept. India has yet to evolve a legal and administrative set-up to protect the green belt.

New Towns and Countermagnets

New towns and countermagnets are also normative concepts that lend additional support to the basic objective of the green belt concept, namely to protect the main city from the flow of new immigrants and rapid physical growth. As the term suggests, new towns have nothing to do with existing towns, but are entirely new in terms of their location, layout plans, and infrastructure. They are conceived as independent townships with residential areas, employment areas, shopping centres, educational and health facilities, and all the basic urban amenities such as water supply, sewerage, and so on. New towns, according to the planners, should be located outside the green belt. The daily interaction between the new town and the city ought to be minimal, while economic activities in the new towns will take advantage of the economies of scale made possible by proximity to the main city. The new town idea has been widely accepted in England, where a large number of such towns have been established around London, Birmingham and other big cities. In India it has not been formally accepted as a planning proposition, in view of the large investment it requires. Nevertheless, a number of townships built by public sector corporations have new town characteristics. The townships built by Hindustan Machine Tools and Hindustan Aeronautics near the metropolitan city of Bangalore, for example, may be cited as examples of new towns in India. But as these townships are not open to the public they could hardly be expected to reduce the pressure of population in the central cities. The new town concept therefore is of limited relevance in India.

A second solution to the problem of unchecked metropolitan growth is to develop existing outer ring towns, or even cities within a distance of about 50 km, as countermagnets to the main city. It is advantageous to locate countermagnet cities farther away to prevent corridor development between the main city and the countermagnet. The countermagnet city, unlike the new town, is an existing city with a well established economic base of its own. Nevertheless, the countermagnet concept also involves large scale investment in infrastructure in the selected countermagnet town. As a result of the new investment, the countermagnets are expected to attract new institutions and industry. Some of the administrative functions of the main city may also be shifted to the countermagnet. In the National Capital Region plan, the contermagnet idea has been given much prominence. But as the idea is yet new, the effectiveness of this approach cannot be evaluated at this stage.

TRANSFORMATION OF THE FRINGE VILLAGES

The villages beyond the limits of a rapidly growing city undergo a process of change that ultimately results in their complete absorption within the physical city. This process of change of the fringe villages may be viewed from two opposite sides: (a) that of people in the main city and (b) that of the people of the village. The first viewpoint has been adequately discussed in the earlier sections; it is pertinent now to focus on the second viewpoint and examine the processes involved in the transformation of the fringe villages, and their effects on both the people and the land over time.

The changes taking place in the fringe villages have, as noted earlier, two fundamental aspects: (a) changes in land-uses within the village (which includes the village settlement as well as the surrounding land which forms part of the revenue village), and (b) changes in the social and economic life-styles of the original people of the village. The mechanism of change in both cases involves interaction between the city and the village. The former aspect, namely land-use change, has more to do with decisions and actions of city dwellers, while the latter is almost entirely the concern of the people of the village. The nature and intensity of interaction between the village and the city in either case increases with time. In order to understand more clearly the processes of change, five stages of transformation of fringe villages have been identified. Each stage in the process of change corresponds to a threshold in terms of accessibility to and interaction with the main city. The five stages are: (a) the rural stage, (b) the stage of agricultural land-use change, (c) the stage of occupational change, (d) the stage of urban land-use growth, and (e) the urban village stage. The processes of change in each of five stages differ significantly and need further elaboration.

The Rural Stage

Initially, the villages located far away from the city and lying just outside the fringe zone are unaffected by the presence of the city. There is, in particular, no daily movement of people from the village to the city for employment or for sale of farm products. However, occasional visits to the city do occur, for medical facilities, purchase of expensive clothing associated with marriages, purchase of agricultural equipment, and so on. The visits to the city are infrequent and irregular and only farmers who are better-off are involved in such visits. For the most part, people in the village carry on their traditional occupations of farming and village crafts and services. The village may have electricity, but rarely any street lights. The streets are invariably unpaved and the drainage system is conspicuous by its absence. The village is not connected to the main city by a bus service. The village houses are mostly built of mud and thatch, and there are very few brick houses. Houses with more than one storey are rare and cement is used very sparingly, if at all, in construction. The physical appearance of the village is not static, for, even in the remote areas, one does encounter social and morphological change. The basic criterion for distinguishing the rural villages from the fringe villages is the lack of daily interaction between city and village.

The Stage of Agricultural Land-use Change

The initial impact of the city is seen on agricultural land-use in the village. The city offers a market for products that the village is in a position to supply, such as milk, vegetables, flowers and fruits. A few enterprising farmers in the village may perceive and take advantage of this opportunity, leading eventually to daily contact with the city. Milk is taken to the city by bicycle, and vegetables by ox- or horse-driven cart. The village, in this manner, becomes the vegetable farm and milk shed of the city. Recent studies of such villages have shown that it is generally the lower and intermediate castes and marginal farmers who have taken advantage of the city market. Well-to-do and upper caste farmers consider it beneath their status to engage in this trade.

What actually triggers this development, this commercialization of agriculture in the village, it is difficult to pin-point, but three factors merit mention. The first has to do with the growth of the city population and, consequently, the demand for products such as milk and vegetables. The second factor has to do with improvement in transportation facilities, particularly the construction or improvement of roads and the introduction of bus services. As a result, the village becomes more accessible than before. The third factor has to do with the village itself. In this case, people's awareness and direct contact with the city increases cumulatively over a period of time, until a threshold for daily movement to the city is attained. All three aspects are inter-related and need to be considered together in understanding the process of change.

The village at this stage is still very rural in character, although some new facilities may make their first appearance. These include dispensaries, higher level schools, and the like. The daily interaction between city and village, in itself, generates a process of social and economic transformation of the village community. The villages in this stage of transformation are by definition a part of the rural-urban fringe, but they also overlap the so-called green belt area. In some cases, such villages are enclosed within a cluster of other villages which have undergone a higher level of transformation. This happens due to their relative inaccessibility in comparison with the surrounding villages.

The Stage of Occupational Change

In this stage, the village population responds to the employment opportunities in the city. In the initial period, salaried employment is sought at the bottom of the scale, as unskilled workers in factories, or as chowkidars, peons, malis, and sweepers in government and business offices. In most cities, the informal commercial sector is dominated by people coming from the fringe villages. Some become daily wage earners doing odd jobs, others are self employed in the city as vendors, hawkers, barbers, and so on. However, it is again the lower castes and the artisan castes in particular, who tend to take the initial steps in this direction.

A concomitant change that occurs in the village is related to the value attached to education. More and more children are sent to schools within and outside the village. The upper castes, who do not want to be left behind, normally take the initiative for higher education in the hope that their children will get better jobs at clerical and supervisory levels in the city. In this they often succeed to such an extent that the social distance between upper and lower castes is maintained even in the city.

The process of occupational change progresses steadily until most families in the village have at least one member working in the city. Farming is carried on as before, but the major responsibility for this falls upon those who have, for some reason, not acquired any educational qualifications. In the process, a new category of part-time farmers also emerges, and as a result the actual farm work is slowly transferred from the peasant castes to landless labourers. Those having no land of their own play a greater role than before in farming. At the same time, women also contribute more labour and time to farming. Very few girls go to school, or seek employment, in the city.

Some enterprising village families also venture into independent businesses in the city, focusing on grocery or clothing stores, cycle repair shops, tea shops, etc. As time passes, the range of private enterprises widens to include almost every type of enterprise.

This stage marks a quantum jump in terms of the spatial mobility of the village population. The village is invariably connected by the city bus service, either as a terminal point or as an important transit point in the network. Bicycles, however, continue to play an important role. In a few cases local trains are the chief means of commutation to the city, especially around metropolitan cities. The village economy is transformed in many ways. Shops selling a variety of urban consumer goods appear within the village itself. Transistors, television sets and other electrical and household gadgets are found in a number of village homes. There is a rapid increase in the number of bicycles, scooters and motor cycles, providing greater personal mobility. Dress and even eating habits undergo change. Houses are rebuilt using cement and bricks. Single-storeyed houses are replaced by two-storeyed and even three-storeyed structures. While houses are improved and better furnished and equipped, the basic amenities, such as water supply, sewage disposal and drainage do not show any improvement; on the other hand, the sanitary conditions in the village tend to deteriorate. Collective action, so vital for the improvement of civic conditions, is hardly in evidence and, as usual, people expect the administration to improve the conditions.

The Stage of Urban Land-use Growth

The growing interaction of the village people with the city, which is the main characteristic of the earlier stage, generates an awareness of the village in the city. The tangible evidence of this awareness is seen in the introduction of distinctly urban land-uses within the village. To begin with, a few plots of land belonging to the farmers in the village are purchased by real estate agents from the city, and developed into residential colonies or industrial sites. The new residential colonies are given names totally unrelated to the village but reflecting the current trend in the city. Plots in the residential colonies are sold to people in the city; this is made possible by the growing awareness of the village location among the city people and the demand for land. Land values in the village tend to increase rapidly as the potential for urban land-uses is recognized both in the village and in the city. The process of land acquisition and its development for urban uses begins slowly at first, but gains momentum within a span of three to five years. As more and more of the agricultural lands of the village are acquired for urban uses, the farmers in the village are compelled by circumstances to give up farming altogether. The transition is rather abrupt in some cases where land is aquired by government or city development authorities. In normal circumstances, lands near the main road connecting the village to the city are first developed for industrial or residential purposes. Lands that are unsuitable for agriculture are also taken up first, mainly because of their availability for sale and lower values. Agricultural lands of high productivity would be sold reluctantly, and are therefore the last pieces of land to be converted for urban uses.

Some of the villages in the fringe zone around Delhi are within the 'urbanizable limits' as defined in the Delhi master plan of 1962. As a result, the farmers in these villages are not allowed to sell their land to private land developers. Instead, they are compelled to sell them to the Delhi Development Authority (DDA), which, by law, is the implementing body for the master plan. From time to time, the DDA purchases land from the people of the villages within the urbanizable limits, often at a price far lower than the market price. Once the land has been acquired, it is developed into residential and industrial areas in conformity with the master plan. Though the urban land-uses introduced in this manner in the village are usually well planned, the beneficiaries are invariably the people from the city, who have no sociological link with the village people. Similar processes of land acquisition and development in the fringe villages is undertaken around other metropolitan cities in India by organizations which have drawn their initial inspiration from the DDA.

The growth of new residential colonies within the village, dramatically alters the demographic and sociological profile of the village. Not only does the village population increase all of a sudden, but it is also partitioned into two distinct social categories. The old village settlement continues to exist almost intact with its original residents, while the new residential colonies house the people from the city. The city people belong to different caste, linguistic and regional groups. The village population is now highly heterogeneous, a fact that is not reflected in the Census data. The social relationships between the residents of the old village and the new colonies is at best tenuous and superficial. The two communities have different values and have totally differing perceptions of the city. There is, however, some contact between the two communities for supply of milk, vegetables, and for domestic services. Much of this interaction is with the lower castes in the village. The upper castes in the village remain isolated from the residents of the new colonies. At times, a third component is introduced into the area. This social group consists of new immigrants from rural areas who have come to the city in search of employment. Finding the city areas more expensive, they settle in the fringe villages, sometimes in squatter slums located near factories, on the roadsides, near drains, and other unhealthy places.

With increasing physical evidence of urbanization around the village, the village site itself receives some attention. Piped water supply, drainage, and street lighting are introduced. This is done by the government agencies, often to allay the hurt feelings of the village people. The houses in the village site also get a face lift; mud walls are replaced by bricks and cement; tiles and other modern building materials are used to improve the existing houses and to expand them. All this improvement in the village site is made possible with the inflow of money through the sale of land and the income from employment in the city. Farming as an occupation sees a progressive decrease in importance, and the way of life in the village is increasingly urbanized.

The Urban Village Stage

The ultimate stage in the transformation of the fringe village is reached when all the land that was in agricultural use is taken up for urban uses. There is now no agricultural land around the village and farming of any kind is not possible. All around the old village site, we have a number of urban residential localities. For example, Kotla Mubarakpur, one of Delhi's several urban villages, has Defence Colony in the east, South Extension in the south, Kasturba Nagar in the north, and Kidwai Nagar in the west, all well known residential areas of middle and high income groups in Delhi. All these areas have been developed from the agricultural land belonging to Kotla Mubarakpur. In all, there are 110 such urban villages in Delhi. Their number has been steadily increasing from one Census to the next, thus clearly demonstrating that the process of transformation of fringe villages is proceeding at a rapid pace around metropolitan Delhi.

In a number of instances, the original village sites are surrounded by low quality residential areas and squatter slums. With the increasing pressure of population on the city, the poorer sections in particular are compelled to seek dwelling space within the original village site. Thus, the population of the original village site acquires a new character with a mix of original dwellers and newcomers. The houses within the village site may change hands. Some, at least, among the well-to-do people from the village move out to better localities in the city. The village begins to decline with the invasion of outsiders into the village site and the exit of the villagers. The level of civic amenities further declines with overcrowding. Neglect of building and poor sanitary conditions reduce the urban village to the status of a slum. The dignity of the original village is lost; in its place is a den of crime and illegal activities including bootlegging. The narrow, winding streets, the difficulty of providing sewage facilities, the impossibility of introducing vehicular traffic inside the village, all preclude any drastic improvement in its condition. The urban village continues its existence as a virtual slum, until it is cleared for 'redevelopment'.

The urban village is in practice and in theory an integral part of the city. It does not come within the rural-urban fringe zone, because it has no longer any agricultural land around it, but it is surrounded on all sides by urban land-use.

THE SPECIAL PROBLEMS OF THE RURAL-URBAN FRINGE

The rural-urban fringe offers, perhaps, the greatest challenges to the urban planner. It is an area of rapid change in land utilization and in population characteristics. While the planner is often aware of the problems, he is unable to do much, given the multiplicity of administrative areas within the fringe. In the following subsections, an attempt is made to outline the major problems of the rural-urban fringe zone and trace the inherent weaknesses of our present administrative framework and its inability to cope with the rapidly changing landscape of the rural-urban fringe.

Land-use Problems

The rural-urban fringe is often described as the garbage and sewage dump of the city. All obnoxious land-uses relevant to the normal life of urban areas are pushed towards the city's outer limits, and often into the fringe villages. The classic examples of such land-uses are garbage dumps, water works, sewage disposal tanks and farms, burial and cremation grounds, airports, timber yards, brick kilns, and so on. The fringe villages are often considered as most suitable for the relocation of city slums. Industries emitting noxious gases or generating chemical effluents are allowed to locate in the city's peripheral fringe villages. The village people have no say in these matters, for the decisions are made by the planners, administrators and the industrialists in the city. This total indifference to village people's opinions is a heritage from colonial days which has not yet been shaken off.

The people of the fringe villages have land which they are willing to sell for urban land-uses at comparatively low prices. Urban land developers, industrialists looking for factory sites, businessmen and others who wish to invest black money, and those people who want to take adavantage of tax laws wherein agricultural incomes are exempted, are all attracted to the fringe village. An offer higher than the current market rate is often sufficient to make people in the fringe villages part with their land. As a result, haphazard residential and industrial development occurs in the fringe areas. The land developers, who are primarily concerned with profits, do not really develop the lands before they are sold. Proper land development involves the construction of approach roads, a proper layout for the residential plots, laying of sewage and water pipes, provision of electricity, street lights, and so on.

The provision of such amenities is beyond the means of private land developers. Consequently, the people who buy land from them have to wait for decades to obtain basic urban amenities.

The proper development and utilization of land in the fringe villages require the preparation of a detailed physical plan for land-use. This plan must: (a) demarcate areas for residential, industrial, recreational, and other public uses in terms of established norms, (b) provide for basic urban amenities such as roads, water supply, sewerage, electricity, telephones, etc., and (c) provide for a network of transportation lines to cope with the increase in the movement of people and goods.

In addition, the fringe areas suffer from concentration of land ownership, speculation on land, and rapidly rising land values. All these require urgent regulation. In particular, it is necessary to remember that land is the most vital asset in urban areas; and in the context of the fringe zone, land can generate the necessary capital, through the taxation of land sale, for investment in urban infra-structure. Far-reaching and bold steps are needed to tackle these problems, but as yet there is no evidence of any initiatives to deal with these problems in any serious manner.

Provision of Urban Amenities and Services

The fringe villages invariably lack most, if not all, of the civic services that are taken for granted by the upper sections of urban society. These include: (a) protected water supply, (b) sewage and drainage, (c) garbage disposal, (d) parks and playgrounds, (e) paved streets, footpaths and street lighting, (f) shopping centres for consumer goods, (g) educational services, particularly high quality public schools, and other English medium schools, and (h) high quality medical services, in the sense of clinics with qualified doctors. In addition, the services rendered by the police, postal authorities and telephone department are definitely of a lower order in the fringe villages. Primary urban facilities, such as water supply, sewerage, etc., are for the most part not available because the city provides these services only to places within the municipal limits. Outside the municipal limits, the small towns and the revenue village lack the necessary administrative infrastructure and the finances to provide these basic amenties. The people living in the fringe villages, however, manage to live without most of the services. Water is obtained from hand pumps, tube wells or ordinary wells. Septic tanks and dry latrines provide an alternative to the sewage system. People do get along with the poor quality of local medical, educational, police and postal services. City bus services are usually available, though infrequent, while other modes of public transportation such as taxis and auto-rickshaws are not often available.

On the other hand, the people in the fringe villages, and the new residential colonies therein, enjoy freedom from payment of civic taxes. They also benefit to a substantial degree from increases in land and property values. It is this aspect that explains the continued demand for land for housing in the fringe villages.

Administration of Fringe Areas

The rural-urban fringe is a problem area for administration. The Indian territorial administrative system was designed at a time when rural-urban fringe development was unknown and in fact totally absent. The institution of municipal administration dates back to the 1860s. At this time, the city ended abruptly and its boundaries over decades were relatively static. City populations remained nearly static from 1872 to 1930. The situation has dramatically changed since Independence. Not only are cities growing rapidly but they are also generating a transitional zone with rural and urban characteristics. However, the Indian administrative system continues to be among the most static institutions in the world. Municipal acts of the 1860s remain unchanged even today. The administration of revenue villages, well established a century ago, has been modified only in the past two decades. The gram panchayats, however, are basically a cosmetic substitute for local self government. They are administratively and financially weak and powerless. It is no wonder, therefore, that the rural-urban fringe remains a virtual administrative jungle with no responsible authority for the management of its complex problems.

The fringe zone comprises gram panchayats or revenue villages and a few nagar panchayats or municipal towns. The gram panchayat is not supported by any administrative personnel; its secretary is often a very minor official with very little knowledge, skill or power to deal with urban affairs. The problems concerning land and land-use are by and large taken care of by the tehsildar and his village representative, designated as *patwari, karnam, shanbag,* etc. The city administration, represented by the municipal corporations, has no regulatory or supervisory power over the tehsildar or the gram panchayat. Problems arising out of the urbanization of the fringe villages remain largely unattended and uncared for under the existing administrative framework.

In all the metropolitan cities and in a number of cities for which master plans have been prepared, the planning of the rural-urban fringe is entrusted to the town planning department of the state government, while the problems of the rural-urban fringe are handled by the offices of the town planning department in the city. However, in actual practice, these departments have only a regulatory function and they cannot directly provide the basic civic amenities to the fringe areas. The master plans for most cities remain for the most part on paper, with no single authority capable of implementing them. The problem is that town planning is a state subject and the states have serious financial constraints; as a result, town planning at the state level remains ineffective.

There are, however, some exceptions to the scenario described above. The Delhi Development Authority has been established by an act of Parliament which gives this organization far-reaching powers to intervene in the affairs and problems of the rural-urban fringe. Thus, the DDA can not only regulate land-use in the entire fringe zone and even beyond, but also acquire, develop and sell land. It has the infrastructure to construct roads, water works, sewage systems and other items requiring major investment, necessary for planned development of the fringe zone. The DDA has built flats, commercial complexes and industrial buildings, in addition to developing land for sale for all these purposes. For the most part, the finances of this body have come from the sale of land over which it has a legal monopoly. This is indeed a novel experiment in urban planning and there is a need to set up similar supra-urban administrative bodies to deal with the problems of the both the city and fringe zone.

A word of caution, however, is legitimate at this stage. The DDA has not, since its inception in 1962, resolved all the problems of the rural-urban fringe. This organization has shown concern for the problems of the city people (including the slum dwellers), while in many ways neglecting the problems of people in the fringe areas. Thus the most obnoxious land-uses, including resettlement colonies, have been shifted to the fringe, while very little is done to improve the civic amenities there. Further, the lands acquired from the village people at a low cost, are used for generating capital which is then used for the benefit of the city people. This is obviously unfair to the fringe people. There is an urgent need to evolve policy guidelines that are equitable to the city and the fringe areas alike.

The Rural-Urban Fringe 321

SELECTED READING

Blizzard, Samuel M. and W. F. Anderson: *Problems in Rural-Urban Research: Conceptualisation and Delineation*, Progress Report No. 89, The Pennsylvania State College of Agricultural Experimentation, State College, Pennsylvania, 1952.

Ganguly, Maya: 'The Nature of the Fringe Areas of Calcutta', *Geographical Review of India*, Vol. 29, 1967, pp. 53–9.

Gopi, K. N.: *The Process of Urban Fringe Development: A Model*, Concept, Delhi, 1978.

Gupta, Kamla: 'Gradients of Urban Influence in the Vicinity of a City—A Case Study of the Urban Influence of Agra City over Its Adjoining Areas, 1971', *Annals of the National Association of Geographers, India*, Vol. 3, No. 1, 1983, pp. 28–37.

Hussain, Irshad M. and N. A. Siddiqui: 'Urban Encroachment of Rural Lands: A Case Study of Saharanpur City (1950–1973)', *The National Geographical Journal of India*, Vol. 28, Parts 3 & 4, 1982, pp. 186–96.

Jadhav, R. S. and G. S. Kulkarni: 'Land-use Planning in the Rural-Urban Fringe of Poona', *The National Geographical Journal of India*, Vol. 13, 1967, pp. 158–67.

Janaki, V. A. and H. M. Ajwani: 'Urban Influence and the Changing Face of a Gujarat Village', *Journal of the Maharaja Sayaji Rao University*, Baroda, Vol. 10, November 1961, pp. 59–87.

Mookherjee, Debnath: 'The Concept of Urban Fringe and Its Delineation', *Geographical Review of India*, Vol. 25, 1963, pp. 47–57.

Nangia, Sudesh: *Delhi Metropolitan Area: A Study in Settlement Geography*, K. B. Publications, New Delhi, 1976.

Prakasa Rao, V. L. S. and V. K. Tiwari: *The Structure of an Indian Metropolis: A Study of Bangalore*, Allied Publishers, Delhi, 1979.

Prakasa Rao, V. L. S.: *Urbanisation in India: Spatial Dimensions*, Concept, New Delhi, 1983, pp. 127–52.

Ramachandran, R. and Bina Srivastava: 'The Rural-Urban Fringe: A Conceptual Frame for the Study of the Transformation of the Rural-Urban Fringe with Particular Reference to the Delhi Metropolitan Area', *The Indian Geeographical Journal*, Vol, 49, No. 1, 1974, pp. 1–9.

Rao, M. S. A.: *Urbanisation and Social Change: A Study of a Rural Community on a Metropolitan Fringe*, Orient Longman, New Delhi, 1970.

Sinha, M. M. P.: *The Impact of Urbanisation on Land-use in the Rural-Urban Fringe: A Case Study of Patna*, Concept, New Delhi, 1980.

Tyagi, V. K.: *Urban Growth and Urban Villages*, Kalyani Publishers, New Delhi, 1982.

Wehrwein, E. G.: 'The Rural-Urban Fringe', *Economic Geography*, Vol. 18, 1942, pp. 217–28.

CHAPTER 11

Urbanization Policy

Soon after Independence in 1947, India embarked on a national programme of economic development and planning. The philosophy of planning encompasses policies regarding various aspects of the national economy and society, which provide the framework for programmes for bringing about orderly change. Urbanization is a natural outgrowth of socio-economic development in general, and industrialization in particular. However, while there are specific and detailed statements of policy for industrial development, agricultural development, population growth and so on, there is no national urbanization policy statement. This, however, does not imply that the government has no policy or policies with respect to urbanization, but only that these policies are not articulated in a collective and coherent document.

The absence of an urbanization policy statement may be explained in terms of the mundane observation that as yet less than a fourth of India's people live in urban areas. Further, the relative proportion of the urban population remained more or less the same during the first two decades of planning. It is only in 1971–81 that this proportion showed some signs of rapid growth. Also urbanization, unlike industrialization, development of transportation, etc., is a spontaneous rather than induced phenomenon. Planning is, by and large, biased in favour of induced changes in society and economy, and is less concerned with spontaneous and voluntary processes. Urbanization is often perceived as a by-product of economic development, rather than as an agent of socio-economic change. As a result, urbanization is at best perceived as a peripheral issue by economists and planners. All the factors noted above explain the general lack of interest in formulating a national urbanization policy for the country.

It is perhaps necessary to assert that urbanization is not a trivial aspect of the processes of socio-economic development in India at the present time. First and foremost, it should be emphasized that a phenomenal concentration of economic activity has occurred around the four major metropolitan cities of India since the 1950s. In lesser measure, concentrated economic growth has occurred in the one-lakh cities, while the rural areas have (with a few exceptions in Punjab and in the South) shown very little dynamism. Cities have been in the forefront of economic growth in the past few decades. More than half the gross national product originates in urban areas, while more than 90 per cent of the government's revenue also comes from the cities. The four major metropolitan cities alone contribute more than 70 per cent of the income tax revenue at the national level. While cities have emerged as the primary locational foci of industries, their role in inducing and promoting modernization of agriculture is also impressive. Towns and cities have become focal service centres for the rural economy. The role of the smaller urban centres is best illustrated by the fact that during 1976–86 over 40,000 branches of scheduled banks have been located in such centres to serve the rural economy and to integrate it with the national economy. Despite the positive role that the cities have played in socio-economic development, the contrast in terms of incomes and amenities between rural and urban areas has widened. Ironically, the expansion of the banking system which was intended to serve the rural areas, has itself become the instrument of transfer of capital from rural to urban areas. All this indicates a need for a rational policy towards the development of urban areas keeping in view the age-old, but rapidly changing, inter-relationships between rural and urban areas.

One major distinction has to be kept in mind in any articulation of national policy on urban areas. First, we have to have a policy with regard to the role of urban places, small and large, in relation to the entire settlement system, which includes both rural and urban places. Secondly, we also need a set of clear policies with regard to the internal problems of cities and towns, such as policies concerning land and land-uses in cities, policies on slums, on urban transportation and so on. The first aspect may be designated as urbanization policy, while the second has to do with urban policy. In the following discussion, the primary focus is on urbanization policy and aspects of urban policy will be touched upon only to the extent that they are relevant to an urbanization policy framework.

A national urbanization policy ought to reflect the national ethos regarding urbanization and urban problems. In India, we have the benefit of long and variegated urban and rural traditions whose interfaces have had remarkable, yet rarely understood, impacts on our culture, traditions and perceptions of both rural and urban ways of life. All the same, the compulsions of the modern age also have a definite bearing on our national policies. This secondary interplay between the traditions of the past and the needs of the present have generated a number of contradictions in the outlook on India's urban future.

Among the many conflicting ideas generated by tradition and modernization, three basic issues stand out prominently. First, there is the fundamental issue of the desirability or otherwise of urbanization on a large scale. The second issue focuses on the choice between an idealized and highly decentralized settlement system with the self-sufficient village as the base and the opposite scenario of a highly centralized urban system, with multi-million metropolises forming the major foci. The third issue has to do with our federal political system, in which urbanization is a state subject. This raises the question whether an urbanization policy should be evolved at the state or national level. All three issues merit further elaboration.

Anti-urban and Pro-urban Philosophies

A recurring theme in Indian thought, from 600 BC to the present time, has been that cities are bad and the city way of life is the embodiment of evil. The opposite view, that the city way of life is an attribute of a civilized people, has an equally long history. Kautilya in the *Arthasastra* and Vatsayana in the *Kamasutra* have defended the urban way of life. The anti-urban and pro-urban viewpoints are linked with the rivalry for power and influence between the three principal *varnas* of the Aryan society between the 8th century and 4th century BC. The brahmanas were always opposed to the urban way of life and all the brahmanical religious texts from the Vedas to the Upanishads have exalted the virtues of the rural way of life as opposed to the urban way of life. In the early stages, the Aryans were essentially a rural people and at this stage, the brahmanas enjoyed unlimited influence and power. The rise of the kshatriya *varna* with the consolidation of territories or *janapadas* under various Aryan tribes, led eventually to the emergence of cities. The anti-urban philsophy has its origins at this stage, when the brahmanas tried to retain their influence using moral tirades against the city-dwelling kshatriyas. The conflict of interests between the different *varnas* led to the emergence of kshatriya religions such as Buddhism and Jainism. Both religions were favourably disposed to the urban way of life and did not see any evil in it. Towns and cities emerged in rapid succession from about the 6th century BC; these continued to flourish and attained a climax during the Mauryan period. The combined influence of the kshatriyas wielding secular power and the vaishyas wielding economic power reduced the influence of the anti-urban values of the brahmanical religion. Later, Kautilya and Vatsayana, both brahmanas, defended the urban way of life. However, the clock turned full circle with the revival of brahmanical Hinduism in the 8th century AD, and the concomitant decline of Buddhism and Jainism. The establishment of Muslim sultanates in North India in the 11th century completely demolished the influence of the kshatriyas and the vaishyas. The anti-urban values enshrined in the brahmanical texts found refuge in rural areas, where, isolated from the mainstream of Indian geopolitics, they have survived to this day.

Ironically, in the 20th century, the brahmanical anti-urban philosophy was expounded with great firmness of belief by the Father of the Nation, who belonged the vaishya *varna*, which was always the most urban oriented. In the post-Independence period, under brahmanical leadership, a definite pro-urban bias has been introduced through the national commitment to socio-economic development. The subtle ironies of the pro-urban and anti-urban schools of thought are difficult to understand even for Indians, and incomprehensible to outsiders. These opposing viewpoints, with their minor variants, will perhaps never be resolved; after all, they have survived for over two thousand years.

The Gandhian opposition to urbanization is well known, and although it has in reality very few adherents, there is strong reluctance on the part of politicians to discard the theory, incongruous though it may be today. An unhappy consequence of this duality is the widening gap between what is stated as policy and what is actually practised.

Decentralization and Centralization Policies

Another policy viewpoint that has come to occupy a major plank in our national thinking is the policy of decentralization of economic activities. This is partly an outgrowth of the belief that the British colonial administration was highly centralized and all power was concentrated in the capital, leaving little scope for initiative at lower levels. On the other hand, Gandhian philosophy underlined an extremely decentralized society and economy based on self-sufficient villages. The need for decentralization is an accepted principle in our national thinking on economic development; an important step supporting this line of thinking is seen in the launching of the community development programme in 1952. The acceptance of the socialistic pattern of society further underlined the need to dilute concentration of economic power in the hands of a few. The spin-off from this rather universal-looking principle in the area of urbanization is a policy for preventing the growth of large metropolitan cities and encouraging the growth of small towns. The metropolitan cities are seen as the outcome of forces of centralization which have to be curbed. Further, big cities have generated big problems, such as housing, transportation, civic services, environmental pollution, and so on. It is at times asserted that big cities are undesirable, while small towns are good for the country and highly desirable. Thus, urban decentralization means the encouragement of urbanization at the level of small and medium towns and the discouragement of urbanization at the metropolitan level. This viewpoint finds strong expression in our national five year plans and in the literature on urbanization in all social sciences. Recently, this principle has been given a high status in a document on national urbanization policy prepared by the Town and Country Planning Organization.

The experience of the decades following Independence, however, does not show any evidence of the effects of decentralization policy in the growth patterns of Indian cities. Despite the criticism of the British period, what has actually happened in independent India is increased centralization in the political, administrative, industrial and urban spheres. Hardly any additional power has gone to the local governments, including municipalities and municipal corporations. In fact, municipalities have been drained of their democratic base and their sphere of action has been constrained or actually taken away by the departments of the state governments, while at the same time, the state governments have become increasingly dependent for finance on the centre. The centre has become more powerful and consequently considerable investment has been concentrated in the national capital, which has grown phenomenally. Delhi is a national primate city in the making, and if we are to judge from past experience, Delhi will definitely emerge as India's leading metropolis, with Bombay following as a poor second. Concomitantly, the other metropolises and even cities are growing rapidly all over the country, while small and medium towns are either stagnant or declining. The proportion of urban population in one-lakh cities has steadily increased decade by decade to over 60 per cent in 1981. The evidence from data on urbanization in India indicates the forces of centralization in action in both the political and economic spheres. There is no trace of decentralization, at least as far as urbanization is concerned. However, decentralization remains a very popular principle, a principle that is affirmed frequently as fundamental. Perhaps this contradiction between belief and reality is unique to India. In trying to rationalize this inherent contradiction, it is noted that centralization is a temporary adjustment for rapid economic growth, while decentralization is only a long term or ultimate objective.

National and State Policies

A third issue in urbanization policy concerns the legitimacy of the very concept of a national urbanization policy within the constitutional and federal framework. The Constitution of India has laid down that local government, including urban government and land, are state subjects, in which only the state governments are empowered to enact legislation. It may be noted that all the existing laws in this area, such as the town planning acts, the land acquisition acts, the rent control acts and the municipal acts, are framed by the state governments and differ from one state to another. The national government in Delhi, according to the Constitution, has no powers or responsibility with regard to urbanization and related problems. Consequently, it may be argued that it is rather unnecessary to frame a national urbanization policy, since there is very little that the central government can do with such a policy statement. Further, it may be asserted that it is up to the state governments to evolve their own urbanization policies. In this respect, urbanization stands on a footing similar to that of agriculture, which is also exclusively a state subject. Nevertheless, the central government in Delhi has a Department of Urban Affairs and does, through the Town and Country Planning Organization, provide advisory services for state governments in India. The Planning Commission in Delhi also has an important role in framing a national urbanization policy through the national five year plans. The national plan is a collective effort, approved by the National Development Council consisting of the chief ministers of various states, and in this sense it is a blueprint for national effort. Nevertheless, national urbanization policy can be stated only in very flexible terms, setting guidelines for action, rather than laying down a rigid policy framework.

The state governments can draw up policy statements on urbanization for implementation at the state level, but hardly any state government has yet contemplated such a step. There is, in fact, a substantial intellectual void in some states. They are not in any position to prepare policy statements, despite the constitutional responsibility given to them in several important areas. During the past 40 years, all the initiatives for policy making and even the programmes for their implementation in the area of urbanization have come from the central government. Often state governments have to be persuaded to take action through substantive financial grants from the centre. This is an unsatisfactory state of affairs. A few states have begun taking independent steps to solve their urban problems, but given the constitutional and administrative framework in the country, it is important that all states recognize their responsibility and take steps to evolve urbanization policies and programmes on their own.

URBANIZATION POLICY AND THE NATIONAL FIVE YEAR PLANS

In some areas of national importance such as industrialization, policy statements have been placed before Parliament from time to time. These statements form the basis for the preparation of plans. In the area of urbanization, such a policy statement has not been placed before Parliament and as such it is not possible to make an appraisal of national policy on urbanization. However, the national five year plans reflect the general policies being followed by the central and state governments.[1] An appraisal of the programmes and occasional policy statements in the five year plans deserve our attention.

---

[1] In August 1988, the National Commission on Urbanization submitted its report, and it is expected that a policy statement on urbanization may be placed before Parliament soon.

The First and Second Five Year Plans

The first and second five year plans were for the most part dominated by the problems of agricultural and industrial development, and urbanization by and large does not appear as a problem worthy of attention. Nevertheless, the first two plans did witness the establishment of institutions for the study of urban problems at the national level and also for the training of manpower in this area.

In the first plan, there is no reference to urban policy. However, the plan did recognize the acute shortage of housing and the rapidly rising land prices in metropolitan areas. It recommended a model act for controlling land prices in urban areas, on which unfortunately no action was ever taken. On the positive side, the first plan period (1951–6) saw massive house construction and land development activity, particularly in Delhi, where several refugee resettlement colonies were established. In addition, a number of new towns were also established in different parts of the country for housing refugees from Pakistan. The response to the refugee problem underlined government policy towards urban housing and land development.

By the end of the first five year plan several institutional set-ups were introduced. A new Ministry of Works and Housing was first established and later renamed as the Ministry of Urban Affairs. The National Buildings Organization was established to design low cost housing. The School of Planning and Architecture in Delhi and a regional and town planning department at the Indian Institute of Technology at Kharagpur were established to train personnel in town and country planning. The Town and Country Planning Organization was also established in 1957 to prepare the Delhi Master Plan and provide advice and policy guidance to the central and state governments on urban problems.

The second plan recognized the need for planned development of cities and towns and also for an integrated approach to rural and urban planning in a regional framework. However, despite the grandiloquent statement, nothing concrete was contemplated or suggested. The Delhi Master Plan was prepared towards the end of the second plan, being the first of its kind in India. The Delhi Development Authority was set up to implement the master plan by an act of Parliament. This, of course, was a major step in initiating city planning and its implementation in India, which later stimulated similar action in some states.

The Third and Fourth Five Year Plans

Urban policy appears to have received major attention in the third and fourth five year plans. The most important contribution of planning at this stage was the diffusion of the idea of town planning from the centre to the states. A model state town planning act was prepared by the Town and Country Planning Organization in Delhi and this led to the enactment of laws in all states. As a result, most states established town planning departments to cope with the problems of urbanization within the state.

The third plan specifically recognized the role of industrialization in urban development. It advocated a policy aimed at the establishment of new industries away from big cities. To accomplish this, the industrial licencing policy was to be used as the primary instrument. In addition, industries were to be encouraged in industrially backward districts and in the smaller cities and towns, which had no industry at all. A variety of incentives, in the form of lower taxation, subsidies for infrastructure, help in land acquisition, provision of electricity, roads and so on, were to be offered. All this, in a small way, contributed to the dispersal of industries towards the one-lakh cities.

The third five year plan made financial provisions for the preparation of master plans for cities and towns in the states. Nearly 400 master plans were prepared as a result of this step. Apart from this, the third plan also made massive contributions to the building of state capitals, necessitated by the reorganization of states in 1956; thus, Gandhinagar in Gujarat, Bhubaneshwar in Orissa, Dispur in Assam, and Bhopal in Madhya Pradesh received specific grants for the construction of new townships. The third plan also initiated urban community development schemes in selected cities as an experimental scheme to solve social and human problems associated with urban slums. This marked a major departure from the earlier approach of slum clearance or slum improvement.

The fourth plan, while discontinuing the aid given to the states for the preparation of master plans, recognized the problem of financing urban development schemes. Towards this end, it established an agency—Housing and Urban Development Corporation (HUDCO)—to provide the funds for metropolitan authorities, state housing boards and other urban institutions to finance schemes for the construction of houses in urban areas. Direct grants were also given to cities with acute problems, such as Calcutta.

The fourth plan also laid considerable stress on the improvement of the administrative structure in cities and towns. It advised the state governments to create planning and development authorities for the larger cities and asked them to give more funds to the municipal bodies. Apart from this, it also made a plea for an urban land policy at the state level. According to the plan document the land policy should aim at: (a) the optimum use of land, (b) making land available for weaker sections, (c) reducing or preventing the concentration of land ownership, rising land values, and speculation on land, and (d) allowing land to be used as a resource for financing the implementation of city development plans.

The Fifth and Sixth Five Year Plans

The fifth and sixth five year plans had separate chapters or sub-chapters on urbanization and urban affairs. The increasing recognition of urban problems and their seriousness was matched by the expression of greater concern for the urban poor. But, as in the past, the laudable objectives stated in the plans were not matched with action programmes. Nevertheless, while the fourth plan was very liberal in advice to the states, the fifth and sixth plans offered more by way of financial incentives, particularly for solving the problems of the under-privileged.

The fifth plan had perhaps the most detailed statement on urban problems and policies. In a separate chapter on urban and regional planning, it laid down the objectives of its urbanization policy: (a) to augment civic services in urban centres, (b) to tackle the problems of metropolitan cities on a regional basis, (c) to promote the development of small towns and new urban centres, (d) to assist inter-state projects or metropolitan projects, and (e) to support industrial townships under government undertakings.

While these objectives were laudable, they betrayed a lack of understanding of the need to deal with urban problems in a holistic rather than piecemeal fashion. The major objectives mentioned in the plan appeared self-contradictory. While small towns were to be encouraged, the plan also wanted to develop metropolitan cities and the lion's share of the funds was actually allocated to a few metropolitan cities.

The fifth plan also suggested actual steps to achieve the objectives set out in its policy statement. These included: (a) differential taxes on urban land depending on various uses; higher taxes on vacant land to discourage speculation; higher taxes on land under non-conforming uses to encourage redevelopment; (b) taxes for mopping up unearned increments in the value of land by means of a recurring tax on capital value of land and property, enhanced stamp duty on sale and transfer of property; conversion tax on change in land-use; and betterment levy on private land owners for indirect benefits accruing to them from development schemes. However, not all the suggestions listed above found favour with the state legislatures. The central government's attempts in this direction were also a failure. For example, the Urban Land (Ceilings and Regulation) Act 1976 aims at a ceiling on the ownership of vacant land in urban agglomerations, but it has numerous loopholes which make it impractical to implement.

The sixth plan also had a special chapter on urban problems. However, these were given subsidiary importance in relation to problems of housing in both rural and urban areas. Still, the plan for the first time took note of regional variations in the levels of urban development. In particular, it noted the low levels of urbanization in the states of Bihar, Orissa and Assam and the high levels of urbanization in Gujarat, Maharashtra and Tamil Nadu. It did not, however, suggest how the problems of regional disparity were to be tackled.

The sixth plan emphasized the role of the small towns in promoting rural development through their function as growth centres. It advocated that the thrust of urbanization policy during the decade should be the provision of adequate infrastructural and other facilities to the small, medium and intermediate towns. Towards this end, a number of schemes were outlined. Two hundred towns were to be identified for integrated development in various states. Grants were to be provided for the development of water supply schemes in 550 towns in the country and sewage projects were to be financed in 110 towns. The plan noted that out of the 3,119 towns, only 118 had sewage facilities; while 1,029 towns did not have a piped water supply system. The plan thus recognized the basic problems of towns and cities and the most unsatisfactory conditions existing in them.

The Seventh Five Year Plan

The seventh plan takes note of the rapid growth of metropolitan cities and one-lakh cities and the slow growth of small and medium towns, lucidly brought out by the 1981 Census. As a result, the plan stresses the need for the integrated development of small and

medium towns and the need for slowing down the growth of metropolitan cities. Towards this end, the plan envisages greater private
industrial investment in small and medium towns to draw the
population away from the larger cities. Further, the programme
for the integrated development of small and medium towns is to be
continued; however, the plan dilutes the criterion for selection of
the small and medium towns to include even cities with populations
of one to three lakhs. It is obvious that the planners are not serious
about their policy statements.

A second major thrust in the seventh plan has to do with the
strengthening of municipal administration and municipal tax laws.
The plan, while noting the sad state of municipal administration,
advises the state governments to give more funds to
municipalities. Further, it suggests land acquisition in concentric
rings around cities, its development for urban uses and resale at
appropriate times for generating finance, and perhaps even more
important, for preventing a rapid rise in land values. The objectives
are obviously contradictory in nature. In addition, the plan would
like the city planners to alter the norms and standards for physical
planning, keeping in view the social realities of India and in
particular the needs of the poor. It also emphasizes the need to
look into the problems of the minorities; reflecting the growing
concern about communal riots in a number of cities.

The seventh plan makes only one major contribution—the
creation of yet another institution, namely the National Urban
Infrastructure Development Finance Corporation, to provide capital
for the development of infrastructure in small and medium towns.

The seventh plan policy statements on urban development are
liberal on advice to the state governments and the private sector,
but deficient in terms of allocation of financial resources for urban
development. The plan, however, makes it clear that rural development should get priority over urban problems, so the tottering
municipal administrations will have to face the problems on their
own.

Critique of the Plans

Urbanization has been given low priority in the five year plans.
Even when its importance is admitted, the measures suggested for
the solution of the problems are half-hearted. There is a tendency
to advise state governments and recommend measures that even
the central government cannot implement. The basic malaise of

an inefficient municipal administration receives only scant reference. The need for regulating urban land values receives strong support in the fifth plan, but there is very little follow-up action.

Certain aspects of the urban economy have received greater attention in the five year plans. These are: (a) finance for housing, (b) slum clearance and improvement, (c) town water supply and sewerage, (d) urban transportation, and (e) the preparation of city master plans and the related problems. In all these areas, the funds allocated are indeed meagre, and even here, the lion's share is allocated to a few major projects in some states, while the other parts of the country hardly receive any funds. There is considerable lip sympathy for the small towns and the weaker sections of society. Achievements on both fronts are minimal.

The five year plan programmes and policy do not exhibit any comprehensive appreciation of India's urban problems, nor do they provide a coherent framework for dealing with the increasing tempo of metropolization and the stagnation of small towns particularly in the less urbanized states. Much of the confusion on urbanization policy has to do with centre-state relations. It is high time that the states took direct initiative in this area.

PERSPECTIVES ON URBANIZATION POLICY

A meaningful and pragmatic urbanization policy should recognize the significance of the spontaneous and voluntary urbanization processes at work in the country. Unfortunately, there has been a consistent tendency on the part of the policy makers to be negative in their approach; it would appear as though the policy has to reverse whatever is happening currently. The opposition to urbanization in general, and the opposition to the growth of big cities in particular, the over concern about rising urban land values in the context of general inflation, the persistent harping on the need for strengthening municipal administration when it is actually crumbling, the continuing emphasis on slum clearance and the reluctance to provide land for the poor within the urban areas, are all indicative of the negative attitude towards the solution of urban problems. Urban policies in India have a Utopian ring. It is necessary to get over this impractical and negative approach to policy making if we are ever to come closer to the treatment of the urban malaise.

In the following paragraphs an attempt is made to outline a

positive approach to urban policy and to identify the basic components and perspectives of such a policy framework. The fundamental
assumptions underlying this approach are: (a) Urbanization is a
natural and desirable process in the modernization of the country.
(b) The processes of centralization, as seen in the rapid growth of
large cities, are inherent in the universal processes of urbanization
which essentially means concentration of people in a small area.
Such centralization is a spontaneous, natural and desirable process.
(c) Within the framework of our Constitution, a successful urbanization policy can be evolved only at the state level. The initiative for
a viable urbanization policy should therefore come from the state
planning boards.

Broadly speaking, an urbanization policy statement at the state
level should cover three major aspects: (a) city size and spacing
policies, (b) rural-urban migration policy and (c) rural-urban
fringe policy. In each area, there is a need to prescribe policy
perspectives that, while contributing to rapid urbanization, will
attempt to minimize the undesirable consequences of the urbanization processes.

City Size and Spacing Policies

India has over 3,000 recognized urban places and well over 12,000
settlements with a population of 5,000 or more persons, which are
likely to emerge as full-fledged urban centres in the decades to come.
While the unrecognized, yet large, settlements may be provided with
additional services to raise them to the level of towns, there is in
fact no need to build new towns. There are, nevertheless, two
exceptional situations where new towns may have to be built.
First, there is a need to build new industrial townships close to
centres of mining or away from metropolitan cities for reasons of
safety and to keep the environment free from pollution. For example,
atomic power stations need to be located far away from cities.
Secondly, in areas where urbanization is at a very low level, new
urban centres may have to be developed for administrative and
developmental purposes, as is the situation in Mizoram and in
Arunachal Pradesh, for example. The policy framework should
identify both the underdeveloped areas and the industrial situations
where new town development is necessary. It should further indicate
the scale of development of new towns in these areas.

There are inequalities in the size and spacing of urban settlements,
not only between states, but also within states. A majority of the

states have a leading city—primate city—with a number of one-lakh cities distributed unevenly and a host of small towns with an even or near even distribution within populated areas. The policy perspective for the development of cities and towns in the states should focus more on the smaller towns. For example, out of the 400-odd districts in India, only four do not have a single urban place; while, on the other hand, the majority of the 5,000-odd community development blocks do not have even a single urban place. Nevertheless, the vast majority of the blocks have large village settlements which serve as focal points for development. There is a need to further strengthen such settlements with investment in infrastructure, such as senior and vocational schools, hospitals, *mandis*, piped water supply, and so on. The growth of primary urban centres at the block level should receive a high priority in any planning process.

There has been unnecessary concern about the emergence of primate cities at the state level. This is an inevitable and, in our opinion, a desirable phenomenon. The state administration is a vital part of the constitutional territorial framework, in which homogeneity in terms of language and culture has laid the foundation for meaningful territorial entities with an identity of their own. For West Bengal, Calcutta is much more than a city, it symbolizes the very essence of modern Bengal; it is a cultural and economic nerve centre, and above all it gives the people of Bengal a sense of belonging. Similar statements can be made in relation to other states. Furthermore, the state administration, like its counterpart at the centre, has intrinsic centralizing qualities and the state capitals are bound to emerge as leading cities even in those states where they are not already so. The general policy, therefore, should be one that encourages the growth of cities, big or small. The bigger cities, in particular, deserve attention for the improvement of water supply, sewerage, transportation, milk supply, and so on. They offer opportunities for land development and provision of housing on a large scale, and the rising land and property values can provide the basic financial resources for such development. The policy framework should aim at a system of self-financing investment in big cities and, if necessary, subsidized investment in the small towns. In small towns, land and property values do not increase so rapidly and the rate of growth is also low. In such a situation, investment, particluarly for infrastructural facilities, needs to be subsidized.

Rural-Urban Migration Policies

An anti-urban bias naturally also generates a negative attitude to rural-urban migration. At one extreme, we have the Gandhian philosophy of 'back to the village', a prescription that is now universally accepted as Utopian. Nevertheless, even those who have no faith in the notion of 'back to the village', tend to cling to the belief that migration to the bigger cities is undesirable and therefore ought to be curbed. However, the Constitution under article 19(1) guarantees to every citizen the right to 'move freely throughout the territory of India' and 'to reside and settle in any part of the territory of India'. While reasonable restrictions on movement for reasons of national security, public order and public health can be made, a total ban on migration of people to cities cannot be sustained under the Constitution. No democratic country in the world can restrict the entry of people into cities for purposes of settling there. Migration is, by and large, voluntary and spontaneous, and there is no point in trying to arrest this process.

The reasons that prompt people to migrate to the cities are many and varied. Apart from dislocations due to war, partition and natural calamities, the root cause of migration lies in the basic urge to better one's life. Rural-urban migration is not restricted to the rural poor or the rural unemployed, as some would have us believe, but is even more common among the rural rich. The upper castes and the richer sections of rural society crave the city way of life, while the poor hope to get rid of their problems by migrating to the city. Nor is the migration of people to the cities a total debt to the city: in fact, the village people bring skills and they often find means of self employment in the city. Further, when the rural rich migrate, capital flows occur from village to city. The city, in fact, is a net beneficiary of rural-urban migration and there is no reason why cities should consider immigration as a burden. It is fashionable to attribute all the city's problems to the influx of people into it, but if we examine the levels of city services in earlier periods and compare them to the present level, most cities are better off today than before, despite immigration. A rational urbanization policy should encourage rather than discourage rural-urban migration.

Rural-urban migration is at the present time confined primarily to metropolitan cities and, to a lesser extent, one-lakh cities. This is the natural consequence of the forces of centralization. The major problem is that while the current policies and programmes adequately serve the interests of the well-to-do immigrants and the richer sections of urban society, the poor immigrants are left to fend for themselves. As a result squatter slums tend to multiply in big cities. It is, therefore, necessary to reorient our policies to provide adequate urban land for the settlement of new immigrants who come from the poorer sections of rural society. The poor people need residential plots of 20 sq. m, on which they can themselves build houses using readily available and cheaper materials. The city residential colonies do not provide for residential plots for the poor. In fact, the provision of 20 sq. m plots in each new residential colony ought to be mandatory and such plots should cover at least one-fourth of the total area of every colony. In India, the rich and poor live side by side and there is a symbiotic relationship between the two. There is absolutely no justification for spatial separation of the rich and the poor, which appears to be the fundamental basis of western city planning.

In the smaller towns, the provision of urban amenities and social infrastructure, although necessary, mainly serves the rural rich. It is imperative that the rural poor are aided by the provision of residential land in the small towns along with employment opportunities. Another area where the poor could be helped is the area of vocational education in small towns. The provision of such facilities in towns at the block level would make education accessible and relevant.

Rural-Urban Fringe Policies

Urbanization policy cannot simply be treated as an isolated problem of cities and towns, but the regional impact of urbanization needs to be examined as well. In particular, the areas in the immediate periphery of large cities deserve the attention of policy makers. The rural-urban fringe has suffered from neglect from both ends— rural as well as urban—of policy and decision making. It is necessary that in framing an urbanization policy in any state, due attention should be given to the rural-urban fringe.

The problems of the fringe zone are indeed many and varied. In particular they encompass three major areas: the growth of urban land-uses, the problem of urban amenities, and the problem of administration. Above all, the problem of the rural-urban fringe is a human problem—the problem of the original residents of the fringe, who are compelled by circumstances to give up the rural way of life. The problems of the original fringe population have totally been neglected in the past, and there is a need for policy orientation to correct this. Such a policy should cover the following areas: (a) fair and just compensation for land acquired for urban uses, (b) provision of adequate facilities for vocational training of youth in the fringe areas, so that they may be gainfully employed in urban occupations, (c) financial and technical help to enable the rural people whose lands are taken away to establish small scale industries, and (d) the improvement of civic amenities in the village site and the improvement of housing therein.

One of the major challenges of the rural-urban fringe is the haphazard location of major urban land-uses. The fringe zone is often used as the peripheral dumping ground, both literally and in a symbolic sense. Most unpleasant land-uses in the city are shifted to or located in the fringe zone. In recent times, the fringe zone has been used for the relocation of slums, which are uprooted from the city. This phenomenon underlines an attitude which is basically unfair, and which has to change. While the fringe may have to be developed for the physical expansion of the city, this expansion ought to be well planned, and the fringe area must be made as attractive as, and perhaps even more attractive than, the city area. There is no reason why fringe areas cannot be developed keeping in mind the quality of the environment. Given a high quality environment, even the rich in the city would migrate to the fringe zone. The present rich-poor relationship between the city areas and fringe areas ought to be reversed by appropriate policy and planning methods. This would require land-use planning and land zoning regulations as well as investment in urban infrastructure and amenities.

The problems of the rural-urban fringe cannot be resolved within the existing administrative framework. There is a need to evolve new patterns of administration of the fringe zone. Unfortunately, even the constitution of supra-urban authorities, such as the Delhi Development Authority, has not solved the problems of the fringe people. In fact, there is a feeling that such authorities are established for solving the problems of the city and not of the fringe. There is no feeling of empathy for the fringe people among the administrators of the supra-urban bodies. The fringe, under these bodies, is treated as the city's dumping ground. The administrative problems of the fringe zone can be solved only by setting up separate bodies or authorities for dealing with the zone. While conflicts between the city planning bodies and the fringe administration are bound to arise, the interests of the fringe zone are not likely to be served by city based planning bodies. A fresh look at the administrative framework for city and city region planning in the Indian context is necessary.

EPILOGUE

The rich historical heritage of urbanization in India has been severely tarnished in the aftermath of the industrial revolution. The medieval Indian city symbolized unity, grandeur and liveliness of culture and trade; this has given way to cities of heterogeneous accretional components tied together by a system of mass transportation of questionable efficiency, with a multitude of unsolved problems of housing, services and employment. The colonial heritage has only complicated the problems, without offering any solutions. Very hesitant and often fumbling attempts have been made since the 1960s to deal with the problems of cities, particularly the metropolitan cities. Much more needs to be done if we are to cope with the rising tide of urbanization. India's urban population may increase from about 160 million in 1981 to over 300 million in the year 2000, with perhaps 40 one-million cities, 500 one-lakh cities, and over 5,000 urban places in all. In many ways, the price of inaction or inadequate action may well fall heavily on metropolitan cities which may break under the strain of their own population growth; while the smaller one-lakh cities, would, in all probability, be able to cope with both the rising populations and problems arising out of the world energy crisis. The infinite resilience and flexibility of the Indian people, and their ability to adjust to new and excruciating circumstances, will save the cities, even if planners and politicians fail to do the right thing at the right time. The indomitable strength of the people provides hope for India's urban future.

SELECTED READING

Aichbhaumik, Debajyoti: 'Indian Policy on Industrialisation, Urbanisation, and Industrial New Town Development', in Gideon Golany, ed., *International Urban Growth Policies*, John Wiley & Sons, New York, 1978, pp. 231–48.

Bhargava, Gopal: *Urban Problems and Policy Perspectives*, Abhinav Publications, New Delhi, 1981, pp. 47–76.

Bose, Ashish: *India's Urbanisation—1901–2001*, Tata McGraw Hill, New Delhi, 1978, pp. 257–333.

—:'Evolution of Urban Policy in India 1947–78', in Hanumantha Rao and P. C.

Joshi, eds., *Reflections on Economic Development and Social Change*, Allied Publications, New Delhi, 1979, pp. 339–62.

Breeze, Gerald: 'Urban Development Problems in India', *Annals of the Association of American Geographers*, Vol. 53, 1963, pp. 253–65.

Harris, B.: 'Urbanisation Policy in India', *Papers and Proceedings of the Regional Science Association*, Vol. 5, 1959, pp. 181–201.

Jakobson, Leo and Ved Prakash, eds.: *Metropolitan Growth: Public Policy for South and Southeast Asia*, Sage Publications, New York, 1974, pp. 259–92.

Lewis J. P.: *Quiet Crisis in India*, Brookings Institute, Washington, D.C., 1962, pp. 197–9.

Prakasa Rao, V. L. S.: *Urbanisation in India: Spatial Dimensions*, Concept, New Delhi, 1983, pp. 291–305.

Misra, R. P.: 'Towards a Perspective Urbanisation Policy', in R. P. Misra, ed., *Million Cities in India*, Vikas Publishing House, Delhi, 1978, pp. 346–66.

National Council of Applied Economic Research: *Market Towns and Spatial Development*, NCAER, New Delhi, 1972, pp. 17–29.

Sundaram, K. V.: *Urban and Regional Planning in India*, Vikas, New Delhi, 1977.

Town and Country Planning Organization: *National Urbanisation Policy: An Approach*, Ministry of Works and Housing, New Delhi, 1974.

Wishwakarma, R. K.: *Urban and Regional Planning Policy in India*, Uppal Publishing House, New Delhi, 1981.

Indian Cities: Selected Characteristics

Name of City/Urban Agglomeration	Population 1981 (in lakhs)	Number of Towns and Other Units in Agglomeration	Growth Rate 1971–1981	Sex Ratio	Literacy Rate	Functional Type	Climatic Type	Year of Origin
1	2	3	4	5	6	7	8	9
Calcutta	91.6	107	30	783	66	Tg(C)	C	1690
Greater Bombay	82.2	—	38	773	68	Mf(B)	C	1532
Delhi	57.1	25	57	808	62	SS(D)	NI	1030
Madras	42.8	49	35	930	66	Tg(C)	C	1639
Bangalore	29.1	97	76	893	63	Mf(C)	P	1700
Hyderabad	25.3	24	41	920	56	Tg(D)	NI	1589
Ahmedabad	25.2	32	44	868	61	Mf(A)	NI	1413
Kanpur	16.9	8	32	810	55	Mf(D)	NI	1800
Pune	16.9	9	48	881	67	Mf(C)	P	1721
Nagpur	13.0	3	40	910	66	Mf(C)	SI	1500
Lucknow	10.1	6	24	832	57	SS(C)	NI	1400
Jaipur	10.0	3	58	867	54	SS(D)	NI	1730
Coimbatore	9.2	17	25	924	66	Tg(C)	SI	1800
Patna	9.2	6	87	816	58	SS(C)	NI	400 BC
Surat	9.1	9	85	843	60	Mf(A)	C	200 BC
Madurai	9.0	10	27	954	67	Mf(C)	SI	300 BC
Indore	8.3	—	47	887	61	Mf(C)	P	1661
Varanasi	7.9	12	31	844	47	MA(C)	NI	600 BC
Agra	7.7	4	21	854	46	Mf(C)	NI	1506
Jabalpur	7.6	17	42	846	61	Mf(D)	NI	200
Vadodara	7.4	2	59	890	68	Mf(D)	NI	1000
Cochin	6.9	5	—	982	78	Tg(D)	C	200
Dhanbad	6.8	17	56	737	50	Tt(A)	NI	1860
Bhopal	6.7	—	75	866	57	SS(B)	P	1500
Jamshedpur	6.7	7	47	846	57	Mf(A)	NI	1911
Ulhasnagar	6.5	6	64	876	64	Mf(A)	C	1950
Allahabad	6.4	3	25	814	59	SS(C)	NI	300 BC
Tiruchirappalli	6.1	12	31	952	69	Tg(B)	SI	850
Ludhiana	6.1	—	51	809	66	Mf(A)	NI	1481
Vishakhapatnam	5.9	3	64	925	57	Tt(C)	C	900
Amritsar	5.9	—	35	838	59	Tg(C)	NI	1500

APPENDIX *(Continued)*

1	2	3	4	5	6	7	8	9
Srinagar	5.9	14	43	870	39	Mt(D)	H	700
Gwalior	5.6	2	38	859	53	Mf(C)	NI	1030
Calicut	5.5	5	—	1007	73	Tg(D)	C	1325
Vijayawada	5.4	6	58	968	59	Tg(A)	SI	629
Meerut	5.4	4	46	842	51	Mf(D)	NI	1030
Hubli-Dharwar	5.3	—	39	912	58	Tg(C)	P	1325
Trivandrum	5.2	3	—	1006	76	SS(B)	C	1700
Salem	5.2	19	24	952	56	Mf(A)	SI	1800
Solapur	5.1	2	—	933	53	Mf(A)	SI	850
Ranchi	5.0	2	96	821	64	Tg(D)	P	1800
Jodhpur	4.9	—	55	875	52	SS(D)	D	1465
Durg-Bhilainagar	4.9	12	100	873	56	Mf(A)	SI	1960
Mysore	4.8	14	34	938	62	Tg(D)	P	1799
Rajkot	4.4	—	48	928	64	Mf(D)	NI	1500
Bareilly	4.4	10	34	843	47	Tg(D)	NI	1500
Nasik	4.3	5	58	838	67	Mf(D)	P	200 BC
Chandigarh	4.2	7	81	776	66	SS(A)	NI	1956
Jalandhar	4.1	—	37	851	60	Mf(C)	NI	700
Thane	3.9	3	87	806	69	Mf(A)	C	1030
Ajmer	3.7	—	42	900	61	Tt(B)	P	700
Guntur	3.7	—	36	966	49	Mf(B)	SI	1500
Asansol	3.7	13	51	787	57	Tt(A)	NI	1860
Kolhapur	3.5	2	31	901	67	Mf(C)	P	1400
Moradabad	3.5	2	28	858	41	Mf(D)	NI	1624
Kota	3.5	—	63	859	55	Mf(D)	NI	1264
Raipur (M.P.)	3.4	—	65	909	57	Tg(C)	SI	1360
Warangal	3.3	—	62	935	52	Mf(C)	SI	200
Faridabad	3.3	—	—	741	57	Mf(A)	NI	1950
Cuttack	3.3	5	42	791	63	Tg(C)	SI	200
Tirunelveli	3.2	11	23	1005	63	Tg(B)	SI	1325
Rourkela	3.2	4	86	792	60	Mf(B)	SI	1960
Aligarh	3.2	—	27	867	45	Mf(D)	NI	1300
Jamnagar	3.2	7	39	915	56	Mf(D)	C	1500
Aurangabad	3.2	3	91	858	59	SS(D)	P	1636
Bhavnagar	3.1	2	36	925	60	Tg(D)	C	1500
Gorakhpur	3.1	4	—	831	59	Tt(B)	NI	200
Durgapur	3.1	—	48	822	67	Mf(A)	NI	1960
Mangalore	3.1	20	37	1007	70	Mf(B)	C	1325
Belgaum	3.0	3	40	894	66	Mf(C)	P	1300
Saharanpur	2.9	—	31	860	49	Tg(C)	NI	1500
Dehra Dun	2.9	6	44	799	67	SS(A)	P	1800
Ghaziabad	2.9	3	129	792	52	Mf(C)	NI	1500

APPENDIX *(Continued)*

1	2	3	4	5	6	7	8	9
Ujjain	2.8	6	35	905	57	Mf(C)	NI	500 BC
Jhansi	2.8	4	42	887	55	Tt(B)	NI	1500
Bikaner	2.8	4	34	886	50	SS(B)	D	1600
Erode	2.8	7	62	922	57	Tg(B)	SI	200
Sangli	2.7	3	33	914	61	Mf(D)	P	1500
Rajahmundry	2.7	4	42	964	55	Tg(B)	SI	850
Amravati	2.6	—	34	915	64	Tg(C)	SI	1500
Bokaro Steel City	2.6	2	144	748	55	Mf(A)	NI	1970
Pondicherry	2.5	3	64	979	61	Mf(D)	C	1630
Tuticorin	2.5	10	38	954	64	Tg(B)	C	200
Vellore	2.5	8	38	980	59	Tg(C)	SI	850
Gaya	2.5	—	37	868	56	Tg(C)	NI	400 BC
Malegaon	2.5	—	28	947	50	Mf(A)	SI	1900
Nellore	2.4	—	77	955	57	Tg(D)	C	500
Kharagpur	2.3	2	46	883	60	Tt(A)	NI	1900
Udaipur	2.3	—	42	866	62	SS(C)	P	1500
Kakinada	2.3	—	38	988	51	Tg(D)	C	850
Akola	2.3	—	34	911	59	Tg(C)	SI	1500
Bhagalpur	2.2	—	29	842	54	MA(D)	NI	500 BC
Bhubaneshwar	2.2	—	108	757	67	SS(A)	SI	1970
Gulbarga	2.2	—	50	906	52	Tg(C)	SI	1347
Tiruppur	2.2	6	43	933	58	Mf(A)	SI	1900
Jammu	2.1	8	36	880	63	SS(C)	NI	1900
Dhule	2.1	—	54	900	61	Mf(C)	SI	1800
Sagar	2.1	7	34	860	61	MA(A)	P	1660
Kurnool	2.1	—	51	928	49	Mf(C)	SI	1650
Patiala	2.1	2	36	873	64	SS(B)	NI	1700
Shahjahanpur	2.1	3	43	864	41	Tg(D)	NI	1600
Rampur	2.0	—	26	893	33	Mf(C)	NI	1650
Firozabad	2.0	—	52	847	39	Mf(A)	NI	1361
Bellary	2.0	—	61	941	50	Tg(D)	SI	1800
Davanagere	2.0	—	62	903	55	Mf(A)	P	1900
Nanded	1.9	—	51	906	54	Mf(D)	SI	1600
Muzaffarpur	1.9	—	50	805	60	Tg(C)	NI	1600
Bilaspur	1.9	6	37	919	60	Tg(D)	SI	1900
Thanjavur	1.8	—	31	943	69	Tg(C)	SI	850
Nizamabad	1.8	—	58	944	43	Tg(B)	SI	1750
Ahmadnagar	1.8	2	22	848	69	Mf(D)	P	1494
Darbanga	1.8	—	33	875	51	Tg(C)	NI	1700
Shillong	1.7	6	41	902	64	SS(A)	H	1850
Muzaffarnagar	1.7	—	50	873	52	Tg(C)	NI	1800
Nagarcoil	1.7	—	21	999	76	MA(D)	C	1700

APPENDIX *(Continued)*

1	2	3	4	5	6	7	8	9
Dindigul	1.7	—	33	961	61	Tg(B)	SI	200
Trichur	1.7	7	—	1045	81	Tg(C)	C	800
Alleppey	1.7	—	6	1023	77	Mf(C)	C	1700
Eluru	1.7	—	32	1006	57	Mf(C)	SI	1700
Bardhaman	1.7	—	17	885	63	Tg(C)	NI	1800
Quilon	1.7	2	—	1015	74	Mf(C)	C	200
Rohtak	1.7	—	34	867	62	Tg(B)	NI	1700
Berhampur (Orissa)	1.6	—	38	924	57	SS(C)	C	1700
Sambalpur	1.6	5	54	880	54	Tg(C)	SI	200
Mathura	1.6	2	15	846	58	Tg(C)	NI	300 BC
Farrukabad-Fatehgarh	1.6	2	45	821	48	Mf(C)	NI	1500
Yamunanagar	1.6	3	—	831	62	Mf(B)	NI	1960
Cannanore	1.6	6	—	1001	76	Mf(C)	C	1800
Ratlam	1.6	2	31	906	61	Tg(D)	NI	1800
Imphal	1.6	—	55	976	64	MA(C)	P	1700
Siliguri	1.5	—	58	793	63	Tg(A)	NI	1800
Shimoga	1.5	—	48	911	63	SS(C)	P	1800
Bihar	1.5	—	51	893	53	Mf(B)	NI	1900
Bijapur	1.5	—	41	925	56	Tg(B)	P	1325
Hardwar	1.5	4	60	817	56	SS(C)	NI	629
Kancheepuram	1.5	4	21	977	60	MA(A)	SI	300 BC
Jalgaon	1.5	—	36	906	64	Tg(C)	SI	1800
Kolar Gold Fields	1.4	3	21	973	65	Mg(A)	P	1900
Nandiad	1.4	—	31	921	66	Mf(C)	NI	1800
Faizabad (Ayodhya)	1.4	3	29	779	55	SS(C)	NI	500 BC
Kumbakonam	1.4	2	18	980	66	Tg(C)	SI	850
Burhanpur (M.P.)	1.4	—	34	939	48	Mf(A)	SI	1417
Alwar	1.4	—	39	853	57	SS(C)	NI	1750
Machilipatnam	1.4	—	23	977	62	Mf(C)	C	200
Panipat	1.4	—	57	868	57	Mf(C)	NI	1500
Hisar	1.4	2	—	803	57	SS(D)	D	1361
Ichkaranji	1.3	—	52	852	56	Mf(A)	P	1960
Porbandar	1.3	2	25	949	62	Mf(C)	C	1500
Bhusaval	1.3	2	26	917	65	Tt(A)	SI	1900
Karnal	1.3	—	42	869	59	SS(C)	NI	1800
Agartala	1.3	—	31	977	75	SS(A)	NI	1900
Wadwan	1.3	3	34	940	61	Mf(C)	NI	1800
Bhadravati	1.3	2	28	916	59	Mf(A)	P	1920
Nabadwip (W.B.)	1.3	5	38	975	59	Mf(B)	NI	1500
Munger	1.3	—	26	863	55	Mf(D)	NI	700
Navasari	1.3	3	61	854	63	Mf(A)	C	1950
Mirzapur-Vindhyachal	1.3	—	21	850	42	Tg(D)	NI	1500

APPENDIX *(Continued)*

1	2	3	4	5	6	7	8	9
Habra (W.B.)	1.3	2	37	960	70	Tg(C)	C	1950
Cuddalore	1.3	—	26	966	60	Tg(D)	C	200
Bathinda	1.3	2	95	819	52	Tg(B)	NI	1190
Murwara (M.P.)	1.3	14	45	897	57	Tg(B)	NI	1900
Arrah	1.2	—	34	855	56	Tg(C)	NI	1500
Raichur	1.2	—	56	934	45	Tg(B)	SI	1200
Bhilwara	1.2	—	49	889	48	Mf(C)	NI	1850
Jalna	1.2	—	34	944	50	SS(D)	P	1800
Katihar	1.2	2	52	801	51	Tg(A)	NI	1200
Ganganagar	1.2	—	35	802	56	Mf(D)	D	1920
Ambala Cant.	1.2	2	—	970	62	Tg(C)	NI	1850
Junagadh	1.2	2	25	938	65	SS(B)	NI	145
Ananthapur	1.2	—	49	912	60	SS(C)	SI	1500
Raniganj	1.2	11	156	720	43	Tg(C)	NI	1860
Tenali	1.2	—	16	982	58	Tg(B)	SI	1800
Palghat	1.2	2	—	1014	71	Tg(C)	SI	1800
Gadag-Betgeri	1.2	—	22	940	56	Mf(A)	P	1800
Valparai	1.2	—	22	949	53	MP(A)	H	1950
Chandrapur	1.2	—	54	907	64	SS(D)	SI	1900
Bhiwandi	1.2	—	45	663	51	Mf(A)	C	1950
Tirupati	1.2	—	75	909	63	Tg(C)	SI	1100
Vizianagaram	1.2	—	33	982	55	Tg(B)	C	1500
Hospet	1.1	4	—	963	43	Mf(B)	SI	1336
Pollachi	1.1	6	22	931	63	Tg(B)	SI	1900
Khandwa (M.P.)	1.1	—	34	916	59	Tg(D)	SI	1900
Belurghat	1.1	3	68	898	66	SS(A)	NI	1850
Amroha	1.1	—	36	894	28	Mf(B)	NI	1200
Etawah	1.1	—	31	873	49	SS(C)	NI	1500
Bharuch	1.1	6	22	920	63	Tg(D)	C	200 BC
Latur	1.1	—	60	889	53	Tg(C)	P	1800
Chapra	1.1	—	34	868	50	Tg(B)	NI	1500
Purnia	1.1	2	54	814	48	SS(B)	NI	1500
Sonipat	1.1	—	75	844	61	Tg(D)	NI	1700
Parbani	1.1	—	78	907	51	SS(B)	SI	1500
Tumkur	1.1	—	55	892	64	Tg(C)	P	1800
Adoni	1.1	—	28	958	39	Mf(A)	SI	1800
Pathankot	1.1	—	42	898	54	SS(B)	NI	1500
Ondal	1.1	16	246	725	40	Tt(A)	NI	1960
Sambal	1.1	—	26	876	25	MA(B)	NI	1200
Proddatur	1.1	—	51	951	48	Mf(A)	SI	1800
Bharatpur	1.1	—	51	834	51	SS(D)	NI	1750
Patan	1.1	2	39	955	45	Tg(D)	C	200 BC

APPENDIX *(Continued)*

1	2	3	4	5	6	7	8	9
Jaunpur	1.0	—	30	875	48	Tg(D)	NI	1359
Ambala City	1.0	—	25	895	66	SS(B)	NI	1500
Bulandshahr	1.0	—	74	869	48	Tg(C)	NI	1500
Hapur	1.0	—	45	867	48	Tg(B)	NI	1500
Cuddapah	1.0	—	56	930	54	Tg(C)	SI	1800
Sikar	1.0	—	45	914	39	Tg(D)	D	1700
Sitapur	1.0	—	52	821	56	—	NI	1500
Bheemavaram	1.0	—	60	932	45	Tg(C)	C	1800
Rajapalayam	1.0	—	17	963	58	Mf(A)	SI	1950
Bermo	1.0	5	46	818	42	Mg(A)	NI	1900
Bhivani	1.0	—	38	836	54	Mf(A)	NI	1800
Puri	1.0	—	39	876	59	SS(B)	C	200 BC
Gurgaon	1.0	2	—	869	66	SS(B)	NI	1800
Batala	1.0	16	32	888	54	Mf(C)	NI	1960
Rewa	1.0	—	45	789	55	SS(C)	NI	1700
Gondia	1.0	—	29	955	64	MA(B)	SI	1800
Mandya	1.0	—	39	910	50	Tg(C)	P	1800
Karaikudi	1.0	7	13	992	63	Tg(C)	SI	1950
Behrampur (W.B.)	1.0	3	27	963	65	SS(B)	NI	1700
Guwahati	1.2	9	—	638	65	Tg(B)	NI	1400

NOTES: Col. 5: Sex ratio is defined as number of females per thousand males
Col. 6: Literacy rate—percentage of literates in total population
Col. 7: Functional type—Based on Asok Mitra's functional clasification of towns, 1971. The symbols indicate the following:
Mf—manufacturing; Mg—mining; MA—artisan; MP—plantation; Tg—trading; Tt—transport; SS—service.
Degree of specialization is indicated by symbol in brackets as follows: A—predominant function highly accentuated; B—predominant function accentuated; C—functions moderately diversified; and D—functions highly diversified.
Col. 8: Climatic types:
C—coastal type; NI—northern inland type; SI—southern inland type; P—plateau type; H—hill station type; and D—desert type
Col. 9: Information on the origins of existing cities compiled from standard books on Indian history. Rounding of the year of origin has been done where information is of a vague and approximate nature.

Subject and Author Index

(Page numbers in italics refer to figures; bold numbers refer to tables.)

Place Index